Infant Mortality and Working-Class Child Care, 1850–1899

Infant Mortality and Working-Class Child Care, 1850–1899

Melanie Reynolds
Oxford Brookes University, UK

First published 2016 by
PALGRAVE MACMILLAN

Palgrave Macmillan in the UK is an imprint of Macmillan Publishers Limited, registered in England, company number 785998, of Houndmills, Basingstoke, Hampshire RG21 6XS.

Palgrave Macmillan in the US is a division of St Martin's Press LLC, 175 Fifth Avenue, New York, NY 10010.

Palgrave Macmillan is the global academic imprint of the above companies and has companies and representatives throughout the world.

Palgrave® and Macmillan® are registered trademarks in the United States, the United Kingdom, Europe and other countries.

ISBN 978–1–137–36903–1

This book is printed on paper suitable for recycling and made from fully managed and sustained forest sources. Logging, pulping and manufacturing processes are expected to conform to the environmental regulations of the country of origin.

A catalogue record for this book is available from the British Library.

Library of Congress Cataloging-in-Publication Data
Reynolds, Melanie, 1959– author.
    Infant mortality and working-class child care, 1850–1899 / Melanie Reynolds.
    pages   cm
    Includes bibliographical references.
    ISBN 978–1–137–36903–1 (hardback)
    1. Child care—Great Britain—History—19th century.   2. Infant mortality—Great Britain—History—19th century.   3. Working class women—Great Britain—Social conditions—19th century.   4. Working mothers—Great Britain—Social conditions—19th century.
    5. Workhouses—Great Britain—History—19th century.   I. Title.
HQ778.7.G7R49 2015
362.7094109'034—dc23   2015029310

To Tim, Lisa and Billy

Contents

List of Figures and Tables

Figures

Tables

Acknowledgements

I have received huge support and encouragement whilst writing this work. First and foremost I wish to acknowledge the debt I owe to Professor Anne-Marie Kilday. She has supported this book throughout and forced me to prove, prove, prove. It is one thing to suspect nineteenth century working-class women were not always bad mothers, but an entirely different and difficult thing to furnish evidence.

I also wish to thank Professor Hilda Kean – her truly inspirational teaching at Ruskin College, Oxford set in store my love of social history which still lives with me today. Enormous thanks also go to Dr Anna Davin for her invaluable comments, sage advice, generosity and hospitality.

Dr Andrew Williams of Northampton General Hospital helped me tackle the nineteenth-century medical debate. Colleagues at Oxford Brookes also played a part in bringing book the book to fruition – most importantly Professor Joanne Bailey, who gave considered and valuable advice freely, as did Dr Alysa Levene. Thanks also go to Dr Tim Philipson, Professor David Nash, Dr Katherine Bradley, Dr Carol Beadle and Dr Katherine Watson. Ruth Collins was also hugely supportive. Thank you! The staff at the Bodleian Library have been enormously helpful, particularly Hannah Chandler, whose knowledge of the Parliamentary Papers is unparalleled. Thanks also go to the *Community Practitioner Journal* who gave me permission to publish some of the ideas presented here in an earlier draft.

My thanks also go to the reviewers whose comments and criticisms have improved this work. My sisters Michele and Ange and friend Barry should not go unmentioned, and last, but by no means least, I wish to thank Tim. His support has known no bounds during my writing and research, and it is to him and my daughter Lisa, and her husband Billy, and Gloria that this book is dedicated. They have all been most patient with me whilst writing a book about northern working-class women – whose experiences of motherhood were far more difficult than mine.

Introduction

During the period 1850–1899, the Infant Mortality Rate (IMR) was significantly high in many parts of Britain.[1] At least 15 per cent of all infant deaths occurred in the industrial northeast and northwest areas.[2] Districts such as Leeds and Manchester feature strongly in these high rates, and the historical demographer Robert Woods has argued it is these areas which should 'command' the historian's attention due to their impact on the national rates during the latter half of the nineteenth century.[3] Joshua Ikin, a medical practitioner working in Leeds during the 1860s, was concerned about these rates, and reiterated the concerns of the Registrars General who lamented 'the evil of the employment of…women in work that requires them to leave their own homes'. They argued that the consequences of this was that the child:

> is deprived of its proper nourishment… and that the fearful death which prevails amongst children, where the mothers work in mills or at any out of doors labour must be accounted for in a large measure by injurious influences. The deduction drawn from manufacturing towns… is that the mother is away during the greater part of the day and the child is left… the mother hardly sees her child from the time she goes to work. It is impossible she should have much of the feelings of the mother, and experience shows that she has very often none…[4]

The belief in the link between the high northern IMR and 'industrial and urban motherhood' during the period 1850–1899 still prevails today in the pertinent scholarship. Condemning nineteenth-century working-class child care is acknowledged as 'controversial', and although mothers' 'indifference' to their infants has not been confirmed, it is still a theory which provides a 'framework' for historians of infant mortality to work from. However, in doing so it labels a whole population of nineteenth-century working-class women as irresponsible child carers – with respected social historians arguing that 'there could be no…[doubt] about the importance

1

of infant-feeding practices and the general problems of maternal ignorance and fecklessness'.[5]

Challenges to this theory are thin on the ground. Identifying the nature and method of positive working-class child care is extremely difficult. Consequently, northern working-class mothers feature infrequently in our history books, and when they do, they are usually labelled as rash, inattentive, and sometime callous mothers, who were impervious to, and unable to provide for, the needs of their young. The present work challenges this perception, the first to do so.

This book provides for the first time, an in-depth look at northern working-class child care in the industrial districts of the north of England between 1850 and 1899. It puts working-class mothers at the heart of infant care and examines their child care practices whilst they worked in factories weaving wool, making nails, bricks and salt, or working at harvest in agriculture. It also explores the 'daily graft' of the workhouse nurses who supposedly mirrored the dispassionate and blasé attitudes of working-class mothers and whose 'care' to infants in the workhouse was said to have been negligent and neglectful. Challenges are also made to the currently prevailing perceptions of the actions of day-carers and baby-minders, who are equally seen as aloof, seeking merely to make money from the minding of infants placed in their care. The book divulges the broad context in which nineteenth-century mothers approached their child care, and reveals the actions they undertook to keep their infants alive. In doing so, it uncovers a new and compelling sense of working-class women's history, where mothers fought and won battles to enhance, rather than diminish, their offspring's chances of survival. By opening this fresh perspective, the shape of working-class women's history in the nineteenth century will be fundamentally altered.

The focus of this work will be a discussion of the high IMR in northern England. This will be followed by an examination of the relative successes and failures of supposed improvements in standards of living, public health and medicine, all of which were nineteenth-century measures introduced in order to reduce the high IMR. However, as we will see, little could be done against the prevalence of a high IMR, and thus we will move on to consider the relationship between infant mortality and northern working-class mothers' child care practices and the research questions which this work will address. The sources and methodology to answer these questions will be introduced below, followed by an outline of the book's structure.

The IMR was significantly high in many parts of Britain during the nineteenth century, and in the northern industrial counties in particular, often excessively and 'depressingly' so.[6] The historical demographer Robert Woods has given a general English mean of 150/1000, with a range of 70–250/1000, and he notes that IMR was far from uniform, with the lowest rates in southern rural districts and the highest in the industrial towns and cities.[7] The midlands and north of England consistently exceeded the national average during 1860–1899, as shown by Williams and Mooney, with Preston and Manchester showing the highest rates in Lancashire, of 209 and 194 respectively, and by Robert Woods, who illustrates the persistent high rates of Yorkshire towns – Leeds and Sheffield having rates up to 249/1000.[8]

Statistical analysis taken from the Registrar General Decennial Supplements by Robert Woods and Nicola Shelton also shows the urban north experienced far higher rates than the rural south.[9] Steven King and Geoffrey Timmins mirror this finding, particularly in the areas of the West Riding of Yorkshire and Preston.[10] Robert Woods hoped he would find the rationale for this phenomenon from the nineteenth-century Registrar General's 'Professional nineteenth century source material', but he reports that it was of little use, other than to say it was the northern regions that were hit hardest.

The areas central to both the high northern IMR and women's waged work are Yorkshire and Lancashire and it is these areas which this work will cover. The West Riding communities of Leeds, Bradford, Halifax, Dewsbury, Batley and Huddersfield witnessed predominantly female employment in the woollen, worsted and flax trades. In Lancashire, women likewise dominated employment in the cotton mills of Manchester, Bolton, Preston and Rochdale. The book will focus on these areas. During our period, Yorkshire was rich in the coal deposits and water essential for industrial concentration and growth, and the expansion of mining, heavy industry and textile production in Yorkshire and Lancashire brought about unprecedented population expansion from the mid-eighteenth century. The introduction of power looms and other 'steam-generated horse-powered machinery' quickly established these centres of textile production as the 'powerhouse of the industrial revolution', which by 1830 had obliterated all competition and accounted for 'up to half of all English exports'.[11]

These innovations in textile production, its consequent economic dominance in the region, and the large numbers of women it employed led to the industry and the regional labour force developing a distinctive female character. These areas of textile production saw the rates of married women's work rise precipitately during 1850–1899; for instance, the numbers rose from 456,956 in 1867 to 720,469 only five years later.[12] This expansion of textile production and the demand for labour meant that there was employment for any woman who wanted it, and, as Emma Griffin notes, 'female participation rates tended to be high wherever there was cotton or wool' to be spun or woven.[13] Married women made up a large percentage of the population in these regions, accounting for up to 79 percent of women aged between 15 and 44, with this age cohort making up 50 to 60 per cent of the regional population.[14] The women who formed the backbone of textile production across the West Riding and Lancashire lived almost exclusively in self-contained towns and cities which were often associated with a specific textile type and which tended to have populations of less than 100,000.[15]

It was in these areas that, according to scholars, waged work separated mothers from their infants, forcing infants into the arms of day-carers and baby-minders and, when severe economic difficulties for the mothers arose, to the welfare bolthole of the workhouse and its nurse. Moreover, it was these areas which concerned contemporaries most of all during the period of the high IMR and forged, in their minds at least, the north–south divide with regard to child care, with northern mothers supposedly caring less for their infants than southern mothers. Indeed, it is still these areas which historians characterise today with high northern IMR and inept working-class child care.[16] Our deliberate geographical focus therefore places the argument within the same set of parameters as those applied by nineteenth century contemporaries and which have informed much of the current historical analysis relating to the high northern IMR. Given this, these counties represent a useful methodological setting in which to test the validity of the attribution of high northern IMR to working-class mothers' child care practices during the second half of the nineteenth century. By using this approach this book will provide much-needed balance in the IMR debate.

Historians have dedicated many hours to the topic of the 'lives lived' during the industrial revolution. One of the particular themes has been to seek whether the population and its offspring prospered or were hindered by industrialisation. The standard of living debate has been one of the defining features of twentieth-century economic and social history. It is not the purpose of this book to rehearse this argument in all its detail; however it is necessary to acknowledge that it does impact on the wider IMR debate, although historians acknowledge there is very little consensus as to what the impact was.[17]

Emma Griffin has recently concluded that globally, gains were made, but the transition from agricultural life to industrial was a painful one for those who had to work through it.[18] This conclusion is of course still a matter of debate. Historians fall into two schools of thought: the optimists noting the advances. The pessimists stressing the losses.[19] Costs and benefits of the nineteenth-century change in the standard of living are discussed in a wide variety of contexts, including wage increases, mortality rates, life expectancy, well-being, height ratios, political rights and literacy levels.[20] What is clear, however, is that for infants of the working class any improvement in standard of living was slight. One of the main problems which beset such infants, and/or their mothers was poverty. The lack of money was a defining feature of life, and was linked to the high IMR that characterised the nineteenth century. Many working-class parents at some time of their life experienced a loss of wages and destitution due to unemployment or illness.

One of the leading proponents of the positive school is Thomas McKeown who, drawing on statistical analysis of English registration data during the period 1837–1914, argues that real increases in income resulted in improved nutrition, which positively influenced the IMR during the late nineteenth century. Nutrition, McKeown argues, played a greater role than any medical intervention in the decline in the IMR because it imparted strength to fight infectious diseases.[21] Robert Millward and Frances Bell mirror this optimistic stand and the role it played in ameliorating the IMR, a view which is also supported by Sumit Guha, who has remarked that 'it is most unlikely that the role of changes in real income, living standards and nutritional status will be found to be a minor one'.[22] This is a view which still dominates the historical narrative.[23]

Simon Szreter, however, argues these views are too optimistic, and that they fail to take into account the detrimental effects than an 'improved' standard of living had upon infants in particular. Based on an analysis of nineteenth-century public health records, he argues that the so-called improvements did more harm than good, especially for weaned infants, due to new food types being infected by pathogens.[24] The pessimist school is densely populated: gains made by infants and their families are doubted by Charles Feinstein, the Webbs and Hammonds, and the Marxist historians Eric Hobsbawm and E.P. Thompson.[25] This view is reiterated in recent publications from Emma Griffin and Kenneth Morgan, who argue that rises in the standard of living gave little to the female working-class work force who fuelled it, and Morgan, though more forgiving of the negative effects of the industrial revolution on women and children, argues that there was actually little to celebrate.[26]

Equally sceptical about the effect of an improved standard of living is Anthony Wohl, who sees little evidence to support the claim that living standards improved, and asserts that any increase had scant benefit for infants, and little effect on IMRs. He argues, instead, that the poor and their infants remained as impoverished and undernourished as they always had been. Moreover, changes in the standard of living had a particularly detrimental effect on pregnant women and the life chances of their infants.[27] This view is complemented by the 1995 study of nine parishes in the north of England by Paul Huck, who argues that there is little evidence of a higher standard of living in the region during the industrial revolution.[28] Even McKeown acknowledges that if an improved standard of living led to higher nutritional standards for the poor, any benefits which accrued to infants would only become evident from the age of two onwards. This suggests that an improved standard of living had real limitations in ameliorating the northern IMR.[29]

Nineteenth-century medical intervention also set a path to reduce the high IMR. Medical practitioners and researchers extended their interest in the causes of infant death and expanded their interest in paediatrics into maternity practices. Contemporaries like William Farr thought the infant mortality problem was a difficult avenue to address medically, and he cautioned against attributing the high rates to individual causes, on the grounds that:

> young infants...were feeble; they are unfinished; the molecules and fibres of brain, muscle, bone are loosely strung together; the heart and the blood, on which life depends, have undergone a complete revolution; the lungs are only just called into play. The baby is helpless...It is not surprising that a certain number of infants should die.[30]

Farr was not confident of finding a single cause for excess IMR, and was well aware of the toll on infant life wrought by disease during the nineteenth century. He catalogued the devastating impact of whooping cough, scarlatina and smallpox during the 1860s.[31] Historians like Kenneth Morgan, Frederick Cartwright, Michael Biddiss and Charles Creighton acknowledge Farr's perspective on the role of disease in pushing up the IMR, as does Anne Hardy, who emphasises that the diseases of 'whooping cough, measles, scarlet fever, diphtheria and atrophy were all serious and life-threatening diseases for the young'.[32] In their statistical analysis of mortality during the period, Robert Woods and Nicola Shelton have added further weight to the argument of a link between disease and the high IMR.[33] Their work illustrates the broad range of disease to which infants were 'especially vulnerable' during the latter half of the nineteenth century. Of these, diseases of the brain or nervous system, of the lung or respiratory system, and diarrhoea, dysentery, and the wasting diseases of atrophy were the most prevalent and deadly.[34]

The rise of scientific medicine during the nineteenth century, which applied new programmes of medical inquiry, new disease concepts and new research practices in order to better understand the causal factors of morbidity and mortality, provided a new opportunity to confront and address the IMR problem during the latter half of the century.[35] One of the pioneers in the field of social history of medicine, Roy Porter, has stressed the importance of scientific advances made by the medical profession during the nineteenth century. The main thrust of his argument has been that the old religious practices in the realm of medicine withered on the vine during the seventeenth century, and that 'the new science of the Enlightenment brought a shift from divine dramatics to more secular practices'.[36] The progress of specialised medical knowledge was, Porter argues, to provide us with a key to unlock health matters, for 'with the accent shifting from the soul's salvation to temporal well-being, medicine took a move towards centre-stage, and medical men and health issues were to command heightened public attention'.[37] Mary Douglas also sees conclusive evidence in the progress of the medical scientific rationale, arguing that 'western medicine over its history had gradually separated itself from spiritual matters'.[38] These arguments form the backbone of the historiography of medicine and are rarely challenged, for, as Loudon remarks, 'even if we dispute the nature and extent of such progress, it is certain that the period from the late eighteenth century to the mid-nineteenth laid the foundations of the medical profession as we know it today'.[39]

The increasing concern over health issues provided a 'professional' vacuum which medical men filled. Anne Hardy remarks that it led to the increased power and prestige of the medical profession during the latter half of the nineteenth century.[40] Roy Porter puts it well when he argues that 'medical men portrayed health and hygiene as the cornerstones of a New Society and the doctor as its priest'.[41] This elevated status, he maintains, facilitated leading reformers like Newsholme, Chadwick and Simon to establish a regular dialogue with the state, which tied the status of the nineteenth century medical profession into a 'close alignment with politicians'.[42] The enhanced prominence of medical doctors led to ever more practitioners entering the political arena, for as Hardy notes, although only three medical doctors were members of the House of Commons during the Vaccination Act debates, including John Lush, MP for Salisbury, and William Brewer, MP for Colchester, this number grew during the nineteenth century. Lyon Playfair emerged as the driving force within the medical–political establishment, and would become 'the leading spokesman for medical and scientific interests' from the 1870s to the end of the nineteenth century.[43] These developments, Hardy argues, led to doctors becoming an 'established authority of medical science in the House of Commons'.[44] The medical profession became commensurately influential in determining policy responses to pressing health concerns such as the IMR during the latter half of the nineteenth century, in large part through their role in commissions into working-class areas and particularly through studies of working-class waged women's work and its impact upon child-caring practices.[45]

This evolution of the role and political position of the medical profession meant that the autonomy which characterised eighteenth-century medical practice became increasingly divorced from the more centralised and ubiquitous role of the nineteenth-century doctor. Loudon argues, 'a transition occurred in which a disunited, pluralistic, or even non-existent medical profession changed to a unified one'.[46] One of the most profound consequences of this new-found importance and cohesive identity was that, as Anne Digby argues, 'medical doctors played an increasingly important role' in diagnosing and prescribing for the working classes, both in the household and in the workhouse.[47]

The significance of these transformations for the IMR in the north of England was that nineteenth-century medics expanded their remit and increasingly saw maternal practice and paediatrics fall within their sphere of influence. However, despite new medical breakthroughs the amelioration of smallpox, infantile diarrhoea and wasting diseases like atrophy, remained difficult.[48] Indeed, these ailments persisted, as Digby notes despite nineteenth-century medical doctors 'expand[ing] their practice with women and child patients', and 'develop[ing] specialisms and institutions' accordingly.[49] As Valerie Fildes notes, these developments drew on a long tradition of paediatric knowledge gained over previous centuries which, Ruth Hodgkinson argues, informed and influenced the role played by the Poor Law medical doctors who sought to right the 'many evils' experienced by the female working classes and their infants during the latter half of the nineteenth century.[50]

Due to the reorientation of relief sentiment in 1834, the workhouse proved to be the arena where the medical profession played their defining role in the lives of thousands of infants during the period, a reality which was cemented by the adoption of Medical Officers of Health in 1848, and which saw 469 medical doctors serving 75 Poor Law Unions across Yorkshire and Lancashire by 1851, and over 4000 nationally by the end of the century.[51]

With infants comprising, up to 38 per cent of the workhouse population during the latter half of the nineteenth century,[52] these medical officers for health fought on the front-line in the battle against infant mortality which, Hodgkinson argues, made them stand out as 'good public servants' fighting for 'positive health measures'.[53] Indeed, Michael Rose has suggested that northern medical doctors did not take their new-found responsibilities lightly: Dr Edward Smith was determined to improve the lot of the infants in the workhouse whose health he considered was bad and who were 'constantly ailing', particularly as a consequence of infantile diarrhoea, and the wasting diseases of atrophy and marasmus.[54]

It was not only Poor Law medical officers, who were interested in the plight of nineteenth-century infants. Paediatricians such as Dr Eustace Smith, Member of the Royal College of Physicians, and Physician to the North-West Free Dispensary for Sick Children, was equally keen to reduce their death rates, as was Factory Inspector and medical doctor Dr Robert Baker.[55] W.R. Lee claims that Baker was peerless in his desire to improve infant health and ameliorate the IMR in the north of England, both within and without the workhouse. Moreover, Baker's efforts led to him being appointed as a Factory Inspector, from which post his analysis of children's factory accidents was produced, laying the foundation upon which the majority of the new laws and regulations on children's working arrangements were built during the final decades of the nineteenth century.[56]

Despite the emergence of scientific medicine directed by an increasingly unified and politically sanctioned medical class, however, the impact which these developments had on the IMR, in the north of England in particular, is questionable. Indeed, although Roy Porter notes that medical science went from 'strength to strength' during the period, and won 'greater public funds and a place in the sun', he cautions against giving too much weight to the ability of 'medical science' to make a positive impact on infant mortality.[57] Wohl echoes these reservations, and argues that medical doctors were at a loss to explain much infant death. Indeed, the extent to which the scientific medical 'revolution' was able to confront and cure diseases which rendered infants ill is highly questionable. For, with the possible exception of the childish disease of smallpox which, Anne Hardy argues, was literally wiped out during the period, the medical profession offered little protection against deadly ailments. Whooping cough, diarrhoea or the myriad atrophic wasting diseases were responsible for urban infant death at 12 months at rates of 694, 3961 and 2734 respectively, and doctors continued to rely on the 'stamina of the child' to avert death, and reduce the IMR.[58]

Public health initiatives were as ineffective as 'scientific medicine' in fighting infant mortality, and historians likewise divide into optimistic and pessimistic camps in the debate. Yet, despite these differing interpretations it has to be acknowledged that the nineteenth century witnessed an unprecedented degree of nationally and locally inspired interventions which aimed to diminish the threat to public health from the urban industrial environment.

Cholera outbreaks during the first half of the nineteenth century highlighted the filth and squalor which existed in urban areas during the nineteenth century and led influential figures like Edwin Chadwick to campaign for radical measures to address the spiralling mortality. For individuals like Chadwick, improvement of public health by means of sanitary reform represented the key that would unlock the door to the armoury housing the weapons needed for the pressing, and indeed depressing, fight against infant mortality.[59] This thinking, combined with the urgency caused by renewed outbreaks of cholera in the 1840s, inspired unprecedented feats of engineering aimed at addressing the inadequacies of sewage disposal, with Joseph Bazalgette's constructions of the London sewers being the most famous example.[60] Although contemporary analysis as to the exact relationship between squalor, filth and diseases such as cholera were flawed, with William Farr being far from alone in believing that it was the stench from untreated waste which resulted in a poisonous miasma, the impetus for measures to improve public health and ameliorate infant mortality passed the tipping point mid-century.[61] Significantly, the increased power of the state, combined with the emergence of powerful metropolitan authorities throughout the provinces, meant that these initiatives were not merely restricted to London, with Liverpool, for example, among the first to obtain a Sanitary Act in 1846.[62] The contemporary analysis of the inadequacies of public health measures, and sanitation in particular, is shared by many historians. Wohl for example argues that the decrepit sewage systems, combined with insufficient privies and overflowing cesspools and exposed dung-heaps,[63] led to 'large amounts of human excrement' entering the houses of the poor in particular.[64] When combined with street refuse and untreated discharges from factories, this filth, argue Bedarida, Wohl and Briggs, was a potent mix which had an adverse effect on infant mortality.[65] Morgan argues that it was not until 1848 that consensus was achieved to back governmental sanitary improvements, and even then when ratepayers and factory owners in towns and cities became aware of the need for their money to fund improvements, they opposed them.[66] Overall, Morgan argues, sanitary improvements until late in the nineteenth century, were slow and piecemeal. Given this, the drive towards public health initiatives such as sanitation improvements, was limited, as Szreter points out. Nigel Morgan draws similar conclusions to Szreter, and by means of a reconstruction of the story of infant mortality in Preston, makes the case that the cause of the high incidence of infant death was the prevalence of horses and their dung. This attracted flies, which in turn 'gave bacteria the power to fly'[67] into the domestic environment, causing bacterial infections within the vulnerable and young infants in particular.[68] Morgan's findings have strong echoes of Naomi Williams's study of infant mortality in Sheffield during the latter half of the nineteenth century.[69] Drawing on a wide range of local source material, including civil death registers, census enumerator books, and employing record linkage, Williams argues that social class was the prime determinant of infant mortality and, like Morgan, finds that there was a distinct seasonality associated with these deaths.[70]

This positivism is not without its critics, however, with McKeown dismissing the role of public health reforms in reducing the IMR.[71] This scepticism is echoed by Woods and Shelton, who likewise argue that sanitary reform had little impact on infant mortality.[72] Sumit Guha, a long-standing vehement critic of Szreter and his ideas, goes further, arguing that to elevate the role of public health measures in the battle against infant mortality is ill-conceived from the outset. In essence, he concludes that 'the classic sanitation diseases...were not controllable through Victorian sanitary measures', and that this is self-evident as 'infantile diarrhoeal rates...maintained their high levels in both town and country...over the last quarter of the nineteenth century'.[73] Anne Hardy acknowledges the prevalence, depth and complexity of the scourge of infantile diarrhoea, which Woods argues was the third highest killer of infants in the towns of Blackburn and Preston during the 1890s.[74] This was despite the evolution in the practice of medicine, something that was highlighted in the growing academic discipline centred on the social history of medicine around the 1970s. Ian Buchanan, for instance, is convinced of the limits of sanitary reform and argues that although steady improvements were indeed evident during the period, innovations in refuse disposal created as many problems as the systems they were meant to replace.[75] Due to these failings, Buchanan places the watershed for effective sanitary improvement as late as the First World War, a view echoed by Anthony Wohl, who has similar reservations concerning the narrative of the triumph of public health reforms throughout the nineteenth century. For Wohl, the significant point is not that 'effective' interventions did not occur, but rather that 'as the nineteenth century drew to a close it was clear, and was common knowledge, that the poor had not shared equally in the improvements of sanitary reform'.[76]

In this respect, both Buchanan and Wohl's pessimism relates to the chronology of effective intervention, as opposed to a straightforward rejection of the efficacy of public health reform in tackling the IMR. This argument in favour of periodic success, as opposed to Szreter's focus on a sustained forward march of effective interventions, is more plausible due to the limited success in reducing infant mortality during the nineteenth century. Moreover, it is important to say that even strong advocates of the effects of public health reform, such as Szreter, acknowledge that its benefits were far from universal. For infants under one year of age, Szreter concedes that 'the public health and preventative measures of the latter half of the nineteenth century could not reasonably be expected to have influenced the infants' environment', a view which is not dissimilar to that held by Wohl. These similarities are less surprising than may first appear, for although public health initiatives had some successes – particularly in the fight against cholera – they had only a marginal impact on infant mortality, which did not begin to abate until the turn of the twentieth century.

Despite diseases and deficiencies in sanitation exacting a heavy toll of infant mortality, the responses of both scientific medicine and public health reform were inadequate during the second half of the nineteenth century. Although historians have sought answers in these grand narratives, the diversity of afflictions and the sheer numbers of infants who succumbed to disease both during and in the wake of the industrial revolution render generalisations difficult, as Geoffrey Timmins and Steven King have argued.[77] This point is forcefully made by Woods and Shelton from their analysis of the Registrar General's Decennial Supplements. They show that there is evidence of diverse regional trends in infant mortality throughout the late nineteenth century.[78] Indeed, even proponents of the role of public health measures in addressing the IMR (albeit in part), such as Szreter and Wohl, allude to the fractured nature of these initiatives, due to the heavy cost, levels of ignorance in respect of their effect, and the degree of local inclination to pursue public health schemes.[79] The clear regional bias identified by Woods and Shelton, whereby the highest and most persistent IMR as a consequence of infantile diarrhoea and its stablemates, atrophy and marasmus, was evident throughout the industrial areas of the midlands and the north is mirrored in the works of Williams and Mooney, who show that the rates in Blackburn, Bolton and Preston remained between 160 and 230/1000 during the 1840s to the 1890s, and who argue that this may be explained in part by the slow adoption of 'improving' initiatives.[80]

Currently, it is beyond doubt that a persuasive body of research has accumulated which indicates that high infant mortality was a largely urban phenomenon with considerable regional variations. Thomas Forbes, for example, has demonstrated clear links between the prevalence of infant mortality and the extent of urbanisation, a point echoed by Robert Millward and Frances Bell in their study of the Yorkshire textile towns of Bradford and Leeds and in Lancashire.[81] The research of Naomi Williams and Graham Mooney reinforces the synergy between industrial, urban population centres in the north, and high levels of infant mortality. These localised studies of the IMR enable the regional and local scale of the IMR problem to be ascertained, and using this approach to explain the northern IMR presents historians with new opportunities to explore the character and nature of infant mortality, and so put forward more grounded and specific arguments in respect of the causal factors which drove these high levels of infant death.

Conclusions drawn from localised studies such as these add nuance to what has become a polarised argument concerning the IMR. Of particular importance is the way in which this research locates the narrative of mortality within specific time-frames and places, thereby allowing the particularity and relative customs of each place to emerge from the obscuring tendency of the general. Whilst this approach can offer new perspectives for the high IMR, the near-universality of high infant mortality across the northern industrial regions can impose limitations on this approach. Clearly, individual communities experienced particular circumstances which contributed to IMRs, which meant that one's birth place affected one's mortality, and the widespread and persistent nature of high IMR throughout northern industrial towns, which doctors were unable to ameliorate, strongly implies that some common causal factors must have existed. This is where the waged work of mothers comes in. Scholars have argued that it was this that drove the persistence of high IMR at this time in these localities. This was the conclusion arrived at by contemporary commentators too. Yet, as working-class women were aware of the limits to which medicine and public health had on the lives of their infants, they continued to work in order to support their families' budgets, and they believed this did not do any harm.[82]

It is within this dichotomy that this book is situated.

In seeking to explore the extent to which working-class mothers were responsible for the high IMR in northern England a vast range of sources has been sought, collated and analysed. They are described below, with their associated strengths and weaknesses. Scholars of social history in the modern era would find it difficult to come across any positive aspects of working-class child care from the sources that have typically been used to address this issue. Nineteenth-century working-class mothers, it seemed, left few records about their infants and how they cared for them. Searches for such evidence, therefore, were mostly fruitless. Those who did have the confidence to write about their experiences during the period 1850–1899 tended to be middle-class social commentators who pass on tales of woe and speak about the ignorance and uncompassionate nature of the mothers concerned. Margaret Hewitt used this tone to write her classic work, *Wives and Mothers in Victorian Industry*, which exemplifies the prevailing orthodoxy of 'feckless mothers.' Yet, surely not all working-class child care was irresponsible and ineffective? Was it inevitable that once industrial work became available the mothers who worked in the industries, and surrogate baby sitters, gave scant attention to the infants they bore or were paid to care for? We need a much more balanced and objective perspective on the history of this subject to identify how child care was managed by mothers and carers. In order to do this, we need to look at a broader range of sources than has previously been explored, to underpin an in-depth analysis of the full range of practices.

In seeking to address the extent to which working-class women's child care was to blame for the high IMR of the north of England, a range of both published and unpublished sources were examined. The first source type to be considered was the published Parliamentary Papers which contained discussions arising from the Commissioned Reports of the Inspectors of Factories to the Secretary of State during 1850–1899 which related to the industrial waged work of women, the high IMR during the period and the child care practices of the women concerned. The catalogues of the Parliamentary Papers were surveyed for a sense of the scale of the official inquiry relating to into the issue of working-class women's waged work and the infant life problem. The method employed was to identify all the official material which appertained to the problem of the high IMR and working-class mothers and carers in particular. This was done to identify the full gamut of official (empirical) records which existed. Moreover, this was also important in pinpointing both the negative and positive aspects of child care by the women concerned. Did all the official sources report similar negative circumstances, or did some differ to paint a more caring picture? This search provided reports of commissions held in the Parliamentary Papers as follows:

- 3476 reports with references to factory work during the period 1850–1899.
- 1644 reports with references to infant life during the period 1850–1899.
- 1292 reports with references to women workers during the period 1850–1899.
- 343 reports with references appertaining to baby-minders during the period 1850–1899.
- 3623 reports with references to women during the period 1850–1899.
- 2765 reports with references to child care during the period 1850–1899.

The large number of these reports allowed for a comprehensive approach to the topic, as they cover the whole of the United Kingdom including Scotland and Ireland. However, once these reports were identified, a specific rationale was adopted to obtain pertinent material which was closely and, crucially, specifically related to discussions relevant to the high IMR in northern England and specifically to northern working-class women's industrial waged work. These sources were thoroughly scrutinised – that is to say that all of the reports were read individually. This slow but concentrated approach was applied particularly to the areas of Yorkshire and Lancashire during 1850–1899. Reports from Factory Inspectors which related to women's factory, metal, salt, brick and agricultural work were sought for the areas of Dewsbury, Batley, Leeds, Huddersfield, Bradford, Halifax, Wakefield, Manchester, Salford, Bolton, Preston and Rochdale. This avenue threw up an abundance of material which would not have arisen through mere keyword searches alone. The sources were further examined for the names of the Factory Inspectors who were sent to explore the above areas during the period 1850–1899, such as Alexander Redgrave, Robert Baker, Leonard Horner, T. J. Howell and Robert J Saunders.

Factory Inspectors made a clear link in their reports between the high northern IMR and the waged work of working-class women, suggesting that there was a case in history to pursue. My next task was to identify from the reports of the Factory Inspectors the IMR in Yorkshire and Lancashire, the causes of disease related to the IMR and the numbers of the women working in industrial arenas. In addition to this it was important to note where they worked, the attitudes of the women towards that work, what areas and what cloths, metals or grains they dealt with, and the times of their working day. In essence, answering these questions led to an understanding of how much time they spent away from home.

Obtaining this information provided good context and insight into the numbers of women workers and their understanding of the importance of their work in terms of its contribution to the family economy. With this information to hand, the next approach was to see if the move from manor to mill turned these dedicated and hard-working women into neglectful and irresponsible mothers, as argued by many historians. This neglect did not seem to fit with the hard-working character of the women concerned: why would they work if the proceeds were not to enhance their family's wellbeing? One hypothesis was that industrialisation did not convert these women into the neglectful creatures we have been presented with, but rather that they had to become more inventive with their child care practices. Evidence of positive child care models were consequently sought in order to build up a more balanced picture of mothers' practices alongside the well-worn negative portrayals. Moreover, narrative from the mothers themselves was sought in the reports, the Factory Inspectors and commissioners often recording women's accounts of the customs of child care, and identifying specific methods. It was important to look closely at what women did with their infants when at work, because if there was evidence of positive child care methods being practised in the factories, workshops and agricultural fields this could mean that these industries were more female-friendly than we have previously been led to believe. The question to ask, therefore, was: did industrialisation allow mothers to cater for their infants and children during waged employment. This would suggest that the factory women and mothers had some control over their working environment. If so, this would mean that overseers ceded some control of the factory environment to the mothers, and sympathised with their approach to combine waged work with child care.

Adopting this close scrutiny was imperative in providing a more balanced approach to this topic. Narrative from overseers was sought to determine whether mothers were valued in the mill, whether they were able to take their infants with them to work, or whether they could they leave the looms to themselves for periods of time to devote themselves to their infants. Narratives were searched for indications of women being able to adapt the material culture or architecture of the mill to suit their needs as mothers, and whether this meant they attended to domestic duties in the mill to ensure their infants' safety and health or were allowed to adopt a flexi-time approach to their work, citing the need to complete domestic duties at home. One fundamental question attached to all of these questions is: were the sanitary conditions in the mill dirty? That is, did infants suffer from diseases incurred in the mill rather than at home? In addition, these sources were searched for statistical information relating to children working in the mill in order to achieve a better understanding of whether it was possible for women to use the children who worked alongside them as 'little nurses' to care for infants in the mill in the same way as they did in the home.

The strength of Parliamentary Paper material (an umbrella term) for this work is that it provides a comprehensive breadth of information relating to waged work of working-class women. These reports were particularly fruitful in this respect, often displaying an interest in the effect of the numbers of hours worked on the health of workers (particularly women and children) and the associated problems of women's waged work in relation to the high northern IMR during the period. These official sources have an authentic nature and are orderly in delivery; they also have a high literary quality, thus they are readable and accessible.[83] This format is important because the commissioners brought a wealth of information back from their research which needed to be catalogued. The Inspectors' reports run to hundreds of pages and were summed up and presented to parliament to give a concise, clear picture of working-class women's work. The appendices to these reports, which contain thousands of questions and answers (for instance one 45-page report contained 32,000 questions) are extremely valuable; particularly useful for this topic because they provide minutely detailed narratives of working-class women's work. The key questions inspectors were instructed to explore about working-class waged work from employers, employees, neighbours, medical men and Poor Law guardians were:

- What sort of work did working-class women do?
- How many hours did they work?
- How many hours were they out of their homes?
- What happened to their children whilst they undertook this work? Who cared for them?
- How did these women feed their children? What was the make-up of the feed?

What kind of world would these sources present of motherhood? Would it be a world in which working women had a strong sense of their own abilities and found innovative ways to preserve their infants' lives whilst they worked? It is from an analysis of the answers to these questions that we get a fuller, clearer, more detailed picture of the real experiences of working-class women.[84] These sources are particularly valuable for the strikingly under-researched topic of working-class child care.

The answers witnesses gave to the inspectors' questions strongly relate to the topic of the high IMR and working-class women's waged work, and the task was to identify if a strong, vivid, detailed picture of women's waged work could be drawn from these sources. Indeed, the verbatim responses of working-class women to the questions evident in these sources are rare examples of the working-class woman's voice. When these reports are linked to other sources they help us to understand whether and how mothers combined work with effective child care. The sources also illuminate the social and cultural customs of nineteenth-century working-class women, their child care and their families. The women talk of the importance of their work for them and their families. They also speak of their views on the Factory Acts as how they combined their work with family and domestic arrangements, and these answers help us to understand whether they felt their work disadvantaged their children. We also hear the inspectors tell us of the innovative and positive steps these women put in place for child care. Indeed, as inspectors pose secondary questions to their interviewees, the answers given contain further details associated with working-class women's working experiences, providing an even wider history of working-class women than might first be assumed from these reports. The reports are evidenced-based and are strictly geared to black-and-white conclusions. They are the official history of working-class women and their child care as presented to parliament; remarkably few historians have picked them apart. Names and addresses of Factory Inspectors, medical doctors, employees, and employers are also provided, thus offering detail which can be confirmed in other sources enabling the reports to be layered with other evidence, giving rise to evidenced-based history.

We see that the research the inspectors were expected to undertake covered the length and breadth of Britain and equipped them with an excellent understanding of the working experiences of working-class women. The depth of research these men undertook led to them being acknowledged as authorities on infant mortality and child care, and their findings were used again and again by various interested groups, although little use has been made of the question-and-answer sets. The reports have further strength in that their context is clear. We know that parliament commissioned the reports in an era of high infant mortality, thus the material arising out of the discussions is strongly linked to the topic of the high IMR. In addition, we know the identity and class of the men who conducted the research: we are given their names and evidence of individuals' special knowledge and personal opinion. The reports also acknowledge the roles which these people played in society, therefore informing us about their politics.[85] As the majority of the men concerned had interests in ameliorating the high IMR we can see that they set out to identify where child care could be improved and the laws and rules which working-class women should adhere to whilst working. Inspectors understood that working-class women had to work. They were expected to be 'open to conviction', 'if not impartial', in listening to the people they interviewed about their problems.[86]

Inspectors' reports also contain statistical information, such as the numbers of infant deaths, their age-range and cause of death. These are classified both nationally and by region. Again, these authentic statistics enable us to see what the official causes of infant deaths were and whether these can be linked to their mother's actions. Moreover, they can be analysed in further detail through other sources such as medical texts as to the character of the diseases and their scope for amelioration.

Whilst the Parliamentary Papers have many strengths, there are evident weaknesses and biases to contend with. As we know when and how the documents arose, we can see that although the researchers and authors were impartial and open to conviction, they were, nonetheless, all upper- and middle-class men who tended to believe that, in an era of high infant mortality, working-class women should not work. Although the inspectors and commissioners understood that working-class women were obliged to work, many wrote in journals and pamphlets about the problems this work caused infants. This philosophy was born of the idea that women should live in the domestic sphere rather than the public arena. They approached the topic with this bias affecting their work, hence the question and answer sets that they used were shaped in a patriarchal manner, giving a distinct impression to the interviewee that they were expected to answer in such a way as to suggest that working-class women conducted little waged work. It also encouraged the notion that they should rarely leave their infants because suitable child care was scarce. Indeed, in this environment women were extremely unlikely to talk of their difficulties in combining waged work with child care. In such a misogynistic environment it would be unlikely that these women would speak of their using child care methods that would seem improper or ill-advised, such as taking their infants to work. Should they do so they might well feel that they were at risk of losing their job because the commissioners could suggest to their employers that they were irresponsible mothers and trouble-makers.

The material provided in the Parliamentary Papers could be considered narrow, biased and weak, but as long as we are aware of these caveats the reports can and should be used because of their strong relation to the ways in which women cared for their infants. A further weakness in the reports concerns the lack of objectivity in the inspectors' evidence. The actual words of interviewees are not available to us. Tape recorders had not been invented when these interviews took place therefore we do not have the spoken words of the working class mothers and the responses to the questions put to them, so we lack 'social clues, the nuances of uncertainty, humour, or pretence' which this oral history could provide.[87] Neither do we have the minutes of evidence nor the inspectors' notes. Thus, the 'best record' we have are the printed texts. We also have to bear in mind that the outcome of the report into infant mortality and its relationship to women's waged work could have hung on a strong personality within the group, such as the Factory Inspector and medical doctor Robert Baker, who thought women's waged work caused many problems for infants and children. Baker's testimony in this respect could have led to laws prohibiting women's waged work – a similar case can be seen with Malthus's Population Report, whose oral evidence given at the Inquiry of Emigration during the 1820s was considered 'decisive'. However, without Baker's minutes of evidence we cannot tell.[88]

Another potential limitation of these sources to be borne in mind is that we do not know the extent to which the reports were built on hearsay and gossip. Indeed, the answers given the questions asked may have been 'streamlined', 'funnelled' and 'shaped' during editing to address the questions asked.[89] We do not know if the inspectors on occasion asked different questions to those set, and in doing so 'doctored' the evidence.[90] We know that the committees who sat on the reports did not have 'blank minds',[91] and did not start their research with a blank canvas. We do not know whether any disputes over findings and 'exchanges of views [were] purged'.[92] Selective inclusion and exclusion of information could have been due to inspectors relating what the Select Committee wanted to hear.

A difficulty with question-and-answer sets such as those which inspectors had is the matter of questions that were left out and not asked –this can often tell us a lot about a report and its intentions. Moreover, we should remember that very few women were commissioned to ask questions about women's waged work until the 1890s. Although these were mainly middle-class women, they understood that working-class women had to work, and were sympathetic to their plight. When faced with male interviewers, working-class women could face an 'intimidating form of interview'.

Weaknesses in the social statistics presented in the reports also have to be acknowledged. Paul Thompson, for instance, argues they 'do not represent actual facts, but represent an individual's viewpoints or an aggregated social perception of facts, and are all in addition subject to social pressures from the context in which they are obtained. With these forms of evidence, what we receive is social meaning, [rather than factual knowledge] and it is this which must be evaluated.'[93] Thompson even doubts that the calculations made by demographers are free from 'manipulation'.[94] Single questions which do not allow for qualification were regularly posed to nineteenth-century populations. For example, when calculating numbers of children, parents were asked how many children they had, but not how many of their children had died. Thus, there may be inaccuracies in the data. Due to these issues with the reports and statistics this work linked its analysis to other documents and materials to get a fuller, clearer, more accurate picture of working-class mothers' child care.

The chapter on women's waged work was supported by evidence from the full range of local and national newspapers in the Yorkshire and Lancashire districts for the years 1850–1899. They were searched for material relating to the actions of working-class mothers. Articles relevant to the topic were taken from newspapers such as *The Leeds Mercury, The Leeds Intelligencer, Bradford Review, Bradford Observer, Huddersfield Chronicle, Huddersfield Examiner, Huddersfield Daily Chronicle, Manchester Courier, Manchester City News, Lancashire General Advertiser, Manchester Guardian, Manchester Times, The Northern Star, The Preston Guardian, Stockport Advertiser, The Yorkshire Factory Times* and the *Cotton Factory Times*.

As newspaper sources were not online at the beginning of this research, websites of local libraries in Leeds, Bradford, Huddersfield, Wakefield, Manchester and Bolton, and national publications held at British Library Newspapers at Colindale were searched, and many telephone calls were made to identify the number of daily and weekly newspapers relating to the northern districts for the period 1850–1899. The above newspapers were available in daily and weekly versions, and their importance cannot be overstated because they provide context for the period with regard to child care. The next approach was to determine from catalogues and archivists (many of whom hold a wealth of knowledge not evident in catalogues and websites) whether the newspapers reported on industrialised areas, the infant mortality problem and IMR, and any association with waged women's work. Due to the interest which surrounded the debates about factory work and the associated Factory Acts it was suspected that this topic would have carried weight for editors and helped them sell to a readership who worked in industry. Archivists confirmed this suspicion and, as suspected, newspapers in the districts identified carried discussions about factories, their workers, their health, the Factory Acts and working-class women and their methods of child care. Close analysis was applied when searching for reports of aspects of child care. Specific words and phrases searched for included factories, metal workshops, agricultural farms, Yorkshire and Lancashire, infant mortality and its rates, positive and negative customs of child care by mothers, workhouse nurses and day-carers, and desertion – including the names, addresses and occupations of the women. The areas specifically analysed were Dewsbury, Batley, Leeds, Wakefield, Preston, Bolton, Manchester and Blackburn. Articles that spoke of what happened to the women who committed neglect, and what happened to infants who were deserted were also consulted, as were reports of investigations into whether women worked on behalf of the state via the Poor Law to care for children outside the workhouse, and the reach and extent of this role. These reports tell of the degree to which the Poor Law employed women to patrol and police other women in the community who were suspected of neglecting infants. To search for the cultures of workhouse nurse care, advertisements in newspapers were analysed in terms of the nature of the advertisement and the character of the nurses sought.

Newspapers were also trawled for articles which commented on Factory Inspectors' reports; edited and pared-down versions were often published in the press. Articles which spoke of local women's factory work, the names of Factory Inspectors themselves and the extent of their reach were analysed. Once the newspapers became available online, stories relating to domestic arrangements in the mills were looked for by keyword searches for terms such as factory work, Factory Acts, holidays (dinners were made for up to two or three thousand people in mills on holidays), dinner times, breakfast times, suckling, and siblings. These sources were selected as they provided information relating to domestic arrangements for factory workers and the space available to them, in addition to workers' time management, false accounting, (neglecting to register women workers) and sanitary arrangements in the mill and any relating diseases.

The strength of using newspapers lies in their provision of evidence and context for the problem of the IMR, its scale and the ways in which it related to northern women's waged work during the period 1850–1899. Journalistic, rather than empirical, they report news stories about nineteenth-century society in both a local and national context. They are sources that are authentic, readable, orderly, have a good 'literary quality' and are accessible.[95]

Newspapers provide extremely good local context in relation to the cultures of child care and also record attitudes and reactions to the IMR and the child care practices. They are also valuable in giving information about factory mills, the context of the mills, the working-class women who worked in the factories, when the women went to work, what that work was, what they experienced at that work, what hours parliament thought their work should consist of, their daily experiences of that work, and the ages of women working in the mills. When these newspapers are combined with the Inspector's reports we can begin to layer the evidence as to the nature of working-class women's child care, the working day of the women concerned, how they combined waged work with child care, when they were responsible and caring and when negligent. In doing so they give extremely valuable colour to the lives of working-class women and also enable rare insight into northern regional child care practices hitherto unknown to us.

A particular strength of newspapers as a source is their ability to tell us that some women received payment from the Poor Law. When combined with the testimony in assize records, this helps us identify whether the community prized infants and acted to limit the neglect they experienced by employing women to police infants suspected to be neglected by their mothers. This information shows us that the Poor Law Guardians in the north of England were engaged in reducing the IMR, and employed poor women in receipt of parish help to help to do so.

However, Victorian newspapers, both elite and popular, do manifest bias, as their owners and journalists were male and middle class. Their reports were also sensational in nature, arguably because there was much competition between newspapers. Also, at times they held a political bias which was often liberal–conservative in nature especially during the 1850–1899 period. Nineteenth-century journalists adhered to this political stance and reported what the editor wished his readership to hear, and shaped and filtered stories to fit this bias.[96] Moreover, they tended to concentrate on the negative aspects or sensational criminal cases (as they sold newspapers). Therefore, the reporting was regularly one-sided. To overcome this, newspapers sources were gleaned for actual testimony about customs of child care and the actual detail inherent in child care which had little obvious political ideology applied to it. Again, we have no records of the notes taken by these journalists so we have to be aware that their stories could be built on hearsay. Hence, articles taken from these newspapers have to be read with these caveats in mind and then stripped of these biases by focusing on the culture of child care, what women did for their infants and children, and not what the editors and journalists thought about that child care.

The published census records at the Oxfordshire Local History Library provided global figures for infant deaths by county. However, these records contain information on number only, there is no information relating to the family details of the infants concerned. To gain a better insight into the deaths of infants in Leeds therefore over two thousand infant death records kept at the Brotherton Library were collated and analysed. These records, taken from Woodhouse Cemetery, hold details of the date of infant death, the names of the parents, the occupation of the father, the disease at death and the address of the parents. The sources were difficult to photocopy so details were spoken into a tape recorder. This unusual style of data collection was slow, but it was important to collect the information as it gave a wealth of detail, vital for this research, about infants who had died in the industrial area of Leeds.

The information on the death records present problems. Errors in recording and transcription are possible, the information to the registrar at the cemetery by either the infants' parents, a relative or neighbour may have been inaccurate as to names, ages, addresses and occupations. We know that embellishments of occupations were made on birth and death certificates as well as censuses – nineteenth-century men and women were often keen to inflate their working status. Nonetheless, with this in mind, and when contrasted with the census, these records can inform us about the infants who lived in Leeds during the latter half of the nineteenth century.

Census records relating to thousands of women were trawled online for information about women's work in the areas of Leeds, Keighley, Bradford, Dewsbury and Batley, Manchester and Preston. Data collected from women's details in these areas were address, work, age and number of children. These census records, when linked with other material, aided our understanding of whether women withdrew from factory works once they reached a certain age.

Census records are a valuable source in the study of women's histories. They are available in a standard readable format and provide a snapshot of particular aspects of Britain. Householders filled out their own forms, which enumerators transferred on to the official census documents. These records give us family details such as women's names, marital status and occupation, and when the census is used in conjunction with other records, such as the mill wage records held in the Leeds Brotherton Library and West Yorkshire Archives (WYAS) for the Dewsbury and Batley districts, they can help us unpick the experiences and individual lives of working-class women. The value matrix which arises out of this record combination adds much-needed depth and understanding to our uneven knowledge of working-class women's lives and their child care: very few women left us any detail, and, indeed, personal accounts of their child care are virtually nonexistent.

Whilst census records hold much important information about working-class women and their children, it has to be noted that some of it may be inaccurate, and there are numerous difficult obstacles to overcome when using them. Eddie Higgs argues the census was a male construct and the data collected from nineteenth century households were severely manipulated by the enumerators who often sought to reflect the domestic and maternal roles of women and mothers rather than their waged work.[97] Elizabeth Roberts argues this was the case in Lancashire, where vast numbers of married women's factory work went unreported and unacknowledged.[98] In addition to ideological issues we have to consider that enumerators could err in transferring the details given to them, and householders themselves might lie about their age, occupations, marital status and the number of children they had; women would be less likely to reveal an occupation in an era when women's work was frowned on; false ages might be given due to the need to conceal identities; householders might misunderstand or misinterpret the questions asked of them. Indeed, women workers might have interpreted their work differently, for example if a woman were occupied in sweated home-work she might consider this as waged work and reflect this on her census return, or might not because the work was not undertaken in the public sphere. This difficulty in understanding might be further compounded by instructions stating that women should only give their waged work when it was other than domestic. As women were discouraged from working in the public sphere, the head of the household (usually the husband) was unlikely to state that his wife was engaged in a waged occupation which would take her out of the domestic sphere. The census can, therefore, be regarded as an uneven source in the matter of women's work.

Testimony was also provided via the published collections dealing with working-class women's waged work by Barbara Hutchins and Margaret Llewelyn Davies. Both these women had a keen interest in the experiences of working-class women's waged work, and their collected works gave voice to the child care practices of women who lived and worked in the industrial districts during the 1850–1890s. Margaret Llewelyn Davies published *Maternity: Letters from Working Women* in 1915. This book holds a unique collection of 160 letters from working-class mothers who worked during the nineteenth century. They were members of the Women's Co-operative Guild (WCG) during the early part of the twentieth century. The WCG was established in 1883 and was headed by Margaret Llewelyn Davies in 1889. The letters were a response to a questionnaire sent out to working-class members of the Guild during the early years of the twentieth century. The questionnaire was geared to collecting information from women about their experiences of maternity whilst working in a range of occupations such as factories, (rag sorting and weaving,[99] laundries, going out to clean and wash,[100] and 'clean and paper',[101] taking in plain washing and sewing[102] and working as a parlour maid.[103] Llewelyn Davies sent questionnaires to 600 women out of the 32,000 who belonged to the Guild; she received 386 replies from women who had become mothers in the nineteenth century.

In approaching this material, the first step was to identify the letters relating to nineteenth century child care. Elizabeth Langford tells us that the letters are a collection from the period, but Angela Davis has argued that these letters confirm Edwardian child care, even though this was not the remit announced by Margaret Llewelyn Davies[104] (she claimed on the back of the book that she was seeking to capture nineteenth-century child care). However, although Llewelyn Davies strips personal details from the letters we can calculate the period that the mothers are writing about: some correspondents give their age at the time of writing and at marriage; if we combine this information with the date when the letters were collected it is a simple matter to calculate the period being described. The letters were published in 1915, and took a number of years to collect. For sake of argument, and to err on the side of caution, we say that the letters were collected in 1914; using this as a benchmark, we can gauge the period in which the women became mothers. Thus, if we look at the author of letter number 9 for instance, she tells us that she was aged 58 in 1914 (or earlier). This tells us she was born in 1856 or earlier, and she tells us that she was 23 when she married and probably 24 when she had her first child. Hence, the child care experience she speaks of begins in 1879/1880. This is nineteenth-century child care, and although we cannot categorically say the mothers all resemble mother number 9, it can be argued that as Davies wanted to capture nineteenth-century child care it was to women around this age that she wrote.

The next issue was to determine how many of the letters were from the northern districts and related to infants aged between 0 and 12 months. As the questionnaires and responses dealt with pregnancy and the immediate care of babies after confinement then the majority of the letters contain this material. However, as the letter headings were stripped of their geographical origin an in-depth search for references to districts in the north of England had to be carried out. This showed that at least 27 of Llewelyn Davies's letters can be linked to the north of England and the West Riding. This small but rare collection of northern working-class mothers' memoirs was then examined for information about child care practices. Further information gleaned included how many children the women had, their experiences of pregnancy and child care overall and what the women ate during their pregnancy as well as their method of feeding after parturition and its duration.

The letters can be used to contrast with the narrative of working class women who give evidence to parliamentary Select Committees. They can be used in conjunction with the Factory Inspectors' and witness narratives to identify whether the women speak with one voice as to how they combined waged work with child care or if there were differences. In addition, they can be contrasted with the Barbara Hutchins collection outlined below.

This source is flawed, however. Firstly, and significantly, there is a tremendous amount of detail *not* available to us from the letters. To conceal the identity of the mothers who responded, Llewelyn Davies purged all their personal details. In addition, the nature and quantity of the responses published were likely to have been affected by Llewelyn Davies' character and her self-portrayal as a middle-class feminist. Llewelyn Davies was sympathetic to the plight of working-class women and lobbied constantly and persistently on their behalf; yet she held deep-seated prejudices about them.[105] As a middle-class, unmarried woman in favour of suffrage and independence, Llewelyn Davies found working-class mothers closed to the idea of suffrage. Moreover, she was appalled by the sight of working-class women sacrificing themselves at the altar of domesticity: she called for them to reject it and all its manifestations.[106] Llewelyn Davies sought to enlighten working-class women, to lift them out of their drudgery by steering them away from 'neighbourhood gossip', choosing instead to debate the merits of 'public life over private life'.[107] Yet, in many respects the trappings of working-class women's lives, their husbands and particularly their infants and children, were ornaments for their respect, and they earned this respect within their communities by looking after their family. Discussions about 'private lives' were the glue which held these female working-class communities together, and Llewelyn Davies, as an independent, unmarried, middle-class woman had very little understanding of this. She could often be scathing of them as a 'class' as a result.[108] This may have limited the number of returns received, and the quality, honesty and content of the replies. That said, the strength of these letters lies in their provision of the 'ordinary'. They document in great detail the everyday occurrences and practices of working-class women's lives, particularly their child care. In this respect, the strengths of the letters far outweigh their weaknesses.

Barbara Hutchins, like Llewelyn Davies, was interested in working-class women's experiences. Hutchins conducted 95 interviews with working-class women who lived in Yorkshire and the West Riding during 1909–10 recalling their child care practices. The testimony given by mothers aged between 40 and 70 were most useful for the purposes of this work, as their narratives relate to mothers who worked in the mills during the latter half of the nineteenth century. These interviews were published in Clementina Black's book, *Married Women's Work* in 1915. Black thought it important to discover the working experiences of women in provincial districts, and the book provides detail about married women's work in Yorkshire, Manchester, Liverpool, Newcastle, Reading, Leicester, Leeds and Macclesfield, and Glasgow in addition to London. Hutchins was a member of the Women's Industrial Council and the Fabian Women's Group during the early years of the twentieth century. She was also a 'school manager, lecturer and writer on factory and social questions'[109] and campaigned to improve women's working conditions during the early part of the twentieth century.[110]

Hutchins spoke to women aged 20 to 70, undertaking the interviews in the women's own homes. The interviews were conducted to establish detail relative to the 'economic and hygienic effects of the industrial employment of married women' and thus provide 'and publish trustworthy information about the conditions of women's work.'[111] The interviews were based around questions which asked details about the worker, including name and address, whether married or not and where they worked. If unemployed, their reasons for not working were documented. Further particulars sought included the women's family and health, their earnings, dependents, number of children, how many had died and whether the mother worked whilst the child was alive. The arrangements for child care were also discussed, as were wages, present economic condition, and the characteristics of trade and legislative and general about the work undertaken.[112]

The strength of the interviews by Hutchins cannot be overstated. She was a regular contributor to pamphlets about married women's work during the early part of the twentieth century and was familiar with the working conditions of factories in Leeds and the West Riding.[113] The women whom she interviewed worked in those factories. They had infants, and they spoke about how they cared for them whilst they undertook their work as weavers (26), spinners (10), wool-combers (17), rag pickers (10) and warpers and winders (11). The older women, aged 40–70, provide some extremely rare testimony on nineteenth-century factory mothers' child care. Indeed, the women aged 50–70 provide testimony on 1870s child care, including whether they breast-fed and if they were able to take their infants to work with them. Details about the reasons for going to work are given, as are their opinions on whether their work was detrimental to their families.[114]

As with Llewelyn Davies's sources, there are class and gender biases to contend with when using Hutchins's work. She was a school manager and perhaps likely to patronise working-class women. Indeed, Hutchins may have possessed what Lucy Delap has characterised as the 'self-development' understanding of feminists in 1913; a model used to preach to women at that time.[115] Again, we do not have the notes taken by Hutchins from which to confirm her findings. She was known in the West Riding area and as a teacher she may have been subject to the same prejudices as Llewelyn Davies with regard to working-class women. Despite these potential weaknesses, the interviews offer an invaluable insight into the working lives of factory mothers, and the women involved seemed less intimidated by Hutchins than Llewelyn Davies's subjects were by their interlocutor.

Further evidence for the voice of the working-class mother was located in the published Vaccination Reports commissioned by parliament during the 1890s. In particular Vaccination Commissions numbered 1897, c 8609, 10, 11,12,13,14 and 15 were examined. These reports concern the outbreak of smallpox, and the subsequent condition of the infants affected. In addition they also give information relating to the child care practices of their mothers in specific northern industrial areas. Held within these reports, especially c. 8615, is testimony from 200 working-class parents given in reply to questions asked by medical doctors as to the care of the infants prior to their illness and/or deaths. These questions were posed in order to ascertain 'cases in which death or non-fatal injury was alleged or suggested to have been caused by or otherwise connected with vaccination'.[116] Hundreds of cases are examined in each report and like the Factory Inspectors' reports; the write up is given in a strict question-and-answer set.

The answers given by working-class mothers provide a wealth of data about child care in the industrial areas of Dewsbury, Salford, Manchester, Leeds and Bradford, and in doing so they reveal much about the social history of child care practice during the period. The testimony as to the modes and models of looking after baby is confirmed by the medical doctors, neighbours and those who had subsidiary care of infants. Infant feeding models were a particular focus for the investigation and analysis of the reports. Once again, the biases in the narrative need to be borne in mind here. Indeed, we have to consider that mothers might embroider and embellish their child care to present it in the best light in order that they could not be held responsible for their infants' ill health or death. Medical doctors, however, do not subject the feeding models to criticism, nor attribute the death of the infants to them, and they do not seem to question or challenge any evidence. Ascertaining the model used was their main aim, in order to assess the general attitude of the mothers towards their infants. Breast feeding was doctors' prescribed way for infants to be fed and if this had been followed or attempted then the prevailing view was that the infant had been well cared for and thus the death had not occurred under suspicious circumstances.

Whilst the first and second chapters of this work examine the work and child care of industrial mothers and how it was managed, the third chapter explores how workhouse nurses cared for pauper children. The next chapter then tests the diet given to them. Evidence cited in the chapters relating to workhouse provision again comes from both unpublished and published material, but largely from sources with more of a medical and welfare focus. Published materials such as the census records at the Oxfordshire Local Records Office and the Poor Law Medical Health Records held at The National Archives at Kew were consulted. In addition, information relating to the Poor Law and medical doctors serving the poor was searched for in sources such as *The British Medical Journal* (*BMJ*) and *Lancet*. Provincial workhouse data was also explored in evidence and reports of parliamentary commissions and unpublished records uncovered at the WYAS.

To ascertain the number of working-class nurses who worked in northern workhouses 16,000 unpublished Poor Law Medical Health Records (MH) held at the National Archives were searched. MH12 was found to be relevant, with over 6,741 Poor Law Medical Health Records. These records showed that Manchester was the workhouse that employed the largest number of such nurses, and provided examples of hundreds of women employed in this context. The search was then narrowed further, specifically to find the Poor Law Medical Health Records for the Yorkshire and Lancashire regions for the years 1850–1899. Once these were to hand each regions headcount of nurses was recorded.

Valuable, but largely unanalysed data concerning the names of the nurses, how long they stayed in their positions, the date of appointment and release was drawn from these sources. We also learnt about the details of the rooms in which they worked. This analysis allowed the identification of a large number of nurses who were trained in Manchester between 1850 and 1899. Overall, these records were extremely valuable and enabled a comparison to be drawn with medical texts, the *BMJ* and *Lancet*, as well as Factory

Inspectors' reports to aid our understanding of infant care during the period and in particular to enable us to see that paediatric intervention, rather than helping infants, often placed them at risk.

Global data concerning the numbers of working-class women who inhabited workhouses, from which analysis could be extrapolated as to who was put to work in workhouses, was collected from published statistical collections and records held at the Oxfordshire Records Office. With these figures to hand the search was narrowed to determine the number of working-class women who lived and worked as nurses in workhouses in Yorkshire and Lancashire in the years 1851, 1871 and 1891. The previous occupations of these women were determined from the population register prior to their entry to the workhouse for the years 1851–1891. This was done to determine the skills of the women put to work to care for infants by the Poor Law Guardians.

The character of the workhouse nurses concerned was explored through contemporary medical sources such as the *BMJ, Lancet,* and through medical texts from luminaries such as Eustace Smith MD. During the Victorian era, the medical profession placed great emphasis on the maternal incompetence of northern working-class mothers, especially those in the Yorkshire and Lancashire workhouses. The women of Leeds, Bradford, Huddersfield, Manchester, Bolton and Preston were particularly singled out as lacking essential maternal knowledge, and it was these inadequacies, it was argued, that led to a high workhouse IMR. These sources contain testimony from medical men such as Dr Eustace Smith relating to working-class women's child care, and also give a deep insight into nineteenth-century medical understanding of infant disease and ailments.

BMJ and *Lancet* records were examined at the Radcliffe Science Library in Oxford. All of the *BMJ*'s 64 volumes relating to 1850–1899 and the 164 volumes of *Lancet* relating to the years 1823–1899 were read, as were various contemporary medical texts. The material was searched for articles and reports relating to northern industrial areas. Of specific interest were articles concerning infant mortality, infant disease and workhouse nurses. By using a focused geographical approach, the volumes were then searched for topics which had relevance to the commissioned inquiry that the *BMJ* and *Lancet* undertook in relation to the high IMR problem in workhouses. Particular discussions relating to the cause of death of infants, the physiology of disease, medical rationale for disease and plans to ameliorate infant deaths were searched for. The power that medical men were imbued with within the workhouse and the relationship they had with workhouse guardians were investigated, to help us to better understand the extent of their influence over workhouse paediatric practices. The nature of the professional relationship which medical men had with workhouse nurses was a subject of particular interest, and information on infants' environment and diet within the workhouse, particularly the ingredients prescribed by the medical profession, was also collected and analysed to establish the propensity to enhance or endanger infant life.

Articles which proffered moral attitudes about workhouse nurses and their child care practices were selected for attention, as were articles which contained discussions about workhouse nurses and baby-farmers, particularly those which dealt with neglect or positive child care in the geographical foci of this research. Using this method, at least 35 reports relating to baby-farmers in the *BMJ* (1850–1899) were found, in addition to a further 267 reports from that period about workhouses, their female staff, paupers and infants. This material was later supplemented by letters found in the archives of Bolton Local Library written by medical men who testified on behalf of the workhouse nurses they worked with.

The strength of the medical sources from the *Lancet* and the *BMJ* lies in their ability to provide a comprehensive approach and context for the period in relation to the problems that infants experienced and medical opinion on the causes of those problems. By researching this we can understand how the nineteenth-century medical profession understood infant health and how it sought to improve it. These sources also tell us about the knowledge that nineteenth-century paediatricians held and how the physiology of infant diseases was understood. Another strength is the information on breast milk and, in particular, the tests which medical doctors performed on it. This enables us to understand the medical perceptions of breast milk and its perceived impact on infant health.

The nineteenth century medical profession was run by middle-class men with little input from women, and the sources have to be read with this bias in mind. Further weaknesses relate to the experiments doctors conducted. We do not have the notes of these experiments, thus we have to take the doctors' word for what transpired. A further caveat is that the medical profession were charged by the government to ameliorate the high IMR. This responsibility and the need to find the cure quickly, may have led medical men to rush their experiments, leading them to the wrong conclusions. Moreover, medical men were keen to prove their worth to nineteenth-century society because they operated in an unregulated, flooded medical market place in which their standing, income and future prospects were threatened. Given this, medical doctors may have been apt to find fault with 'others' who had the care of infants, and label them as neglectful. Expressions of moral approbation have to be considered in this light.

In addition to the above sources, newspapers, and pamphlets from middle-class commentators such as Louisa Twining, Florence Nightingale and the medical doctors Joseph Rogers, T.M. Dolan and Alfred Sheen have also been utilised. These newspapers and commentaries were subject to the same scrutiny as described above. Medical knowledge of paediatricians who prescribed for mother and infant paupers was also investigated through the published works of Dr Edward Smith. Smith was commissioned to write a report in 1866 on the sufficiency of existing arrangements for the care of the sick in 48 provincial workhouses. Included in his remit was the care of pregnant women and infants. A second commission was set up later that same year to examine dietary provision in 65 provincial pauper workhouses, which similarly included cataloguing the diets of mothers and babies in the lying-in wards. Smith's past work on the knowledge of nutrition identified him as the ideal candidate to undertake the surveys. His particular interested lay in the workings of the body, physiological chemistry and of the relationship between diet and health, and which foods proved the most useful and beneficial.[117] In addition he had a desire to improve the health of the population through the food which they consumed and bought.[118] He was duly appointed as a doctor and physician and then as an inspector and medical doctor to the Poor Law Board in 1865.[119] The next approach was to explore the survey for information relating to infants and mothers and lying-in wards. This was available in abundance in the areas under consideration.

Both works from Edward Smith (1819–1874) are extremely relevant and useful for this study. His remit was to delve into the problems associated with provincial workhouses, rather than adopt a merely London-centric approach, and his work pre-dates the *BMJ*'s surveys of parochial workhouses in the 1890s. The reports are extremely valuable as Smith's remit was to identify abuses within workhouses such as inadequate diet, lack of care, incapable nurses and the multitude of problems associated with the role of medical doctors, going on to perform a survey and write up his findings. As mothers and infants inhabited the provincial workhouses, Smith's work is pivotal for this study providing an abundance of information relating to the experiences of these paupers. The information relating to infant diet and its quantities can also be contrasted with the medical pamphlets and texts written by other medical doctors to confirm its authenticity and accuracy. Not only do Smith's reports relay information about daily experiences and diet, but they also analyse the domestic environment. His own views are evident, and this tells us how he views the mothers, the wards they lived in, the plans of the workhouses, the doctors and their daily routines. He also gives information about the medical staff, even naming some of them on occasion. We also have the number of nurses employed, his opinion on their capability and character, and details of the daily tasks performed in different workhouses. He also documents the furniture and sleeping arrangements in the workhouses, affording a unique insight into how infants and mothers lived.

There are a few factors to bear in mind when utilising Edward Smith's work. First, he was a medical doctor. As we have already seen, his profession was in conflict with workhouse guardians during the 1860s over wages and the extent of the work medical doctors had to do. Consequently, and in order to portray the guardians in a bad light, he may have played down the diets and experiences of paupers in the workhouses. In contrast, he may have been tempted to display medical doctors in a good light and to do so he may have embellished the experiences of paupers, both infant and mother, who were under the jurisdiction of the medical officer in the workhouse. On reading all of his reports, however, he seems balanced and objective. Nevertheless, we have to consider the possibility that transcription errors may have been made in transferring the material from his notes to the official record (we do not have his original notes). We also need to remember that the rationale for conducting the dietary surveys was led by a desire to provide the best quality food at the lowest cost to the workhouse guardians. This might suggest that Smith was keen to curry favour with the guardians and help them reduce costs by reporting the diets and quantities as better than he found, but as Smith was a supposed expert in nutrition we might expect that he gave an accurate description, though we do not have access to the notes he took.

More detailed information about northern workhouses came from the archives in Leeds, Bradford, Huddersfield and Wakefield collectively known as the WYAS, and unpublished material in catalogues relating to Poor Law material from the West Yorkshire Archives of Hemsworth, Hunslet, Holbeck, Leeds, Keighley, Holbeck, North Bierley, and Wakefield for the years 1850–1899 was surveyed. This search revealed 64 volumes of Minute Books and 10 Admission and Discharge Books, and additional items related to Poor Law local history constituting some 148 minute books. A minute book record-ing infant death was found at the Leeds Thackrah Medical Museum, and inmate records were also identified at Leeds Sheepscar. Admission and Dis-charge books explain why infants were in the Yorkshire workhouses in the first instance. Bradford and Leeds Sheepscar WYAS provided this informa-tion and disclosed how many infants were deserted by their mothers, and what happened to the infants and mothers concerned. Did they go to the workhouse? If so, how long did the infants remain there and how many survived?

In general, Poor Law minute books mainly contain detail about workhouse economics, so material relating to working-class women is well hidden. This lacuna was compounded as neither 'working-class women' nor 'infants' were specific headings in any of the Poor Law materials and as the minute books do not carry indexes the only approach was to sit in the West Yorkshire Archive and go through the books page by page and line by line. This necessitated a patient approach, not least because of the difficulty in locat-ing narratives relating to the ideology or policy associated with infants and poor working-class women. Most of the Poor Law minutes relate to how and where they spent their money, and even when this is noted, the infor-mation recorded gives historians little to go on as the categories are often unspecified. Much of the detail of where the money was spent is difficult to decipher as single words are used to categorise a whole range of costs. There-fore, every Poor Law minute book, admission and discharge book which Hemsworth, Hunslet, Leeds, Keighley, Holbeck, North Bierley, Dewsbury,

Batley and Wakefield held for the years 1850–1899 was read. Close scrutiny was also applied to note how much money guardians allocated to working-class women with infants – Was it for indoor or outdoor relief? How was this applied? What was the job of the relieving officers? Were they left to their own devices or given instructions to police working-class women with infants? In essence, these volumes were examined in an effort to discover if any working-class women were targeted by the Poor Law and if the women were under any duress in relation to their child care practices.

Poor Law was the official body which dealt with economic problems encountered by working-class women and also dealt with vulnerable infants. Poor Law sources are vital for determining how working-class women and their infants were treated when they needed welfare support. Consequently their contribution to this study was invaluable because they contained verbatim accounts telling us what workhouse Guardians thought about working-class women and their child care. This information is under-utilised in the current historiography. Questions asked of this material were: What approach and philosophy did the Poor Law authorities hold towards working-class women and infants? Further, was the Poor Law accommodating to mothers who turned to it for help? Were policies constructive and practical, or harmful? Admission books were also useful in this respect as they contained information relating to infants and working-class mothers, supplementing the minute books in helping to answer questions such as: Who was admitted? For what reasons? What happened to the infants of the women concerned?

Historians have to navigate certain problems when using Poor Law material. It is patchy and the records are few in number, rarely allowing a comprehensive or comparative approach. Moreover, as we have seen, narratives relating to the topic of infant mortality and working-class women are extremely rare. The records are mostly economic in focus with the Guardians at pains to tell where they spent their money, giving little information on policy or practices. Indeed, the position of 'Guardian' of the workhouse changed from year to year, and record-keeping is extremely inconsistent as a result. Moreover, the records, and the Poor Law in general, was run by middle-class men with very little input from women. Poor Law and medical sources provide information relating to workhouse nurses, to doctors' relationship with the nurses, and to doctors' reach and power within the workhouse and wider community. They also give an insight into how doctors sought to improve the conditions for infants within the workhouse and their relationship with the Guardians as to how they could work together to improve and secure infant lives.

Much of the evidence described in this section contradicts the way in which mothers have been portrayed by scholars. Material has come to light which will give us a more balanced perspective on working-class mothers. Nevertheless, material on ineffective motherhood was also obtained for the Yorkshire and Lancashire districts over the 1850–1899 period. Indictment files and Crown Minute Books of the Northern Assizes were examined at the National Archives, yielding 1200 cases. Eight Crown Minute Books, ASSI 41/21 – ASSI 41/31 for the years 1849–1889, contained hundreds of cases each, and Indictments files relating to ASSI 51 and 52 contained around 50 cases each. Prison catalogue calendars HO 27 and HO 184, were also searched in relation to the name of those indicted.

Whilst these sources threw up negative aspects of infant care, court cases, surprisingly, also help us to identify positive child care practices, for they introduce us to a small, rare collection of day-carers and baby-minders. These women and their testimony play an important part in infanticide trials over the period 1850–1899 as a consequence of the judiciary trying to identify the links between child killing and the high IMR. Day-carers and baby-minders were questioned about how often the mothers saw their infants, how regular their payments were and the amounts concerned. Indeed, the judges who put baby-minders on the stand tended to question them at length on how long they had been a carer, why the mother needed child care in the first instance, and the steps that had been taken to keep the infants alive. In these few but rare and important cases we hear the difficulties of mothers who turned to this form of child care and why they did so. Surprisingly, this material provided a new way of identifying responsible and caring child care during the 1850–1899 period which could then be regularly contrasted with the actions of more felonious individuals. Using these records in isolation of course presents a skewed picture of baby-minding, and in order to provide a more accurate picture other forms of evidence such as Vaccination Records and Parliamentary Papers have been used to supplement this material. This approach of record linkage runs through the whole work, maximising the benefits from the materials uncovered.

Structure

Chapter 1 reviews the current debate concerning women's waged work and the child care practices of these women. As we will see, working-class women earned their crust through a variety of occupations. Chapter 2 addresses the relationship between working-class women's industrial work and the IMR, and specifically analyses whether this work led to a decline in maternal care or whether sagacious new child care models were adopted. The relationship between the work of pauper nurses and the high workhouse IMR is explored in Chapter 3. This chapter examines in depth the responsibilities and character of workhouse nurses through the eyes of those who worked alongside them. Chapter 4 establishes the effect the workhouse infant diet had on levels of infant mortality. By focusing on a rich archival legacy in northern workhouses – broadly representative of northern urban and industrial indoor provision, this chapter provides a more detailed analysis of the nature of infant mortality than has previously been available. The degree to which day-carers were involved in the high northern IMR is examined in chapter 5 by using new, rare, and atypical case studies.

It is to the first chapter that we now turn. This addresses the current scholarship in light of the extent of working-class women's work and the child care practices they adopted.

1
The Scholarship on Working-class Women's Work and their Child Care Models

This chapter will deal with the long, complex trajectory of women's waged and unwaged work. Studies show that women have historically provided for their families and the family economy to a considerable degree. As a high IMR coincided with northern women's introduction to industrialisation, contemporaries made, and historians have continued to make, strong connections between women's work and a high infant mortality rate, with particular emphasis being placed on the culpability of factory work.

Women have always worked. It was mainly working-class women who engaged in waged work, because their personal and family economies and/or cultures dictated it. Female factory work characterised the nineteenth century, though working-class women also carried out unwaged work as they were responsible for a range of domestic duties for which there was no pay. We will see that women were not strangers to waged labour, contributing in a wide range of roles to their family's income, although that work was subject to ebb and flow.

This chapter will begin by discussing the barriers to women taking up waged work, and the strength of feeling against it. By promoting a domestic ideology, patriarchy sought to control working-class women's lives by limiting their recourse to, and availability for, waged work. Home sweated labour and its associated low wage was a distinctive feature of women's work during the latter half of the nineteenth century. One of the justifications offered for the patriarchal ideology was that home-working mothers could care for their infants at home rather than having to pass them over to a carer when going out to work; however, this reduced their families to poverty which had a knock-on effect on the health of the family, particularly women and their children. To alleviate the pressure of poverty, working-class women sold their labour in a variety of guises, and, through their waged labour, played a larger part in supporting their families than has generally been allowed for.

It is to the obstacles to working-class women's work that we first turn.

Barriers to waged work – the domestic ideal

Nineteenth-century censuses were meant to record the numbers of working women in any occupation, but, as a source, census data are controversial due to the way that the numbers were captured and categorised. The works of Eddie Higgs, Sonya O. Rose, Jane Humphries and Sara Horrell give us good reason to suspect that many women's occupations slipped through the net of the nineteenth-century's censuses for various reasons (although Michael Anderson suggests that for all its problems the census 'is the best indicator we have at present'[1]). The debate over the numbers of women workers looms large in women's and economic history, but it is clear that the idea of the working woman in the nineteenth century was constantly under attack, and this may have resulted in regular under-recording.

Industrialisation changed the working-class woman's life: the rationale which had informed their working day during the pre-industrial period began to disappear and with it the home-labour by which they had provided for their families. Historians have argued that industrialisation reduced employment opportunities for women in general, and generated particular problems for mothers as work in factories forced maternal separation.[2] Another complication for working class women who found work was that they were obliged to move into the public sphere, which was a significant barrier to obtaining work. One of the strongest ideological forces operating against women's waged work was, and still is, patriarchy, which identified nineteenth-century working-class mothers who worked as 'out of their sex' and 'feckless'.[3] Further character assassination averted to them being morally culpable for the deaths of their infants.[4] As Sonia O. Rose notes, 'mothering and breadwinning were oppositional constructs'.[5] Carolyn Malone argues that a strong link was made between 'work and maternity' by Drs Bridges and Holmes, who had been commissioned by government in 1873 to investigate the effect that women's waged work had on infant mortality.[6] A collective opinion of these doctors and 130 others asserted in the strongest terms, by a vote of 101 out of 132, that women's waged work 'increased the rate of infant mortality'.[7]

Prescriptions of the best model of motherhood abounded during the nineteenth century, nearly all drawn from the middle-class model of mothers who did not work and therefore were able to focus their love and attention on their families.[8] These women were characterised as the 'angel of the house', whose sole raison d'être was to steer and nurture their families.[9] This opinion shaped the nineteenth-century Factory Acts, which aimed to limit women's work.

Although the domestic ideal was prescribed, working-class women had little control of the family's purse. Without access to waged work they had to rely on a steady income from their husbands and lovers; this made wives' daily existence tricky to navigate and often reduced the family to penury.

Anna Clark points to the struggle for the 'breeches' during the late eighteenth and nineteenth centuries, as women strove to take control of the family's budget from husbands prone to give their wages to the landlord of the public house rather than contribute to 'housekeeping' – a cause of many rows and arguments in plebeian families.[10] The male head of the household was not compelled to 'tip up' his wages to his wife, irrespective of whether the family had enough money to provide for the necessities of life. As Amanda Vickery reminds us, patriarchy was a useful device by which to control the family. The social order – 'master, mistress, and children, with servants and perhaps apprentices, remained a universally recognised ideal type'.[11]

The promotion of gender and its associated notions stained the character of working women, painting women who undertook work in a vulgar and crude hue. Although Amanda Vickery argues against a 'golden age' for women during the pre-industrial era, when domesticity was supposedly an obtainable ideal for working women, Joan Scott identified the 'sexual difference'[12] and ideas about femininity and masculinity which acted to limit women's waged work though gendered notions which labelled the 'dangerous and immoral trades' women worked in and facilitated the passing of dangerous-trade legislation against their work.[13] Alex Shepherd and Garthine Walker have examined this lens and argue it is a powerful heuristic device by which 'historians [can] explore not only relations between the sexes or sexuality but also markets, classes, [and] diplomacy....'[14] Anxieties emanated from men not wishing to be involved in domestication with their family and, particularly during the nineteenth century, desperate not to be seen 'pushing the pram'. The scourge of patriarchy ran wide and deep during the eighteenth, nineteenth and twentieth centuries, and whilst it is not as strong as previously, it still has some bite today. Historians have argued that nineteenth-century working-class women had little political power to fight against controls on their behaviour. The need to adhere to patriarchal models when taking up waged work in the twentieth century was as strong for some women as in the eighteenth century. (For instance, Pat Ayers interviewed the wife of a Liverpool dock worker during the 1930s, who remarked that she did indeed work but hid it from her husband for if he had known, 'he would have gone berserk'[15]). Although there was some change in attitudes in the nineteenth century, Elaine Chalus has argued that 'there is no neat, whiggish trajectory that can be traced for women and politics across 1700–1850', while in the seventeenth century 'the idea of enfranchised women was so outlandish that they could only be imagined satirically'.[16] As a consequence, it has been declared that 'women have been unable to lobby and instigate policy for their own needs.' In her brief chronology Gerry Holloway shows us how, although blighted by patriarchy, women fought this powerlessness and were able to take control of their working lives.[17]

The patriarchal model is challenged by Bridget Hill, who argues it was the middle-class mode of capitalist production, not merely patriarchy, that posed the most problems for working-class women: She argues: 'Once work took husband or wife, or both, away from the home, there could be no approximation to a working relationship between them'.[18] She contends that the onward march of capitalism drove a wedge between men and women, causing men to be in competition with women in the workplace, and it was to ease this competition that the latter were identified as the weaker sex,[19] 'which led to a feminization of women's work' and the 'gendered division of labour'.[20] This feminization promoted women as creatures in need of protection. Medical men and the government concurred with this notion, so we see a whole raft of legislation during the nineteenth century which sought not merely to limit women's work but actually to prohibit it. For working-class women who needed to work to support their families, this environment meant they were in for an extremely difficult time of it.

In a further bid to limit women's work, women workers also faced discrimination in respect of their skill set. Many of the skills they learned during the pre-industrialisation period lost their utility during industrialisation. As Freifeld shows, the de-skilling of women's work in the cotton industries meant that fewer spinning jobs were open to them[21] and without recourse to a trade union women who worked in these cotton industries had few or no means of obtaining redress for grievances.[22] Gerry Holloway shows that us 'women tended to feature in the less skilled lighter end of the trade where employers could justify lower wages.'[23] Lacking skilled positions, women's wages were lower in general than men's, which contributed to a lack of respect from men and husbands who disapproved of working for low pay.[24]

Factory Acts, particularly those of 1847, 1850 and 1853, further compounded women's problems, as they linked women with children supposed to be in need of protection against the dangers of waged work. Carolyn Malone has commented in depth on the volume of legislation restricting the employment space for women during the nineteenth century.[25] Notions of patriarchy deemed many roles 'unfit' for women.[26] Women's identity was determined in the 'domestic sphere', where they could attend to their families. Indeed, not only was it considered that women needed protecting against waged work but also it was held to affect their ability to produce children: a committee reporting on the nail and chain trades concluded that work in this trade 'imperilled women's reproductive functions'.[27] It was suggested that lead poisoning impacted on the ability of women to 'bear children'.[28] Indeed, as Anna Davin has shown us, working-class women were blamed for the poor physique and weak health of the soldiers sent to fight in the Boar War –medical men claimed that recruits had been ill cared-for by their mothers.[29]

The depth of patriarchal feeling led to a reduction in the amount of women's, and in particular married women's, work during the latter half of the nineteenth century. Susie Steinbach points out that: 'Over time, married women found it more difficult than single women to find work. In 1851 75% of married women performed waged work but by 1911 only 10% of married women were recorded as employed.'[30] The marriage bar and unequal pay further compounded women's waged-working roles and although the First and Second World Wars punctured this ideology, the 1950s and 1960s re-entrenched the idea that women's participation in the waged workforce should be extremely limited.[31] Historians argue these barriers acted as a significant bulwark against women's waged work, but working-class women who could not depend on their husbands' wages and were in need of money to contribute towards their families' subsistence had to sell their labour to the highest bidder in their geographical location. Thus, despite the 'rhetoric' employed against them for working, they had little option but to disregard the prevailing ideology and join the ranks of the employed.

Types of work

Working-class waged work

Some of the best-documented accounts of working-class women's waged work are of factory work during the industrialisation period in the northern districts of England. Historians have noted the degree of fervour this work provoked amongst nineteenth-century commentators, but as Judith Bennett, Elizabeth Ewan and Joyce Burnette show us, as early as the medieval period women were earning a wage.[32] Judith Bennett and Joyce Burnette note, for example, that single and married women were in charge of beer brewing and sale from c.1300 to the eighteenth century. The women who were engaged in this trade were known as brewsters or alewives, and their brewing capabilities were widely acknowledged and applauded. Nevertheless, by the eighteenth century this skill had gradually passed over to males, who virtually monopolised the occupation.[33] In large part this transfer was a consequence of the production of beer changing from a small scale operation run in private homes into a much larger industrial capitalist enterprise.[34]

These female manual workers were usurped in the early modern period by men, unlike the women who worked as domestic servants, which was the largest category of women workers from 1700 well in the twentieth century.[35] Domestic service covered a multitude of roles such as barmaid, nurserymaid, housemaid and the keeping of lodging and drinking houses. Tom Meldrum and Carolyn Steedman have argued that domestic service usually meant working in a middle-class family house, with a role as an extra pair of arms and legs.[36] Bridget Hill and Jean Hecht point to the high number of servants in the eighteenth century as 'an expanding outlet' saving women from unemployment, though its rate of growth declined in the nineteenth century.[37] The extent to which there was a demographic cleavage of domestic service employment between the centuries is contested by Leonard Schwarz and Carolyn Steedman. They question the number of eighteenth-century domestic servants, arguing that there were not enough 'young unmarried women' to fill demand.[38] That said, Steedman notes the 'ubiquitous' character of domestic servants throughout both eighteenth and nineteenth centuries, but concedes that ascertaining the true figures is difficult for, as Hannah Barker and Elaine Chalus note, humble women are 'poorly recorded in historical sources'.[39] The numbers, not only of domestic servants but of all waged women workers, in the pre-modern and modern era are debatable, therefore, not least because, as Eddie Higgs tells us, 'domestic service' was a catch-all category of occupation which included domestic servants who worked on farms as well as those who worked in an urban household. Joyce Burnette estimates that in the mid-nineteenth century domestic servants made up between 18 and 40 percent of women workers.[40] The wages earned by such women were fairly static. Joyce Burnette calculates that a young, single, live-in domestic servant in an urban area like Rochdale could earn up to £10 per year.[41] In addition her wage was supplemented by bed and board – though this gain had to be set against loss of freedom as servants had to be available for up to 24 hours a day, and at times had to endure unwanted sexual attention and harassment from their master.[42]

Domestic servants were put to good use by their employer. Not only did they carry out household tasks they often also cared for their employer's children. In contrast to its lack of regard for working-class women, the state provided support for some ersatz care for the children of middle class women: in 1792, William Pitt ended the maidservant tax, which had been introduced in 1785,[43] enabling middle class women to take on more domestic servants. Joanne Bailey and Elizabeth Foyster, whose work relates to the history of the family and in particular to child care and parenting in Georgian England, describe working-class domestic servants involved in the upbringing and daily care of infants and children.[44] Amanda Vickery wrote in 1998 that the 'care and responsibility of young children fell principally to the mother, [who was] supported by a nursery maid'.[45] When advising young domestic servants in 1787 of the role a housemaid was expected to undertake, Ann Walker warned, 'if you happen to live in a family where the mistress either suckles, or brings an infant up by hand, part of the duty of a nurse will fall to your share'.[46] Steedman believes that servants played much more of a hands-on role than Bailey and Vickery allow; arguing that middle-class women who had the resources to take on servants and provide them with food and living space were effectively giving over the 'physical care and management of their children to subordinates'.[47] Control was maintained by strict rules and regulations; working-class domestic servants were thought to have no natural aptitude for the care and management of children. Ann Walker counselled against 'carelessness' with her children whilst servants dressed, played, fed, and washed them, and this ideology extended to the washing of nappies, which was expected 'from the word go'.[48] Steedman notes that parents reserved to themselves the right of chastisement, however.

Our recognition of the roles which women have played in waged work has strengthened since the induction of women's history into the mainstream, and great strides have been made in documenting occupations other than domestic service. We can see that although women were replaced by men in the brewing industry, women replaced men in other industrial arenas during the nineteenth century. During the eighteenth and early nineteenth century, before moving from cottage to mill, women had been involved in proto-industry alongside their husbands, working as 'spinners, silk throwers, lace-makers and framework knitters', but once their work was replaced by mechanical processes, it was women rather than men who were recruited to work the technology.[49] The experiences of these women have captured historians' imagination, not only because of the amount of work they did, but also because they leapfrogged over men to obtain that work and because of the value of their work both to the nation and to their families' economy. Their physique was ripe for capitalist exploitation: their small hands suited the new machines better; also, they were cheaper to employ than men. Neil McKendrick notes the increased wage-earning opportunities industrialisation gave to working-class women, which was fuelled by an increasing 'home demand'.[50] Susie Steinbach mirrors this view and acknowledges Kathryn Gleadles's understanding of the important role that women played in the factories, noting that by '1899 over half a million women worked in [them].'[51] Ivy Pinchbeck, Maxine Berg, Pat Hudson, Pamela Sharpe and, more recently, Katrina Honeyman observe that these female workers contributed enormously to the British economy, with Pat Hudson arguing that 'the extent and incorporation of female and child labour into the most rapidly expanding commercial manufacturing sectors (in households, workshops and factories) and its association with increased intensification and labour discipline was unprecedented'.[52] She notes further that 'the high proportions of female and child workers in the industrial revolution were influenced by innovation'[53] and, as Emma Griffin remarks, this innovation demanded 'back-breaking' efforts to achieve the required outputs.[54] For Katrina Honeyman, the involvement of women in industrialisation shaped and paved the way for its future.[55] The regional and local dynamics of this work in the industrial period are extremely well documented in Nigel Goose's edited work.[56] Recent work from Selina Todd reminds us that women worked in large numbers in factories during the First and Second World Wars, and that munitions women were put on semi-skilled work as a consequence of the Bedaux System. This system, which broke a job down into small components so that only one part of it was required to be learned by the women workers, obviated the need to learn the whole job, meaning that the women could not claim a skilled worker's rate of pay.[57]

It was not only industrial work which gave women a wage. In addition, British women were involved in the nation's food-making processes.[58] Female salt-workers were pictured working alongside their husbands as early as 1556, and this important female occupation continued well into the nineteenth century.[59] In the 'Cheshire wiches' and in Manchester, women worked in the saltworks, which 'demanded, for the most part, sheer physical strength'.[60] The salt was all prepared by hand, without machinery, and the method of work 'consisted of raking, shovelling, carrying and wheeling immense quantities of salt and coal'.[61] The hours of work were extremely long, albeit punctuated by breaks in order for colleagues to prepare 'droughts'.[62]

Women also made dairy products. They were known for their skill in making cheese, butter and milk tasks for which 'a large part of their time [was spent] in productive work on the farm'.[63] These agricultural jobs, like factory work, could demand heavy labour. For example, in the eighteenth century 'A famous dairy-woman used to make her Butter in balls of Thirty or Forty pounds Weight', and, Jo Stanley and Bronwen Griffiths assert, this butter was delivered to houses by women 'bearing buckets on the end of heavy yokes', a practice that continued until the end of the 1870s.[64] Jo Stanley further testifies to the need for women to replace men in this field in the war era, citing a newspaper advertisement from the Second World War:

> DAIRY – Owing to men joining the army, 2 or 3 strong young women for cart and pram rounds, easy work; only those willing to do the work need apply (Wimbledon Park Farm).[65]

In addition to this, women who worked in agriculture also kept chickens and pigs, and cultivated cottage gardens.[66] Women who worked in a dairy in the early part of the eighteenth century in the Cheshire region earned between £2 and £5 per year, which had risen to £2 to £6 per annum by the latter half of the eighteenth century. Using statistics collected by Arthur Young from his tours of the north and south of England, Bridget Hill argues that in 1770 the number of women who worked in rural areas in husbandry and as servants was 167,247 compared to 222,996 males.[67] These female servants, who worked on the farm and in the farmhouse, were paid yearly in two ways: board and lodging in either the farmer's house or nearby building, which included the washing of clothes; and monetary payment of £2 7s 6d which could increase to £3 8s 6d, but which was subject to regional variation and age, and could sometimes be fixed.[68] Hill accepts the severe fall in numbers of agricultural domestic servants as given by Ann Kussmaul and argues that by 1851 'when service was already far gone in decline, females were recorded as constituting slightly less than a third of the total (213 males to 100 females).[69] Deborah Valenze has recently plotted the history of the dairy industry and of the skill and dedication of the women devoted to this work who were engaged in the farming.[70] Ann Kussmaul and Keith Snell note the importance of these women to the food-production industry between 1600 and 1900, and Kussmaul adds to this by giving an anatomised quantitative analysis and social historical account of the women, whose skills were learned from their indentured apprenticeship on the farm.[71] The apprenticeships provided for women in the southern counties in the eighteenth century enabled their involvement in a range of occupations such as butcher, baker, brewer, tallow chandler, miller, coatmaker, framework knitter, lacemaker, shoebinder and brushmaker.[72] This tells us that women were expected to work on behalf of the family, and that this work was vital for their prosperity.[73]

Migration

The coming of the agricultural revolution during the eighteenth century and the enclosures which went hand in hand with it meant that parents, particularly mothers, who had previously been able to support their families through common rights now had to sell their labour. The demise of agrarian England and the rise of enclosure meant the death-knell of common rights to grow food and breed livestock. Enclosure, as Jane Humphries argues, eroded the ability of women to take the 'common rights', available to them which had previously used for example to grow food and feed their families.[74] Grazing rights on which 'ten sheep could be kept' or cows which provided milk and butter for the families, which had been purchasable for 6d in Westmoreland, were no longer available.[75] In tandem with this termination were lost privileges in:

> shrubs, woods, undergrowth, stone quarries and gravel pits, thereby obtaining fuel for cooking, and wood for repairing houses, useful dietary supplements from the wild birds and animal life, crab apples and cob nuts, from the hedgerows, brambles, whortles, and juniper berries, from the heaths and mint, thyme, balm, tansy and other wild herbs from any other little patch of waste ... Almost every living thing in the parish however insignificant could be turned to some good use.[76]

Young women who had served their apprenticeship working for farming families found themselves redundant and obliged to seek work elsewhere.

This agricultural redundancy did not occur overnight of course, and, as Keith Snell points out, there had been some small need prior to the agricultural revolution for both men and women to earn a wage. Widows in the pre-industrial era, for example, worked at the harvest, but this had to be combined with other waged employments.[77] Working-class widows rarely had the luxury of the kind of inheritance which gave comfort to some middle-class women on the death of their husbands.[78] The poverty of widowhood did not provoke sympathy in the hearts of creditors and landlords in the eighteenth century, and they would call their money in. Thus, widows had to earn their keep, and would, for example, take in washing or turn washerwoman, going out to do the washing for other women.[79] The waged work of working-class widows was extremely important to their family's survival, even though widows could re marry. Bridget Hill makes the point that widows were less keen on finding another husband than widowers were a wife, an attitude which prevailed from the sixteenth century to the mid-nineteenth.[80] For this reason Peter Laslett has shown that the number of widows made up one fifth of the population in early modern England.[81]

We can see the extent to which common rights gave women the ability to provide food and warmth for their families; once enclosure was enacted these provisions had to be paid for – money had to be earned. Hannah Barker reminds us that agricultural work was subject to regional variation and that married women also provided support to farmers who needed to fill in the unemployment gaps when there was a shortage of male labour. This 'filling in' – one or more of a variety of roles, such as working during the harvest or sowing seeds – was one way married women could earn money. Some agricultural areas changed with the times: straw-plaiting for hatmaking in Hertfordshire gave work to young women who could earn between 6s and 12s per week, but overall the agricultural revolution was unable to provide work for many women.[82] Jane Humphries is clear: 'the eighteenth century saw a long term reduction in women's work, and paved the way for migration'.[83] Barker and Chalus argue that the agricultural revolution marked the end of an old way of life for young girls who migrated to towns in greater numbers than men between 1700 and 1850.[84] June Purvis demonstrates that the move from agricultural areas to urban areas may not have been sharply felt for some because young men and women were used to moving away 'to work in the houses of others as servants'.[85] The reasons for the move, however, included the opportunity for employment. As Sharpe notes, migration was not only pushed by reduced work opportunities in agricultural areas, but also pulled by increasing demand for female labour in towns: migration was 'as often a positive move as a result of despair'.[86]

The move from rural agricultural communities to urban centres brought changes in the demography of young women in the nineteenth century. They reached adulthood at 21, and their ability to improve their economic and marriage prospects contributed to an urban population growth.[87] Urban living offered industrial factory and metal work to young women, as well as providing employment in domestic service. Historians have studied the numbers of female migrants to urban areas and linked them to employment and marriage rates. Michael Anderson and Keith Snell argue that women who earned their living by working as domestic servants married no earlier than their eighteenth-century agricultural counterparts,[88] but, that said,

Nigel Goose sees strong evidence for earlier marriage rates in the coalfield districts, and Robert Woods identifies textile districts as manifesting a distinctive urban marriage tradition.[89] Family history searches provide some much-needed balance to Woods's assertion, however, as they reveal relatively low marriage rates in some textile districts such as Calverley, Leeds.[90] However, wage-earning women were proving themselves to be good marriage material, capable of providing support for a family by working in factories. The resulting population growth generated a large number of infants in urban areas, whose standard of living is much debated, and the care of whom had to be combined with waged work.[91]

Whilst these women worked in daylight, Joyce Burnette recognises the part women miners played in the industrial revolution when working in coal, lead, copper and tin mines.[92] The 1842 Mines Act forbade women working underground, but in 1851 the census captured 2,535 'coal women' in Yorkshire and Lancashire.[93] The number of coal women was probably higher as women dressed as men to circumvent the act, and inspectors in Wigan found 200 women working illegally.[94] Joyce Burnette notes that women featured as casualties of mining accidents, but, even so, men were keen for their wives and daughters to work in the mines and themselves refused to do so if this was not accepted.[95] The work that women did in these mines, and their working practices and wages, varied from region to region. Angela John notes in her work *By the Sweat of their Brow* that in the coalfields of Wigan 'women had worked in coal mines for centuries, [both] wives and daughters playing a vital role in the family's economy', earning 1/6d to 1/8d per day – not more than 10s for a full week's work.[96] Barker and Chalus note the number of women who worked underground in the regional mining industry of Bo'ness in West Lothian during the 1760s and in the nineteenth century in Pembrokeshire constituted 30 per cent of the mine workers.[97] Robert Shoemaker records pits in the northeast of England and the midlands employing mining women who worked as 'bearers carrying coal from the face to the surface'.[98] Women in Lancashire and Yorkshire undertook this work on a daily basis and were mainly known as drawers, but this could be termed differently, depending on the locality. Their job was to 'pull sledges or tubs along the pit floor or on planks from the coal face to the bottom of the shaft'.[99] This was done by 'drawers crawling along the floors harnessed to their tubs by a belt of leather or rope'.[100] This was hard manual labour and came to the attention of middle-class contemporaries during the nineteenth century because the coal women wore few clothes due to the heat. These practices were said to depict women as unfeminine and at risk of ravishment from their male colleagues. Reformers attempted to remove women from the pit, but women were able to resist this cull and it was not until 1972 when 'the last two British female surface workers were made redundant and left their work on 1 July 1972'.[101] As Angela John points out, this was some '130 years after legislation had forbidden the employment of women below ground'.[102] This example of women's hard graft, or manual labour, was paralleled by women who worked in nail- and chain-making manufactures and by those in the white lead trade and pottery industry.[103] Women who worked in the nail-making industry worked with steam hammers, and women in the white lead trades 'worked in its most dangerous sectors' making white lead from scratch, which could induce lead poisoning.[104] The women earned 2s to 2s 6d for each 'dangerous' shift they worked, giving an average of 12s 8d per week, but this weekly wage could be increased if they worked two shifts per day, which meant they could earn up to and over £1 per week.[105] Double shifts were barred in June 1898.[106] Working in the potteries was also a dangerous occupation, as women could incur pulmonary disease if they inhaled the clay dust and flint in addition to lead poisoning from the colours and glazes used to decorate the pots.[107] Carolyn Malone argues that this work was often done by widows and deserted women who had to support their families singlehandedly.[108]

These 'dangerous trades' have to be contrasted with others that were less harmful. Whilst the Cadbury firm supposedly employed few married women in the nineteenth century Sonia O. Rose acknowledges that it occasionally made exceptions for those in 'poor circumstances' and hired widows to clean for a couple of hours per day.[109] Nursing also contrasts strongly with the dangerous trades which gave employment to women through the early and modern periods. For example, workhouse nursing, midwifery and baby-minding were considered appropriate roles for women through the early modern period and beyond.[110] Workhouse nurses were drawn from the female pauper population and were widely believed to have few actual nursing and medical skills or show little interest in their patients (and when they did, popular opinion held, their nursing practice left much to be desired).[111] Shackled to the workhouse as a consequence of their poverty, these women have received a bad press in the historiography of workhouse nursing hitherto, and been given little credit for any endeavours made in their work.[112]

For women who moved away from their families to work in urban industries, day-carers and baby-minders could act as surrogate kin, providing child care when and where needed, for a fee.[113] The narrative of day-carers, however, is immersed in a sea of neglect, their characters being compared to the likes of Margaret Waters and Amelia Dyer, baby farmers who operated in the south of England and drowned and half-starved infants placed in their care.[114] The extent to which the same dangerous and cruel characteristics typify day-carers who operated in the northern industrial districts, however, has not been researched: this topic will be discussed in Chapter 5.

Nurses who tended to the ill on a daily basis could earn up to 6d per night but some could command much higher prices. For example one nurse earned 42s over a three-week period for nursing someone with smallpox.

Midwives delivered babies in the community, but also tended to the sick and dying.[115] Midwives in the nineteenth century who looked after pregnant women through their confinements were paid 4s per week.[116] Wise-women persisted in Britain until the nineteenth century, and their stories have been documented since the seventeenth century. Lynn Abrams notes an example flourishing well into the nineteenth century and she introduces us to women such as Maggie Winwick (1820–95), who practised her art in Shetland 'in the absence of trained medical provision' as 'an un-trained midwife'.[117]

So far we have noted the orthodox, staple sites of women's work, such as domestic service, industrial and agricultural work, mining and nursing. However a much clearer and more nuanced picture of the myriad ways women earned a living is now available to us from more recent scholarship. Susie Steinbach, for instance, shows that women took on a wide range of occupations during the long nineteenth century and that women's work changed dramatically.[118] Joyce Burnette comments similarly, remarking that 'the participation of women [in the labour market] was widespread and not strictly confined to a small set of occupations'.[119] Drawing on an analysis of the range of women's work which she found in the 1851 Census, Burnette lists women's involvement in not only the staple industries indicated above, but also includes transport and communication, paper and printing, chemicals, leather and skins, and metal manufacture and chemicals.[120] To this collection we need to add women who worked as workhouse matrons. Nor, as Sonia O. Rose, Gerry Holloway and Susie Steinbach note, must we forget the home-work in which hundreds of thousands of women were engaged.[121] This work was often called 'slop-work', or 'sweated home-work', due to its unskilled status. Women outworkers would 'make, mend and finish lace, seam and embroider hosiery, sew gloves, cover and sew buttons and plait straw' in addition to working in the needle trades making shirts, trousers and waistcoats or repairing frayed collars and buttonholes.[122] Women often worked from 5 o'clock in the morning until midnight in a bid to provide for their families, but could not earn more than 5s per week for doing so.[123] This paltry sum was not enough for women to support their families so they had to find other occupations to combine it with, often taking in washing. We also have to include prostitution in this arena of labour, for this was an avenue of employment, in both rural and urban environments, which women could and did turn to when the need arose. Hannah Barker argues that the rise in prostitution has historical links with unemployment, and it was usually a part of a woman's economy of makeshifts, when waged work was in limited supply and the need to make ends meet on a temporary basis.[124]

Research into sweated home-working, and information gleaned from various twentieth-century oral history projects, testify to a set of occupations even more diverse than that given in Burnette's census data. Hannah Barker tells us of the fisher wives in nineteenth-century Banffshire who assist in dragging the boats on the beach, and launching them. They sometimes in frosty weather, and at unseasonable hours, carry their husbands on board, to keep them dry. They receive the fish from the boats, carry them, fresh or after salting to their customers, and to market at the distance, sometimes of many miles.[125]

Annie Spark, who gave an interview for an oral history project, spoke about her mother who was born in the early twentieth century and who 'drove a horse and cart with every kind of vegetable, coal and all – and newspapers' to provide for her family.[126] Annie herself, who lived in Hackney, London, had a more conventional form of employment as she worked in a biscuit factory where she 'had to fill sixty packets of biscuits a minute'.[127] Winifred Salisbury was a full-time fire-fighter during the Second World War, and recalls how the work influenced her life: 'Prior to the war I was rather a quiet personality but once having joined the fire service, how life changed! The comradeship of the other girls and the work really changed my life.'[128]

The move to different forms of work was aided by conscription during the First and Second World Wars to the extent that by August 1941, 87,000 women had volunteered and had been accepted into the women's auxiliary services or worked in industry.[129] Previously male-dominated jobs provided waged work for women during the Second World War. Although working in a diluted skill format – the war government did not encourage women to learn a skill[130] – the young single women in these employments were taken out of the domestic service market, which, as Selina Todd tells us, left middle-class women servantless and obliged to fend for themselves.[131] Rural agricultural work also needed women and over 80,000 were employed by the Women's Land Army, earning slightly over £1 for a week's work.[132]

The job opportunities open to women from the end of the Second World War to the end of the twentieth century were limited to some extent by a glass ceiling that blocked women, irrespective of their skill and capability, from progressing up the ladder. More importantly, they were expected to relinquish their waged-work role and give way to men returning from the war. Attitudes towards women's work changed after the 1950s and although advances in contraception gave women some choice in determining their family size, a woman's role during these years was determined by family life. Women were expected to be at the centre of the family, and their role was expected to dovetail with the notion of the companionate marriage and the reinforcement of the notion of the male breadwinner.[133] This family-centred role was to provide children who had experienced the horrors of war and the dislocation of family, with security and domestication. Mothers were seen as the linchpin of the family's future, nurturing its growth.[134] The routes by which young women could enter work were narrow and obscure: few opportunities were open to women. Thus, Holloway argues, to ensure women were discouraged from working, the opportunities that young women were offered were of the 'less-skilled, lower paid variety, reflecting the normative assumption of what sort of work a woman should undertake', such as textile workers, shorthand typists and canteen cooks.[135]

The aim of providing for a family was no more attainable for women who worked in the latter half of the twentieth century: working options still lay in less skilled jobs. Halloway sums up this difficulty succinctly by quoting G Joseph:

> the typical woman worker, at the turn of the century was … a city dweller, a widow or a spinster aged twenty five years, employed as a domestic servant or in a textile factory. By the seventies, the typical female worker, aged forty years, is married, has returned to work after some years of economic inactivity, and works part-time in a clerical job.[136]

Economic decline gave rise to an increased number of working roles for women, whose waged opportunities included working in technology as a consequence of Britain joining the EEC in 1973 or, typically, 'retail, factory, clerical and caring.'[137] Whilst we can see that women's role in the labour market developed during this period, no real understanding of its change and continuity exists for, as Holloway remarks, 'the history of women's work in the last thirty years of the twentieth century has yet to be written'.[138]

In reading the testament to waged work of working-class women it is essential to remember that they did all of this whilst bearing and raising children. How, then, did they juggle this work and their parental responsibilities?

Child care of waged working-class women

The pre-industrial era

As we can see, waged work has been vital to working-class or plebeian women throughout the centuries. The ways in which women have cared for their children whilst working has been the subject of much debate. Accounts of the failings associated with waged work and working-class child care have flowed from contemporary observers and historians alike. Female experiences have been much picked over by historians, but women have always had to combine their waged work with child care. If the work was done in the home, such as in the pre-industrial era with brewing, spinning, straw plaiting in the eighteenth century, glove-making or midwifery in the nineteenth century, or taking in washing in the twentieth century, then it was combined with child care – women were in effect doing two jobs at the same time. Combining waged work with child care was possible but extremely tiring for the women concerned, and Hannah Barker has argued that the pre-industrial era was not 'any sort of economic idyll for women'.[139] Experiences of the combined role women undertook, of working in the home and caring for children, are not known to us because very little research has been undertaken into the combined role of waged work and child care. It is seen as a given that to be practised effectively mothers needed not only to be on hand to care for their children but also had to manage the difficult task of combining waged work with breast feeding. Historians argue that the issues of child care and breast feeding arose for mothers with the onset of industrialisation; this proposition will be discussed and tested in Chapter 2. During the pre-industrial period the parish offered support to women with children. In particular to widows. Although widows were often loth to apply to the parish, preferring 'independence and near starvation', the parish usually assumed some responsibility for these women, especially those with large numbers of children, and would provide materials to enable home-work, such as 'bundles of straw' to make into hats, or sometimes provide them with a skill such as midwifery.[140] This provision of work in the home enabled women to combine their waged work with child care, a practice which Sonia O. Rose sees persisting into the nineteenth century for widows in London.[141] Pre-industrial mothers therefore were seen in the child care debate as 'safe', for their work was done at home, where the children were, so that work and child care could run alongside each other effectively.

Domestic servants

One of the issues which looms large in the history of child care relates to the difficulties which domestic servants encountered. When domestic servants brought children into the world they faced huge problems. Domestic servants were mainly single and 'lived' in'. It has long been accepted wisdom that any woman who became pregnant in this context was deemed to be carrying a bastard and guilty of moral impropriety; she was a woman of ill-repute and immediately lost her job and home because of her supposed immoral character. This perception is now challenged. Tanya Evans, for instance, finds that some employers were more sympathetic than this and had a range of 'survival networks' to help servants out of their maternal predicament.[142]

Some mistresses took pity on their domestic servants, and gave them both monetary and emotional support, as they saw them as the victims of unscrupulous men who had duped them and rescinded promises of marriage.[143] After these offers of support were exhausted, domestic servants approached the London Foundling Hospital, founded by Thomas Coram, often with a letter of support from their employers to provide for the education and maintenance of their children.[144] Others sought more dangerous alternatives to rid themselves of the burden of illegitimacy. Whilst these issues are important for our understanding of the extent to which domestic servants were able to combine waged work with caring for their children, little or no research has been done on the situation of nineteenth-century domestic servants in the north to parallel Tanya Evans's observations related to the south. Northern districts were home to a burgeoning middle class, who needed domestic servants. The demand for domestic servants, therefore, grew, and we know that illegitimacy may not always have been the route to disaster we have been led to believe. Carolyn Steedman provides us with the example of the Reverend John Murgatroyd from Yorkshire, who helped his servant with her lying-in in 1802 and allowed her, along with her child, to remain with him throughout the rest of his life.[145] If an employer could show kindness to a domestic when pregnant, and flexible attitudes to illegitimacy were reinforced by case law, which determined that 'a maid-servant, got with child could *not*[146] be dismissed from her service' because 'unmarried women being with child' were 'not guilty of any crime, or even misdemeanour at common law',[147] why have historians argued that domestic servants could not work with children?

The growth in urban population threw young people together, giving rise to both population increase and illegitimacy, coinciding with an upsurge in demand for young women to work in cotton and wool factories. The practice of having children out of wedlock has been noted by Emma Griffin, who has found couples cohabiting before marriage because they did not have enough money to marry.[148] Indeed, the rise of the factory gave young women a choice of employment, with some preferring to work in factories because it gave them more freedom than that of tethered domestic servants under the eye of their mistresses for the most of the day. How, then, did employers seeking domestic servants attract them into their houses and families? Especially if their duties included caring for their employer's children, a job which many domestics hated? Employers needed the work doing and employees needed the wages, so did employers make concessions if prospective employees had children themselves? These questions will be answered in the following chapters of the book.

Concerns over how workhouse nurses looked after children placed *in their care* is also a topic which has been widely discussed by historians, with Frank Crompton being particularly dismissive of care they gave to infants. He argues that southern workhouse nurses shirked their responsibilities towards their wards, effectively abandoning them to their fate within the workhouse.[149] The extent to which this characterisation reflects northern workhouse nurses will be explored in Chapters 3 and 4 of this book. They will look at the responsibilities of the nurses towards the infants placed in their care; the environment in which they worked, and the working relationships they had with the workhouse medical doctors.

Industrial work

Juggling work and child care was not easy for women who worked in industrialised occupations, not least because married working-class mothers with children who earned their living in factories did not leave work on becoming pregnant. As Susie Steinbach notes, 'few working-class families could survive on a single man's wage',[150] therefore wives with children worked in the mines,[151] the Bryant and May factories,[152] and the white lead and pottery trades.[153] For instance, one woman with six children worked in the most dangerous section of the Newcastle white lead trade.[154] Deserted women and widows also worked in these sectors, supporting their families singlehandedly.[155] Ray Strachey records a case of a woman with fourteen children who worked in the nail- and chain-making industry.[156] Working wives with children, therefore, contributed in great measure to the family economy and national economy, in both the north and the south, by making woollens, cottons, cheese, pots, matches, nails and chains, by working at the harvest, and providing support to communities via nursing whilst also bringing up their children. When women wanted to earn money for their families they could find work, but what did they do with their children?

Mothers working in industrial areas during the nineteenth century, unlike middle-class mothers who were spared taxes on servants, had little support from the state, as parliament deemed that working-class parents should be responsible for their own child care. Consequently, historians have argued that industrialisation created child care problems for women who worked because they could not take their children to work with them.[157] Separation forced women to turn to kin, neighbours and friends to care for their children whilst they worked, and if neighbour and friends charged then they had to pay the going rate.

Historians have devoted considerable effort to the matter of child care. Sonia O. Rose points to Margaret Hewitt's work, which was conducted in 1958 using the 1851 census of Lancashire. Hewitt calculated that 'grandmothers or an elderly aunt' were often on hand to help with women workers' child care. Rose contends that this number had fallen to less than 6 per cent in 1881.[158] Hewitt argues further that mothers working at the factories sought out 'nurses' to care for their children, either on a daily or longer basis, and that each nurse had the care of two to three infants. She maintains that 'the normal practice was for the mother to carry her baby to the nurse on her way to the mill at 5.30 in the morning, and to collect it or have it brought home by the nurse in the evening'.[159] Elizabeth Roberts recognises the significance of day-carers in the Lancashire industrial districts, noting that working mothers regularly placed their infants with these women; entrusting them to do their duty by them.[160] Anna Davin has shown that another option for working mothers was to turn to their eldest daughters to fulfil the day-care role, and that they often became the sole carer of young infants at as young an age as seven years.[161] A further option was to approach a baby-farmer, a woman who looked after infants and children on a longer-term basis than a day-carer. Margaret Hewitt asserts that these individuals were 'criminal characters' whose child care could be characterised as 'abuse';[162] and June Purvis remarks that 'childminders... were alleged to be a poor moral influence'.[163] But, Meg Arnot has called baby farmers a 'welcome ally' for women who needed child care.[164] Industrial mothers tended to approach day-carers rather than baby-farmers as their need for care was on a short-term daily basis. The cost of this baby-sitting service during the latter half of the nineteenth century was between 2s and 5s per week, which cut heavily into the family budget as in general throughout Britain in the nineteenth century 'women's wages were 1/6th of men's'.[165]

These child care practices are driven by the separation issue: mothers being unable to take their infants with them to work. A consequence of this practice was the extent to which infants suffered from unsuitable, unhealthy food given to them by child minders, often leading, as noted by Margaret Hewitt in 1958 and Robert Millward and Frances Bell in 2001, to infants suffering from gastroenteritis and diarrhoeal diseases.[166] The number of mothers who needed child care was significant; in 1851, Susie Steinbach notes, '75% of married women performed waged work' through a variety of roles involving hard labour (mining), dextrous practices, (lace-making), agricultural work (harvest) and domestic work.[167] Waged work was pivotal to the survival of working-class women's families. Carol Dyhouse, too, recognises that during the 1895–1914 period mothers who worked in factories did so to ensure their families' well-being.[168] Interestingly, Dyhouse points us to a study carried out in Birmingham in 1908 in which babies were regularly visited to check their health. It was found that the infants of women who worked in industry had a lower death rate than those of mothers who did not work.[169] Dyhouse, however is a lone and singular voice in the advocacy of mother's industrial work tending to increase a family's well-being. Few dents have been made in the arguments put forward in 1958 by Margaret Hewitt, that mothers who worked in mills put their children's lives at severe risk, not least because they gave their infants over to the care of others and the separation meant that breast feeding of their infants was difficult. Hewitt argued that mothers found breast feeding incompatible with their work, thus subjecting the infant to 'artificial foods', rendering them susceptible to gastroenteritis and diarrhoea.[170] Although Hewitt was well meaning and, writing in 1958, was lobbying for mothers to stay at home and look after their children, running with the 1950s fashion of the stay-at-home mum, she labelled the many women who worked in industry during the nineteenth century as irresponsible, setting a trend which has been followed by historians. Indeed, Robert Millward and Frances Bell have claimed that the highest levels of infant mortality diarrhoeal diseases afflicted children born to northern textile-worker mothers.[171] As the rise of industrialisation coincided with an increase in the rate of infant death, working-class women incurred the wrath of middle-class contemporaries and observers, who supposed a cause and effect. Although not stigmatised as severely as unmarried domestic servants who found themselves pregnant, mothers who worked were nonetheless blamed for the rise of infant mortality due to their supposed callous and irresponsible attitude, putting work before children. In an effort to address the problem, the government sought to force working-class women to take responsibility for the care of their infants by reducing the woman's working day from 12 hours to ten, then ten to nine, through the Factory Acts of 1833, 1847, and 1874. This, it was hoped, would encourage working women to devote more time to their families.[172]

These acts did not always work in practice, however, as female workers could get around the rules and after all, two hours meant little difference to women whose eldest daughters were fulfilling the child care role. Again, we seem to see these women struggle with the problems their infants posed to them whilst earning a wage for their families, but to what extent was this a true reflection of how working-class women combined waged work with child care in this period? Sonya Rose argues that 'employers structured factory jobs as though they were to be held by people without household responsibilities, and certainly by non-mothers, that is by men'.[173] Yet the numbers of women with household responsibilities who actually filled these jobs in the West Riding districts of Yorkshire and Lancashire grew exponentially during the nineteenth century.[174] Moreover, she acknowledges that 'the belief that individual women were responsible for social reproduction, by which... [is meant] childbearing and caring for family members on a daily basis, was enshrined in law as well as in local custom'.[175] The idea that working-class women were on their own, with no entitlement to assistance in law or custom, in securing the safety of their infants during industrialisation is cemented in our minds. Yet as the agricultural revolution progressed, contemporaries were noting the problems which enclosure posed to plebeian and working-class women with infants. Thomas Spence, for instance, was so concerned about the losses infants would incur from the changes afoot in enclosure, that he argued that the nineteenth century should become the era of 'the rights of infants.[176] These rights would be secured by mothers, and included a provision for 'the proper nourishment for the young', the 'right to the milk from their [mothers'] breasts', the 'right for mothers to have food to make milk of', 'good nursing', 'cleanliness', and 'comfortable clothing and lodging'.[177] These rights were to be obtained by women through their own endeavours, mothers who would 'labour for [them] selves and infants' through their right to work.[178] Thomas Spence argued that working mothers would know what was best for their infants as 'nature has implanted into the breasts of all mothers the most pure and unequivocal concern for their young, which no bribes can buy, nor threats annihilate, be assured we will stand true to the interest of our babes'.[179] Working mothers, according to Spence 'had the spirit to assert them', but how this was to be enacted during industrialisation, and what the customary rights these women were imbued with, elude us, because historians of child care have not taken up Spence's rhetoric but rather have generally cleaved to the view that working-class mothers reneged on this responsibility, and made others responsible for their infants.

It has been customary for historians to surmise that working-class women had little control over their own lives, and were unable to act on behalf of their infants when waged work in factories made its call. The historian J.G. Williamson has argued that factory workers could make certain 'demands' as compensation for working in the factories; therefore, we need to see whether mothers took action on behalf of their infants. This book will consider whether we can find evidence of these mothers recognising their rights to secure their infants' safety and security whilst having them at work with them during industrialisation.[180] It will also aim to identify if others were aware of this right; ask if so, what did they do? What steps did mothers themselves take? How far could their demands be enacted? and attempt to identify the child care practices that arose.

Whilst we are aware of the help which kin and older siblings gave to mothers who worked in industry, working-class mothers were reluctant to place their infants in 'nurseries', suspecting that their children could be harmed.[181] Yet, if they chose not to place their infants in nurseries then what did they do with them? Aversity to nurseries might be associated with cost, as the need for industrial mothers to retain money was clear. They worked for a reason – to contribute to the family's economy and make a better life for their families. So, keeping their children in the bosom of their families saved the expense of child care. We also know that working-class women preferred to breast feed their infants. Tanya Evans says that 'the cult of breast feeding made little impact on the lives of the poor because they had no choice but to nurse their own children.'[182] Alysa Levene argues that breast feeding was important to working-class mothers as it was known to provide some protection against pregnancy; Margaret Llewelyn Davies saw this choice persist into the twentieth century. During the new industrial era women had to think about what to do with their children whilst they worked; although working-class women had to acknowledge that infant life was precarious, Jane Lewis has noted that child health was 'indeed an urgent maternal concern'.[183] Edward Bedoes, a contemporary, remarked they 'anxiously watched' over their infants when they were ill.[184] This interest in securing infant life can be seen in the northern districts as it was in London, where Julie Marie Strange has recognised that grief at death was evident and that working-class women did 'all they could' for their children.[185] The money earned by working mothers was not for themselves but for their family, so why were northern factory mothers particularly maligned and singled out by nineteenth-century observers, and historians since, for their negligence of infants? Was the reluctance to place infants in nurseries born out the strong desire to keep their children with them so that children were under maternal watch and could be breast fed, benefitting from a food which would aid their health and obviating the need for 'artificial foods'? Although Dyhouse has shown that mothers' industrial work lowered the high IMR in Birmingham, no significant study has been undertaken to identify if women acted on behalf of their infants in the northern districts, where working-class women have been the victims of callous rhetoric directed against their child care practices.[186] Indeed, the purpose of working-class women's waged work was to provide for their families, including the preservation of their infants' health. We need to ask why they would go to so much effort to earn money to keep their children alive while at the same time neglecting their very existence. This chapter will look at the West Riding of Yorkshire to investigate if mothers who worked could improve their children's life chances and if so, attempt to describe how they did it. The questions the chapter will ask are: Did mothers recognise their right, as defined by Spence, to safeguard their infants whilst at work? Did others, such as employers, recognise this right? The decisions about breast feeding seem to be linked to whether a mother worked outside the home or not,[187] but was this always the case? Indeed, could mothers breast feed at work? (To do so would mean they had the right to have their children with them or else that they had to devise some 'cunning plan' to get them there.) In essence, the chapter will explore whether working women in the industrial north developed new models of child care which enabled them to combine their waged work with child care as they had during the pre-industrial era.

War period and after

We know little of these individual positive endeavours by nineteenth-century working-class women to act on behalf of their infants and safeguard them. We have been led to believe that it was through governmental policy, such as was developed and applied during the Second World War, that infant safety was enhanced. Penny Summerfield points out that government policy provided a blanket cover of child care;[188] nurseries and crèches were set up, giving mothers some maternal security whilst they worked in factory production. Once the war was over, women were expected to take up what was deemed their primary maternal role and retreat to the home. As the twentieth century progressed however, women's participation in work increased – between 1975 and 1997 it went up from 60 per cent to 71 per cent, and continued to rise.[189] It is important, therefore, to identify any 'rights' women were imbued with to secure infant safety because it may have an impact on women today who have to choose between work and home. Forces of 'separation' are still in operation today, despite a concerted campaign by twentieth- and twenty-first-century feminists who have struggled to defeat the baleful idea and practice of separation.

Patriarchy in the workplace

The social constructs obstructing women's access to waged work in the nineteenth century were strong. However, recent work suggests that there were other forces opposing women's work. Joyce Burnette does not see gender as a heuristic device through which women's working opportunities are diminished; rather, the lack of work was related to women's lack of strength.[190] Yet we can see that women were capable of heavy labour – as Jo Stanley remarks, men replaced women delivering milk when carts instead of yokes were introduced from the 1870s.[191] Women today still face patriarchy in the work place. Unequal pay and the lack of affordable quality child care mean that women still face obstacles when wishing to work.[192] They have to judge whether the money they bring in benefits the family or sets it at a disadvantage owing to them not completing their domestic tasks and having to pay for child care. Whilst these ideas have been thoroughly debated in working-class women's history, Joyce Burnette's work, which picks apart the cultural working practices of the nineteenth century, suggests that whilst patriarchy played a part, 'gender divisions were driven by market forces', rather than a wholly patriarchal model.[193] Moreover, competition was useful for waged women workers in that it 'sorted women into the least strength-intensive occupations'.[194] For a mother, the less strength she spent in work the more she had for her children. So, did women gravitate to these less arduous jobs in order to save their 'strength' for their infants and children? Expending less strength did not mean that women were less interested in their work than men, nor less focused in its practice: they were entitled to their rightful wage. Indeed, we can note that during a labour dispute in West Yorkshire in 1875, male workers in the mills of the West Riding recognised female colleagues' trade-union capabilities and preferred a female committee, rather than a male one, to fight the dispute.[195]

Unwaged working-class women

Historians have the patriarchal line; that working-class waged work posed severe problems for infants, particularly during the nineteenth century. The result was that many working-class women hid their waged work, and others were driven out of the marketplace altogether. Jane Humphries contends that during the nineteenth century married women only worked in crisis, generally providing for their families through their domestic skills, for example, growing and preparing foodstuffs, and making clothes.[196] In ceding to the dictates of patriarchy and retreating from the public sphere these women aimed to play what Tanya Evans has termed their 'fundamentally gendered' and 'natural role' of 'the angel of the house'.[197] Some women themselves believed their waged work contributed little to the household. Mothers in Lincolnshire, Berkshire, Northamptonshire, Devon, Surrey and Wiltshire believed that few gains could be made by actually going out to work.[198] Susie Steinbach notes the comment by one Mrs Hoot, of Surrey, who remarked that she 'used to go to work, and then had to sit up at nights to wash'. Elizabeth Roberts, who conducted oral history interviews of women who worked in the mills during the twentieth century, remarks on their preference for home-work of the sweated trades rather than factory work because they could combine it with their housework and child care and they did not have to pay for prepared or processed foods.[199] In this sense, patriarchy might seem to have pulled the wool from many working-class mothers' eyes. In advocating women should not go out to work but conduct their work in the home and on behalf of their families, the prevailing ideology released them at a stroke from the 'double shift' which many were expected to do.

Yet, for many women working at home took a great deal of energy. Even though the work was unwaged, housework needed to be completed daily: it was all-consuming, carried great responsibility, and was no easy option, particularly, as Bridget Hill has shown, in the eighteenth century.[200] Thus, through either waged or unwaged labour, working-class women had working responsibilities throughout their lives, which was an important part of their daily existence. Hill tells us how single married women earned their stripes in housework through their indentured service as young female agricultural apprentices. They were taught housework through a holistic approach which encompassed both agricultural and domestic skills. In this way they would become capable housewives, who could 'manage the dairy...look after the suckling of calves and house lambs...and cure horses cows and sheep'.[201] Whilst widows and wives of the pre-industrial era made their living through both outwork and housework, their economic role was dissolved during the late eighteenth and early nineteenth century and it was no longer considered necessary for them to play a waged part in the family's economy.[202] That responsibility was placed on the male head of the household, with wives left to work within the confines of the house and garden.

The responsibilities of unwaged working-class women were numerous. They encompassed, providing 'shelter from the elements and a source of warmth, the means to cook food, the materials for providing a minimum of light, and the ability of inhabitants to keep themselves, their clothes, their cooking utensils and the house itself moderately (but only moderately) clean'.[203] Doing all this for the family was a demanding task. Hill notes for example the difficulty of getting water for cooking, drinking, washing and cleaning because 'there was no piped water to the house...no system of drainage, no sewerage, and no privy'. Vegetables had to be carried to a stream to be washed, 'local ponds, streams and springs were commonly used by women for washing clothes and linen...Water butts were a distance from the house...to raise a bucket from a well was difficult' – a bucket could contain from one to three gallons (weighing 10 to 30 pounds).[204] The importance of water to the household was such that that people would be employed to fetch it.[205] Washing up of dishes and the washing of clothes needed soap but not all households could afford it due to the soap tax, so many women had to make their own.[206] Food had to be prepared and the fuel for the fire needed to be collected before this could even be begun.[207] Women went into the forest to find wood and the hedgerows to collect twigs, and collected cow dung and horse dung to dry for fuel.[208]

Although many nineteenth-century wives had ranges on which to cook, their days were still consumed by housework. June Purvis notes it was 'arduous, physically demanding and time-consuming',[209] covering a whole range of jobs: it demanded that women 'shopped, cooked, cleaned, laundered, and sewed apparently ceaselessly', even when pregnant.[210] As Susie Steinbach notes, 'the working-class home was a part of the world, and not a refuge from it'.[211] Hannah Mitchell of Derby, born in 1872, recalled 'one Friday, having done my weekend cleaning and baked a batch of bread during the day, I hoped for a good night's rest, but I scarcely had retired before my labour began. My baby was not born until the following evening after 24 hours of intense suffering....'[212]

Hannah's difficulties would be compounded by having to fetch water from the 'communal tap', a practice that lasted well into the inter-war years. Her daily routine included having to stand for long hours at the 'dolly tub' pounding away at the clothes with a wooden dolly, then forcing the wet garments through a mangle to get rid of the water.[213] It seems that little changed from the work women had to do in the nineteenth century to the twentieth; Mrs Mitchell, Hannah's mother, recalled having to endure similar circumstances to that of her daughter. Whilst most had a tap from which to get clean water, washing took an enormous amount of time. The boiler in which the washing was done had to be filled by

a lading can, a huge cup with a big handle and filled it at the tap, pour it in this boiler till this big iron boiler inside was full of water, and then you waited till that got hot, then they put all the clothes in after they were steeped all night. They were put in and they were all boiled in there. They would boil for so long, and then it all came and...they would go in this butt of water to rinse. Then they would have a good rinse and be taken out of there, put through an old-fashioned wooden wringer. It was solid, you had to drag them out, you couldn't move, made of solid iron with huge wooden rollers.[214]

Mothers needed their children to help them with this. Once this was done the next step was to starch and whiten the clothes. This was done by placing them in a potion of 'dolly blue' then taking them all out and once again putting them through the mangle. The final stage was to place them on the washing line outside. As Mrs Mitchell notes, 'she [her mother] must have been up early' for her to complete all of this in one day, alongside all of their other tasks, not least because working-class women often had large families – washing for all could involve eight or nine sets of clothes, bed linen and sometimes furnishing fabrics.[215] Elizabeth Roberts describes the working-class woman's role in the twentieth century as rooted in the home, and this idea was planted in the minds of these women at an early age.[216]

Thus, the routine of 'housework', or baking bread, mending clothes, buying provisions and cooking them was unending and all-consuming for eighteenth-, nineteenth- and twentieth-century wives. Margaret Llewelyn Davies argued in 1915 that the unwaged exertions of nineteenth-century mothers – of 'cooking, scrubbing, and cleaning at the wash tub, in lifting and carrying heavy weights, is just as severe manual labour as many industrial operations in factories'.[217] Due to the demands of this work, Susie Steinbach records, mothers often cajoled their eldest daughter to help.[218]

The exertions of working-class women were compounded by another role: it was usually their sole responsibility to balance the family budget. Alannah Tomkins, Susie Steinbach, Anna Davin, Alan Kidd, Jane Humphries and Sara Horrell have reflected deeply on the multitasking of nineteenth-century working-class wives.[219] Anna Davin comments on the 'control' mothers had on the family purse;[220] Susie Steinbach stresses the importance of this role for working-class women;[221] and Jane Lewis memorably characterises this as 'solving the food/rent equation'.[222] Women's calculations were based on the male contribution, and wives did not always know what their husbands' earnings were. The men's contribution to the household budget could vary from week to week; some could be counted on to 'divvy' up all their wage, others not. But however these men viewed their responsibilities to their families, they often 'top-sliced their wages, creaming off a share to finance their personal expenditure...' such as tobacco, ale or gambling.[223] By secreting a portion of their wages from a job that did not provide a 'family wage' in the first place, husbands put working-class wives and mothers in a perilous position[224] as they had to plan with scarce resources.[225] Anna Davin and Alannah Tomkins have noted that the boom and bust of the nineteenth century economy gave rise to a precarious nature of life for working-class women whose husbands were subject to slumps in trade.[226] When male unemployment increased, working-class mothers enrolled in the sweated trades we have already identified. When East End children got home from school or the street their mothers might be 'busy at the table' making matches, or they might be taking in washing.[227] This was not always a regular occupation and did not deliver a weekly wage, unlike other sweated work, but could be done on an ad-hoc basis when the need for money arose.[228] Shani D'Cruze points out to us women who earned money intermittently by delivering 'bundles' back to women who had taken clothes to the pawnbroker but did not want to be seen in the queue to redeem pawned goods, as working-class women were often extremely ashamed to need the services of the pawnbroker.[229] The life of the working-class woman was often beset by 'scheming and planning to make ends meet' and this often meant robbing Peter to pay Paul,[230] not least to keep themselves and their families out of the workhouse. The strategy Joyce Crump of Lambeth employed during the 1930s was to work as a housekeeper for a man who had two children. Joyce had been a Barnardo's child and when in hospital having her first baby had been told of a man who needed a housekeeper. The job entailed far more than housekeeping, however. She found that her would-be employer, Rick, actually needed someone to care for his children. He and his wife had split up and the children were in care because he had no one to take care of them during the day. Joyce agreed to become a surrogate mother and carry out the domestic jobs. There was no sexual relationship between the couple but otherwise they lived as a family, with both 'muck[ing] in together', to bring up the children, both his and hers.[231]

Money difficulties could presage disaster and unwaged mothers had to apply a wide range of strategies to forestall it. One way to do so was by taking the wages of their older children. Alannah Tomkins has shown that working-class women would turn to their kin in times of economic need, but this was not the full extent of their networks.[232] Pawning was another option which working-class women could adopt to help manage their money difficulties.[233] During the 1884 depression, for instance, women pawned their wedding rings. For one woman this was particularly significant: arguably, her ring was almost never on her finger after she became pregnant three times in quick succession.[234] Shani D'Cruze notes the support which women gave to each other during lean times; she records that women would in turn lend and borrow from each other, a method which was vital to 'smooth over the gaps'.[235] Cracks in cash flow could be papered over by approaching money lenders.[236] During the nineteenth century many working-class women employed a strategy of malnutrition, eating very little, rather than deal with these often predatory suppliers of credit.

Child care of unwaged working-class women

By 'being at home', working-class women throughout the centuries conducted their child care indoors. This is the patriarchal defining example, aping the middle-class model. These women either cared for their children alone or with the help of their older children. The atypical example of Joyce Crump shows us that she not only cared for her own children but Rick's children too. In conforming to the 'housewife' role, Joyce conformed to the gender stereotype prescribed for her. Women like Joyce would be on hand to care for their infant's needs, breast feed her own children at will and perhaps live up to the nineteenth-century expectation of the 'angel' mother. Susie Steinbach notes the significant gains nineteenth century 'stay-at-home mums' could enjoy. They did not need to pay for child care, nor for prepared or processed food as they could prepare it at home. Thus, as she argues, 'with more time to shop and to prepare food, they could manage money more carefully and spend more time raising their children; these in turn increased their status in the family and the community'.[237] Steinbach goes on to argue that these women not only benefitted in economic terms but by staying at home were able to comfort their husband more, reducing the risk of domestic violence.[238] By rejecting waged work, stay-at-home mothers were at least on hand to ensure their infants and children came to no harm. Yet, even when women conformed to the gender stereotype, they did not escape vilification as careless mothers. Anna Davin argued the idea of the maternally ignorant working-class mother and her 'faulty maternal hygiene' emanated from medical doctors, particularly during the nineteenth century.[239] Alice Reid points out that to 'overcome such maternal ignorance', health visitors were introduced into the northern districts of Manchester and Salford.[240]

The extent to which unwaged mothers were better able than their waged counterparts to provide their infants with breast milk is debatable, however. We have seen that breast feeding was, out of necessity, the normal practice.[241] Anna Davin remarks that during the twentieth century the importance of this milk was widely recognised and that 'neighbours would do it' for infants whose mothers could not provide.[242] This gave infants the important colostrum necessary to provide them with a better chance to resist disease. Unwaged women, however, were at risk of losing their milk due to a lack of food. The irregular nature of their sweated and ad hoc work had an effect on the amount of food they could buy, which in turn had an impact on their ability to make milk to feed their infants. As John Burnett tells us, for most working-class families food could be 'deficient' but it was 'the wife who fared worst of all'. For:

> on Sundays she generally obtains a moderately good dinner, but on other days the food consists mainly of bread with a little butter or dripping, a plain pudding and vegetables for dinner or super and weak tea. She may obtain a little bacon at dinner once, twice, or three a week; but more commonly she does not obtain it.[243]

The best of the working-class diet was given 'to their husbands'.[244]

Anna Davin notes that older and growing children could also take the best of the food, and that working-class women went hungry as 'Mrs. H., a tidy respectable young woman with a husband in regular work, though with small wages, found that her growing children ate all the dinner. She always took a bit of bread. Now it has come to my turn I don't like it.'[245] Anna Davin recognised the problems that a lack of food posed to working-class women, remarking that 'on a diet of bread and tea nursing mothers soon lost their milk.'[246] Ellen Ross acknowledges the sense of self denial and sacrifice of working-class mothers. She notes that 'a pregnancy could denote a 'period of special hardship' . . . , it involved more work, often less food than usual and could be accompanied by great anxiety, as women prepared for the confinement and tried to equip themselves for the new baby'.[247] Doctors at London's General Lying Hospital revealed that the lack of food troubled working-class women when pregnant and one woman, when asked about the amount of food she was eating, cried.[248] Twentieth-century pregnant working-class women seemed to fare little better: Ellen Ross reports 'some of the saddest cases': Evelyn Bunting, for instance, observed at the Saint Pancras School for Mothers in the 1900s 'women who were in the last months of pregnancy, but were weak with hunger'.[249] The child care of unwaged working-class women was clearly affected by hunger, thus casting doubt on the perceived idea that home-work was best for the mother in respect of her ability to care for her children. For if breast milk was not available then 'artificial foods' would have to be given, making a significant impact on the health of infants. We can see the abject poverty of mothers who were unable to provide milk and infants who were unable to take it, thus June Purvis, is right to argue that infant mortality was closely related to poverty.[250] Ellen Ross notes the continual pregnancies of working-class women in London, a state of affairs no different to that in the north. The average number of children per family would reach five by the 1860s.[251]

Being at home, however, did not mean that working-class mothers had unlimited hours to spend with their infants. Child care had to be combined with the ceaseless housework. Infants and children had to fight for their mother's attention, and felt put out when a new infant and sibling came along. When domestic work had to be combined with the sweated home-work, infants were often given over to the care of older children, particularly girls, whom Anna Davin has called the 'little nurses', and were often called home from school to help out.[252] Emma Griffin notes the dangerous aspects of this practice, whilst Sally Alexander plots the apprenticeship these young girls served under their mothers in order to 'become a woman' and give them the competence to play such a role.[253] These young girls often took their little charges into the street in an effort to keep contact with their friends and siblings.[254] If they were not on hand to help then, Jane Lewis tells us, infants were strapped either into high chairs or 'into ordinary seats, waiting in frustration for an older sibling to return from school and take them out'.[255] Despite the furore raised by nineteenth-century commentators and observers arguing that the home was best for mother because it made the lives of infants safer, the home environment could sometimes be dangerous, because mothers had to give their attention elsewhere. Washing, cooking and cleaning had to be done, whether women were pregnant or not, and arguably standing for hours at the wash tub was little different to the standing at the loom all day, other than the lack of pay, and the supposed benefits of having their children with them.

The space in which unwaged working-class women tackled their domestic duties was cramped, the poorest, perhaps, being 'cellar dwellings, the worst form of urban accommodation, comprising one or at most two dark, damp, low-ceilinged rooms with poor ventilation'.[256] The consequences of this environment for infants would often be respiratory ailments, and this may be why mothers sent their infants outside with their older siblings. It is no surprise that June Purvis remarks that 'infant mortality was high in Sunderland, where women did little paid work, and low in other towns where paid work was more common'.[257]

The range of strategies working-class women employed whilst trying to combine either waged or unwaged work with child care was vast. The variety and scope of labour encompassed leads us to suspect that few of these women evaded any of their responsibilities to their families.

Conclusion

Historically, women have always worked, taking on a diverse range of occupations, bending with the capitalist wind when their families needed them to. The effort made by working-class women on behalf of their families is clear: long hours, and, in the pre-industrial era in particular, long days for women who had to combine waged work with child care in the home. This employment was often heavy labour such as working in mines, making heavy cheeses, or working with deadly substances such as white lead which poisoned both women and their infants. Although Amanda Vickery argues against a 'golden age' for women during pre-industrialisation it may have been easier for women to combine waged work with child care in the home. The extent to which this ability to combine the two roles eroded as women were moved from manor to mill with the onset of industrialisation is well articulated in the historical literature.

Since the onset of the industrial revolution women who needed to earn a wage have met with difficulties when children came along. The middle-class control of the mode of production obliged women and mothers who needed to contribute to their family economy to take up new roles, learn new skills when the need dictated whilst at the same time being vilified by contemporary witnesses whose sensibilities were affronted by this waged work – this role did not fit with the female image held by middle-class observers. However, coinciding with the rise of industrialisation was a notable increase in the number of baby-minders and of workhouse nurses who recruited by the Guardians. Once this badge of honour was given, female paupers were responsible for the care of the inmates of the workhouse.

Although many middle-class sensibilities were affronted by working-class women's waged work, this sentiment did not lead to the provision of working-class mothers with the funds to stay in their homes and care for their children. Thus, working-class women had to continue with their employment, contributing in great measure towards their family's finances in both northern and southern regions by making woollens, cottons, cheese, pots, matches, nails and chains.[258] Historians argue that the separation issue forced northern mothers to give their infants over to a carer, be it kin, a baby minder or workhouse nurse, and all were maligned and subjected to scorn, ridicule and scrutiny from contemporaries who concluded that they were irresponsible. The perceived relationship between waged work and child care in the northern districts, therefore, was characterised as unacceptable, because if a mother was prepared to 'go out to work' and the carer was prepared to take money for the care of an infant then neither were responsible women. However, we can see that either waged or unwaged work in all its guises colonised much of the working-class mother's day.

Northern factory mothers however, have been singled out as being the worst perpetrators of neglect, the antithesis of motherhood; uncaring and irresponsible mothers in a period of a high northern IMR. This is despite women who worked in the southern white lead trade, for example, also receiving criticism.[259] For as Thomas Maudsley, the secretary for the Committee for Promoting the Nine Hour Act, remarked in 1872: 'The prolonged absence from home of the wife and mother causes an enormous amount of infant mortality and it must cause the elder children to be more or less neglected'.[260]

Indeed, the white lead trade was also suspected to harm the unborn infants of women who worked in it.[261] Yet, the reasons why women who worked in the factories of the north, and the day-carers and baby-minders who looked after their children whilst they did so, not to mention the workhouse nurses who were in loco parentis, seemingly placed their infants at higher risk than those who sought child care from kith and kin and neighbours can only be guessed at. What we do know is that this neglect features widely in both the contemporary and historiographical view. One of the reasons for the latter being the availability of a wealth of primary source material emanating from nineteenth century observers claiming to have witnessed neglect or its consequences.

The options, historians argue, open to working-class women when children came along were either to engage in 'waged work' and enlist carers to help, or to stay at home and tend to their children themselves. This binary choice meant that if women wanted or needed wages they either had to obtain help with child care or stay at home and undertake sweated labour, meanwhile relying on the wages of their oldest children to supplement the family income. But as we have seen, both options posed problems for working-class women. They were subjected to ridicule and scorn when they engaged in factory work, and they were exposed to alarming poverty when they stayed at home. Yet, there was little difference for working-class women in the work they took part in: work was an omnipresent part of the day and, as Spence argues, the perils of industrialisation would impose harm on to their young if they did not ensure their well-being. Spence reminds us that working-class women were the ones required to look out for their infants and, as we have seen, they were not workshy, and employers needed them to work, so we should ask if they developed a third way of caring for their children which at present eludes us.

Carol Dyhouse set the ball rolling by showing us that working-class mothers who worked in industry were able to improve their families' lot. Was this so in the West Riding? And if so how did they do it? This book seeks to take Dyhouse's ideas further and discover whether there were similar positive aspects to women's child care in the north as in Birmingham. Did factory mothers, day-carers and workhouse nurses heed Spence's words to take care of infants? Is the separation issue for industrial mothers as evident as historians argue it is? If so, is it due to the burgeoning work opportunities for working class women? Have contemporaries and historians exaggerated the irresponsible actions of factory mothers and used it as a cloak for neglect? To answer these questions we now need to explore the child care practice of mothers in industrial waged work.

2
Industrial Mothers

How did mothers' waged work work impact on the northern IMR?

> What do they do with the infants of the mothers who work in the mills? 'Oh', the Rector replied 'they bring them to me, and I take care of them in the churchyard!'[1]

The previous chapters introduced the topic of high rates of infant mortality in the northern districts. They also explained the need for northern women to work; the range and expanse of the occupations they undertook, and the inherent child care models these hard-working and hard-pressed women used whilst labouring in the industrial sectors. This chapter will move beyond this context and explore the extent to which the model identified by the Rector and Dickens in the quotation above reflected the reality of nineteenth-century child care for northern working-class women.

The structure of this chapter will be to address the criticisms of the employment of mothers, then the actual child care practices of working-class women will be described for women who worked in agriculture, heavy labour such as nail- and chain-making, bricklaying, salt works and, finally, textile work.

Criticisms of the employment of mothers

The answer Charles Dickens received from the Rector convinced him that female factory work caused high rates of infant mortality. He particularly viewed the tri-part relationship of the mill, married women, and infants, as an unhealthy combination which led children to an early grave.[2] In speaking and writing against married women's work Dickens was but one of many critics who sought to push working-class women out of 'industry'. For the working-class themselves, however, it was not unusual or undesirable to see married women working.[3] After all, as we have seen, staying at home for these women meant subjecting their families to severe and all-consuming poverty. Thus, the mill gates came to be regarded as an awkward, but necessary portal to enter.

Although the mill was by no means the only form of employment for northern mothers in this period, factory work was the particular *bête noire* of many social commentators who echoed Dickens concerns with regard to the northern IMR.[4] These anxieties prompted many parliamentary enquiries.[5] Influential men such as Herbert Asquith the Home Secretary in 1893 and medical doctors such as William Farr were adamant during this period in placing the blame for the high IMR on the shoulders of working women. Mr Asquith remarked that 'the main reason' for the high IMR, 'one of the most melancholy features of our vital statistics... was the employment of young married women in factories'.[6] His analysis has led the factory to be seen as a particularly destructive force in relation to infant health, and it is viewed as a catalyst for infant neglect in that it removed mothers from both their children and the domestic sphere.[7]

The moral barriers against female waged work were as forbidding for factory work as any other occupation, and more imposing than most. Asquith argued that, during this age of the 'deification of the home', the married working factory operative was at odds with the feminine ideal of the 'housewife' due to the length of time she was at work and consequently out of the home. Moreover, as factory work gave women independence – or more independence than domestic service allowed – the female factory worker was even further distant from the feminine norms of the nineteenth century. As they were not under the watchful eye of their employers, as domestic servants were, they were supposed to have more liberty during the working day, which led them to be characterised as 'unchaste' and lacking in the appropriate maternal skills. Historian Nigel Goose notes that factory work, and in particular married women's factory work, had 'dominated contemporary discussion out of all proportion...' and forged a 'protracted debate' during the nineteenth century as it was 'of central concern' to nineteenth century observers.[8]

Middle-class men disliked their wives working. The idea was put forward under the guise of protection, arguing that the public sphere was no place for a woman and waged work was anathema to their sex. Middle-class women in turn frowned on the waged work of working-class women who sought 'independent careers' like 'impertinent mill girls who refused the paternalistic principle of domestic service... and who might also... refuse to fit the role of a respectable man's working wife.'[9] Whilst middle-class men could 'protect' their women from this so-called danger, as they had enough money to support their wives, working-class men had to allow their wives to work because their wages were needed – hence, husbands were unable to keep them away from supposed harm and associated sexual dangers. According to the prevailing moral perspective, working-class women entering the public sphere were philosophically engaged in a role which was anathema to their sex.[10] Waged work identified working-class women as members of the public sphere – albeit poor ones – causing tension between women due to the independence it gave working-class women that was denied to middle-class women.[11] Femininity was shaped by domesticity, not waged work; the 'Angel of the House' was the ideal to which all nineteenth-century women were to aspire.[12]

This philosophy was well rooted in the nineteenth century for, as historian Deborah Valenze remarks, 'long before the nineteenth century Victorian ideals of womanhood, eighteenth century moralists regarded the female Sex for domestic Life only'. As Carolyn Malone argues, this ideal became more entrenched in the century which followed.[13] The link between the domestic sphere and its inhabitants put the mother who cared for her children at the head, and sanctified motherhood. As contemporaries remarked, 'The child receives nurture, warmth, affection, admonition, education from a good mother; who, with the child in her arms, is in the eyes of all European nations surrounded by a sanctity which is only expressed in the highest works of art'.[14] There was disapproval levelled at mothers who transgressed this ideal; some even said it represented an emasculation of the husbands who permitted their wives to enter the public sphere.[15]

The contemporary medical doctor George Newman, who became the first chief Officer to the Ministry of Health in the twentieth century, remarked at the end of the nineteenth century of his deep concerned over the high IMR. Using statistical records collected by medical officers of health and published by the Registrar General, Newman produced reports on the infant mortality problem, and he concluded that the problem was one of 'motherhood'. Moreover, he 'placed the mother as the single most important influence on an infant's chances of survival', and was convinced that the problem was not medical but social.[16] Newman arrived at this hypothesis after becoming disillusioned with the extent to which medicine was able to make any improvement in the IMR and he sought public office to establish the correct procedures of infant health through a policy of the education of mothers. This prescriptive role took on a more determined character when he became a part-time medical officer for the Clerkenwell borough in London, before attaining a lifetime ambition to become Chief Medical Officer of Health for Education in 1907 and in the Ministry of Health in 1919, where he sought to take control of working-class child care practice.[17]

Newman took his lead from the Yorkshire medical doctors such as John Ikin of Leeds, George Reid, Edwin Chadwick, and Dr Lankester.[18] Due to the concern over the number of infants who were dying in Leeds, Dr Ikin and his colleagues arranged a forum where these men could discuss this issue. The group consensus was that working-class mothers and their waged work was a significant cause of the problem because the factory separated the mother and child.[19] These findings were published in a pamphlet which was distributed locally in the *Leeds Mercury*.[20]

Although Newman found common ground with men like Ikin as to the dangers that married mothers' factory work caused infants, he himself conceded that he 'found it difficult to establish the case in a way that proved completely convincing'.[21] This caveat is a salutary reminder of how tacit conclusions based on statistics collected from the Registrar General and the medical reports which arose out of them, but lacking any content on the experiences of women's lives and child care, have maligned working-class women's characters and child care practices. Criticisms and condemnations were composed and circulated with little evidence to substantiate them. Yet, despite the lack of proof, Newman's words exerted and have continued to exert great influence in the northern IMR debate, as in the works of historians Robert Woods, Alice Reid and Margaret Hewitt, all of whom rely on Newman's rhetoric and the statistics of the Registrar General as they remark on the 'maternal ignorance' of working-class mothers, as a result of which 'health visitors had been first introduced in 1862 by the Ladies' Sanitary Reform Association of Manchester and Salford, in order to overcome such maternal ignorance'.[22] Robert Woods's work shows that the highest rates of IMR occurred in the industrial districts of the north, and this statistic is repeated by Robert Millward and Frances Bell who have shown that the highest levels of infant mortality applied to those born to northern textile mothers.[23]

Northern mothers and agricultural work

The figures given by Millward and Bell show that whereas mothers employed in agriculture endured an IMR of 125/1000, and those engaged in the proto-industrial metal trades a rate of 190/1000, infant mortality amongst female factory workers registered the high figure of 200/1000.[24] From this evidence it appears that there was more than a grain of truth in Margaret Hewitt's claim that mothers' waged work during the latter part of the nineteenth century in Lancashire and Yorkshire factories posed significant problems for married women with children.[25] When trying to ascertain the impact of female waged work on the IMR, and whether factory work represented a disproportionate risk to infants, however, we need to consider the range of these modes of employment and the child care practices which they fostered. With this in mind, we first examine the maternal experience of those employed in agriculture during the period.

Despite the number of women employed in agriculture almost halving over the second half of the nineteenth century, working on the land remained an option for a significant number of women. Despite being characterised by industrial and urban growth during the period, the north still retained an agricultural base which provided waged work for women, particularly in the North and East Ridings, Northumberland, and even parts of Lancashire.[26] Agricultural work gave women both seasonal and all-year-round employment, offering them some flexibility. Historians Ivy Pinchbeck and Bridget Hill note that this work particularly appealed to mothers, as it allowed them to combine domestic and work responsibilities, with even 'servants in husbandry and cottagers' wives, whose husbands eked out their small allotments by occasional earnings as day labourers... [were] often accustomed to work for wages at hay and harvest.'[27] At a local level, mothers were employed in higher numbers than men, and, as a Royal Commission reported, not only was there a tradition of female workers in the fields, but the 'majority of the women who work in the fields are... generally married.'[28] Richard Jefferies described the nature of women's agricultural work during the 1870s:

> From the earliest dawn to latest night they swing the sickles, staying with their husbands, and brothers, and friends, till the moon silvers the yellow corn. The reason is because reaping is piece-work and... the longer and harder they work the more money is earned... Grasping the straw continuously cuts and wounds the hand, and even gloves will hardly give perfect protection. The woman's bare neck is turned to the colour of her tan; her thin muscular arms bronze right up to the shoulder. Short time is allowed for refreshment; right through the hottest part of the day they labour. It is remarkable that very few cases of sunstroke occur. Cases of vertigo and vomiting are frequent, but pass off in a few hours.[29]

Giving evidence to the Royal Commission, Mr Joseph Henley, MP for Oxfordshire until 1878 and member of the Board of Trade during the 1850s, remarked that across the agricultural north, 'women are extensively employed throughout the whole year, and their labour is considered essential for the cultivation of the land'.[30] The essentially female nature of the northern agricultural labour force was, argued Charles Borthwick of Lancaster, born of necessity, as farmers 'couldn't get males to work'.[31] The statements by witnesses to Royal Commissions are, of course, less a reflection of any 'truth' than of the stance an individual wished to take to the Royal Commission, and Henley and Borthwick may have been putting a positive spin on mothers' work because it was necessary and cheap for the farmer. This is surprising in light of the overall desire for farmers to hide the true extent of women, and especially mothers, employed in field work, but the statistics support the witnesses' evidence that field work was done by numbers of women and mothers. For example, around Durham, 40 single women were reported as working in the fields, but 55 married women.[32] Ever adaptable, these women did 'a great many out-of-door tasks including "slingling and quickening"',[33] leading one observer to note that 'the women who do this labour are physically a splendid race'.[34] Whether single or married however, women formed the core of the northern agricultural workforce. The absence of sufficient male labour was only one reason for this, however: as the witnesses noted, among the landowners around Doncaster in Yorkshire there was a preference for women as their labour was 'the most economical the farmer can employ'.[35]

Despite agricultural employment waning during the second half of the nineteenth century, women still worked in agriculture throughout the north. This included a substantial body of married women and is significant in respect of the infant mortality debate, for it allows the child care practices used by these women to be evaluated and compared with those employed by factory workers.

Margaret Hewitt damned the impact of female agricultural work on levels of infant mortality. Arguing that this work was impossible to combine with effective motherhood, she concluded that the mothers engaged in this work abandoned their children at home, or delegated their child care to siblings, leading to injury and even death for infants.[36] These depictions of neglect and abandonment for agricultural mothers contrast with those advanced by witnesses reporting on agricultural employment, however. Inspections of York, Goole, Howden, Holderness, Beverley, Driffield, Pocklington, Malton, Thirsk, York, Northallerton, Richmond, Hawes, Settle, Guisborough, Wakefield and Rotherham, and of Northumberland led witnesses to state that married agricultural workers, 'take their children with them to work', where 'they are kept in sight all day long.'[37] Although Mr Portman of York remarked in 1867 that he thought 'mothers with young children were better off at home', the majority of witnesses to the Royal Commission did not share this view.[38] Agricultural mothers did not compromise the safety of their infants when they were forced to sell their labour to farmers. This maternal practice was similar to that used by mothers in Sussex in 1833 where:

> the custom of the mother of a family carrying her infant with her in its cradle into the field, rather than lose the opportunity of adding her earnings to the general stock, though partially practiced before, is becoming very much more general now.[39]

Mrs. Britton from Wiltshire remarked that she 'frequently carried the baby' with her, as she 'could not go home to nurse' it whilst she 'worked in the fields'.[40] Northern agricultural mothers considered it highly advantageous that this employment gave them the opportunity to combine agricultural work with feeding their infants, who were breast fed for 'a year and a half or 2 years frequently'.[41] Once fed, infants were 'placed on a heap of coats or shawls in the shade of a hedge where they would be watched over by one of the older children'.[42] Thus, not only did mothers' agricultural work present them with a way of having their infants with them, but their older children also, enabling mothers to keep a close eye on both age-groups, abandoning neither, despite accusations to the contrary set at them. Despite being physically demanding, agricultural work did not appear to impact on the health of mothers, which in turn meant that their ability to care for their infants was not affected. Of course, agricultural work does not always equate to rude health and we should be wary, as Everslay has cautioned, of perpetuating this myth, but the witnesses to the Commission were positive about the well-being of these women, remarking that:[43]

> married women bear the labour in the fields extremely well; that he has never observed any other effects on their general health than colds, from which they suffer occasionally, caught from wet and exposure to the weather; he was sure that they were even peculiarly subject to colds; women in the family-way, or suckling children, are not hurt. He does not think that their work is too hard for them, or injurious, even taking into account the fact of their generally having insufficient food. The out-door work is rather healthy than otherwise.[44]

Indeed, as Mr James Barwick of Barrow suggested, the agrarian lifestyle seemed particularly suited to mothers, as it provided a welcome addition to the family income without compromising their independence.[45]

These observations are important for the IMR debate as they indicate that agricultural work gave mothers the opportunity to combine the difficult tasks of waged work and maternal obligation.[46] The farmer was perhaps willing for mothers to take their children with them as it improved the chances to which they would turn up for work. Despite the physical and outdoor nature of agricultural work, the latitude it afforded mothers facilitated infant care whilst they worked and provided them with an effective check against infant mortality. This explains why the IMR among these workers was less than that experienced by their contemporaries employed in metal works and factories at 'only' 125/1000.[47]

Northern mothers and heavy labour

Although the textile trades clearly moved towards more concentrated modes of factory production over the course of the nineteenth century, some industries resisted this trend, with production still carried out along cottage or proto-industrial lines.[48] Industries like the glass and pottery trades, and centres of nail-and chain-making all proved slow to change, and continued to provide work for northern women throughout the nineteenth century.[49] Indeed, as witnesses to a Commission remarked of the nail and chain trade, 'very few men of average strength continue in the trade'.[50] Thus, Robert Baker was probably correct when remarking that the northern nail making trade was mainly the preserve of single and married women.[51] Wages for female workers in the metal industries were around 9s per week, which was not a high wage for women during this period.[52] One of the main benefits of this work however, was that it allowed mothers to work with their family as part of a family unit, for as the witnesses noted 'it was not an uncommon sight to witness a man, his wife, and three, four, or five daughters working in the same shop, and...mingled with these, a son and two or three men who work as journeymen.'[53]

Despite enabling mothers to be with their families within the work place, these trades were marked by social commentators as both dangerous and unsuitable for women to perform, and posing a risk to the well-being of infants. Reports submitted to the Royal Commission raised concerns in respect of the impact that these working conditions had on the welfare of infants. Their survey of northern nail makers, for instance, illustrated the extreme nature of the working environment to which even infants were subjected. The heat emanating from the forges for example, meant that many women preferred to work during the night, when it was cooler, with infants in tow. Should the infants wake from the noise of the hammers, mothers would delegate their older female children to attend to them and ensure that they were kept away from the sparks. The witnesses were not instilled with confidence at the sight of 'girls...each of whom carried a baby.'[54] The practices of hanging infants from a hook on the wall in slings after feeding, in order to soothe them, or 'placing infants in a wooden belt' which 'limited their exercise area whilst their parents got on with their work' were unlikely to inspire confidence either.[55]

Whilst providing mothers with an opportunity to combine waged work with child care and breast feeding, the trade raised problems of safety because infants were in the workshop itself. Recognising this, mothers attempted to make their infants as safe as possible so, as Robert Sherard, author of *The White Slaves of England*, remarked in 1897, they erected poles at the workshops to which they would attach slings into which they would place their infants, whom they would rock to and fro.[56] Female witnesses to the Royal Commission investigating this form of work in 1894, remarked that mothers perched their infants 'on a warm heap of fuel or dangled them in an egg-box from the shop ceiling'.[57] These contemporary accounts are supported by the historian Sheila Lewenhak, who likewise argues that it was not uncommon to see infants 'hanging in little swing chairs from poles so that while working the hammers [mothers] could rock their infants'.[58]

In general, witnesses were positive about the impact of these working arrangements, remarking that 'there does not appear to be anything in their employment to be at all injurious to health'.[59] Further, they stated that 'the health of the nail makers *as a class* is very good; they are not subject to any specific disease; as a rule they live long, their occupation being one not too exhausting'.[60] We have already seen that the IMR amongst this operative class was around 190/1000. This rate does not appear to mirror these positive evaluations, and suggests that the close association between the working and maternal environment did not promote infant well-being or health. That said, however, the number of deaths of nail-makers was less than that recorded amongst female factory workers.[61] Indeed, although the working environment in the nail making industry was difficult for infants, because infants were not separated from their mothers the risk set to them was relatively small.

These innovative models of child care practiced by northern mothers during industrialisation have tended to go unnoticed by historians. No less creative were the married women who processed brine in the Cheshire, Manchester and Droitwich salt mines. These mothers were employed to boil brine in pans, which made the sheds 'very hot'.[62] Extremes in temperatures at the sheds were common: workers could 'be met by a chilling wind,' if working on a different side of the shed. Despite the flux in temperature, mothers thought the industry quite suitable to combine with child care for, when a new baby was born, as the Inspector of Factories Mr Fitton reported, they 'bring their infants into the streaming sheds to be suckled, and lay them down in the hot drying sheds to sleep at intervals while they, the mothers, are occupied in the laborious work of dragging the salt from the bottom of the pans with heavy iron rakes.'[63] The ardent maternal nature of these women, who were accused by contemporary commentators of lacking motherly feeling, is summed up by the historian Brian Didsbury, who tells us 'Groups of weary women (some with babies wrapped in their shawls) and sleepy-eyed children made their way through the pitch darkness towards the Wych houses. Many lived within a short distance of the saltworks in cottages rented from the proprietor but others had to walk up to two miles.'[64] Robert Baker (who erroneously stated that during the latter half of the nineteenth century mothers left their infants in the care of others) was clearly aware of these child care practices operated by the mothers who worked in the salt works – yet this did little to dent his ambition to provide Select Committees with the inaccurate testimony about the negative aspects of working mothers' child care upon which Margaret Hewitt's classic and George Newman's tome is built.[65]

Mothers who manufactured bricks in Manchester and the West Midlands were equally proactive and tender when managing their child care in times of work, despite the 'hard graft' their labour asked of them. Pregnant women worked in the brickyards where they soldiered on at their work shortly before being confined.[66] The MP Charles Owen O'Conor reported to the Select Committee in 1876 of the tenacity of these mothers who 'take their little ones along with them to the brickyards'.[67] Moreover, the parents remarked that this was not unusual and was the custom on which infants of brickmakers were 'brought up' for he remarked 'I saw some of the parents last night, and they said that they were almost born and bred in the brickyard. And on the continuance of this ritual he said: 'Their little ones are taken there, and there are little corners in Messrs Rufford's works which are screened off for the little ones. I have seen them many and many a time kicking and tossing about'.[68]

Mr O'Conor reported the legality of this practice to the Select Committee and agreed with the Committee's conclusion that it was an extremely effective child care method as the infants 'were looked after better than if they were at home', for the 'mothers bring their meals in the morning and cook them in the brick yards.[69] The children are under their eye the whole of the day, and they take them off home again by the time that the father comes home from work'.[70] These youngsters were watched over by both their mothers and their older siblings who would often strain themselves in getting to know their new siblings by carrying them around the brick works.[71]

Other safety measures were also used. William Henry Edwards remembers his mother working the brick yards and how he was placed out of harm's way:

> I had a little swing fixed up for me on the beam opposite the horse and round and round I would go all day. If the horse dropped anything, it had to be cleared away immediately to keep the path from becoming greasy and in bad condition. So as I travelled round and round, I kept a diligent watch for this, and was delighted when I could call out, 'Tom, Old Jack's messing again'

This was a first-rate method of child care, allowing Edwards's mother to get on with her job, knowing her son was along with her. It enabled her to earn the money she needed to raise her family, for, as historian Jane Humphries acknowledges, she was 'a good hand', at making tiles and 'made hundreds and thousands'.[72]

Agricultural, metal, salt and brick work were all significant employers of northern women where infants were kept close and were breast fed, and where mothers ensured their children's safety as far as they could. To what extent were factory mothers able to display the same mother craft qualities? It is to them that we now turn.

First, we examine the extent to which contemporary criticism of this work described it as being detrimental to infant health and a key driver of infant mortality.

Northern mothers and the textile industry

Northern working mothers were caught in the rise of centralised industrial production which was, as Pat Hudson argues, 'a distinct period in which the commercial employment of female labour increased in an unprecedented fashion'.[73] As the domestic process moved from manor to mill it did not take with it the expensive male labour force, but drew, as Maxine Berg has remarked, on a 'large cheap female labour force'.[74] As women were increasingly shaken out of agriculture by economic change, the factory gave them a chance to carry on working and keep their wage – a process aided by the feminisation of technology which, argues Maxine Berg, was the driving force which led to the eventual 'sexual division of labour'.[75]

Although historians Eleanor Gordon and Esther Breitenbach note that the 'figure of the factory-or mill-girl was not typical of women workers in the nineteenth century', they nonetheless concur that 'the sheer scale of the textile industries as sources of employment for women makes them impossible to ignore'.[76] Moreover, as these 'new methods and new machines had real potential to 'eradicate [an old] trade and with it the assumption of work for the rest of a person's lifetime',[77] women who were young enough to adapt and learn new technologies consequently flocked to the mills and the supposed security they offered. For example, in 1841 at the Leslie Parish in Scotland, the Prinlaw mill employed a vast number of women, totalling some 74 per cent of the workforce, and throughout Britain females were employed as tenters, spinners, warpers, weavers and reelers.[78]

The growth in demand for manufactured cloth such as cotton, wool, linen and silk during the nineteenth century led to its manufacture in ever larger premises, which in turn led to areas of manufacturing specialism. Lancashire became famous for cotton processing and spinning, and Yorkshire and the West Country for woollen weaving. What all these areas had in common was that these industrial processes were performed by an overwhelmingly female workforce.[79]

For married women, particularly those in Lancashire and the West Riding, this meant there was work for the women who needed and wanted it.[80] Whilst the Lancashire district needed women mainly to spin cotton, Yorkshire mothers were asked to weave wool, worsted and flax which, according to Maxine Berg, was the largest and most important growth industry of the nineteenth century.[81] Of a total of 703 woollen and worsted mills in Britain during 1867–8, employing 131,896 workers, Yorkshire held 626 mills with 121,117 employees, a local monopoly which was retained throughout the nineteenth century.[82] As with the cotton mills of Lancashire, the workforce was predominantly female.[83] The historian Emma Griffin confirms that there was a high female participation rate in regions of cotton and wool manufacture.[84]

According to the historiography reviewed in the introduction, the infants of the mothers who worked in these industries were subject to maternal separation. Of course, we have to remember that not all women who worked in the textile industries were married with children. As the number of married women workers is largely unknown, the figure of infants at risk to this separation is also contested. Nineteenth-century censuses sought to capture the number and type of occupations working-class mothers were engaged in and the results show that few mothers claimed to be accomplished in the art of power loom weaving – either in wool or cotton.[85] Leigh Shaw-Taylor notes the low figure as do her fellow-scholars Michael Anderson, Jane Humphries and Sara Horrell.[86] Eddie Higgs even goes so far as to argue that the figures were actually much higher than those recorded,[87] and Patricia Branca asserts that the low numbers in census returns do not reflect the true numbers but are a mirage intended to deliberately conjure a mean picture of waged mother's work.[88] The historian and demographer Paul Laxton reminds us the 'numbers listed in factory inspectors' reports do not collate on to the census records', and thus this may have been a determined effort by nineteenth-century working-class mothers to keep up appearances, and not divulge their waged work during a period of high infant mortality.[89]

Any definitive conclusion to the statistics debate is unlikely to be forth-coming. It is clear, however, that in the cotton districts of Lancashire mothers were strongly represented in the women earning an income from factory work. Historian Rosalind Hall has argued that they featured promi-nently among the 500,000 factory operatives employed in the 2,300 mills in the period from the 1860s to the 1900s.[90] Elizabeth Roberts has noted the high rates of married women who were employed in the cotton mills in Lancashire, where their wage was crucial to the family economy.[91] Burnley is a good case in point, for, as historian Jutta Schwarzkopf has argued, this Lancashire town 'boasted 400,000 spindles along with 99,000 looms', most of which were operated by women, single and married.[92] Lancashire was the centre of the cotton industry and Hewitt points out that the area had strong associations with married women's work, estimating that around 58 per cent of female workers in the Lancashire district were married and mothers.[93] Family responsibilities were taken on by Lancashire mothers: on a visit to the Lancashire mills in 1862, the author Ellen Barlee remarked that:

> the temptation [for wives] to work is great; for, so large is the demand for female labour, that fifty women can find employment where the man fails. Thus, it is quite true that many women do keep their husbands and families, the men merely doing such jobbing work as they can pick up.[94]

Given this scenario, the historian Joan Scott could be right to say that women not taking a job in a factory town were 'looked on as lazy'.[95]

In the West Riding districts of Yorkshire Emma Griffin and Elizabeth Roberts remark on the high female participation rates of up to 50 percent, but they caution against making too much of these figures, noting that 'it may never be possible' to quantify participation accurately.[96] Yet, it has to be considered that the numbers of women workers conveyed to us by factory inspectors in their reports relay a truer picture than our historiog-raphy suggests, as some working-class women concealed their waged work from the census records, despite their role in supporting their families. Jane Humphries has argued that women withdrew from the factory once their children were old enough to replace them, but irrespective of the age of the children, if poverty came in at the window then any 'choice' women had over leaving work and relying on their children's wages flew out of the door. Indeed, if destitution reared its ugly head, usually in the form of a bare food cupboard, then women sought and took whatever work their region provided. Poverty was a driver of waged work for these women, even with its associated moral approbation, which probably continued even when children were old enough to bring in a wage. The nineteenth-century social reformer and activist Barbara Hutchins tells us of the 95 women she interviewed in the West Riding who worked mainly because of their husbands' unemployment.[97]

Other reasons given for West Riding wives to walk through the factory portals were widowhood, the refusal or reluctance of husbands to hand over their wages (preferring sometimes to give their money to the pub landlord)[98] desertion and separation.[99] Hutchins's survey is extremely small and not representative of all married factory operatives, but we see that two-thirds of mothers in the West Riding had to support their families single-handedly. Others had to work to prop up their husbands' low wages – wives worked in the West Riding during the latter half of the nineteenth century because work for their husbands could be scarce, and even if work was found it paid very little.[100] Very few mothers said they had 'preference for outside work'; these mothers went out to work out of necessity.[101]

Whilst most women worked full-time, part-time work was also available. When full-time women were ill they would be replaced by a woman known as a 'sick weaver'. These women worked as and when needed, such as the anonymous Mother A2 in Barbara Hutchins's survey who worked as a sick weaver during the 1880s and 1890s, replacing her colleagues who were ill.[102] These women were also likely to stand in for pregnant women, such as Emma Riley who lived and worked in the Leeds mills as a weaver. She was aged 19 and was married to a rag merchant, John Riley.[103] The narratives of 160 mothers who gave the reasons for their work to Margaret Llewelyn also confirm the conclusion that male unemployment, low wages and drink were their key motivations.[104]

The husbands of the wives in Hutchins's and Llewelyn's surveys in the West Riding districts worked in the same industries as those captured in the Leeds Brotherton infant death records – husbands subject to the same low wages and unemployment.[105] We can confirm this by using the census to search for the parents of dead children. Thus we see that although Alfred Crosland, the husband of Rosina, said he was a paper merchant (but may have embellished his working status and was probably employed in the paper industry), he was actually unemployed. Given this desperate economic scenario Rosina, who gave no occupation on the census, was likely to get work where she could find it. Mary Ash lived in the same district of

Brotherton; her husband was a painter, as were 32 other men in Brotherton, and she may have been equally pressed to say he was employed when not. Of course, even when in work he was subject to a low wage.[106] The same situation may have arisen for Ann Thorpe. Her husband was a respectable master mason in Leeds, but when work was slack, with four children to keep, Ann may have had to put food in the cupboard – as would Jane Simpson whose husband was a basket maker in the same district. Rosina, Mary, Ann and Jane may not have felt too indignant at having to go out to work, as other wives who lived not too distant from them did so. Mary Birmingham, aged 29, was a wife and a spinner; Mary Bretham, aged 39, was also a wife and a mill hand; Catherine Perkins, a widow aged 30, worked and spun in the mill.[107] Seeking and undertaking this work would have been difficult, but as mothers, it was better than starvation.[108] The wages earned might be from full- or part-time work. In any event, as historians Carol Dyhouse and Ivy Pinchbeck have commented, they made a significant contribution to the family's economy.[109]

May Abrahams visited mills as part of the investigations of the Royal Commission on Labour: The Employment of Women to identify 'the effect of work on married women, on the health on themselves and their children' in the northern districts in the 1890s. She wrote in her report of its necessity, and noted that only four mills in the whole of the West Riding area mentioned their dislike of it, whilst the others 'regarded it with indifference'.[110] As the female inspectors commented,

> many workers fear the immediate result of a complete withdrawal of married women working from the mills, and fear the effect upon homes practically maintained by the wife's labour, either where the husband is dead or disabled from work, or where he is unemployed. [Where he is able bodied] the withdrawal from the mill of his wife would not necessarily be followed by the substitution of himself.

From this it could be surmised that the inspectors did not disapprove of married women's work as the balance of the family's economic prosperity was often in the mothers' hands.[111] In an unnamed mill in the West Riding, Abrahams reported that married women accounted for some 97 per cent of the 'preparers', 19 per cent of the spinners, 32 per cent of the warpers and reelers, 14 per cent of the winders and 34 per cent of the weavers.[112] Preparing was the most popular occupation for married women because, as the manager reported, it was 'owing to the work being of such a nature that it could be taken up by the casual worker, who is driven into the mill by pressure of circumstance'.[113] The mothers who feature as parents of the infants recorded in the Leeds death registers are not asked for their occupation, but they could be dipping in and out of work when the need arose, despite their reluctance to acknowledge any occupational status in the census.

The factory inspector, Robert Baker, lamented the numbers of working married mothers and related its growth from the 1870s in Yorkshire and Lancashire, remarking that:

> if the employment of married women has increased with the employment of females generally, then we can probably arrive at some idea of their amount. In 1850 the number of females employed in our textile factories alone, exclusive of children was 329,577. In 1867 it was 479,596 or an increase of 45 per cent. In 1872 they amounted to 720,468, independent of those in thousands of workshops that are as yet unregistered. It cannot be doubted therefore that the employment of married women has greatly increased.[114]

The West Riding districts of Dewsbury and Batley, like Leeds and Lancashire, had a predominantly female work force. By the mid-nineteenth century the majority of woollen weavers were women – hence this area experienced a gender occupational crossover.[115] In the West Riding towns of Leeds, Bradford, Dewsbury and Batley this was reflected in a six to four ratio favouring women in woollen weaving by 1872.[116] This had been facilitated by the open nature of the trade due to the decline of the apprenticeship system and the gradual introduction of power-looms, which were capable of being operated by women.[117] The small town of Batley alone, for example, had at least 50 mills to its name, which were mainly worked by married women.[118] The cloth these mothers worked on, woollens and worsted, was specific to this area. The town grew and prospered on the back of the mungo and shoddy trade, developed in the 1860s, which turned old rags into new cloths and became the fastest growing textile trade during the period, selling mungo and shoddy cloth throughout Britain.[119]

Responsibility for pushing up the rates of married factory operatives seems to have lain with the mothers themselves. A conclusion to the debate about numbers of married women workers may rest in the hands of historians, but the female factory workers of the nineteenth century exerted some jurisdiction over membership of their sorority. As factory work during this period was characterised by 'irrespectability', the women working in the mills disliked mothers of illegitimate children tending to the looms. They wanted only 'married' and 'respectable' women. Margaret Hewitt contends that marriage may have been a prerequisite for procuring a job in the factory as manufacturers, reflecting the views of their workforce, were not keen to employ unmarried mothers.[120] Married mothers in Lancashire frowned on unmarried mothers, as illegitimacy was synonymous and emblematic of the supposed immorality they were keen to avoid, and they sought to limit it.[121] They policed courting couples and if a pregnancy occurred before marriage they would subject the mother to the humiliation of 'private punishment and public humiliation'.[122] Factory mothers in the West Riding of

Yorkshire seemed proud to have a husband, despite the anxiety their low wages incurred, and Dewsbury and Batley women were keen to show their 'respectability'. When the all-female 'Heavy Woollen Weavers' Trade Union Committee' posed for pictures in 1875, they ensured their wedding rings were on show.[123] In claiming the moral high ground these factory mothers give us a sense of their pride in themselves and their work.

The extent to which their morals had any effect on the unmarried mothers concerned is debateable but we have seen that working-class mothers in the West Riding needed to work, and they worked for the high wages on offer in Leeds. Although Leeds during the 1860s and 1870s has not been noted as a typical mill town, it had a legacy of textile work and high wages for mothers during the early part of the nineteenth century. It was known for its textile innovation, and Leeds manufacturers received royal assent from Prince Albert and Queen Victoria. This acknowledgement of excellence and services rendered may have pleased both worker and mill owner, but it was the wages of up to £1 a week associated with this work which particularly attracted women and mothers.[124] The manufacturer William Hirst drew mothers into his factories during the early part of the nineteenth century using a high-wage strategy, to 'encourage his weavers to make a good article' on his new machine he had developed to weave a new cloth, 'superfine merino', paying 'from 5s to up to a £1 extra in wages' for his workers to do so.[125] This high wage was necessary as it was a continuation of the fee women could command during the eighteenth century,[126] which Nigel Goose acknowledges was given to women in the weaving districts.[127] Hirst believed that it was necessary to build and secure a workforce to weave the new cloth, which sold at double the price of ordinary material.[128] The cloth had a distinct 'lustre' and 'shine' like no other,[129] and was of a 'perfectly different style to any of which had been previously made in Yorkshire'.[130] Hirst also devised ways of speeding up production rates by using hydraulic presses, double-rod mules, and the Lewis cutter which worked at a faster speed than those of competitors because it added seven cutters to each machine.[131, 132]

The cloth sold well, and Hirst offered his patent to other Leeds manufacturers and in the West Riding mills[133] (who presented him with a silver cup for his efforts).[134] In doing so he made both the work and the wage available to other factory mothers working in the 67 mills that the Leeds manufacturers had built and rented in order to profit from the cloth.[135] The demand for the cloth was high in Britain, Europe and America, and Leeds secured the trade – thus decimating the West of England woollen trade.[136] The American financial crash in 1825 put Hirst out of business but other mills in Leeds were able to carry on through the economic difficulty. The market secured, factory workers produced this cloth throughout the second half of the nineteenth century, making the women workers in Leeds 'better off'.[137] In 1840, mothers were amongst 17,000 'families' who worked in the mills producing this cloth.[138] Women such as Martha Marshall, Ruth Wilson, Hannah Adams,

Ruth Jackson and Maria Hartley all worked with numbers of children, from one to five each, and could be fairly confident of their wage to support their families.[139] The wage books of Holly Park Mills in Calverley and John Briggs Mill of Keighley also show mothers on the payroll, among them Hannah Adams, Emily Marshall, Sarah Wright, and others, such as Mary Ann Moore, Rebecca Buckley, Martha Feather, and Mary Ann Smith, worked in unnamed mills, being paid up to £1 per week.[140]

These mothers were noted in the Leeds woollen and worsted mills by William Dodd. He described a city which had an 'immense number of factories in the neighbourhood, each vomiting forth clouds of smoke, which collect in dense masses, and poison the surrounding atmosphere, and from which are continually falling particles of dirt and soot' [in which] 'many thousands of women and children are employed.'[141] The lure of employment outweighed the unremitting harshness of the conditions endured by women workers in Yorkshire and Lancashire. As the contemporary author James Haslam remarked of a Lancashire cotton factory in 1904:

> the ear was deafened by the roar of 'flies and spindles', the whirr of wheels and the squeaking of straps ever going round and round...Women attended carding engines...with the hurry, scurry and commotion of ants in danger of losing their lives...The whole work room seemed under an irresistible spell of continuous din and haste...some could be seen coughing, some heads were bent in oppressive labour, and mothers of large families [were] sitting on upturned skips, or on bobbins piled in skips and tins, stealing forty winks in order to rest their tired bodies or help sooth their pulsating limbs.[142]

The responsibilities of the weavers increased, as from around 1847 there was a tendency for 'each operative to be in charge of a greater amount of machinery, and for machinery to be driven at greater speed.'[143] This put pressure on the women in charge of these machines and the contemporary journalist and historian, Whately Cooke Taylor, remarked that 'women could not withdraw without affecting the work of the whole factory'.[144]

A contemporary report, informing the arguments made by Lord Ashley to the Select Committee during the 1844 Ten Hours debate, states that a manufacturer conceded that:

> he 'gives a decided preference to married females, especially those who have families at home to support'. And why? Because, he says, 'they are attentive, docile, more so than unmarried females, and are compelled to use their utmost exertions to procure the necessaries of life'.[145]

Thus, 'he only employed women at his power looms' as they 'were easier to manage and cost less'.[146] This suggests the women ceded to the patriarchal mode. Yet, this liking for employing female workers was also born out of the value of the women's work, from which the majority of the Yorkshire mills' profit was made.[147] This gave the women a cachet in the mills, and their value was something which the manufacturers acknowledged and wanted to keep. As Hutchins argued 'even in 1840 a woman working a power-loom could do "twice as much" as a man with a hand-loom, and the assistant commissioner who made this observation added the prophecy that in another generation women only would be employed, save a few men for the necessary superintendence and care of the machinery.'[148]

Manufacturers in the West Riding were thus keen to offload any men they had and 'offered 5/- to men working in the mills to go elsewhere'.[149] Employers were extremely 'indifferen[t]' to married mothers working in the West Riding districts because they knew that if employment could not be given by them, the mothers would not retreat to their homes but would seek it elsewhere.[150] Manufacturers who turned married women away gave a valuable asset to their competitors. Moreover, they would be giving away women who could offset further costs to the manufacturers for, unlike male workers, who were apt to abuse the children working in the mill violently, incurring prosecution costs from visiting factory inspectors, women practised a much more gentle approach[151] which did not incur these costs and overall, 'softened the hardships of their children's lives' by reducing the risk of abuse.[152] When children were naughty and mischievous, when they 'ran about' with the 'utmost unconcern', and when they played 'gymnastics on a revolving shaft', and when 'wilfully amusing themselves and playing', it was their mothers who intervened and stopped them.[153] Through their omnipresent and omnipotent eye, mothers took charge of their older children by getting them to settle down to work in a routine fashion;[154] working with their mothers on a frame, the children were less disruptive and worked in a regular pattern.[155]

As we have seen, the reasons for married women's work were varied, not only for the mothers themselves but for the manufacturers, but what about their child care? In 1872 Robert Baker lamented the number of married women involved in textile work in Yorkshire, and he agreed with Jevons that 'there were many evils arising from the employment of married women'.[156] In 1860 he had also remarked that 'infantile deaths are concurrent with the increase of manufactories, and the abstraction of females from their homes and domestic occupations for mill labour'.[157] This meant that when towns such as Leeds and Batley were singled out by the Registrar General as having particularly high levels of infant mortality these two issues were conflated, with the result that the crusade against the IMR also became a crusade against women's factory work throughout the northern industrial regions.[158] Whateley Cooke Taylor argued that the mothers who worked in the factory spent much of their lives at the loom rather than with their infants and although 'manufacturing mothers are organised like other mothers, in the first instance ... they do not commonly nurse their own children, because of the inexorable demands made on their time at the factory.'[159] These infants, Factory Inspectors Alexander Redgrave and Robert Baker argued, had to be artificially fed, a practice which retained and exacerbated the northern IMR. As Baker noted in 1871, 'experience can scarcely speak in sufficiently strong terms of condemnation' in respect of the 'employment of young married women ... in factories and workshops, especially those who are having families', as this condemned infants to be fed artificial food 'day in day out', which led to diarrhoea and exacerbated the IMR.[160] Were these contemporaries right, or are their musings merely a tool with which they could argue for limitations on married women's work?

The historian and sociologist Margaret Hewitt has argued that irrespective of the 'exaggerated social commentators' accounts', factory work undoubtedly impacted on the time women were able to devote to the home, and that consequently 'beyond doubt, the employment of mothers was a threat to the health and well-being of their babies'.[161] Sheila Rowbotham arrives at much the same conclusion, arguing that the archetypal northern factory represented 'the separation of work and home and the new discipline of the factory made their diverse activities less easy to combine'.[162] As Susie Steinbach tells us, decisions about breast feeding were linked to whether mothers worked outside the home or not.[163] Wanda Neff, Margaret Hewitt, Joyce Burnette and Jane Humphries also run with the separation issue, asserting that throughout the latter half of the nineteenth century when mothers worked at the Yorkshire and Lancashire mills it marred the amount of time they could spend with their infants.[164]

Clearly, some historians have come to regard mothers' industrial factory work as clearly damaging to the maternal bond. At the forefront of Hewitt and Rowbotham's analysis is the impact that this employment had on the time mothers could spend with their children.[165] Jane Humphries points us to the enforced costs of child care, often sought from neighbours, that factory work prescribed.[166] Sonia O Rose reminds us of the wider problems this separation rendered for factory mothers.[167]

It is clear that mothers had to spend much of their time at the factory, and Baker's musings are not without merit. The introduction of 'self-acting' machinery, for example, meant that constant attention was required from female operatives, who also had to 'set anything right that may happen to go wrong with it'.[168] These demanding working conditions meant that, as Baker noted, nursing mothers who lived any distance from the factory were simply unable to go home during the lunch break to breast feed their infants; consequently they were fed a sweetened 'pap', prepared before the women left for work.[169]

Administering this 'pap' to infants was, through necessity, delegated to others. If families were 'kin-rich' then this task would be undertaken by relatives. If this was not possible, then it was not uncommon for mothers to solicit the help of others to feed their infants.[170] Contemporaries reported that in Lancashire it was common practice for mothers to pay other women to feed the infant in the family home, in addition to carrying out most of the domestic tasks.[171] In Yorkshire, the custom was different, William Dodd recording the sight of mothers in the morning, who at the 'first sound of the factory bell' ran with their infants to 'some woman or girl' who would care for the infant and administer the artificial food.[172]

Robert Baker was also acquainted with this practice, and agreed that it was commonplace for infants to be 'nursed' by women other than their mothers during the day. he noted that this was the case throughout the West Riding, citing the example of one handloom weaver from Bradford who 'having two children, one an infant and the other under four years of age, at this moment places one out to nurse with her father at 2s 6d a week, and the other 3s-6d a week to a female.'[173] Such expenses would have wiped out much of a mother's income but in an era of economic flux, when male employment was subject to peaks and troughs and low wages, women needed to be the breadwinners and had to continue with this work despite the costs it incurred. Some families may have reduced the child care costs by using the husband during slack times to care for the children at home, as cited in Barbara Hutchins's survey. However, when employment was available for both parents they took it, and when both parents were away from home other resorts were taken: the contemporary travel writer Angus Reach confirmed Baker's observations, citing the case of a girl of seven looking after her younger siblings due to their mother's employment in one of Dewsbury's textile mills.[174] For the majority of factory women it seems, therefore, that the demands of their employment meant that there was little or no opportunity to breast-feed their infants.

The anxieties associated with married women's work were twofold: firstly they represented an affront to the ideal of motherhood noted earlier; and second, the separation of infant from mother rendered infants vulnerable to the care of others, who would feed them dangerous artificial food. Due to the need to work, the first morally charged objection has little significance for this research. However, the second objection needs closer inspection, for artificial food posed real danger to infants due to its lack of nutrients essential for infant growth and development. Due to the dietary medical prescription and its cheapness, the unboiled 'pap' which contemporaries argued was found in some factory mothers' homes had the same ingredients as given to workhouse infants. Further, it was delivered via what Dr Farr, the nineteenth-century medical statistician, and Drs W.S. Jevons, Kinnaird, Wiltshire, Benson Baker and Robert Baker called the 'fungus-bearing bottle' – it was often left dirty and gave the infants diarrhoea.[175]

As the historical demographers Robert Woods and Nicola Shelton have identified, the northern industrial towns like Liverpool, Manchester, Sheffield and Leeds experienced a disproportionately high rate of infantile

diarrhoea. In Leeds the recorded IMR figure was 20–44.9/1000 from infantile diarrhoea alone.[176] This cause and effect for the northern IMR appeared
clear.[177] This rationale contained more than a grain of truth, for if mothers were to make up the pap without refrigeration it was apt to go off and
become sour, then they compensated for this by adding 'an excess of sugar
in it to make [the] food palatable'.[178] As Dr Andrew Williams, paediatrician
at Northampton Hospital has argued, even the smallest amount of sugar
when given to infants on a daily basis, would be highly detrimental to their
health, and could induce the wasting diseases of diarrhoea and atrophy.[179]
That this sweetener was administered at all was due to the belief that it was
a necessary addition to cow's milk, and to its availability and cheapness.
As G.N. Johnstone has noted, due to technological changes in production
and refining processes, and a period of free trade from around the mid-
nineteenth century, sugar was transformed from a luxury item to a staple
of the working-class diet.[180] This low price led the historian John Burnett to
the working-class had great use for it in amounts of '7½oz for adults weekly
and 33¾as a family.'[181] Sugar was sold at the corner shop and added to tea
to make 'an important and essential part of the urban diet of all classes',
and during times of economic distress, was even used as a substitute for ani-
mal fat.[182] Consequently, as contemporary social realist novelists Elizabeth
Gaskell and George Gissing remarked, it was always found in larders, even
when tea and milk were in short supply.[183]

Despite individuals like Robert Baker imploring female factory mothers to
refrain from adding sugar to infant milk in his many lectures such as *No'butt
and Niver Heed*, the high rates of fatal infant diarrhoea recorded throughout the northern industrial regions suggest that the mothers rejected his
pleas.[184] However, when specific causal factors of infant death are analysed,
although the incidence of fatal diarrhoea was indeed high, and may have
been induced by the adulteration of infant milk by sugar, the extent to
which this indicates a causal link between female factory work and the IMR
is difficult to assess.

Using data drawn from the detailed Leeds Burial Registers, it is possible to
reconstruct the causal factors of infant death in the city between the years
1865 and 1873 – a period when there was particular concern over the high
northern IMR. Although identifying the occupational status of the mothers of deceased infants is notoriously difficult, as we have seen, we know
that factory work, and textile work in particular, was the principal employer
of female married labour during the second half of the nineteenth century
in the West Riding, including Leeds. The wider employment profile of the
region suggests that factory employment was typical for married women of
Leeds, and these burial registers are, therefore, essentially a record of the
mortality of the infants of waged-working mothers.[185]

As Table 2.1 indicates, when the 2260 infant deaths recorded in the Leeds
burial registers for the period 1866–1873 are compiled by contemporary

Table 2.1 Recorded causes of infant death, Leeds 1866–1873

Cause of death	Proportion of deaths (%)
Epidemic, Endemic and Contagious Disease	19.3
Sporadic Diseases of the Nervous System	18.5
Sporadic Diseases of the Respiratory Organs	13.1
Sporadic Diseases of Uncertain Seat (Including Infantile Wasting Diseases)	48.7
Sporadic Diseases of the Organs of Circulation	0.2
Sporadic Diseases of the Digestive Organs	0.2
Sporadic Diseases of the Urinary Organs	—
Sporadic Diseases of the Organs of Generation	—
Sporadic Diseases of the Organs of Locomotion	—
Sporadic Diseases of the Integumentary System	—

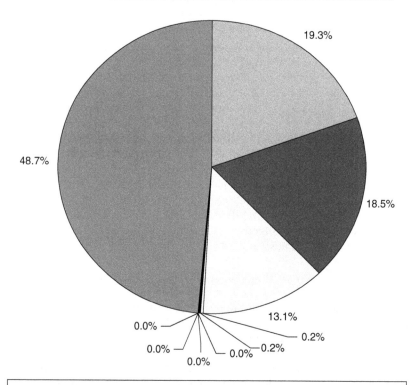

mortality classifications, infant mortality was essentially driven by four broad typologies: epidemic and endemic contagious disease; sporadic diseases of the nervous system; sporadic diseases of the respiratory organs; and sporadic diseases of uncertain seat (which included the various wasting conditions). With 451 infants stillborn, and only two deaths recorded as being due to 'natural causes', the figures clearly indicate a fundamentally unhealthy environment for infants in Leeds during this period – a situation which was undoubtedly mirrored throughout the northern industrial regions.[186] Whereas some diagnoses were related to specific environmental factors – like the incidence of sporadic diseases of the respiratory organs, which may have been due to damp housing – of interest for the purposes of this discussion is the incidence of 'epidemic diseases', which include 186 infant deaths attributed to infantile diarrhoea, giving an IMR of 18.4/1000. This suggests that some mothers may have artificially fed their infants thus inducing infantile diarrhoea, lending weight to the idea that infant mortality was indeed a consequence of factory mothers' or carers' artificial feeding.

Although it suggests a link between factory work and levels of infant mortality, Table 2.1 supports another, more nuanced reading. The IMR of 18.4/1000 pertaining to diarrhoea in Leeds is below that of the general rate of 20.4–44.9/1000 for the area shown by Woods.[187] Of course, this difference can be explained by several factors. The place-specific nature of the Leeds burial registers may not represent an exact 'fit' in respect of the aggregate figures arrived at within Woods's exhaustive national study. Also the analysis of the Leeds data is based in part on a set of assumptions relating to the occupational status of the mothers of the deceased infants. Despite these possibilities it is argued here that the analysis is robust, for, as noted above, this area was disproportionately characterised by high-wage mothers' factory work, and due to this concentration and the squalid urban environment, levels of fatal infant diarrhoea would be expected to be towards the high end of the spectrum, rather than below the aggregate calculated by Woods.

If lower levels of diarrhoea are evident in Leeds, where mothers' factory work predominated, is it possible that Leeds mothers reduced them by having their infants with them to breast feed in the mills? Flying in the face of the comments made by Baker and Dodd, B.L. Hutchins, who interviewed 95 women in the West Riding districts, has provided evidence which suggests that this was the case. Although 95 interviews are not representative of the West Riding district overall, they give us a narrative from the women who actually worked in the mills themselves during the 1860s and 1870s. May Tennant remarked that factory mothers breast fed their infants but that this posed difficulties for them whilst combining it with factory work.[188] William Dodd acknowledged that manufacturers disliked it because it 'hinder[ed] work'.[189] Whether these testimonies witness an 'objective view' of the textile owners is of course open to question. Falling victim to machinery Dodd had numerous accidents which crippled him for life and this may have coloured his experiences of factory mills. He may have wished to paint the mill owners and overseers in a bad light. Jane Humphries sees Dodd as a confidence trickster, whose agenda was to embellish his account in order to prise money from his sponsors,[190] but concedes that not this does not mean that all of Dodd's musings of life in the factories were inaccurate.

Yet the evidence from May Tennant, B.L. Hutchins and Margaret Llewelyn Davies, collected from working-class women themselves bears consideration for accounts of the maternal infrastructure in the nineteenth century textile mills. These institutions provide a more positive account of factory mothers, as the mothers who worked there took their infants to work *with* them.[191] Moreover, when their account is woven with Select Committee reports with regard to the maternal environment which mills provided, they together suggest that working mothers and mill owners came to some agreement in respect of combining the needs of motherhood with those of waged textile employment – and in an era of high infant mortality perhaps we should not be surprised that each sought to come to an agreement. It seems clear that mothers understood the merits of breast feeding; they recognised its importance and that it could be integrated into the factory work regime. The mill owners for their part acquiesced in light of the value of mothers' work in the factory.

We know that working-class mothers preferred to breast feed their infants themselves, rather than give them 'artificial food' because they found artificial foods, 'inadequate'.[192] Sian Pooley tells us that working-class parents feared 'the uncontrolled consumption of unsuitable food outside of the parental home'.[193] Indeed, as 'mother fifty one' from Llewelyn Davies's collections tells us, working-class women baulked at giving babies the 'inadequate' artificial food and warned other mothers to 'shun all patent foods rusks etc. as they would shun the devil himself, for an infant will have to be born with a digestion like a horse if it is to digest solid food in the early stages'.[194] The dangers of this food for infants were seemingly clear for working-class mothers, and breast feeding was a contraceptive, was cheaper than buying artificial foods, and was seen as having significant benefits for mothers – some medical men advertised it as way of reducing the risk of cancer.[195] Indeed, breast feeding also gave comfort to mothers, for retaining the extra milk was extremely painful. As one Manchester mother reported 'my breasts have given me the most frightful pain, and I have been dripping wet with milk'.[196] Medical men such as Sidney Coupland who interviewed working-class mothers from the Yorkshire districts heard that out of 100 women, 70 spoke of their breast feeding methods whilst 12 admitted to a mixture of artificial and breast.[197] Forty nine gave details of suckling infants, of whom 42 claimed to breast feed solely. The doctors gave no reason to suspect these women were being economical with the truth. Thus, in an era of high infant mortality, when the child care practices of working-class mothers were under scrutiny, and when the advantages of breast feeding to health, comfort and in reducing costs were widely appreciated, we should not be surprised that many working-class mothers fed their infants in this way.

Whilst historians and contemporaries argued that the factory walls created a fortress which the maternal relationship could not penetrate, Richard Stanway's Enderly Mills at Newcastle bucked this trend and provided a 'playroom and a cot-room...being equipped with cradles which were gently rocked by steam machinery.'[198] This room was strictly for factory mothers and their infants.[199] When mother and infant came together, breast feeding took place. Radical measures were also taken by the mothers themselves to metaphorically break down the walls. The mothers who worked at Tean Hall Mills at Stoke-on-Trent for instance, got around the blockade by breast feeding their infants through a breast hole. As local historian Joy Dunicliff has noted, for 'the women [who] worked in the part of the mill near High Street...there was a hole not much bigger than the span of a man's fingers, from thumb to little finger, in the wall, covered by a vertical sliding shutter and through this a nursing mother could feed her baby. The baby would be brought by its baby minder, usually by an aunt or an older sister, the foreman would fasten up the shutter on its cord, and with the baby being held to the outside of the hole, the feeding could be managed.'[200] Yorkshire factory mothers were no less innovative and found ways of having their infants at work with them and feeding them themselves. Northern mother 105 from Llewelyn Davies' data reported that if infants 'were at the breast, you must take baby with you'.[201] A weaver who worked in the Yorkshire West Riding districts during the 1860s acknowledged to an investigator from the Women's Industrial Council in 1909 that just as at Newcastle and Stoke-on-Trent, this is exactly what she did when she worked in the West Riding mills during the 1860s: 'she had them at the mill, and put them in a basket out of the way, till she was ready to go home'.[202] Taking infants to work early in the morning would have been a cold affair as the manufacturer Mr J. Booth remarked 'it was a hardship...(more especially women with infants) must suffer'[203] Mother 53 in Llewelyn Davies's dataset tells us it was 'their duty' to take them to work with them, which produced babies who were 'strong and healthy'.[204] This practice was in keeping with the cultural feeding practices of other industrial mothers such as those who worked in agriculture, metal, brick and salt works. For instance, although when her new baby was born, mother A26 left it at home with her mother and went home to suckle it; should the grandmother be unavailable then the basket served as an ideal place in which to place her new baby, for infants were no strangers to mills.[205]

The importance of taking infants to the mills seemed to have grown out of the idea that once mothers began breast feeding it was their duty to continue to do so, and this may be the reason why Llewelyn's mother remarked 'take baby with you'.[206] If child minders were used, they had the responsibility of ensuring the infant's progression even if the mothers had to be brought out of work. When a babysitter was speaking to a medical doctor who was enquiring about the family history of an infant whose mother worked as a servant, the babysitter said due to the hunger of the male infant 'I had to send for the mother in the middle of the day about half past two because he was crying'.[207] This tells us that employers understood the feeding scenario and the needs of infants and allowed mothers to go home and feed their babies. This is a picture which offers a different perspective about infant mortality and waged work when aiming to bring up infants. One of the earliest practices used by mill owners to entice mothers out of their homes and into the factories was to adopt or build 'burling-sheds' where women were employed to do the 'burling, stuff weaving and flax spinning' – these were female-only spaces.[208] These sheds offered the mothers privacy to combine breast feeding with waged work, like the sorting and picking sheds which operated in Leeds late into the nineteenth century.[209] These sheds facilitated a strong 'female group consciousness', enabling mothers to discuss their child care practices whilst they 'exchanged views and gossip'.[210]

When larger sheds were built, anonymous mother A26 in Hutchins's survey remarked that she worked at the mill whilst using the baskets to bring up most of her 15 children. She took her infants to work – there was no barriers to her doing so – and as a power loom weaver during the 1860s she earned 34–40 shillings per week with her children by the side of her in a basket.[211] However, it is difficult to gauge the extent of this practice in the West Riding for, as we have seen, overseers did not think it important to identify whether women were married or not.[212] Of course we also have to consider the ease of this practice. Unlike today, nineteenth-century artificial infant feeding vessels were difficult to transport, so for working-class women who had to fit work and children together, breast feeding at work was the most useful method, and it meant that they were on hand to feed when their infants became hungry.

Although the mothers in Llewelyn Davies's and Hutchins's datasets tell us they took their infants to the mills, where they were able to breast feed and place their infants in baskets, their practice cannot be held to represent the West Riding in general. Nonetheless, in knowing this we can see how 13 other factory mothers in Llewelyn Davies managed to breast feed their infants whilst working at the mills.[213] For, as mother 13 tells us, whilst she worked at the mill her infant was given the breast 'till she was twelve months old'.[214] This could only have been managed in continuation if she took her infant to the mill with her. This method may have contributed to the health of these infants and kept them away from the dreaded diarrhoea and gastroenteritis which infants in the Leeds death registers experienced. The practice was also in tune with the length of time middle-class mothers breast-fed their infants,[215] a length of time recommended and prescribed by medical doctors,[216] who stated that weaning should not take place until the age of 10 months, or 'until their first teeth appear, as this indicates the digestive organs are developed' and the infant's body could then digest solid food.[217] As we know, some infants can walk at nine months, so some mothers may have walked their infants to the mill, placing them in a basket until ready for a feed. Not only did the factory mothers who breast fed in the mill reduce the chances of their infants incurring diarrhoea, they also prevented the babies 'getting a rash', which stemmed from bottle feeding. This could cause great concern for mother: as Mrs D8 in the Hutchins dataset who worked in the mills in the 1870s tells us, 'the anxiety about it [was] killing her'.[218] Breast feeding at work reflects a 'medley of surety', for the 60 women (out of 95) who cited 'insufficiency of husband's earnings' as a reason for working at the factory.[219] This method brought together women's work and child care in industry, which operated a path of best practice against infant mortality, poverty and isolation. Indeed, as nineteenth-century northern women were apt to notice, working from home brought little reward as one woman remarked it 'worried her to be continually laying down her work to attend to the baby or to see to something in the house'.[220]

Whilst Baker and Dodd paint a bleak scenario of mothers leaving infants with nurses, the picture painted here, based on the evidence of northern factory mothers, is much warmer. We see mothers working at their loom with their infants by their side in a basket; mothers keen to preserve the maternal bond, just like female agricultural, metal, and salt workers. When women worked in industry they took their babies with them, and factory mothers were no different –taking baby to work fitted in with the infant-feeding culture of nineteenth-century industrial mothers.

The mills were not only a place where factory mothers could take their infants; the infrastructure provided security for the infants in their baskets. In this respect the mothers were allowed to ensure their infants safety by adapting the factory architecture to suit their maternal needs. There were baskets aplenty in the Leeds flax mills, as in the West Riding woollen mills, and they were used as makeshift cots. A picture taken of the inside of the Wilkinson's Flax Mill shows numerous baskets for the mothers to choose from and a wide space in which to place their infants at the side of their looms. There were similar spaces at Marshall's Mill from 1800 to 1880.[221] These would be useful for, as Selina Cooper, who worked in the Lancashire weaving sheds from 1876, recalled, some women 'would give birth at the looms'.[222] The weave of the baskets, both large and small, was very similar to the weave of the baskets which agricultural mothers placed their infants in at work. These 'makeshift cots' were similar to the ones made by the St Pancras School for Mothers, who turned banana boxes into cradles and sold them to mothers in the belief that it was safer to place babies in these at night than in their beds.[223] Objects had multiple purposes during this period, as is shown by Bernard Cotton who notes the vast number of uses a vernacular piece of furniture provided.[224] Indeed, at home, infants were placed in the drawer of a sideboard to sleep, and Margaret Macmillan's mothers spoke of placing older infants on chairs in the corner whilst they worked.[225]

Like the mothers who worked in the salt mines and brickworks, factory mothers displayed their responsible and nurturing maternal practice by walking to their work with their infants in their arms. Mother A26 from Hutchins's survey would be seen thus, weaving her way through the streets of the West Riding carrying her infant to the mill with her – a scene repeated in Manchester, where women and men walked 'through the streets with cradles in their arms, ... and women with their babies in their arms wrapped in shawls to protect them as much as possible'.[226] Eyre Crowe depicted Lancashire mothers, like their Yorkshire sisters, breast feeding their infants in the mill yards.[227] These are scenes reminiscent of salt workers who walked to work with their children in tow.

'Rights of Infants' and accommodations made

Looking after children while at work was clearly important to working-class women, flying in the face of current historiography which portrays their lack of maternal care. Significantly, working-class women took their infants to work with them because they had the right to do so. Indeed, as Thomas Spence, the English Radical Reformer, tells us, during the advent of the industrial revolution working women would have to assert their rights to ensure their infants' well-being and they did so under the aegis of the 'rights of infants'.[228] The historian, John Williamson, argues that workers in industry during the nineteenth century were compensated through 'rights' for the disadvantages industrialisation imposed on them.[229] Whilst Williamson makes claims for the rights of men, here we can see mothers claiming the right to keep their infants with them whilst at work, in the name of ensuring their health. During the 1860s and 1870s manufacturers did not seek to change mothers' established working patterns or destroy the maternal bond when mothers moved from manor to mill in the West Riding, arguably because they knew that the mothers needed to work, that they needed the mothers' labour *and* because they recognised that mothers needed to ensure the safety of their infants. In 1876 the MP Charles Owen O'Conor confirmed it their 'legal right' and entitlement for them to have their infants at work.[230] Not only do we see this practice in the West Riding but this 'right' was also evident in the West Midlands. The 'majority of mothers' who worked in the brickyards, for instance, did not leave their infants at home when they went to work but 'the parents take their little ones along with them'.[231] O'Conor remarked further that this descended from the old custom of parents taking their infants with them to work and that the infants are 'taken there and there are little corners in Messrs. Rufford's works which are screened off for the little ones'. As O'Conor acknowledged, this enabled mothers to ensure their infants safety as 'the mothers bring their meals in the morning, and cook them and the children are under their eye the whole of the day, and they take them off home again by the time that the father comes home from work'.[232] For working-class parents work was a necessary part of their lives and mothers had to contribute to a family's progress and prosperity. The ability to take infants to work meant that, as workers, neither nineteenth century mothers, nor their infants, lost out.

By exercising this 'right' we can see that mothers in the West Riding had little need for baby-minding. This was acknowledged and reported by the *Huddersfield Daily Chronicle* in 1896 with a sense of pride.[233] Indeed, as the Leeds census data indicates, again with a sense of dignity, there was only one baby-minder and one wet nurse during the 1831–1871 period.[234] Thus, older women who might have made a living out of child care, gravitated to the outskirts of villages, making way for mothers to live near the mills, which would have helped when carrying infants to and from work.[235] This also benefitted the infants' siblings old enough to work alongside their mothers. The highest number of children working in mills in the country were to be found in the West Riding areas of Dewsbury, Batley and Leeds, where worsted, woollen and flax manufacture dominated.[236]

Not only did mothers apply safety measures by keeping infants in baskets, and by keeping them away from the looms, but they employed their older children as baby sitters in the mills. The relationship between women and children gave mothers an ally when needing help with their infants at work. In Leeds and the West Riding areas of Batley, Holbeck, Hounslow and Hunslet during the 1860s children were kept away from school to be on hand to ensure the safety of infants and to help with child care inside the mill.[237] Children's factory certificates from Stubley's mill in Dewsbury from 1871 show 37 children working; they would have acted as surrogate parents when the need arose.[238] This was a practice which two of the factory workers, Eliza Day and Elizabeth Sykes, would have used as they were the mothers of infants but also had their older children working with them at the mill who were on hand to baby-sit. The 1871 census records that women aged in their thirties and forties who acknowledged working and who had children aged one and under had between two eight children. That these women were not ashamed to give their working status could be linked to their pride in providing and caring for their children whilst at work, knowing they were safe. Linking the census with factory certificates and wage books provides a new way of identifying positive child care methods: if all three are available, if the mother has an infant and older children working at the same mill with her then this 'family unit' may be definable as a team of workers and infant carers aiming to preserve infant health. We can see examples from Keighley factory certificates – Betty Denby worked at the mill with an infant and eight older children; Mary Ann Moore had four older children working alongside her.[239] This was similar to the practice in Birmingham, where mothers placed their older children in charge of their infants when they took them to work at button factories. Babies were placed in tubs filled with sawdust for safety.[240] The son of a button factory worker recalled in 1850:

> I was a nurse at five years old, and had sometimes to mind the children at home that they did not set their pinafores on fire, and sometimes I had to go to the factory to attend to the infant. My mother was allowed to take it with her, and it used to lie in a tub of sawdust, and sleep or roll about till it wanted the breast. I was obliged to watch over it and amuse it. I was put to work at the buttons at seven years of age, and I thought myself very fortunate in being relieved from the disagreeable labour of nursing the baby.[241]

Again, the dedication of these mothers in the industrial sector, who breast fed their infants and employed their older children as baby sitters, is a new phenomenon for historians of child care.

A domestic workplace

Breast feeding mothers needed to ensure they were sufficiently nourished to produce enough milk. Again, the mills were adapted by them for this purpose because mothers knew that 'good plain food' was necessary to ensure good quality breast milk.[242] To enable appropriate feeding whilst at work, women altered the factory space to suit their needs: a 'cookshop' was often erected.[243] Angus Reach, who visited the Leeds and West Riding mills, reported that cookshops had seats on which mothers and children could come together to eat, and where the breast feeding mothers could feed their infants at lunch time. Relatives brought pies to the mill 'with under baked crusts',[244] which were placed on a makeshift oven, often the 'surface of the steam engine', which allowed for 'every girl who pleases [to bring] her dinner, ready cooked but disposed in a dish so as to allow it to be warmed up again'.[245]

In one mill Reach saw three hundred dinners prepared this way; 'they were handed out through a sort of buttery-hatch to each ... as she shouted the number of her cording machine or spinning frame or loom.'[246] Reach testifies to 'one woman helping herself to potatoes using the shears she used to cut the rags with'.[247] Drinks were also available, and Lady Commissioners visiting the West Riding mills saw in Mark Oldroyd's mill at Batley that 'hot water and milk are given free to the workers',[248] and in a nearby mill 'attendants provide tea, coffee, or cocoa for the women workers'.[249] Should mothers require anything further for their infants during the lunch hour at the factory such as 'camomile tea', (which was given to both infants and their older children), then mothers could ask a girl who was employed by the mill solely to run errands to fetch it.[250] As the nineteenth century wore on, further provisions to make the care of children easier were made, and facilities for washing, combing hair, and cleaning, which had been frowned on during the early part of the century, were allowed.[251] To improve the arrangements further, Dr Williamson even instructed that baths should be provided.[252] Large quantities of soap were purchased monthly by Marshall's mill.[253]

If the mothers found the factory floor rooms unsuitable then other spaces could be found. The *Leeds Intelligencer* and *Leeds Mercury* tell us of workers such as Margaret Kay and Nancy Mortimer, who worked at Morley and Joseph Wilson's mills, Rawfolds, Leeds respectively, retreating to the upper rooms of mills in order to take their meals.[254] Similar rooms where workers congregated to eat were also available to factory workers in Bolton.[255] Eating at regular meal times was the best foundation for ensuring that breast milk was made, as the infants needed a number of feeds whilst they were in the mills with their mothers. Indeed, breast feeding was a time-consuming practice, the usual pattern during this period being 6 or 7 times a day, (beginning at 7 a.m. with the last feed being given at 10 p.m.), and children were fed this way for up to two years.[256] Although May Tennant claimed that breast feeding was incompatible with factory work because the looms needed constant attention, by the 1860s power looms had started to become less demanding of the worker, and 'one weaver could manage four to six looms'.[257] Great breakthroughs came with 'winded parallel sided pirns' becoming available. This was a marked difference from earlier versions of the loom, which needed perpetual close attention. As a result it became easier for workers to give more care to infants.[258] The workers' key tasks were to replace the empty shuttle with 'weft and [they had to] repair the waft and weft breaks'.[259] The new looms only rarely suffered from broken yarn and, as Leon Faucher remarked on his visit to a mill, the young women who worked them 'had so little to do they occupied themselves with needlework for intervals of half an hour and an hour together, without rising from their seats'.[260] As long as the machines in Manchester seemed to be in good working order there seemed to be no need to incur the expense of training women on new machines which provided nothing new to the manufacturer.[261] The West Riding manufacturers were less concerned by these costs, so in Yorkshire the new machinery was purchased and the mothers mastered its techniques. Having done so they found time to breast feed whilst waiting for the shuttle to empty. Given this, Robert Baker and William Dodd resolved not to focus on this innovation when writing their accounts of the child care actions of mothers in the mills. Indeed we read the contemporary clinician Dr Dolan account of witnessing mothers feeding their infants at 'breakfast' and 'dinner times', we realise that he meant at the mill, and not at home.[262] This mirrors the research by Elizabeth Roberts, who argues factory mothers in Lancashire breast fed at the mill as their minders brought their babies to them.

The wait at the loom for the shuttle explains how Yorkshire mothers could find time to attend to their infants. As the historian Michael Huberman points out, work, rather than being constant 'mixed bouts of intense labor and idleness', which workers took advantage of. Factory mothers would use this 'slack' time effectively by attending to their infants.[263] Late deliveries also punctuated work,[264] and as infants needed ad hoc attention, this environment would suit the mothers, who were, perhaps, glad of the time it made available for their infants.[265] These breaks were an overhang from the earlier period in 1843 when work practices allowed both adults and children to come and go to the factory as they pleased when work was plentiful. As Anthony Austin, commissioned to observe the metal trades, remarked:

> The adults and children come and go as they please; there is not any necessity for finishing any quantity of work. What they have done is weighed and paid for at the usual hour of the day, and then they may leave. This is a common occurrence amongst all manufacturing concerns...[266]

It was possible for women in the West Riding textile factories to work this way because they were paid either by the 'warp', 'pick' or 'string', which were all equal to three yards three inches in length. Thus the worker and the overseer were able to see exactly how much work had been done, and should a mother need to take her infant out of the factory to go home or for a walk she would receive payment (typically 10d for 50 picks) for the number of picks woven.[267]

The mother attending to her looms and her infants in tandem was working to a similar rhythm undertaken to that of the pre-industrial era. Their waged work, as in metal-working factory, salt-mine, brickyard and field, was punctuated by the hunger of their infants, who demanded feeding every three hours. It was this which gave the factory mothers their time-discipline. These women were fully alive to the importance of the 'necessary and inevitable' attention required for infants as they combined waged work with child care, and aimed to produce little 'conflict between work and labour'.[268] This sense of time was, according to Norbert Elias, a 'gift'. Yet rather than mothers having an imperfect sense of time, 'The mother of young children has an imperfect sense [today as in the factory] of time and attends to other human tides. She has not yet altogether moved out of the conventions of "pre-industrial" society, [either today or in the nineteenth century factory].' This understanding of time and its framework for women's daily lives was a form of 'structure' and 'communication' for employers, and its importance was noted by those wishing to impose the concept of time in the mills.[269] The public face of breast feeding was a common aspect of female working-class culture, which Leonore Davidoff and Catherine Hall argue was frowned on by middle-class women, yet, despite being regarded as a display of vulgarity, breast feeding served waged working-class mothers well because it was a healthy response to the necessity of combining waged work with child care and the feeding of infants.[270]

Infants of factory mothers were also given 'fresh air' by being taken out of the factory. For example if a walk was needed after a feed, mothers could 'demand' time out of the factory 'from overseers' who knew they 'had to be at liberty' to take this time, which was usually 'half an hour'.[271] Thus, infants would be placed in a basket carriage or pram,[272] taken out of the factory doors and walked in the street. Richard Stanway's mills in Newcastle also provided a pram which the factory mothers could rent, which made 'carrying their babies to and from the mill much easier.'[273] The West Riding factory mothers, like mothers in Bethnal Green, were alert to the importance of taking infants out into the fresh air. Mrs Layton, born in 1855, when aged 8 used to push London babies around Victoria Park in a pram which was hired by several mothers but managed by the older children.[274] The carriages used by the West Riding mothers were often supplied by mill owners on the suggestion of Robert Baker, who knew the necessary apparatus needed to cater for mothers with infants and children, and pressed mill owners to provide 'cradles, chairs, cots, or for those bigger than cradle size ... a sofa'.[275]

The legal maternal aspects of mother care in the factories ran to textile mothers dictating their own working hours; they 'made demand[s] to that effect', without fear of retribution. Thus mill owners and overseers understood the problems faced by factory mothers and helped to accommodate them, often conceding lengthy periods of time out of the factory if they wished, thus enabling them to juggle work with 'attending to their household duties'.[276] Martha Ann Hirstwood seems to have had an excellent working arrangement when she worked at J. & W.H. Sykes in Huddersfield: she worked 'out of hours', justified by the knowledge that 'she could do the work anytime'.[277]

Overseers and manufacturers were aware of domestic life and its exigencies and had to allow mothers to start late if they so wished.[278] They stated plainly that they could not make mothers come in early if they wanted to, and factory mothers often did 'not show up at 6 [when supposed to] but [at] 8' because 'they cannot turn out before breakfast'.[279] Concern about mothers' night work was widely felt, but even though the Factory Acts legislated against female night shift patterns they continued. John Marshall, the owner of Marshall's flax mill in Leeds, remarked on the common practice of night shift working in Leeds and confirmed to select committees that he often asked his mill girls to 'Give me as many nights as you can'.[280] For new mother Sarah Dawson, the work as a flax weaver at Marshall's was a welcome wage as it contributed to the family's income along with that of her husband Edwin, and enabled them to keep their infant off the Leeds death register.[281] These violations were not exclusive to Leeds factories, as the Factory Inspector Mr Saunders conceded. Despite the restrictions laid down in the Factory Acts, it was still commonplace for women to work during the night.[282] It is no wonder that factory mothers considered themselves to be blameless when it came to the infant mortality rate, for they did all they could to enable them to continue breast feeding whilst working in the factory.[283]

The well-intentioned factory inspector Robert Baker misread the situation when he remarked that the working day was rigid. He was relying on adherence to the Factory Acts [which introduced a 10 hour maximum working day for factory mothers and a half day on Saturday] and their resolution that 'in all mills in which steam power [was] used to move the machinery, the hours ... within which work and meal-times are to be done, are fixed'.[284] The presumption that the use of 'steam power' rather than the ebb and flow of production governed the working day seriously underplayed and misrepresented the opportunities that factory mothers had to devote to their infants well-being. Whilst Baker sought to enforce the law, it was difficult to do so, and the absence of any systematic legal oversight suited the factory owners, who were reluctant to be bound by inspectors' rules and regulations and who, in Leeds in particular, voiced the 'most urgent objections about the act'.[285] These flexible working patterns were also evident in Lancashire. Power loom weavers John O'Neill, and his daughter Jane found the overseer very amenable when it came to time off or time out. John was given leave to spend time with his brother at very short notice from the overseer who was visiting,[286] and John's daughter Jane felt at ease to dictate her own working hours, delaying her trip to work and staying in bed because she was tired.[287]

However, even these pliable overseers were determined that certain tasks had to be done by the women in the mill and had to be combined with waged work and child care. Some women were 'employed for nothing else but to clean the floors of two of the rooms, [with] the others being done by the workpeople' and also for 'cleaning the looms when in motion'.[288] Yet, there was recognition that mill owners were aware of the needs of nursing mothers for it was understood that 'they like[d] a decent place in which to eat the food they bring in with them.' In addition they required good sanitary arrangements, for 'they like to be able to wash and tidy before walking home'.[289] This chimes with the comment made by Barbara Hutchins who notes the West Riding factory mothers were 'fiercely domesticated'.[290] These washroom facilities were not unique to Leeds: a 'woman's room' was set up at a mill in Essex in 1851, which provided 'hooks for their clothes, and a supply of water, towels and soap'.[291]

For mothers, cleanliness meant shielding infants from the dust by ensuring that they kept their 'territory' around their machines as clean as possible,[292] '[keeping] bright the portions of stone floor, over which they preside'.[293] In this respect we can see that when these northern working women stepped out of their private sphere into the public one, repeating some of the domestic duties they had performed whilst working at home, and contending with all of the pejorative connotations which went with the transfer, they retained their sense of self as mothers, despite working for their living and no longer residing solely in the domestic environment.[294] Given this we can see why factory mothers such as Rose Holdsworth, who worked at the Holly Park Mill in Leeds, felt able to record on the census that she worked in the 'domestic' rather than textile industry.

The extended efforts on behalf of factory mothers to keep their infants well fed and safe in the mill is clear. But as Millward and Bell testify, infants of factory mothers died at a higher rate than other mothers who worked, so why was this? As mothers breast fed in the mill then why were there not lower rates of infantile diarrhoea? In Yorkshire, this might have been a consequence of the insanitary conditions in the factory. Marshall's Mill, and Holdsworth and Barrett's Mill in Leeds both had outbreaks of cholera in 1854.[295] Insanitary conditions caused numerous deaths amongst the factory operatives but despite this, the greatest opposition to any sanitary improvements came from factory owners, and factories were extremely slow to adopt and pay for water closets, using instead privies that had to be cleaned out.[296] The mills were thus extremely dangerous places as the privy was used by all in the mill and faeces leaked onto the factory floor when it became full. Responsibility for cleaning up this waste was tasked to the women in the mill.[297] They had 'the option to clean it themselves or pay someone else to do it'. Either way, women in the factory came into contact with the waste matter which would get onto their hands. If they did not wash their hands thoroughly afterwards, faeces could give children bacterial diseases and lead to diarrhoea.[298] The Lady Commissioners found these conditions existed throughout the West riding mills and had done since the earlier part of the nineteenth century.[299] The same insanitary conditions were found at Messrs Palmer and Hault, Pin Manufacturers, at Lancaster in 1843. R.D. Grainger, the commissioner who was sent to observe the conditions in the factory, found that 'the privy was not fit for anyone to enter' and evidence about the conditions in the factory from Maria Field, a superintendent at the factory, confirmed this view, remarking that the workers at the factory were not able to use the privy 'as it is not in a fit state for a dog to go into'.[300] The same perilous conditions were found in the Dewsbury mills' closets, where Ann Ellis the female Trade Union Leader in Dewsbury, requested a need for their significant 'improvement'.

Although some houses had water closets by the mid-nineteenth century, the majority still disposed of their waste through the old fashioned method of 'bucket privies, dung carts, and cesspits'; in Leeds in 1860 these old methods outnumbered the new at a rate of three to one.[301] The sanitary conditions in the factories contributed to workers contracting bacterial infections which were passed on to their infants, contributing to the 32/1000 death rate from infantile diarrhoeal diseases calculated by Millward and Bell. If Emma Riley aged 19, who lived at Lady Lane, St John's Square and worked at a Leeds woollen factory, had to clean out the privy then her daughter, who died of diarrhoea in 1871 as recorded in the Leeds Brotherton death registers, was likely to have contracted the disease through her mother's hands rather than as a result of any reluctance to breast feed.[302] The *Huddersfield Chronicle* reported on the insanitary conditions at the convent at Carlisle Place Westminster leading to the deaths of many infants in 1877. A total of 1528 infants were admitted to the convent, 54 aged one month and under. Of the 54 month-old infants, 49 died, the other five being removed.[303] What these conditions tell us is that whilst this work may well show that mothers were not to blame for the high northern IMR, the foul and dirty floors in factories militated against the efforts of the pro-active, cautious and caring factory mothers.

Even with this hard-won work ethic, the idea that working-class women had 'rights' is not easy to comprehend. Historians have associated few human rights with nineteenth-century working-class women, even less their exercise of options within the work place. However, here we see them working on behalf of their families' interests earning wages and simultaneously ensuring their infants' safety. In this respect we can see why middle-class women were challenged by the independence of working-women; after all, few women have this right today. This is why the Leeds factory mothers such as Maria Hartley, aged 36, a wool weaver with children aged ten, seven, four, two and one month, was able to keep her children off the Leeds Death Register. As did Ruth Holdsworth, of Alma Place in Calverley, aged 27, working as a woollen warper in Leeds with three children aged five, three and one. Sarah Lister, aged 33, is a further example of this 'mothercare' of women working in the textile districts with children aged 11, seven, five and one; as is Maria Hartley whose children were aged ten, seven, four, two and one. Indeed, a random search on ancestry.com reveals another 16 factory mothers aged in their thirties and forties with infants alive in 1870 and 1871 all escaping the death register. As these women had at least two children each, some having eight, it is likely that if they undertook waged work they operated in similar conditions as did their colleagues, with baby-sitters on hand to provide extra care in the mill.[304] The independence this gave factory mothers meant that they were able to continue working and functioning as caring parents alongside their families as they grew older. This limited but strongly linked evidence gives us reason to see that infants of factory mothers were cared for and survived the high northern IMR, and that their child care methods allowed mothers to continue working as the need dictated.

Working at the mill was a way to stave off poverty for women with infants. When their husbands lost their jobs, gave their money to pub landlords, or deserted them the mill was a way in which they could support themselves. There was little leisure for these mothers to trade and, during a period of wage rises – as Emma Griffin and Jan de Vries argue – their work was merely a part of a growing 'industriousness'.[305] After all, mothers were acutely aware of how much money the family needed to survive. They 'went to the mill', taking their infants with them, to ensure money was earned when their husbands could not provide enough.[306]

Conclusion

This discussion of how working-class mothers who worked in industry combined their work with child care has shown that they adopted innovative and unorthodox maternal practices, and took their infants to work with them to keep them close, breast feed them, and in doing so guarded against the dangers of artificial foods and prevent levels of infant mortality spiralling upwards. The demands of industry did not negate their maternal feeling and through exercising their 'rights' as mothers with infants they were allowed to adapt their working environment to fit their maternal needs. In doing so they continued to combine waged work with child care as they did in the proto-industrial home.

Having noted the extent to which working-class women sought to protect their infants' well-being when working, the next chapter will address the extent to which northern workhouse nurses were likely to neglect the infants placed in their care. The rates of infant mortality in the workhouse were said to be equally high.

3
Workhouse Nurses

We saw in the previous chapter how mothers cared for their infants whilst working in factories and mills. The problem of combining work with child care is a continuing theme: this chapter will investigate how nineteenth-century workhouse nurses tended vulnerable pauper infants, in *loco parentis* whilst the babies were under the jurisdiction of the workhouse. It will begin by raising what is seen as the key problem for pauper infants, go on to investigate the welfare philosophy for them, and conclude by examining nurses' duties and daily routine.

The problem nurse

According to Frank Crompton, Pat Thane and Angela Negrine, infants were forced into the workhouse for several reasons. Destitution was a prime cause: infants accompanied parents who entered as a consequence of 'family poverty.'[1] It was, however, possible for infants to enter alone, without kin: for some mothers a newborn infant could be the straw that broke the economic back of the household. This was a method, Frank Crompton argues, used by mothers to keep the rest of the family out of the workhouse and allay economic ruin.[2] The largest category of workhouse infants, however, was the 'orphaned, bastards, or deserted' – consequences of a mother's widowhood, divorce or desertion by her husband.[3]

Although the workhouse was not originally intended to care for infants, Guardians usually had no option but to accept them. Once inside, infants were classified as amongst the 'vulnerable' who the guardians recognised could not care for themselves, and were placed into the care of the workhouse nurse.

The nineteenth-century social commentators and social reformers Louisa Twining and Florence Nightingale, claimed that workhouse nurses contributed to the high IMR because of a lack of care they gave to infants. In effect, they argued, workhouse nurses were 'too old, too weak, and too drunken' to care for pauper infants properly.[4] Sidney and Beatrice Webb repeated these words and accepted these sentiments when examining work-house infant care during the twentieth century. They claimed that work-house nurses were responsible for the deaths of some of the thousands of infants who contributed annually to the death rate recorded in workhouses outside London.[5] For the Webbs, the 'ignorant and often careless' workhouse nurse, combined with the severity of the indoor relief regime, meant that infants who inhabited the nurseries and lying-in wards experienced a death rate 'twice or thrice that of the nation as a whole'.[6] This sentiment influences the more recent writings of Jonathan Reinarz and Leonard Schwarz who, despite presenting new work which aims to 'break down some general statistics in regional and key diagnostic groups', acknowledge that the mortality of infants in workhouses was high.[7] These figures were a blot on the landscape for social reformers. As Ruth Richardson notes, their view was that workhouse nurses and the 'care' that they provided to the vulnerable infant paupers, was 'dismal'.[8]

Like the factory mother, therefore, the workhouse nurse was one of the 'usual suspects' when social commentators sought out the causes of the high northern IMR during the late nineteenth century. The prevailing view was clearly stated by Florence Nightingale when she remarked that work-house nurses were 'absolutely in charge' of infants 'perhaps for the first and last time of their lives'. She also asserted that it was essential to determine whether the nurses who were responsible for the infants' 'care and comfort' by 'day and night' were violent, old, lazy, drunken, inexperienced women whose negligence harmed infants.[9]

The practice of drawing pauper nurses from the female inmate population and putting them to work in order to pay for their keep was common in the nineteenth-century.[10] Responsible for the day-to-day care of the infant, and also for the cleaning of the infants' ward, pauper nurses performed key roles within the workhouse during the latter half of the century.[11] As the comments of the Webbs and Ruth Richardson indicate, the suspicion prevailed amongst traditional historians and contemporaries that, in part as a consequence of their desperation at being in the workhouse in the first place, these women neglected the infants in their care. Consequently they bore a large part of the responsibility for the 50-plus per cent annual death rate of infants in parochial and northern workhouses during the latter half of the nineteenth century.[12]

These accusations were based on two premises: the physical demeanour of these nurses, and the degree and length of time for which they were responsible for the day-to-day care of infants.[13] As Abel-Smith points out, pauper nurses were often selected on the basis of their availability to under-take nursing duties. This, according to historian Anne Digby, resulted in the employment of women who were 'marginally less infirm than the patient, and were untrained in nursing procedures'.[14] For example, a 'professional' or paid nurse who worked in the Rotherhithe workhouse during the 1860s, reported that pauper nurses were violent towards the paupers and were liable to 'steal their food'.[15] Historians have taken reports like this as clear indicators of the quality of care that infants received, for, as contemporary observers noted, 'as the matron was rarely seen among the wards, it was the pauper nurse who controlled the workhouse ward'.[16]

Pauper nurses had an extensive and wide-ranging presence in the workhouse, and despite the vital role they performed – particularly for infants – they feature little in the historiography of nursing. This could be a consequence of workhouses not being initially intended for infants, meaning that little material was collected as to the nature and conduct or practice of the workhouse nurses who cared for them.[17] In the absence of any comprehensive historical narratives therefore, the pauper nurse has been unable to counter much of the historical understanding of their nature and role; they have been reduced to little more than a caricature. The indolent and inebriated Dickensian figure of Mrs Gamp, for instance, has passed from the pages of fiction to inform our understanding of the workhouse nurse as rough, cruel and tyrannical, as depicted by Abel-Smith and Crompton.[18]

Jonas Hanway, the eighteenth-century philanthropist and foundling hospital benefactor is a source of much of the popular reputation of pauper nurses, maligning much of the infant care in workhouses during the Old Poor Law. He remarked that pauper nurses contributed towards 'the misery and neglect amidst which the children of the parish grew up', and 'the mortality which prevailed amongst them, [which was] positively frightful'.[19] Hanway's criticisms were meant to emphasise the disreputable nature and decrepitude of the pauper nurse. Florence Nightingale and Louisa Twining reported the same circumstances in the workhouse in the nineteenth century.

For Nightingale, the 'true test of a nurse was whether or not she could care for an infant', and on their visits to workhouses to provide religious instruction, both Twining and Nightingale found much to criticise.[20] They reported that, although nominally responsible for 'the personal cleanliness of each [infant] under [their] charge, the care and cleanliness of the [their] room', and ensuring that the 'furniture and utensils of each [were] clean,'[21] pauper nurses were not up to the task of caring for infants, as they had little experience and exposed infants to significant risk.[22]

Determined to right the supposed wrongs of the pauper nurse in the workhouse, Louisa Twining formed the Workhouse Visiting Society (WVS), and encouraged many middle-class female philanthropists, such as Mrs Shepherd, and Frances Power Cobbe, to visit workhouses in both the northern and southern regions on her behalf. They published their findings in the organisation's journal, the *Workhouse Visiting Society*. On her visits to workhouses, Frances Power Cobbe noted the same abuses as Twining, remarking that the able-bodied women who undertook nursing and infant duties in the workhouse were the most 'wretched' specimens.[23]

It is not to be doubted that Twining and her supporters had the best interests of infants at heart and acted in good faith, with genuine concern for the welfare of infants:

> Nothing can be more important, in any endeavour to discover or ameliorate the condition of workhouses, than to be furnished with the means of drawing comparisons between the state of mortality, and sickness in different institutions, for such materials (combined with other information) would give an excellent test of the care bestowed on the inmates, *especially infants*.[24]

This rhetoric influenced the historiography of workhouse nursery care, and its influence can be detected the works of Abel-Smith, Crompton and Lionel Rose, who have tended to take these remarks at face value and gone on to generalise about a whole cohort of pauper nurses. If these depictions of negligent workhouse nursing practices are valid, then they would indeed go a long way to explain why levels of infant mortality within workhouses were so high. This raises the question as to how accurate these depictions are.[25]

Although the criticisms made by Twining and Nightingale of the inadequate care and attention given to infants are clear and backed by impressive authority, achieving a genuine understanding of the workhouse nurse and the care she gave is fraught with difficulty because the infant inmate experience seldom features in the available sources or scholarship on welfare.[26] The testimony of John Rowlands, for instance, is a rare example of a first-hand account of the harsh life he experienced as an infant in the workhouse.[27] As historians Alysa Levene and Gertrude Himmelfarb remark, the 'infant inmate experience of mortality largely remains invisible'.[28]

Despite their inability to observe the real practice of workhouse care, contemporary social commentators – and subsequent historians drawing on their testimony – argue that there is a clear link between the high IMR in the north and the use of pauper nurses. Mortality rose when increasing numbers of infants entered the workhouse during the latter part of the nineteenth century. As historians Kim Price and Tanya Evans point out, compassion for illegitimate infants waned towards the end of the eighteenth century, with the result that these 'unfortunate objects' increasingly found themselves placed into workhouses, as opposed to charitable institutions like foundling hospitals.[29]

Welfare and middle class philosophy

This change in sentiment, of which Malthus was a leading architect, was supported by both the clergy and the middling sorts. Claiming the moral high ground, these observers sought to restrict any entry into charitable institutions, and – as critics of relief policy –to restrict outdoor payments, to single mothers, aiming to discourage illegitimacy, indolence and vice. Henceforth, poor women and their children had to receive their welfare in the workhouse.[30] The economic and practical help which had been the hallmark of the philanthropic spirit towards the infant poor consequently declined during the period.[31] Mr Hillis, owner of the foundling hospital in Leeds, is evidence of this decline. During the latter half of the nineteenth century he decided that he no longer wished to give this support to infants and closed his hospital.[32] Hillis's action supports William Burke Ryan's view that these charitable institutions were being written off in the harsh sentimental climate.[33]

Although some orphanages continued to operate during this period, their decline in number led to the parish becoming the prime provider of infant welfare.[34] As historian M.A. Crowther notes, during the New Poor Law this sentiment took hold and grew, with deserted and orphaned infants now classified as part of the 'undeserving poor'.[35] As Lionel Rose has argued, the workhouse became the main residence for illegitimate infants in particular[36] because charitable lying-in institutions did not welcome unmarried women, leading to their ever-greater dependence on the Poor Law.[37] Indeed, even if unmarried women had money to pay for lying-in institutions, and for their infants' subsequent care, their morally compromised status could prevent them getting help.

Levene has argued that the rise in illegitimate infants under the sole responsibility of their mothers heightened this dependence on the workhouse, due to the nature of the problems that these infants posed.[38] These arguments are supported by Frank Crompton's valuable study of the Worcester workhouse, which indicates that there was a move to confine orphaned and deserted infants in workhouses, an impulse which was evident not only across the industrial north but country-wide during the middle and later part of the nineteenth century.[39] The workhouse filled the vacuum left by the deserting philanthropists.

In these circumstances, according to contemporaries and historians alike, infants were left at the mercy of a system whose ideology was 'less eligibility'; a prospect which did not augur well for the standard of nursing and conditions that infants could expect to receive. Indeed as the workhouse operated a policy of forced separation, particularly in respect of unmarried mothers, contact between mothers and infants was scarce and heavily policed, with the result that most infants 'remained in the care of the pauper nurse'.[40]

This forced separation meant that infants had to be artificially fed. It is unrealistic to say that the workhouse never allowed mothers to breast feed their infants, but it is reasonable to argue that this contact, if allowed, was rarely prolonged, as official intent was to deter unmarried women from having children.[41] The advent of the New Poor Law was responsible for the workhouse 'care' of an increasing number of infants, thus rendering the workhouse nurse extremely important for infants.[42] On visits to 48 provincial workhouses during the 1860s, including unions in the northern districts of Leeds, Manchester, Derby, Nottingham, Newcastle, Sheffield and Stockport, to identify their dietary provision to the inmates, Dr Edward Smith noted that the majority of workhouses did indeed provide the diet for infants.[43]

To what extent were the nurses culpable for the worryingly high IMR throughout the northern industrial regions? Twining received much support in her defamation of the nurse. Contemporary newspapers catalogued apparent abuses: for instance, the *Yorkshire Gazette* condemned the actions of the Tadcaster pauper nurse Catherine Levers in 1865. In addition to her abuse of the elderly Elizabeth Daley, the cruel Levers directed her anger against her younger children.[44] She flogged George Standeven and kicked and beat other youngsters in the Tadcaster workhouse with a brush.[45] Levers had a cruel streak, which went beyond the abuse of infants, and was fond of telling the older children to stick their tongues out before smashing their jaws together, causing them to bite and lacerate their tongues.[46] William Crossley testified that a young boy and girl, named Townend, were both beaten 'black and blue' by her, and that when stripped of clothes, the boy 'was black from his shoulders down to his hip.'[47] This abuse was not confined to Tadcaster: Ella Gilespie, a workhouse pauper nurse in Bolton, was similarly charged with the assault of children.[48] Protection from this sort of 'care' was difficult for the vulnerably orphaned and deserted as they had few family members to turn to in the workhouse. Moreover, even when infants were in the workhouse with their mothers, the *BMJ* concluded that isolation was commonplace, especially in northern provincial workhouses, as infants were only allowed to spend time together with their mothers on 'visiting days'.[49]

This neglect and abuse was noted by Frederick Engels during his investigations of Manchester workhouses during the 1840s. Engels was critical of the workhouse system per-se, but he particularly disliked the harsh treatment meted out to infants, when they were 'locked up in a "dog-hole" for three days and nights'.[50] For Twining this behaviour was attributable to the culture of drunkenness that existed amongst workhouse nurses. It was the case that both pauper nurses and some *paid* nurses were apt to indulge in 'drink'. Indeed, Poor Law records during the 1860s and 1870s indicate that drunkenness was widespread amongst paid nurses.[51] For example, Sarah Allsop, employed as a nurse by the Manchester Union with a salary of £16 per annum, was discharged in October 1871 for inebriation; Elizabeth Hepworth, appointed in February 1872, was forced to resign due to neglect of duty whilst drunk;[52] Georgina Partington, taken on by the Leeds Union on February 1878, was likewise discharged in November 1879 for intoxication; and Susannah Witham, also employed at Leeds in December 1879, was discharged in March 1880 for insubordination.[53] Alcohol was not an uncommon feature of workhouse life.

Nurses' drinking was in keeping with customs in the workhouse, for, as both *The Lancet* and the *BMJ* remarked at the time, although there were dangers involved in nurses consuming alcohol, it was sometimes easier (although dangerous) for a nurse to have had a drink of alcohol prior to carrying out some of their medical duties, as it helped them cope with the great number of disagreeable and repulsive medical cases.[54] As contemporary commentator Joseph Rogers remarked, during this period 'the responsible duties they had to perform were remunerated by an amended dietary and a pint of beer', whilst for laying out the dead, and other especially repulsive duties, they had a glass of gin.[55] The Guardians often provided pauper workhouse nurses with a small allowance of beer daily as part of their wage, as a recognition of the many difficult tasks they had to perform.[56] Beer or stout drinking was the custom of working-class women when pregnant, and as it was thought to help make breast milk. So, when workhouses nurses were pregnant they had a two-fold justification for drinking.[57]

The suggestion by Twining and others that drink was emblematic of a nurse's negligence displayed a degree of ignorance of the role of alcohol in the workhouse, the actual functions that nurses performed, and the circumstances under which they were obliged to work. Poor Law Unions were not reluctant to dismiss those who neglected their duty when drink had been taken to excess. So, although the consumption of alcohol had the potential to impact on infant care in workhouses, it is doubtful whether it made a significant contribution to the driving up of the northern IMR.

The degree of responsibility borne by workhouse nurses for the high IMR throughout the northern industrial regions is, therefore, not as clear-cut, or indeed as great, as Louisa Twining and historians have since argued. One possible cause of error was a failure by the WVS to visit workhouses on a regular basis. Minutes of Poor Law records suggest that the WVS was not as ubiquitous as Twining would have liked: some unions reported that 'if [the WVS] does visit, there are no records kept',[58] and that often 'the visiting society did not visit at all'.[59] The *Lancet,* although remarking on much of the valuable work which the WVS performed in the field of workhouse improvements,[60] also noted that Twining's ladies did not visit as often as they should, because 'workhouse visiting is not popular among ladies'.[61] Edward Smith also concluded from his visits to 34 northern workhouses that the Visiting Committee 'infrequently' inspected workhouses and as a consequence many 'defects' went unreported.[62]

Although the work which Twining and her society set out to undertake was laudable, it seems that the lack of visits from both her and the WVS made them unqualified to pass any informed judgement on the quality of care delivered by the nurses in the workhouse. Of course, Guardians who disliked the WVS visiting may have placed obstacles in the society's way. Nonetheless, it seems that the conclusions the WVS drew and promulgated were based on a combination of preconceptions and mere snapshots derived from occasional visits. Moreover, in light of the primary purpose of the WVS being to provide religious instruction to the workhouse pauper population, the extent to which Twining and her supporters actually set out to document practices of infant 'care' on a long-term basis is questionable.

Nursing skill and dedication

The conduct of workhouse nurses came under increased scrutiny during the latter half of the nineteenth century. The *BMJ* and *The Lancet*, for example, carried out investigations across Yorkshire and Lancashire into the supposed link between negligent workhouse nursing and the high northern IMR.[63] Contrary to the damning verdict of Louisa Twining and the WVS, the medical journals noted that, in general 'parish or union nurses could demonstrate the best side of parish nursing',[64] that 'most of [the nurses] have been in office for long terms of years', and that 'they seem on the whole well-conducted, zealous, and well managed... and anxious to deserve good opinion.'[65] For example, at St Luke's, Halifax, the head pauper nurse was 'a widow of superior address', her nurses were 'well conducted and their assistants considered 'good natured'.[66] The conduct of the nurses in respect of the lying-in wards and infant nurseries was particularly praised by *The Lancet*, which stated that although the rooms were 'often low and small and ill-lighted', workhouse nurses nevertheless ensured that:

> they had an aspect of cheerfulness and comfort, as they coloured the walls cheerfully. There were prints hanging on the walls, and a few ornaments about the fire-places. The linen was very clean, and here two clean sheets are allowed per week, every ward had a supply of bed rests for patients, this was important for the infants who would often have bed sores... The patients were cheerful... and kept as to their faces and hair, and their personal linen. And there is an abundance of playthings for the children.[67]

As a result of their investigation, the *Lancet* concluded that pauper nurses could be both 'very intelligent' and 'active'.[68] These verdicts mirror the experiences of the Poor Law Unions themselves: Dr Robert Patrick of the Bolton Union workhouse noted the excellence of children's nurse, Rose, and her predecessor Mary-Jane Allen,[69] and the Bradford Poor Law Guardians praised the dedication and conduct of their nursing staff;[70] even Miss Pringle, a philanthropist and close companion of Florence Nightingale, remarked that 'some of the nurses [in Liverpool] were of the best type of women, clever dutiful, cheerful and caring, [and] endowed above all with the motherliness of nature which is the most precious attribute of a nurse'.[71] Edward Smith reiterated this approval and stated in clear terms that he 'had met with pauper nurses who have been employed for many years, and have gained the confidence of the medical officer and the sick'.[72] Smith felt the need to go further on this issue when reporting on the character of pauper nurses in the northern districts:

> It is all hastily assumed that all the female inmates of a workhouse are either too old or too ill-conducted to make trustworthy nurses; but omitting reference to the fact that not a few had previous experience in nursing before their admission, it is needful to state that there are many respectable persons who have been deserted by their husbands and having been left with a number of children, had no alternative but to enter the workhouse. Such remain in the workhouse for many years, and acquire an aptitude for nursing quite equal to that of paid nurses in general. Here is material from which efficient nurses might be made.'[73]

This testimony does not, of course, absolve all workhouse nurses from complicity in the unsatisfactory northern IMR, but it does challenge characterisations which have been informed by notorious yet isolated cases of abuse and neglect like Catherine Levers at Tadcaster. Indeed, if weight is given to the testimony of *The Lancet* and the Poor Law Unions, then it may be suggested that the quality of care delivered by these women may have limited, rather than contributed to the northern IMR. If this was the case, how can their competency be accounted for?

To a large extent, this would be dependent on the kind of women in workhouses who were selected to act as pauper nurses. As we have previously seen, historians like Brian Abel-Smith, Anne Digby and, more recently, Ruth Richardson have been dismissive of the physical attributes of those selected to undertake nursing duties.[74] The number of infants within the nineteenth-century workhouse might have posed difficulties for aged and infirm workhouse nurses; a point which was recognised by Poor Law Guardians, who preferred nursing duties to be carried out by younger women when possible.[75] Notwithstanding this expressed preference, however, Abel-Smith argues that it was rarely borne out in practice, as younger women 'were not always plentiful' in the workhouse, which meant Guardians were obliged to recruit many of their nurses from the older female workhouse population.[76]

The extent to which the 'aged sot' was representative of the pauper nurse is, however, debatable, as new research suggests that Brian Abel-Smith is wrong about the ages of pauper nurses, and that infant nursing, in particular, was performed by much younger women. Whilst walking the many wards in the northern workhouses Edward Smith found the pauper nurses:

> Are not necessarily old or of bad character, but are often young or in middle life, with health and energy which they cannot take to any other market, since they cannot leave the workhouse and take their children

with them. Hence they are as effectually restricted to the workhouse as if it were a prison, and as in most cases their children are well treated and well educated whilst in the workhouse, they become resigned and are ready to give their aid in performing the work assigned to them.[77]

By analysing census material which shows workhouse female populations across the latter half of the nineteenth century in the areas of the south midlands, the south-eastern counties, the north west and Yorkshire, it is possible to confirm Edward Smith's view by taking a broad survey of those who were in the workhouse, and therefore on hand to nurse infant inmates during the years of high IMR.

Although census data are useful in determining workhouse population cohorts and occupational backgrounds of inmates, it is clear that these data have their limitations. Providing a mere snapshot of the workhouse population, the census cannot be used to determine length of residency for inmates. Poor Law minutes for Leeds however, appear to indicate that young women represented a significant cohort of the workhouse population and that throughout the period 1875–6 their residency seems to have been protracted, indicating that there were enough young women to form a nursing 'pool'.

The census data in Figure 3.1 reveal that women of childbearing age (defined as 15–44) never represented less than 10 per cent of the female workhouse population across regions and years, and often exceeded this

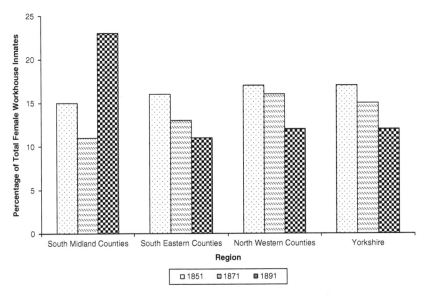

Figure 3.1   Regional female workhouse inmates aged 15–44

markedly during the period of heightened concern over the Northern IMR, a fact that has largely been neglected in accounts of workhouse nursing.[78] Younger women like Emma Wilson, aged 19, and Lily Smith, aged 20, were resident in the Leeds workhouse in 1875, and available to nurse for the Poor Law Guardians; this is a new lens through which we can view both the infant institutional experience and institutional infant mortality.[79] As the *Leeds Mercury* reported on 24 June 1865, Guardians considered the preferred age for workhouse nurses to range 'between the ages of twenty five to forty'; looking at Figure 3.1, it is clear that there was no shortage of these younger candidates, not only in Yorkshire, but across most northern regions. Presented with this younger cohort, given the Guardians' preference, it was they who made up the core of nursing provision in workhouses.

The large proportion of younger women in the workhouse confirms the reorientation of sentiment in relation to relief policy noted previously. As Steven King and Pat Thane have argued, the New Poor Law increasingly stigmatised and marginalised both the single and married female poor, forcing them to seek refuge in the workhouse in ever greater numbers in the latter half of the nineteenth century.[80] The jury is still out on the extent to which indoor relief eclipsed outdoor relief, due mainly to the cost of indoor care, but young women like 'Molly' (no surname), aged 20, and Phoebe Smith, 22, were resident in the Bradford workhouse along with their children, and were put to work nursing infant inmates.[81] The significance of using these women was that they were both mothers, experienced in caring for infants. These skills were very valuable in a workhouse where as many as six infants a week were being born.[82]

This is not to say that all the younger women in the workhouse had the same level of skill in infant care. Even if they did, many contemporary social commentators dismissed their capabilities, stating that they were unable to perform the simplest of tasks such as 'nursing baby', or 'cooking, scrubbing, cleaning house and mending clothes'.[83] One anonymous commentator remarked that female inmates not only could not look after babies, they even had difficulty taking care of themselves – 'their clothes are given them to put on, their food is prepared and placed before them to eat ... [they have] no contact with the daily objects of everyday life.'[84] This was not the picture painted in *The Lancet's* surveys of northern workhouses during the latter half of the nineteenth century. These women often had domestic service experience, rendering them excellent nurses.

As Figure 3.2 indicates, there were few named nurses in the workhouse – they were almost entirely absent in the sample of northern workhouses in 1861 and 1881: in 1881 Liverpool named its sole nurse, and only one there. This echoes Marjorie Levine Clark's work on the Rye workhouse.[85] What they did have, however, as shown in Figure 3.2, was a number of experienced domestic servants, possessing an array of skills, and it is this which was key to the effectiveness of workhouse nurses in suppressing the IMR.

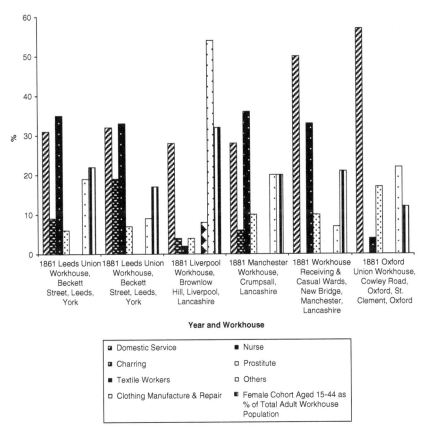

Figure 3.2 Occupational proportionate breakdown of female workhouse inmate cohort 15–44

'Domestic service' was an umbrella term for an array of female employments, including general servant, second girl, cook, laundress, chambermaid, waitress, housekeeper and *nurse*.[86] It was a skill set which nineteenth-century commentators like Lucy Maynard-Salmon knew was associated with domestic service both in England and America.[87] A common expectation of private employers of domestic servants was that they would 'care for baby' and 'nurse the infants'. They had vital training and experience which was put to use in the workhouse.[88] Mrs Warren's domestic servants were routinely engaged in bathing, dressing and walking her son, John and daughter Edith,[89] and this was no anomaly. William Cobbett remarked in 1802 that servants were only necessary when *children came along* because until then wives could do the work.[90] Once children came along, the use of servants to care for them was widespread.[91] Historians Joanne Bailey and Amanda

Vickery both support this view of servants caring for children, and argue that although knowledge of the exact split in 'parental' responsibility eludes us, with domestics often 'indistinct figures fading into the background', their role, was intrinsic to the rearing of employers' children.[92] Work by Caroline Steedman has likewise shown that a servant's workload undoubtedly increased during the eighteenth century due to an expanding range of child care duties.[93] For every Betty Ramsden, the dutiful mistress of the house who gave up 'visiting [her friends] entirely', and for whom motherhood devoured 'almost all reserves of physical and emotional energy', there was a multitude of domestics like 19-year-old Elizabeth Rothwell of Salford who found herself compelled to look after her mistress' new-born child, in addition to her ten other children.[94] This practice endured well into the nineteenth century: we see Mary Ann Green, a domestic servant in Huddersfield in 1887, being left in charge of her employer's infant 'all day long'.[95] Mary got little respite from her child care duties, as her employer's neighbours, Mrs Abel and Mrs Jane Thornton, remarked that the child 'repeatedly' slept with Mary and she was the sole carer during the weekend, from 'Friday night to Monday morning'.[96]

George Reynolds, the author of *Mary Price: or the Memoirs of a Servant Maid*, records the extent of the care which domestic servants were expected to provide to infants and children during this period.[97] If domestics without these skills were taken on then, argued Mrs Baines, Governor of the British Lying-In Institution during the latter half of the nineteenth century, because of the fragility of infant life, it was the *duty* of the mistress of the house to instruct the servants as to their 'expected' infant nursing duties.[98] In a similar vein, Lucy Maynard-Salmon pointed out that it was vital that domestic servants 'must understand washing, dressing, and feeding', in addition to the 'general care and health and the well-being of children'.[99] One consequence of this was that 'many housekeepers [were] obliged to conduct in their own households a training-school on a limited scale' for their servants.[100] Written instructions on what was considered proper child care were compulsory reading in the middle-class household during the latter half of the nineteenth century, and were highly influential in determining the range and standard of nursing skills that were inculcated into domestic servants.[101] Through her 'general reading' of influential medical texts like those of Drs Conquest and Allbutt, and Dr. Thomas Bull's *Hints to Mothers*, written in 1838, but still used at the end of the nineteenth century, Baines sent direct instructions to middle-class homes on infant care.[102]

Although mistresses like Mrs Dalton remarked that directing her domestic servants in infant care was taking more time than she wished, she also acknowledged that this role was important, and so 'great pains [were] to be taken in instructing them.[103] Of most importance was that the servants 'change[d] the infant three times daily', and if baby cried, 'the first thing' that should be done was to 'check them for dirt'.[104] This was crucial in keeping them 'dry and comfortable', as the cotton or linen nappies of the period were not very good at absorbing excretions.[105] Even the introduction of towelling nappies during the nineteenth century, which were more effective at keeping babies drier than the earlier nappies, did not entirely keep children dry as 'a thick piece of flannel called a pilch or saver' had to be inserted as a liner for the nappy during the night in order to ensure it did not leak.[106]

Even routine tasks like pinning new nappies required patience and skill, domestics had to use between eight to twelve ordinary dressmaker's pins in one nappy, hence proper care and attention had to be taken to ensure domestic did not prick the baby they were caring for.[107] The high level of competence domestics brought to these tasks led women like the Manchester born Mrs Stewart, a friend of the feminist Josephine Butler, to remark on the enormous debt which middle-class women owed to these working-class women, who, through often thankless, dedicated hard work and excellence 'made and washed [their] clothes, cooked [their] food and nursed [their] children'.[108] Mr Twisden, the husband of Mrs Twisden who employed the domestic servant Mary Price, was equally complimentary about the child care Mary gave to their three children, which included a young baby.[109] Competence in child care was a long-established prerequisite for obtaining a position of domestic servant, as shown in eighteenth-century instruction manuals.[110]

The knowledge and skills commanded by domestic servants were rated at a premium inside the workhouse. When Maria Brookes left her position in a Bradford middle-class household on account of her master's 'rudeness' and placed herself at the mercy of the workhouse, she was immediately put to nurse in the workhouse, the Guardians 'seeing nothing wrong in their action' because Maria had been working for her employers as a nurse for at least two years.[111]

The education and training which domestics received before going into the workhouse was, of course, useful, but guardians thought it important to advance their child care knowledge further once inside the workhouse by providing instruction in the workhouse itself. In Manchester, due to the Guardians being 'most assiduous in the care of children',[112] a training school for female pauper nurses was established in 1879, instructing pauper nurses (such as Annie Roberts) over a year-long course in the art of correct and effective infant nursing.[113] Although the Webbs argued that northern guardians did not identify with the needs of infants until 1894, the evidence from Manchester clearly suggests otherwise.[114] It also indicates that the female nursing cohort had a degree of professionalism which was put to use countering the northern IMR.

Despite the abundance of experienced young infant nurses within the workhouse, contemporaries and historians seem to have little confidence in these women. Rather, they note the absence of paid infant nurses in workhouses.[115] It was true that Guardians were reluctant to pay for infant care. Alice Broomer and Emma Cullum, for example, were almost unique in their status as paid 'infant nurses' when they were employed by the Manchester Guardians during the 1870s.[116] Indeed, when Alice Greenhatch resigned from the Manchester lying-in ward after a year's work there in 1871, the Guardians stated that they did 'not at present propose to fill up the vacancy'.[117] Lamenting the low number of paid infant nurses Frances Power Cobbe and Joseph Rogers thought that refusing to re-advertise the nursing post put infants in the workhouse at risk.[118] Yet, it seems that nursing per-se was routinely condemned by these reformers: not only did they criticise the low number of professional nurses, but, even when paid nurses were employed they argued the women were of poor quality.

So, like their counterparts, the pauper nurses, salaried infant carers in the workhouse were deemed as unfit for purpose – reformers maintaining that this was because of inadequate vetting procedures. In this respect, at least, critics like Joseph Rogers had a point, as candidates for jobs as paid workhouse nurses were seldom grilled during the interview. They were simply asked about their 'religious views and so forth and whether they had been accustomed to nursing a certain number of patients.'[119] As an unnamed nineteenth-century doctor noted during discussions of work-house nurse reform, Guardians were apt to 'take them without evidence of character'.[120]

In light of the guardians' knowledge of the skills that domestic servants commanded, this narrow interview technique should be placed in context. Of course, some women tried to get a job with false references, as in Leeds in 1876. The Guardians, under pressure from reformers like Rogers, appointed Annie McDougall as a paid workhouse nurse. She had no experience of domestic service, and was thus unable to show competency of infant care; so, she supplied the name of a Dr Thomas, who worked at the Royal Infirmary in Glasgow, as a character witness. On checking her reference, the Leeds Union Board found, however, that the infirmary could not confirm that Annie had worked there, and Dr Thomas had 'no recollection of her and that it must be some years since she was so employed at that Infirmary'.[121] Without proof of identity or character, and despite being unable to show any competency with regard to infant care, Annie was nevertheless taken on and provided with a contract worth £25 per annum.[122] This arguably reckless approach was probably due to the pressure of middle-class reform-ers like Rogers and Frances Power Cobbe, who would lobby rate-payers and government administrators if they did not get their way. This may be why incompetent salaried nurses were kept on, despite being incapable of caring for infants, and why, as Brian-Abel Smith noted, a woman who 'had been six-teen times in the House of Correction...was a woman given to drink,...of a violent, ungovernable temper, and [who] caused great misery to [those] under her control', was able to get a job in a workhouse.[123]

Despite their shortcomings, these lax vetting and recruitment procedures were on the whole not significant for the care of infants in the workhouse and its associated impact on the northern IMR. For, as we have seen, paid nurses were few, perhaps as a consequence of their 'character', and the workhouses already held a sizeable population of young women who were capable of providing effective care to infants. Indeed, the fact that the Guardians were acutely aware of the pool of cheap nursing talent available and on tap within the workhouse explains why they were so reluctant to spend rate-payers' money on salaried nurses, as they regarded them an unnecessary and incompetent expense.[124] Edward Smith acknowledged the skill of the resident northern pauper nurse who worked in both the children's and lying-in wards and 'who had acquire[d] an aptitude for nursing quite equal to that of paid nurses in general'.[125] He mused further that

> nothing would be easier than to convert such persons into paid nurses, and if they are fit to discharge the duties of nurse they should, I think, be removed from the rank of pauper, and installed as paid officers … This has been done in numerous instances and when the position rations and apartments of officers are assigned to them they increase in self-respect and efficiency and the sick inmates soon respect them'.[126]

Workhouse failings

If reformers like Nightingale, Twining and Rogers were wrong about the child care abilities of workhouse nurses, to what extent were they right about their personal qualities? The criticisms made of nurses cited their supposed laziness, their lack of rigour when undertaking their duties, and their lack of attention to hygiene and cleanliness. A lack of hygiene was a contributory factor to premature infant mortality in workhouses, as Lara Mark's study of workhouses throughout Britain has shown.[127] Despite the stigma attached to the lying-in ward of the workhouse, Lara Marks argues that most poor women depended on its services when confined, and infant mortality rates were due to the vulnerability of infants to the dirt and disease which often characterised these places.[128] To what extent is Marks correct in saying that lying-in wards were one of the key components of infant death? What blame can be attached to the pauper nurses responsible for these wards?[129]

Alfred Sheen, Senior Surgeon and Poor Law Medical Officer, who practised in England, Scotland and Wales throughout the nineteenth century, took great interest in labour wards and the possible impact they had on infant mortality. Sheen noted that as the infants' first experience of the workhouse was the lying-in ward, it was crucial that they were 'exceptionally clean', and that in order to keep infants safe from infection 'great cleanliness' should be enforced on the workhouse nurses.[130] *The Lancet* questioned the cleanliness of the northern pauper nurses in respect of these wards and reported the conclusions of a survey of northern workhouses during the 1860s, that 'the majority of the labour beds were found to be filthy and in a matted state'.[131] Moreover, the beds were frequently 'filthy, with crusted blood and discharges.'[132] Even women about to give birth were found to be unkempt, the bed-linen on which the infants were to be born was unclean, the 'utensils with which to bring forth the labour were also very dirty and the bath and towels which the new born infant was to be placed on were black with dirt'.[133] Throughout the country, from London to Stockport, the picture painted by *The Lancet* report was almost unremittingly pessimistic, and highlighted the problems that new-born infants had to contend with during their first few hours of life. To what extent were these infants at risk as a consequence of the actions or neglect of northern workhouse nurses?

Edward Smith found northern pauper nurses were 'devoted' to their duties in the children's and lying-in wards and argued they carried them out with 'patience, cleanliness and tidiness'.[134] But despite the concerted effort made by the pauper nurses on behalf of their patients, part of the problems experienced within the lying-in wards in particular stemmed from a deficiency of appropriate equipment, which caused malady and adversity for both infants and mothers, rather than the personal failings of nurses. For example, it was the duty of the workhouse to ensure that regulation labour beds which had 'an elevated rim around its margin' and 'lead sheeting to prevent stains on the floor' were provided.[135] These beds, if purchased, would have prevented matter from the women's labour seeping onto the floor, and reduced the work which workhouse nurses had to do to keep the ward clean and infants free from infection. Yet, obtaining permission to purchase these beds from the workhouse governors and rate payers was notoriously difficult, because the 'Board of Guardians had never been told' to run maternity wards.[136]

Failure to provide appropriate equipment was only one aspect of a workhouse management ruled by a wider culture of 'economy'. Although lying-in wards are clearly evident in the Guildford workhouse in Surrey for example, any clear-cut labour arrangements are less easy to see in northern workhouses.[137] The 'fairly suitable' four-bed labour ward at Guildford was a far cry from the cramped makeshift lying-in provision that was common throughout the north, and which sometimes meant that when 'several [northern] women were in labour at the same time', some had to be 'confined in general wards'.[138] The Leeds workhouse placed lying-in women in the body of the workhouse as the lying-in ward was housed in the main building.[139] As Poor Law Inspector Dr Edward Smith noted in 1867, the pauper nurse 'attends to the lying-in ward' but there was no specific 'night nursing' other than the pauper nurses should they be 'willing to attend'. Therefore, should a birth occur during the night it was likely that the residue from the birth was not cleaned up until the following morning due to the demands placed on the pauper nurses.[140] The duties placed nurses under great stress, for in Leeds they had up to 77 children to care for and 50 to 60 lying-in cases per year. Before they could attend to confinements, nurses might have to clean up from the night duty, in addition to doing nearly 'everything for the women and babies' and 'delivering them also'.[141] Their burden was made even heavier because they were also 'responsible for the distribution of food for meals', and undertaking other general nursing duties such as dispensing medicine throughout the whole workhouse.[142]

Under these circumstances – the amount of work the workhouse nurses had to undertake and the arduous regime – newborn infants were extremely vulnerable. Mary Jane Allen, a workhouse nurse in Bolton during the 1870s, confessed that the work was 'far too much for her', and that her 'health had given way under it'.[143] Mary Jane was replaced by Rose Morris, who also found the work exhausting, and likewise left the Bolton workhouse.[144] Even when nurses like Mary Jane 'had help [in] each ward' they still found the workload 'impossible', for 'even with the most fatiguous exertions', the labour was far too onerous.[145] The long hours were particularly criticised in Liverpool,[146] as was the physically demanding nature of the work, and nurses in Liverpool commented that whilst carrying the clean and dirty linen to and fro they 'almost broke [their] arms; and the nurses were out of breath after carrying them'.[147] The duties placed on an assistant nurse at Leeds who had charge of both the lying-in ward and those who lived in the 'main body of the house' were equally evident. Although women in the lying-in wards needed special care, nurses were unable to provide this due to the time devoted in getting around to the other pauper patients who were 'scattered about' with 'no classification of cases, and young and old, children and adults, mix[ed] together in the same ward'.[148] The arduous and unrelenting duties demanded of these nurses increasing the number of avoidable instances of infant mortality that were not the fault of the workhouse nurse.

It was not only nurses who complained about the heavy workload: doctors also witnessed it. Of particular concern for the *BMJ* was that due to the time constraints placed on nurses, infants would be the last in line for attention.[149] For 'as these nurses were responsible for the personal cleanliness of each infant under her care, and for the care and cleanliness of their room', her duties were 'so manifest that she can give but a fraction of attention to each.'[150] Dr Edward Smith reiterated these concerns, noting that as paupers were 'scattered about' such as at Leeds and this meant that nurses would sometimes have 'to walk 200 yards from one ward to another', which made it difficult to get around to each child.[151] To reduce the time constraints of the nurses such as at Leeds, and aid them in giving more attention to the lying-in wards, Edward Smith suggested that 'paid servants' should be employed to 'clean the wards and wash the linen.'[152]

With workhouses in cities like Manchester accommodating in excess of 2000 inmates, infants were in significant danger.[153] In the Bradford workhouse for example, Mary Brook was charged with scalding an infant in her care, which occurred as a result of her seeking to save time.[154] When questioned about the incident, Mary stated in her defence that 'she had left the infant in the bath whilst carrying out her other duties',[155] indicating that when viewed through the medium of the time demands placed on nurses, what may at first appear to be clear instances of neglect need more complex explanations. Indeed, although infants were clearly in danger this was not because of any wilful neglect on the part of the workhouse nurses. Nurses themselves expressed concern over the conditions placed on them. One unnamed pauper nurse at the Leeds workhouse remarked that as she was in charge of, and dispensed, the 'medicine' for the 'sixty patients under her care', disposed in seven wards, she found it very it very difficult to get to all of her patients, and that 'infants suffered' as a consequence.[156]

Although they were supposed to work an eight-hour day, many nurses actually worked much longer, sometimes into the night, although as few nurses could muster enough energy to work these long hours, the inmates, including infants, were generally put to bed at eight o'clock in the evening.[157] Even if pauper nurses did on occasion agree to work the night shift, this was often far too much for them to deal with, which caused them many problems, leaving *The Lancet* to remark of one nurse who did this work that it 'should not have been thrust on her' as 'it was impossible for her to carry it out'.[158] During the day it was noted that 'nurses...poor things never sit', rendering them physically exhausted and totally unfit to attend adequately to anyone during day and night.[159]

For nurses labouring under these conditions, it was therefore likely that if Twining should chance on some infants they would have 'high temperatures with their "whole being" in a sorry state and many having bed sores.'[160]

The guidelines in workhouses, which were beyond the control of nurses, commonly required infants to be placed in hammocks, slings, or cribs and kennels, with straw linings and blankets for extra warmth, like those illustrated in Figure 3.3, a practice carried over from the late eighteenth century.[161] In these circumstances, it was possible that infants may have been out of sight and mind if nurses had so much to do when going about their duties, – often attending to in excess of 27 wards – leading to the bed sores noted by Twinning.[162] The Webbs were scathing of the infants' workhouse environment, noting that they were housed in nursery wards, children's wards, or kennels and lamented that 'infants are kept too much in these rooms and are not taken into the fresh air to the extent they should be'.[163] The Webbs were not alone in voicing concerns; *The Lancet* also stated that the space provided for infants was 'very small', which left them 'very badly

Figure 3.3   Crib for Workhouse Infants
Source: K. Morrison, *The Workhouse, a Study of Poor Law Buildings in England*, p. 34

off'.[164] Recounting a visit to one unnamed northern ward, *The Lancet* report continued:

> It was a miserable and dark little room on the ground floor; the door that gives access to it opens directly off a court, and has no screen or porch to break the draught. It faces another door and to the left of it is the fireplace ... There is no proper lavatory attached to this ward, nor any bathing accommodation other than a moveable bath. A few commode chairs were standing in a recess behind the door.'[165]

An onerous workload and inadequate infant accommodation therefore contributed to the infant mortality rates in northern workhouses. The significance of this is that even if the northern IMR was affected by the workhouse regime, it would be misleading to lay the blame for this solely at the hands of the pauper nurses in these institutions, a view supported by contemporary doctors, who lobbied workhouses to take on extra pauper nursing staff specifically to care for infants.

The conclusions drawn from the Select Committee report on nursing in workhouses led Drs Smith and Farnell to argue that nursing staff were 'especially' necessary 'for the Northern nursery and children's wards', as well as 'for the lying-in ward'.[166] Rather than being critical of the pauper nurse therefore, the medical profession was supportive of them, and acknowledging their 'excellence', argued for the continuation of their employment.[167] The medical doctor at Leeds remarked that he was satisfied with his nurses, confirming that his 'cases [did] well'.[168] As the Leeds nurse attended the lying-in ward every day, although we are not aware of the actual times, it could be suggested that she had some control over her ward, the women within it and the condition of both mother and baby.[169] Equally, Edward Smith lauded the pauper nurses at Loughborough in 1866, one of whom had nursed and tended to the pauper inmates for nine years and received glowing praise from the medical officer, master and matron for doing so. Smith remarked in particular on the excellence of her midwifery skills and the 'homely aspect' of the female wards where 'each patient' had their own articles such as 'comb and brush', 'soap, wash-hand basins'.. 'a basket for clothes', 'rocking chairs' and the all-important 'mackintosh sheeting' for the lying-in beds for their individual use.[170] Both pauper nurses at Loughborough carried out their 'duties in a most satisfactory manner', and as a consequence, Smith felt unable to quarrel with the Guardians who were disinclined to appoint a paid nurse.[171]

Indeed, through their role as Poor Law medical officers, doctors were very well placed to gain a first-hand insight into the proficiency of these women, and this led them to remark that 'reformers were overstating the inadequacies of the nineteenth-century nurses'.[172] Although Lionel Rose has argued that the medical profession was the enemy of the female nursing profession, it is clear that this was not entirely the case; this supports Margaret Pelling's suggestion that the idea that nurses were the victims of a dominant and patriarchal medical class has been overplayed.[173]

Advocacy on behalf of skilled nurses by the medical profession was not merely confined to generalised utterances of support. J. Stallard, for example, looked into the condition of workhouses and their nursing staff during the nineteenth century, and noted that the relationship between the workhouse doctor and nurse could be very close due to the amount of work they undertook together.[174] Further, some doctors were known to directly intervene on behalf of nurses who experienced problems with their health due to the amount of work they did. For example, the Bolton nurse, Mary Jane Allen, stated that the 'medical man tells me, if I continue to do the work I am now required to do it will be at the risk of my life'.[175] These examples indicate that not only did some local medical practitioners recognise the contribution made by pauper nurses, but that they also acknowledged that nurses were expected to perform their duties under very trying circumstances, and that these circumstances could result in the neglect and even premature death of infants. Indeed, rather than blame nurses for the ills accruing to workhouse infants, Dr Dolan of Halifax remarked that doctors were sometimes guilty of not spotting disease within the workhouse quickly enough, and they themselves, on occasions endangered the lives of entire wards of infants and children.[176] When seeking to understand the causal factors behind northern infant mortality within workhouses, therefore, the focus needs to be widened to encompass actors and factors beyond the humble workhouse nurse.

Conclusion

At times of concern about the high IMR in northern workhouses, many voices blamed pauper nurses for the wilful neglect and premature death of infants. Yet, following a visit to Bradford during the 1870s, a female investigator for the WVS remarked that the problems in northern workhouses stemmed from a combination of 'defective management and overworked nurses'.[177] These observations raise important questions in relation to the characterisation of the workhouse nurse during the period, and show that it is too simplistic to lay the blame for infant mortality in workhouses solely at their feet. Indeed, much of what we read in the literature is based on or influenced by the ill-informed, perhaps jaundiced judgements of reformers like Louisa Twining. An important point to draw from this chapter is that due to the philosophical and sentimental shifts which characterised the provision of public welfare from the New Poor Law Amendment Act of 1834, the workhouse was able to draw on the excellent services of a cohort of young women who worked in the workhouse as pauper nurses and whose characters challenge the myth of the supposed 'old sot'; they were women who did not resemble the 'Mrs Gamp' archetype. Detailed analysis of the occupational background of these women reveals that a sizeable proportion *were* well versed in maternal skills, derived from their domestic service employment.

Yet, despite the deployment of these skilled workhouse nurses – a point acknowledged by medical journals like *The Lancet* – the IMR still remained stubbornly high in northern workhouses. This should not detract from the contribution made by the majority of the workhouse nurses: as the report of her visits to the workhouse made by a member of the WVS indicates, it was managerial shortcomings which were the main problem in workhouses, and which the diligent nurses found hard to surmount. Inadequate buildings, poor or non-existent equipment, and the ruinous workload heaped on the shoulders of workhouse nurses fed into infant mortality statistics in northern institutions. The difficulties these nurses faced on a daily basis were acknowledged by medical officers, indicating that even contemporaries recognised that the frustrating battle against the IMR was more complex than claimed by campaigners like Florence Nightingale, Louisa Twining, and indeed some modern historians. This is not to state that abuses at the hands of workhouse nurses did not occur, but rather that the administration of infant care was governed by complex forces and characterised by structural failings to a greater extent than has hitherto been acknowledged. Understanding this, and recognising its importance for the workhouse nurse debate, leads to a more nuanced reading of the relationship between workhouse nurses and the northern IMR.

Infant mortality in workhouses remained high, and with this in mind, the infant diet in workhouses, and the culpability of the nurses who administered it, is now examined.

4
Workhouse Infant Diet

As we have seen in the previous chapter, workhouse nurses were not dis-inclined to tend to pauper infants, but to what extent did they feed them dangerous foods when they got around to offering care? This chapter will analyse the feeding practices in the workhouse, and identify when and where the workhouse took on responsibility for feeding infants. We begin by relating the contemporary view of workhouse nurse feeding:

> Experience has repeatedly shown that the congregation of several hand-fed infants in infant-nurseries, workhouses and elsewhere entails almost certain disease and death. Sooner or later, they are attacked by aph-thae [atrophy] or diarrhoea, and no amount of care or attention will avert their death. In one instance, mentioned by Dr. Routh, where the infants...were received in an infant-nursery, an average of four out of five died...[1]

Despite the endeavours of workhouse nurses to do their best for pauper infants, as the contemporary report in *The British Medical Journal* (*BMJ*) cited above indicates, the incidence of infant mortality, particularly within the workhouse, remained a concern for the medical establishment.[2] These concerns are shared by historians like Ruth Richardson, Angela Negrine, Jonathan Reinarz, Leonard Schwarz and the Webbs in particular, who argued that indoor pauper infants who lived in workhouses 'outside of London' experienced an annual death rate of a third of all infants, and these high rates continued into the early twentieth century.[3] Such figures were abysmal. As Ruth Richardson notes, the workhouse nurses and the 'care' that they were able to provide to infant paupers was 'dismal.'[4]

Undertaking an in-depth survey into the causes of the high IMR and attempting to explain it, the Webbs placed particular emphasis on the common feeding practices in workhouses, mirroring the conclusions drawn by the *BMJ*.[5] Although we have seen in Chapter 3 that the hard-pressed pauper nurse often carried out her duties under trying circumstances, we still need to ask whether some blame could be attached to the pauper nurse's infant-feeding practices when looking for the causes of the high level of infant mortality in northern workhouses. Essential first steps are to revisit the nature of infant mortality in the workhouse, the feeding practices of workhouse nurses, and the practical and medical rationale for them. Only after this analysis can we determine the extent to which blame for the appalling levels of infant mortality in workhouses can be allocated to pauper nurses.

It should be made clear from the outset that many of the ailments which afflicted infants in northern workhouses went beyond the remit of nineteenth century Poor Law Unions, who were obligated to provide 'succour' to the poverty-stricken. Some ailments were, nevertheless, attributable to the care, or rather the lack of it, within the workhouse. The prevalence of conditions like rickets, for instance, shows that the workhouse diet lacked Vitamin D. The nurses who gave the infants their diet, attracted criticism from social commentators throughout the nineteenth century, just as criticisms of wet-nurses characterised the eighteenth century.[6] An eighteenth-century case in point was the infamous London wet-nurse Mary Poole, who was employed by the Poor Law to feed pauper infants. The remarkable death-rate of infants in her care led the philanthropist Jonas Hanway to ask: [7]

> Would not any man in his senses conclude, after the death of three or four children in one woman's hands, that the nurse was very unfortunate; and after five or six, that she was very ignorant or very wicked? But when in so short a period, the mortality of seven or eight had happened, would it not create a suspicion that she starved them...And would not the same common-sense and candour lead one to think that on seeing the eighteenth child brought within this parish nurse's den that those who sent them preferred that they should die? And what is preferring that a child should die but something too shocking to mention or think of? But it has been said and continues, in many parishes to be so common a practice, that this violence on humanity...is become as familiar in these renowned cities, as the use of the bowstring in Morocco for those who offend the Emperor.[8]

Hanway was clearly outraged by things he had seen and heard on his travels and this led him to campaign for workhouse feeding reform. Yet, whilst noting that some infants were starved whilst in the care of workhouse nurses, historian Valerie Fildes argues that it was not only workhouse nurses who bore responsibility for the high IMR; rather, the parish authorities were also culpable as they sometimes failed to pay wet-nurses for their services. This led to the nurses being unable to buy food for themselves, which in turn reduced the amount of milk they could make to give infants in return.[9]

Although, as Rose has argued, the tradition of wet-nursing waned during the nineteenth century, to be replaced by artificial feeding beyond the first month of an infant's life, which limited opportunity for nurses to neglect infants, the rates of infant death in the workhouse as a result of diarrhoea and wasting diseases during the latter half of the nineteenth century were still high.[10]

One of the main causes for the high rates of infantile diarrhoea was the practice of feeding cows' milk to infants. In his survey of 48 northern workhouses in 1866, Dr Edward Smith found this practice was universal.[11] Cows' milk is totally unsuitable for infants due to its nutritional deficiencies, yet nineteenth-century doctors approved its use in the workhouse. As nurses merely followed the directions given to them, they may be absolved from some of the blame of inducing rickets. Cows' milk was thought to be suitable for infants because the eminent Dr Eustace Smith, MRCP and Physician to the North-West Free Dispensary for Sick Children, a man who took a keen interest in infant nutrition and its effects on IMR, said so. He remarked that infants should drink asses' milk which bore the closest resemblance to human milk, but if that was not available, then they should be given cows' milk.[12] As asses' milk was more costly than cows' milk, the workhouse preferred the latter.[13]

The use of cows' milk was a continuation of eighteenth-century infant feeding practices. Dr. Hugh Smith argued as early as 1772 that when it was necessary to 'bring up a child by hand' he preferred 'cows' milk to every other kind of nourishment, in the early months'.[14] Margaret Baines reiterated this advice in her 1862 pamphlet on how to stay infant mortality.[15] Clearly then, and despite its nutritional deficiencies, the feeding of cows' milk to infants was medical orthodoxy by the late nineteenth century. Laurence Weaver and P.J. Atkins have noted the extent to which unpasteurised milk led to debilitating illnesses for infants of the independent poor, reflected in high rates of tuberculosis, gastroenteritis and diarrhoea, and, as Table 4.1 indicates, these illnesses were prevalent and deadly in the Leeds workhouse.[16]

The risk posed to infants was further compounded by the belief of Dr Eustace Smith that cows' milk given to infants 'must not be boiled, but that the cold mixture must be warmed by dipping the bottle containing it, for a few minutes in hot water.'[17] Again, these directions reflected eighteenth-century medical orthodoxy, with Cadogan, for example, stressing that 'boiled milk harmed infants'.[18]

As a consequence of the incorrect medical advice, compounded by the lack of pasteurisation, it is little wonder that Leeds infants like John William Hudson, Josh Hardwick and George Amos, in addition to many others recorded within the Leeds Infant Death records during 1879–1883, suffered from diarrhoea whilst in the workhouse and subsequently died, making their own tragic contribution to the northern IMR.

Table 4.1 Causes of infant deaths in the Leeds workhouse, 1879–1883

Cause of death	Number of deaths
Epidemic, Endemic and Contagious Disease	18
Sporadic Diseases of the Nervous System	10
Sporadic Diseases of the Respiratory Organs	37
Sporadic Diseases of Uncertain Seat (Including Infantile Wasting Diseases)	32
Sporadic Diseases of the Organs of Circulation	0
Sporadic Diseases of the Digestive Organs	2
Sporadic Diseases of the Urinary Organs	1
Sporadic Diseases of the Organs of Generation	3
Sporadic Diseases of the Organs of Locomotion	6
Sporadic Diseases of the Integumentary System	0

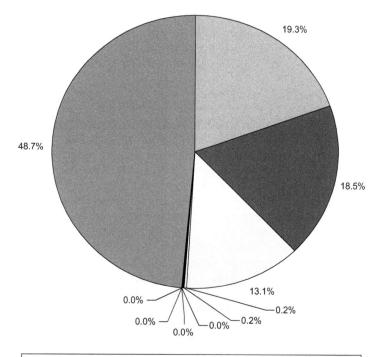

☐ Epidemic, Endemic and Contagious Disease   ☐ Sporadic Deseases of the Urinary Organs

■ Sporadic Diseases of the Nervous System   ☐ Sporadic Diseases of the Organs of Generation

☐ Sporadic Diseases of the Respiratory Organs   ☐ Sporadic Diseases of the Organs of Locomotion

☐ Sporadic Diseases of the Organs of Circulation   ■ Sporadic Diseases of the Intergumentary System

■ Sporadic Diseases of the Digestive Organs   ☐ Sporadic Diseases of Uncertain Seat (Including Infantile Wasting Diseases)

Despite workhouse nurses being skilled in maternal care, their position in the hierarchy of the workhouse rendered it difficult for them to question the efficacy of the infant diet, assuming that they identified it as contributing to the levels of infant mortality in the first place. In this respect then, workhouse nurses were merely the *servants* of the institution: they were simply carrying out the orders of the guardians and medical officers, who claimed to understand what was in the best nutritional interests of infants, but which in some instances, could prove fatal.

Doctor Alfred Sheen, who worked for the England and Wales Poor Law Board as well as being the author of influential paediatric texts, was adamant that the responsibility for infant diet in the workhouse lay with medical officers.[19] In the case of the Leeds Union during the late nineteenth century, this meant that Dr Allen was responsible for the infant diet and not the workhouse nurses: they were merely doing his bidding.[20] This is not, of course, to state that potentially fatal dietary guidelines were borne of any malicious intent, but rather that they were considered sound by contemporaries as they were based on flawed nineteenth-century medical reasoning. Ill-founded medical thinking was not restricted to the consumption of milk; it also influenced wider dietary policy, which had further devastating consequences for infant mortality in northern workhouses.

This was particularly evident in the incidence of atrophy, or marasmus, which accounted for 29 per cent of infant deaths in the Leeds workhouse during the period 1879–1883. These rates and the reasons for them were a mystery to most nineteenth century medical men, and they were categorised as 'diseases of uncertain seat'. The uncertainty of the causes of these deaths, and the scale of infant mortality which arose from them, was of great concern to nineteenth-century medicine. The number of infant deaths attributed to wasting diseases in the Leeds workhouse amounted to 32 out of 109 recorded over four years.[21] So, to what extent was the pauper nurse responsible for these deaths?

Nineteenth century doctor William Farr linked the incidence of atrophy to starvation, a view endorsed by historian Simon Fowler, who argues that the infants fed by pauper nurses suffered from a lack of food.[22] Lionel Rose and Frank Crompton have drawn similar conclusions.[23] If this was the case, then the workhouse nurse could re-enter the frame when blame for the IMR in northern workhouses is apportioned. To what extent were pauper nurses responsible for infants suffering from marasmus and atrophy?

An alternative explanation for the atrophy rates, other than starvation, can be found in the words of Dr Robert Baker: nineteenth-century Poor Law medical officer and factory inspector. He had trained at Guy's Hospital, London, was qualified as a Surgeon Apothecary, and latterly a MRCS in London and then became the Poor Law medical officer at Leeds during the 1830s. Baker was a severe critic of the artificial diet given to infants. In particular, he argued that the infant diet contained an excess of sugar which had a profound effect on infants, leading them to ail from the wasting conditions of atrophy and marasmus. As Baker starkly put it: 'more children die of sugar than of anything.'[24]

It was not only Baker who held this view. He took his lead from the French physiologist Francois Magendie, who had developed an understanding of the influences of sugar on the basis of the work on infant feeding by the German physiologist Justus von Liebig during the nineteenth century. Magendie found through experimentation on dogs that although sugar was an essential part of the diet, when consumed in *excess*, it warranted effects that led infants to develop 'a general atrophy [wasting] of the muscular structure.'[25] Despite these concerns about the use of sugar, Dr Edward Smith, Medical Officer to the Poor Law, advocated that all infants residing in Poor Law Unions should receive it when the mother was unable to produce enough breast milk, and once weaning had been completed.[26] In order to assess the accuracy of the criticisms made against sugar in a nineteenth-century infant diet, modern-day medical expertise was sought. Current paediatricians like Dr Andrew Williams of Northampton General Hospital, agrees that if sugar were given to infants at half an ounce daily – as prescribed for example by Alfred Sheen and Dr Allen at Leeds – it would severely impact on their health, inducing wasting diseases and stunted development.[27] Infants would become pale, pasty, lethargic, quiet, and rendered with a 'frozen watchfulness' leading to atrophy, marasmus, and/or diarrhoea, and ultimately tissue loss.[28]

The workhouse, under the jurisdiction of doctors, rather than pauper nurses, subjected infants to a sweetened diet which, as the contemporary testimony from the *BMJ* shows, was still thought appropriate some 20 years after Edward Smith proposed it. Medical orthodoxy, rather than pauper nurse ignorance, exacerbated levels of infant mortality in workhouses during the late nineteenth century.[29] These practices were not new: the use of sugar in sweetening cows' milk was a continuation of a method used in the early modern period.[30] Sugar in addition to spice and honey, was also considered to 'add bulk to milk' during the latter half of the nineteenth century, and Margaret Baines argued in her pamphlets and also at a *NAPSS* meeting in Bradford during the 1870s that cows' milk was only safe to use for infants when 'other substances' were added.[31]

Whilst the *BMJ* reported that workhouse day nurses took 'charge of serving the infant diets in turn for a week at a time', which in practice meant giving the infants their food,[32] it is clear that as with the feeding of cows' milk, the workhouse nurses were not responsible for the make-up and dangerous nature of the food they were providing. They were merely carrying out the dietary orders of the workhouse management –themselves influenced by medical opinion and orthodoxy.

The flawed medical advice of giving sugar to infants in measurements higher than half an ounce a day is evident in the northern workhouses.

Edward Smith's project of surveying 65 provincial workhouses yields valuable information with regard to the diet of northern workhouses, as Smith recorded the diets of 34 of the unions. This analysis revealed that the practice of adding sugar to the infant diet was common. Whilst Kirby Moorside added no sugar to the infant diet, like 21 other northern unions, the four unions in the West Riding, including the urban areas of Hunslet and Great Preston in Leeds, did. Another thirteen areas, seven of which were in Yorkshire, included sugar.[33] At Hunslet, in Leeds, infants were fed a 'pap' which comprised 4 ounces of bread, 4 ounces of cows' milk, and 2 ounces of sugar daily, whereas at the Halifax workhouse, the medical officer, Dr T. M. Dolan, prescribed 'three pints of sweetened milk during the day'; and that after 'nine months, four ounces of bread should be added to the milk' to make the 'pap'.[34] This sweetened diet was also found in Hemsworth, Wakefield, where 4 ounces of bread to which sugar, milk and water were added was the staple. Rotherham, Scarborough and Knaresborough did not add sugar, but in the areas of Yorkshire, and in particular in the urban area of Hunslet, where pauper nurses were said to be culpable for the high rates of infant mortality, it was included. A similar diet was found in Cardiff, where Dr Sheen remarked that the infants in workhouse from 'birth to nine months' received:

> 2 ¼pt milk daily and from nine months to twelve months their 'pap' was made up of 2 ¼pint milk, ½oz loaf sugar and 6oz bread. If weaned from six to twelve months the 'pap' was made up from 4oz bread and 1 pint milk daily, and 2oz loaf sugar weekly.[35]

The rationale for this adulteration of the infant diet was the belief that as cows' milk contained less sugar than working-class mothers' breast milk, it was important to make up this deficiency in towns where pauper inmates were drawn from the industrial districts.[36] Moreover, nurses were also instructed to add it to mask the taste of limewater which was added to reduce the acidity of cows' milk.[37]

Although seemingly certain as to what the *correct* diet for infants was, doctors were extremely ignorant of the problems which this *incorrect* diet caused infants, and of the influence this had on the mortality rates in the workhouse. Even august medical journals like *The Lancet* could give little explanation for the prevalence of wasting diseases like atrophy or marasmus, which had caused the deaths of infants like Fanny Henkinson and Edward Craig, both born in the Leeds workhouse, and who died at the age of eight weeks and four months respectively in 1879.[38] Even the eminent Dr Eustace Smith himself, Senior Physician to Shadwell Children's Hospital in London, who was responsible for the infant workhouse diet, and who influenced workhouse medics like Dr Allen of Leeds and Dr Alfred Sheen amongst others, was at a loss to explain why so many workhouse infants succumbed to wasting diseases.[39] Smith's pamphlet *The Wasting Diseases of Infants and Children* written in 1868, for example, questions why so many infants died of atrophy, marasmus and diarrhoea, yet also contains the prescription to add sugar to the infants' feed.[40] The review of Smith's work by the *BMJ* tells us much about the state of ignorance that prevailed with regard to the effects of feeding too much sugar to infants. Although lengthy, the review merits restatement:

> In this small volume, the author groups together the various affections that entail, as a common result, the production of a condition which is generally somewhat vaguely spoken of as one of 'marasmus', 'tabes', or 'atrophy'. The condition itself, amongst infants and young children, more especially in our crowded cities and towns, is one of the greatest frequency, obtruding itself on the busy practitioner at every turn; and we feel assured that the careful and judicious way in which Dr. Eustace Smith has treated his subject will ensure its favourable reception as a most useful and valuable contribution to our medical literature. The author assigns as his reason for grouping these affections, that 'he had not long begun the study of children's diseases, before he found that even the best systematic treatises dealt but imperfectly with the clinical condition of chronic wasting, and did not consider together, in the way required for every-day use in practice, the various disorders to which it may be due'. After some general introductory remarks of a practical character, Dr. Smith, treats, in successive chapters, of the various forms of Chronic Wasting, resulting from In-sufficient nourishment. It would be impossible now for us to follow Dr. Smith in his exposition of these various subjects; and, although we might differ from him in some matters of detail, we can most honestly recommend the volume as one full of valuable practical information, not only concerning the diseases of children of which it treats, but also as to their food and general hygienic management. The book is essentially clinical in its character; and, as the author observes, 'he has limited himself to matters of direct practical significance, and has indulged little in considerations of a purely speculative kind', in the pathological department of his subject. The author has evidently spared no pains in order to make his book as useful as possible; and we have little doubt that it will soon be a work in the possession of a large majority of busy practitioners, who have not too much time for reading.[41]

Although Magendie and Baker saw the deleterious effects of putting sugar into the infants' feed of cows' milk, most medical doctors did not understand the dangers of sugar, unboiled milk, and the dirty bottle. Medical doctors undertook vigorous analysis of artificial foods to understand why so many infants succumbed to the conditions of marasmus and atrophy, but as a profession, their discipline was flawed and failed to establish a link between sugar and wasting diseases. For, despite advances in medical paediatric knowledge, the President of the Obstetrics Society of London and Professor of Midwifery at Birmingham University in 1904 admitted that 'in some cases, the want of knowledge of doctors themselves with regard to the most elementary principles of infant feeding is lamentable . . . Infant dietetics might be better taught in medical schools [as] it is a subject that is not taught properly [but] picked up by degrees'.[42] Despite good intentions, the medically prescribed diet did more harm than good to infants in workhouses and drove up the level of northern infant mortality.

The workhouse was not only detrimental to infants eating artificial food; new-born infants also suffered from malnutrition. Dr Joseph Rogers, a London Poor Law medical doctor and workhouse reformer, found that the mothers of new-born infants were provided with little nutrition as they were only allowed to have fluid for the first five days whilst both mother and infant lived in the lying-in ward.[43] William Rathbone, a middle-class philanthropist, and Florence Nightingale, found similar conditions on their visits to the Liverpool workhouse, where Nightingale commented that 'food was at starvation level'.[44] This would have severe implications for the mothers themselves who were dependent on receiving food from pauper nurses to enable them to feed their children. The motive for supplying such poor rations, argued Rogers, was that guardians wished to deter single mothers from resorting to the workhouse.[45]

Smith's survey of northern lying-in wards reveals the lack of food available to new nursing mothers in the Leeds workhouse. He reports the diet consisted of the following:[46]

Within one week after confinement after birth:

Breakfast:	5oz bread, 1 pint tea, ½ oz sugar ½ oz butter.
Lunch:	1 pint milk, 4oz bread, 4oz sago.
Supper:	5oz bread with gruel, 1 ½ pints of tea, ½ oz sugar.

Within one month after confinement and birth and afterwards, in Leeds, during whole period of suckling:

Breakfast: 6oz bread,
                 1 pint tea,
                 ½ oz of sugar.

Dinner: 4oz meat,
                 8oz potatoes,
                 or other vegetable,
                 3oz bread.

Supper: 6oz bread,
                 1 pint tea,
                 ½ oz sugar.

Smith argued that this diet was inadequate for nursing mothers to provide sufficient nutrients to enable their infants to thrive, and he argued that other doctors were of the same mind.[47]

The quality of the breast milk of mothers taking this diet would have put infants at risk, but it did contain the 'antibody-rich colostrums', as noted by Alysa Levene: 'breast was best, because it gives protection against certain diseases'. Notwithstanding the mothers' diet, the contemporary perception of working-class breast milk was that, like cows' milk it had deficiencies. Indeed, Eustace Smith argued it was less sufficient, and of a lower class than the breast milk of a middle-class counterpart because it lacked certain nutrients.[48] Eustace Smith was convinced that working-class women provided insufficient nutrition to their infants, arguing that:

> from the researches of MM Vernois and Becquerel we find that the richest milk is far from being secreted by women of the greatest muscular development. On the contrary, their investigations tend to show that a robust figure is inferior in milk-producing power to one slighter and less apparently vigorous. Under the first head (strong constitution) they place brunettes, with well-developed muscles, fresh complexions, moderate plumpness, and all the other external signs of constitutional strength. Under the second head they range fair-complexioned women with light or red hair, flabby muscles, and sluggish muscular contraction.[49]

Smith's analysis is shown in Table 4.2.

The conclusions Smith drew from these 'researches' was that 'It will thus be seen that in women ranked under the head of strong constitution the deficiency in the amount of the sugar and the casein is very remarkable, while in those of apparently weaker constitution these elements very nearly attain the normal standard.'[50] The imperfection of breast milk, Smith argued, was most seen in women with 'well developed muscles... and all the other signs of constitutional strength' attained through waged work and which was to be counter-balanced by providing 'lump sugar to nursing mothers'.[51]

Table 4.2 Eustace Smith's analysis of breast milk for three categories of female constitution

	Constitution		
	Strong	**Weak**	**Normal**
Specific gravity	1032.97	1031.90	1032.67
Water	911.19	887.59	889.08
Solid parts	88.81	112.41	110.92
Sugar	32.55	42.88	43.64
Casein	28.98	39.21	39.24
Butter	25.96	28.78	26.66
Salts	1.32	1.54	1.38

To remedy these deficiencies and tackle the high IMR, therefore, Smith recommended working-class mothers to increase their intake of sugar whilst breast feeding. We see the added sugar was given to nursing mothers in Leeds at breakfast, dinner and supper. In addition, to ensure enough sugar flowed into the infants' veins, Smith recommended working-class pauper women should limit their breast feeding to 'twice a day' and the rest of the feeds should be made up of 'three to four ounces of cows' milk sweetened with a teaspoon of sugar every two hours'. When their infants were a little older, 'the breast should be given twice a day' with the rest of the feeds being 'pap', which should be made up of cows' milk, bread, and the all-important sugar.[52] Smith published his findings in his book *The Wasting Diseases of Infants and Children*, which influenced other students of nineteenth-century infant mortality[53] and which led to another 27 doctors prescribing the sweet supplement to mothers in workhouses such as Holbeck, Bramley and Howden in Leeds, Helmsley, Wakefield and Kirby Moorside, North Yorkshire.[54]

Smith's testimony led *The Lancet* to prescribe this augmented diet for working-class mothers in lying-in rooms. The prescription 'for women at the breast an extra one pint of milk and 1oz of sugar daily in addition to [their ordinary] diet until the child is one month old', was the prime response to the widespread concern about the apparent undernourishment of mothers in the workhouse.[55] In the 35 Yorkshire unions, a strong and wide belief in sugar and its nutritional benefit to working-class infants and mothers was evident. As Smith himself remarked, Leeds workhouse doctors were extremely grateful to the Guardians for instituting the recommended dietary enhancements, noting the 'considerations which his suggestions have been received, and for the generous readiness with which most of them have been carried into effect'.[56] The flawed logic of providing sugar to working-class mothers and infants was highly significant, as it tapped into wider social and political concerns centred on the northern IMR.

Doctors believed that mothers and infants prospered whilst in the workhouse during the month they were allowed to be together in the lying-in ward. Margaret Hewitt reiterated this view by arguing that the vigorous health of working-class infants and mothers was largely due to the fact that 'mothers who were admitted into the maternity ward of the workhouse had a full month's rest after their confinement, during which time they were able to give their infants their full care',[57] which the *BMJ* argued made them 'quite strong'.[58] Although mothers had a limited diet, the time they spent with their infants providing breast feeding on demand, gave positive results. However, doctors' conviction that working-class mother's breast milk was flawed, and their belief that artificial food had better ingredients, led them to seek to bring poor working-class mothers into the workhouse in ever-larger numbers during this period. The medical profession saw this as an opportunity to produce fit and healthy infants, so addressing the problem of the high northern IMR. Infant mortality measured the health of the community, and the Poor Law and medical profession were under pressure to reduce the IMR whenever and however possible.

The workhouse enabled the medical profession to control the diet of working-class infants as part of the efffort to reduce infant mortality.[59] Public health measures had improved adult mortality rates, and it was considered by medical practitioners like Dr. Dolan of Halifax that the workhouse as an avenue of public health could improve infant health too. Indeed, control of early diet would enable 'the children grow up strong and be in after life of service to the state'.[60] The workhouse was the front-line in the battle against the IMR, taking control of the feeding practices of northern mothers on outdoor relief. Justification for this policy lay, as with many contemporary theories, in the supposed inadequacies of the poor mothers themselves, seen as lacking maternal skill and, in the case of those who had robust characteristics due to the waged work they performed, deficient in the quality of their milk.[61]

The workhouse, therefore, embarked on a programme of recruiting new mothers and their infants, aiming to take direct control of their diets. Yet, doing so caused difficulties, as medical officers had no powers to separate even the 'most neglected or ill-used child' from its parents. And doctors were unable to prescribe special foods for outdoor mothers, for, as the Webbs noted 'it [was] unfortunate during the latter half of the nineteenth century that ... no particular instructions [were] issued to Relieving Officers to grant special food to women ... about to become mothers'.[62] The help which poor mothers received was therefore limited to a midwife attending the birth. There was no post-partum support from 'nurses', and the outdoor relief for new-born infants amounted to only a shilling or two, with 'nothing for the mother'.[63] Thus if doctors were to help these women they had to get them into the workhouse, so the workhouse targeted poor women on outdoor relief during the 1860s and 1870s, and 'compelled them' to seek 'assistance' within the workhouse.

Mr Earnshaw, relieving officer for Leeds and Wakefield, was sent to police the individual circumstances of new mothers and infants receiving outdoor relief. As a result, women like 'Sarah Rusby and her children' were subject to 'an order made out for their admission to the House', as were Ellen Sykes of Ackworth and her two illegitimate children.[64] These cases were part of a wide trend to capture and control the maternal experience within the workhouse. When Louisa Dobson was 'recently confined of an illegitimate child' in 1862, she immediately came to the attention of the Guardians, who resolved to enquire and report on the situation.[65] Similar treatment was evident in the same year in the case of Martha Smeaton, 'due to her recently being confined of an illegitimate child'.[66] Likewise, for Mary Bulmer and Caroline Brook, each mothers to two infants, Anne Richardson and her infant, Annie Walker of Leeds and her child, and Emma Standfield, 'a poor person belonging to Great Houghton and her children', relief was likewise conditional on complying with an 'order' to go into the house.[67]

Indeed, the desire to 'rescue' infants from inadequate working-class mothers' milk was so strong that unions were prepared to pre-empt some cases. In Leeds, the Guardians were particularly concerned with pauper Jane Waddington, who was merely considered likely to become pregnant sometime in the future. The Leeds Guardians sought to prevent any such pregnancy and Mr Earnshaw, the relieving officer, reported to the Leeds and Wakefield Guardians that 'she had just buried a bastard child and it was feared [she] would soon have another' without any intervention, and so it was 'strongly recommend[ed] that a Workhouse Order should be sent for her'.[68] Consequently, 'The Clerk produce[d] a letter from Mr Barras on the 14th inst declining to give out-relief to Jane Waddington and requesting that an order might be sent for her admission into our workhouse and an order was duly made out accordingly.'[69] Jane was a single mother; we would be justified in a suspicion that the Guardians' interest in her was to stop her becoming pregnant again, as the costs for maintaining the child would fall on the ratepayers. However, it may well be that the Guardians may have been seeking to head off the conception of what they feared was another child likely to contribute to the high IMR in Leeds.

These cases support Pat Thane's theories on the surveillance of single and widowed women.[70] None the less, the actions of Guardians and doctors in Leeds and Wakefield suggest that these acts of social control were at least in part a logical result of an attempt to improve the nutrition of the infants of poor women. At a clinical level, these 'policies' took infant nutrition away from the mother and placed it under the control of the pauper nurses who, on instructions from the medical officer, gave artificial foods to the infants. This had the perceived advantage of reducing the possibility of the pauper infants inheriting the 'bad characteristics' of the mother through 'tainted' breast milk.[71] This may explain why it was considered appropriate to separate an infant from its mother 'immediately' when they entered the Wigan workhouse,[72] but retain both mother and child within the workhouse for as long as possible.

Indeed, as Steven King has argued, women 'vulnerable to poverty' tended to end up in the workhouse along with their children, and once admitted, children tended to remain there 'for a long time'.[73] In Leeds, for mothers of illegitimate children, 'the workhouse had the capacity to become just as much a prison'.[74] As Appendix 2 shows, 40 per cent of the women who went into the Leeds workhouse were there for 180 days at least, providing doctors with what they considered was the required time to augment and 'improve' the diet of mothers and their infants. This was a 'custom in common' across the north, with both Liverpool and Manchester operating similar policies, and it also has resonances with the Chaley Union in the south, where guardians urged single mothers with young infants to 'stay' in the workhouse.[75] One consequence of this was that as Figure 4.1 indicates, women of child-bearing age constituted 15 percent of the workhouse population during the period of heightened concern over the northern IMR, which perversely resulted in ever more infants being rendered vulnerable to premature mortality as a direct result of a policy which sought to ameliorate, rather than exacerbate the problem.

Figure 4.1 clearly supports this view, and illustrates that infants represented a sizeable proportion of the workhouse population during the second half of the nineteenth century. Their diet came under the remit of workhouse medical officers and subject to their 'nutritional theories'. As Robert Baker had predicted, the consequence of the widespread adoption of an infant diet laced with sugar was the polar opposite of that envisaged by workhouse medical officers. Far from reducing the IMR within northern workhouses, Leeds for example would return infant mortality figures of 257/1000 in 1879–1883, which was significantly higher than the national average of 150/1000, and which was largely driven through a high incidence of atrophic wasting diseases.[76] These levels and causes of infant mortality point to the need to question the role of the workhouse diet as a direct cause of infant mortality.

Doctors did not, of course, set out to cause distress or harm to infants under their care. They were insistent that infants should not leave the lying-in ward until they were well enough, and they also forwarded details of the condition of infant inmates and their surroundings in both the lying-in ward and nurseries to *The Lancet* Commission and the *BMJ* throughout the latter half of the nineteenth century, both of which journals fought long campaigns to improve workhouse conditions for infants.[77] This policy however, was firmly opposed by Guardians and Poor Law Boards who sought to keep the Poor Rates to a minimum. They gave little financial support to

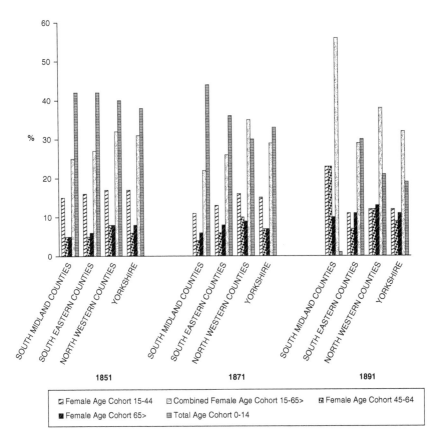

Figure 4.1   Female and child workhouse population for the years 1851, 1871 and 1891

improving the lot of infants, thereby thwarting the efforts of the medical profession.

Reducing the frequency of breast feeding meant that infants had to be fed workhouse pap by the bottle,[78] and this was done with a vessel called the 'bubby pot', invented by Dr Hugh Smith:[79]

> The pot is somewhat in form like an urn; it contains a little more than a quarter of a pint, its handle, and neck or spout, are not unlike those of a coffee pot, except that the neck of this arises from the very bottom of the pot and is very small; in short, it is on the same principle as those gravy-pots which separate the gravy from the oily fat. The end of the spout is a little raised, and forms a roundish knob, somewhat in appearance like a small heart; this is perforated by three or four small holes; a piece of fine rag is tied loosely over it, which serves the child to play with instead of the nipple, and through which by the infants sucking, the milk in constantly strained. The child is equally satisfied as it would be with the breast; it

never wets him in the least; he is obliged to labour for every drop he receives in the manner as when at the breast; and greatly in recommendation of this contrivance, the nurses confess it is more convenient than a boat, and that it saves a great deal of trouble in the feeding of an infant; which is the greatest security to parents, that their servants will use it, when they themselves are not present.[80]

This was a humane method of feeding as infants were fed with something which resembled their mothers' nipple.[81] When infants grew older, the 'bubby pot' enabled infants to feed themselves – which was vital for the survival of infants who had been separated from their mothers for whatever reason and fed by nurses who had little time to do it. However, the pot was a dangerous mechanism for feeding because although its rag was meant to act as a filter, it could at times allow small pieces of bread to flow into the infants' mouths, causing the youngsters to choke.[82] Thus bread, or 'solid food, when given to infants, became "bullets"',[83] endangering the lives of the young inmates. As a result, the 'bubby pot' was replaced by the 'Maw's feeding bottle' – more commonly known as the tube vessel.[84] This method was better for weaning infants as the thin tube allowed less bread to pass through. The feed bottle was placed into a dish on a ledge, and the tube was left to dangle down to the floor, from where infants could grab the tubing and suck.[85] It was also made in a smaller metal version, allowing the infants to use it in their cots. Dr Eustace Smith remarked during the 1860s that it was 'the best kind of bottle' for feeding infants, and the *BMJ* reported that it was commonly used in workhouses.[86] The tube method, therefore, enabled the youngsters to wean themselves, and eat some of the solid foods that would form their diet at a later stage.

For overstretched nurses, this feeding method was extremely useful. The WVS remarked, 'it was well that these infants were so capable of looking after themselves', when they saw 'an infant lying in a large bed...placidly sucking a tube feeding bottle'.[87] Although useful, the tube bottle was very difficult to clean, and a dirty bottle led to bacterial infection resulting in gastroenterital infections such as diarrhoea. Given this scenario, it is little wonder that rather than ameliorating the IMR within northern workhouses, the combination of cows' milk enriched with sugar, forced separation, and the substitution of breast milk with unsuitable 'pap' in dirty tube-feeding vessels had a detrimental impact on infant mortality rates within the northern workhouses – and all at the instigation of the medical officers. Equally importantly, although workhouse nurses fed infants, their role was just that – to feed the food prescribed by doctors, using the vessel provided. They were not involved in the make-up of the food, nor in the choice of bottle.

Conclusion

Pauper nurses have been much maligned, subjected to criticism for the feeding practices they used in northern workhouses during the latter half of the nineteenth century. The Leeds workhouse infant mortality stemmed from wide systemic failings: wasting diseases in the workhouse are a new key to the incidence and cause of infant mortality.

Believing that poor women's breast milk was of poor quality and nutritionally deficient, doctors set in train a course of dietary reform that imposed sugar as a compulsory supplement to infants' and mothers' diet, despite the dangers highlighted by Baker. This induced fatal wasting conditions in infants. Moreover, under pressure to address the high northern IMR, the 'logic' of nutritional reform led Guardians and medical officers to bring young women with children into the workhouse, so that their perceived nutritional failings could be brought under the control of the Poor Law and its modern nutritional practice.

The ideologically driven separation of mothers and infants meant that the result of medical and welfare policy was to expose infants to a harrowing death as they were fed a damaging mixture, usually from a dirty bottle.This practice absolves the pauper nurse from blame, as they were working under the assumption of the benefits of sugar relayed to them firstly by middle class women and secondly by workhouse doctors.

What this chapter demonstrates is that the scorn directed at pauper nurses was misplaced, and fails to take account of their position and actions in a wider hierarchy of responsibility. In providing context to the workhouse infant diet debate, we have seen the workhouse infant experience and its relationship to workhouse nurses more clearly. The book now explores the child care privided by day-carers and baby-minders.

5
Day-care and Baby-Minding

Continuing the theme of previous chapters on how infants fared at the hands of mother-surrogates, this chapter will visit the conventions of child care of working-class day-carers and baby-minders to identify the part they played in the high northern IMR. It will explore how day-carers and baby-minders looked after the infants they were paid to supervise and protect on a daily or weekly form. It will firstly address the historiography of the women employed in this occupation. Then, through individual case studies, it will investigate the relationship between carers and infants in Lancashire in particular (day-care was less common in Yorkshire, as mothers there could often take their infants to work with them). The discussion will then move on to consider in broad terms the practice of *loco-parentis*, examining its nature and characteristics in more detail to identify whether the actions of day-carers and baby-minders had a detrimental effect on the northern infant mortality rate.

'She asked me if I would nurse Lewis who was three weeks of age, I agreed for the sum of 5s per week'.[1]

In 1877, Lewis, the infant son of Jane Jones, was cared for by the baby-minder Isabella Mason, of Darwen, Lancashire, whilst his mother went to work. For working-class mothers like Jane Jones, the infant- and child-care services provided by self-employed, private child carers like Mason were essential. Dr E. J. Syson, a contemporary medically qualified observer, remarked that two-thirds of married mothers who worked in Lancashire's mills put their children out to nurse.[2] The demand for this service was enormous: women like Isabella, who would look after the infants of working women on a daily and weekly basis,[3] caring for them until the end of the working day (usually around 6–7pm[4]) were 'besieged with applications'.[5] The historian Elizabeth Roberts acknowledges the common practice of Lancashire married mothers turning to day-carers when needing to support their families through factory work through the nineteenth and early twentieth centuries.[6]

More recently, the historian David Bentley has also noted the importance of this child care and argued that the need for it was substantial in the north of England, and particularly in the Lancashire regions, during the latter half of the nineteenth century.[7] Isabella, and women like her were, therefore, a crucial element of the support of families like Jane's. This relationship also provided succour to Isabella, who earned money from minding to support her own family. Isabella was one of the numbers of women who, for reasons unknown to us, chose not to go out to work but to earn her living through child-minding. This was the 'critical' role Isabella defined for herself whilst she contributed to 'the management of the family budget'.[8] Mothers paid between 3s 6d and 5s per week for this service, easing the poverty of child-minders.[9] Should child-minders take in more children, perhaps up to three, this could provide a 'comfortable income'.[10] The women electing to look after babies, usually identified as 'day-nurses', tended to be elderly. They were typically under severe pressure; not only was their child care under scrutiny from the mothers of the infants they cared for, but also from medical men. This meant that the demands made on the values of the 'Angel in the house' were more acute for child carers than for other women. If they were to make a living out of this employment, securing their status as a reliable day-carer, they would have to draw on *all* of their mothering skills irrespective of the poverty they faced. The position of child carer during the latter half of the nineteenth century was arguably a lonely and isolated one. They had no 'body', either public or private, to lobby on their behalf. Nineteenth-century feminists such as Emma Paterson gave their support to working women who entered the public sphere, giving them licence to move away from their 'female status', for she wanted to bring these 'outdoor' working women into line with men, but this option was not available to child carers because to lose any of their feminine identity would have been detrimental to their work, pinned as it was to their maternal skills.[11] Margaret Hewitt questioned the maternal values of nineteenth-century Lancashire day-carers: she argued that they 'regarded day nursing as merely a potential source of income' and that acts of 'kindness' were rare.[12] However, Elizabeth Roberts characterises the women chosen to care for the infants of industrial mothers in Lancashire during the twentieth century as 'some reliable person',[13] and Jane Lewis informs us that nineteenth-century 'neighbourhood public opinion was intensely hostile to those suspected of cruelty to children'.[14] She records that in certain communities such as the East End of London, should infants be harmed the mothers' enmity was publicly displayed, 'strong-arm[ing]' the women concerned. They 'mobbed and hooted women accused of starving "farmed out" infants when they appeared in court, and extra police guards were sometimes required'.[15] Whilst this evidence may tend to allay fears about metropolitan child carers to some extent, we should investigate the northern experience during the latter half of the nineteenth century.

Contemporary medical men such as Dr E.J. Syson remarked that Manchester day-carers were in it for the money; that the infants given to nurse were mere tiny tots of two weeks of age, and the women who were asked to look after the babies were of a lower class than the mothers.[16] Not surprisingly, rhetoric such as this resulted in the day nurse often being seen as resembling the criminal character of the baby farmer. According to the historians David Bentley, Jim Hinks and Lionel Rose, and nineteenth-century social commentators William Charley, MP for Salford, Ernest Hart, Editor of the *British Medical Journal*, the medical man John Ikin, and the Reverend John Clay, the future for babies like Lewis was not bright. Contemporaries and historians alike labelled the thousands of Lancashire baby-minders as having the same criminal character as that of 'baby farmers' who disposed of the infants they were paid to care for. These premature deaths in turn impacted on the northern IMR.[17] The sense of moral panic over baby-minding fed the belief that neglect was common. Indeed, James Greenwood, the nineteenth-century journalist, lamented the evils of the practice and asked:

> Was there no remedy for [the modern and murderous institution known as baby farming]? Would it not be possible, at least, to issue licenses to baby-keepers as they are at present issued to cow-keepers? It may appear a brutal way of putting the matter, but it becomes less so when one considers how much at present the brutes have the best of it.[18]

The character of these day-carers was summed up in a *BMJ* article by Dr Reid and Mr Asquith which asserted that these women were responsible for the high infant mortality rates which existed in factory districts where young mothers had to rely on someone willing to care.[19]

Irrespective of the Commissioners finding little evidence of industrial mothers in Lancashire placing their infants out for 'lump sums', as with baby-farming, Dr E.J. Syson testified to the select committee that infants *were* vulnerable in day-care, and that 'a great number of them die[d]'[20] – 80–90 per cent of those aged under one year.[21] Contemporary commentators believed that infants like Lewis were as vulnerable when placed in day-care as they were with a baby farmer. Yet, little is known about the actual practices of Lancashire day-carers and it is now time to visit this topic to see whether and how they affected the high northern IMR. Before we do so, however, it is important to note that the child carer was a necessary form of child care support. As the 1851 census illustrates, 50 per cent of women in the prime of life, of whom many were mothers, were unsupported by a husband, leading to a vacuum in familial provision.[22] As the New Poor Law failed to address the economic problems which these women experienced, and as Lancashire mothers were unable to take their infants to work with them, many northern working-class women in waged work were obliged to turn to the private baby-minder.[23] For a fortunate few, support from the extended family was available: Michael Anderson has pointed us to the numbers of grandmothers in Lancashire who provided much-needed day-care help for their daughters in the factories.[24]

For single mothers engaged in waged work, the dilemma was acute. As Margaret Arnot notes, most mothers of illegitimate children could not care for their children at the same time as supporting themselves.[25] Consequently, these women had to turn to those who provided a 'minding' service, as without them, as Lionel Rose has argued, they ran the real risk of being sent to the workhouse, where independence was lost, separation ensured, and maternal care was handed over to institutional nurses.[26] Single women were extremely disadvantaged when it came to choosing who would care for their children whilst they worked because they could not approach anyone in receipt of 'welfare' (an outdoor Poor Law payment). Indeed, if it was known that such a person was caring for a 'bastard' child, their relief would be discontinued and they faced an accusation of aiding and abetting illegitimacy, or even prosecution for harbouring an illegitimate child.[27] Arguably, it was those in receipt of relief who needed the work the most, but nineteenth-century Poor Law legislation forbade it. Widows were likewise compelled to seek the services offered by 'baby-minders' when in need of child care support. Pat Thane notes that widowed women were often 'left to support children on their own', which led them to consider someone who would take on their infants as a 'welcome ally'.[28]

Clearly, baby-minders were an established part of the canon of child care arrangements available to, and utilised by, working-class women during the late nineteenth century and after.[29]

Despite the valuable service these arrangements provided to working women, medical journals persisted in characterising working-class carers as 'feckless, selfish and uncaring', holding to the belief that both the women who were employed as carers and the mothers who used their service were responsible for the many cases of infant death.[30] Indeed, the belief that the IMR was adversely affected by day-care led to the Infant Life Protection Acts of 1872 and 1897, which sought to regulate the practice and restrict the number of infants that day-carers could take on to just one.[31]

The emergence of new social history and second-wave feminism from the social and political movements of the 1960s and 1970s led to a critique of the existing historiography concerning infant mortality. Historians like Anna Davin challenged many of the negative assumptions which underpinned judgement of working-class women's maternal practices.[32] Noting the extent to which the high rates of infant mortality dominated the discourse of nineteenth-century public health officials and medicine, Davin persuades us that there was an increasing tendency for these commentators to lay the blame for the death or ill-health of infants at the working-class woman's door in her role as mother or child carer.[33]

In a similar vein, June Purvis notes that, in general, working-class child-minders were alleged to be a poor moral influence, and 'regularly dosed their infants with opiates'. However, she argues, such comments should not be taken out of context, as 'bland food and regular rest were necessary components of good child care'.[34] Elizabeth Roberts demonstrates that there is 'no evidence' whatsoever that child-minders neglected the children they cared for; rather, these Lancashire women were 'generally fond' of the children they minded during the day and that 'they brought [them] up in the same way as their mothers before them'.[35] Indeed, any 'neglect' of children meant that a carer would no longer be considered as reliable and the community they lived in would ostracise them.[36] For women who earned their living in this way, such rejection meant they lost their 'wage'. Awareness of any neglect spread amongst the factory mothers quickly, helping to prevent any future harm to other children. Of course not all minders were women; Mrs A11 in Margaret Llewelyn Davies' survey, which was conducted to identify the maternal problems posed to working-class mothers, entrusted the care of her ill child to her husband when she worked in the Yorkshire mills during the latter half of the nineteenth century.[37] This supports Ruth Homrighaus's view that child-rearing practices were more complex than we have been led to believe.

Despite this acknowledgement, much of the historiography concerning the baby-minder still paints her in an unpleasant and menacing hue. This lends weight to Margaret Arnot's claim that although much of the sensationalised rhetoric centred on 'one or two cases of neglect', this led to the vilification of 'whole groups of women'.[38] It is clear that there were northern day-care nurses who were guilty of neglect. Bentley cites the case of Sophie Todd of Manchester, who strangled a three-week-old infant in her care.[39] Likewise, Rose documents four cases of northern 'board-minding', including the Mancunian Francis Rogers, who was sentenced to 20 years imprisonment for her 'wilful negligence' of the infants in her charge.[40]

It is also clear that, for northern women, child care represented only one support alternative among many. Family support for child care was not uncommon: when the unmarried Mary Ann Addey gave birth in 1860, her father informed her that the family would help her with child care.[41] Neighbours would also support mothers who lived away from home and away from their kith and kin with an overnight baby-sitting service.[42] This ad-hoc form of baby-sitting was also needed on washdays, when babies were taken to a neighbour's house for a few hours whilst the washtub and mangle took over the mother's time.[43]

For daily or weekly care in the northern districts it was often a network of women who stepped in when baby-minding was needed. As the single mother named E.S. reported to Dr Theodore Dyke Acland at the Vaccination

Commission on 17 April 1892, when she required help to care for her new-born son after she gave birth to him on 25 September 1891 she found she could count on the support of many women around her.[44] Not only was help provided in the form of living accommodation but also in medical care when her child became ill. With no permanent fixed abode but a baby to care for, E.S. went to live at her boyfriend's father's house taking her baby with her. Two weeks later she left this home and approached a Mrs B for help who duly obliged to take him in. Three weeks after this, for reasons unknown, she approached a Mrs A.C. to care for the child whilst she worked. Although having several children herself (who took up a great deal of her time), Mrs A.C. agreed, at a price of 3s per week. The baby remained at Mrs A.C.'s house for around twelve weeks, being visited regularly by his mother until three weeks after 'Christmas'. During this time when the boy became ill with what Mrs A.C. suspected was 'bronchitis', she 'dressed it with oil, and put flannel shirts on and I used it the same as I should one of my own'. Mrs A.C. took on further responsibility on behalf of the baby in her care. Knowing that her brother's wife was taking her own infant to be vaccinated, she asked her 14-year-old daughter to take the baby along too. When complications arose with the vaccinated arm, Mrs A.C. washed the baby's arm 'well' remarking 'I washed it two or three times a day, every day for about a week'. I also put some Fuller's Earth on the arm after I had washed it'. I did this for a day or two. I did all this with the view of relieving the inflammation'.[45] When the boy's father visited his son at Mrs A.C.'s he found him ill, and in his desire for the infant to spend as much time with his mother as possible he sought out other accommodation, as Mrs A.C. did not have room for both the infant and his mother. New lodgings where infant and mother could come together were found at Mrs S's.[46] This case shows us that both carer and father were capable of tenderness to the boy and also that vaccinating infants seemed to be an important aspect of 'infant care'. Indeed, taking infants to be vaccinated seemed to be the done thing and was also practised in Salford when in 1892 Mrs B took a neighbour's child to be 'vaccinated' and 'also on the eighth day to be inspected'.[47] This was also the case for an infant female baby during the year 1888 who was taken for post-inoculation inspection by her neighbour.[48]

Whilst, as we can see, help was available for mothers in need of daily, weekly and even hourly care, some sought not to pursue these arrangements but to take a different path altogether. Indeed, the case of Catherine Holme reminds us of the options that were open to women with children when faced with the dilemma of balancing motherhood and waged work. As *The Leeds Mercury* of September 1860 reported under the headline 'Selling children near Rochdale', Holmes clearly decided that the most practicable way out of her predicament was to sell her child at the Whitworth Wakes; even 'bartering in order to secure the highest price':[49]

On Thursday she offered for sale what she said was her own child – a fine looking boy – at the public house called the Chapel Inn. She asked £1.00 for him. One of the company, a stone mason, said he only had 14s and 10½d which she accepted. The child appears to be about 11 months old. The woman left the place soon after she had effected the sale and had not been heard of since.[50]

When the empirical source base is widened it is even possible to use Assize cases to discern positive narratives of day-care in Lancashire.[51] The Assize holds records of mothers who committed infanticide, yet in reading these indictments they reveal that the women who provided the day-care and baby-minding service for these mothers prior to their infants' deaths were capable and responsible women, and that the infants in their care met their deaths only when they were *returned* to their mothers.[52]

As pointed out previously, when using Assize sources to investigate the character of day-care we have to be aware that they may present a skewed picture. The day-carers giving testimony would wish to present a positive image of the time and attention they gave to infants they were paid to take care of. They needed to present their case in the best possible light and pre- serve their maternal character, for any blemish would severely impact on their ability to earn their living this way. As we will see, any ambiguity regarding the circumstances of care they gave is resolved by the words of others, and we see the actual practice of their care coming alive.

This atypical evidence testifies to the ideas presented in Elizabeth Roberts's work, *A Woman's Place*, where she found effective and responsible baby- minding was revealed, in the twentieth century and where we see Rosanne Walker adhering to this child-minding ideal in the nineteenth century. Rosanne lived in Bolton in 1876 and was paid to take daily charge of the child of Ann Berry whilst Ann went to work at the cotton mill of Messrs. Cross and Winkworth. Both Rosanne and Ann seemed happy with their arrangement, and, according to neighbours, Rosanne and the infant 'were often seen walking out together'.[53] The case of Elizabeth Ingham, also pro- vides testimony to support the notion that child-minding was a positive support to mothers, built on reputation and trust. Elizabeth was employed to care for the child of her Lancashire neighbour Mary Ann Charnley, a fac- tory worker, in 1884. Charnley remarked to the Assize that she employed Elizabeth for 'over a year.'[54]

Elizabeth is an excellent example of a working-class woman who worked as a baby-minder and gave careful and considered care to the infants she looked after in her own home on a daily basis. It is likely that Elizabeth was chosen as she lived in the Billington area, which was local to Mary. Moreover, Elizabeth could be considered 'respectable' as she was married to James and by 1884 was well known to the waged female factory mothers who needed help with their children. The money Elizabeth earned from caring for infants went towards supporting her own family, which comprised four children: two sons aged nine and four, William and John, and two daughters aged two and 11 months, Emma and Isabella.[55] Elizabeth's character was probably regarded favourably in factory floor gossip when mothers discussed their child-care arrangements.

Indeed, the further example of Elizabeth Seddon and a Mrs Hughes indicates that northern carers provided a welcome haven for infants in the Lancashire of 1877 whilst their mothers worked. Mary Jones was the infant daughter of single mother Emily Jones, and she was well provided for by baby-minders Elizabeth Seddon and Mrs Hughes. A doctor stated in his deposition to the Lancashire Assizes that prior to Mary's strangulation at the hands of her mother, she had been 'well nourished' by Hughes.[56] The actions of the baby-minder Isabella Mason similarly challenge many of the assumptions that have accumulated around this mode of infant care. When Jane Jones, a single mother of two children, found herself desperately in need of a nurse for her three-week-old son Lewis in 1889 – because she was about to be married and her husband would not accept the responsibility of Lewis – she sought the assistance of Mason. The terms for his care were agreed at the cost of 5s per week, and, due to Jane's distant employment in Blackpool, she agreed to send Isabella her fee via the post.[57]

We have no direct evidence from Mason of the quality of care that was given to Lewis, but it is possible to deduce from the evidence and testimonies in the Assize Court records that he seems to have received good and compassionate care from her. Indeed, he appeared to flourish whilst under the care of Isabella, which Jane herself concurred with when she remarked that Lewis was given good care within a good home.[58] Moreover, he was also provided with plenty of clothes, which, as it was noted at the Assizes, were of excellent quality.[59] That he was provided with clothes at all from a baby-minder is worthy of remark; the northern women who cared for infants described in this chapter seem far removed from the felonious depictions of some historians and contemporaries.[60] Furthermore, when Lewis's mother 'began to fall off in her payments,'[61] Isabella took Lewis to Blackpool to his mother, only to be told that Jane 'dare not take him', because her husband refused to allow him in the house.

Rather than 'do away' with him, Mason remained compassionate and continued to care for him for a number of weeks whilst reminding Jane of her responsibilities. Although Jane owed Isabella a significant sum of money, Lewis did not perish whilst under the care of his nurse, but rather she remained an 'abiding' maternal 'presence' during his short life, and he only met his downfall when he was finally returned to his mother.[62]

What these cases indicate above all is that for some northern working mothers who needed child care, baby-minders were undoubtedly a 'welcome ally', enabling these women to maintain some economic independence.[63]

The importance of this 'beneficial' day-care was acknowledged in testimonies given by Commissioners who reported to the Select Committee on their findings on day-carers. For example, Dr E.J. Syson, although suspicious of day-carers, had to concede that they were known to the mothers who employed them as they were usually a neighbour. Moreover, as Dr Whitehead found during the 1870s in the northern districts, between the day-carers and mothers 'there is a feeling of kindness existing between neighbours... and it is partially done out of kindness and partially for a little addition to the general income of the family'.[64]

The relationship between mother and day-carer was strong; the day-carer often opened her home to the mother to come and feed the infant during the day so the child could take breast milk.[65] If not, the mother would provide the day-carers with a pint of milk for each child. The mother would be in constant contact with her day-carer as she would call on her way home from work each day to pick up her child.[66] Moreover, it was inferred by the Select Committee that the day-carers employed by the factory operatives were reliable and responsible and that the infants' Lancashire operative parents were a 'well to-do, well dressed cleanly people',[67] who would not place their infants with someone who did not come up to the mark. Familiarity with day-carers, and cleanliness, were extremely important to the Lancashire operatives. Indeed, despite Dr Whitehead running a charitable crèche whose charges were much less than the day-carers, the Lancashire operatives shunned his establishment, preferring to pay their neighbour. Dr Whitehead was astonished that they did so and was moved to declare to the Select Committee that his establishment was a moral and upstanding one.[68] However, when questioned by the Select Committee, who were most interested to find out why the Lancashire operatives chose a neighbour over Dr Whitehead's cheaper option, it was conceded that the crèche was 'three miles out of their way' and that the infants in his institution were 'riddled with vermin'.[69] Whilst acknowledging the spirit of philanthropy in which his nursery was established, the Select Committee put it to Dr Whitehead that perhaps the reason why factory operatives chose their neighbour over his institution was because they lived nearer, 'they had a dislike of vermin', knew better than him, and wanted to choose their own day-care and place their infants with people they knew and could rely on.[70] Crucially, it has to be considered that Dr Whitehead's nursery probably took in the infants that the day-carers rejected. Day-carers probably knew that to take in lice-ridden infants would jeopardise their reputation amongst factory mothers.

This Select Committee of 1871 revealed that William Farr had a clear understanding that the day-care service provided by neighbours of mill mothers in Lancashire was:

> a beneficial operation of infant nurseries in the districts where children of working women are taken in for a small charge. Particularly relative to the satisfactory working of some infant day nurseries in Manchester

and Salford – there is increasing confidence being shown by the people in these institutions. Children being well cared for at a moderate charge.'[71]

Indeed, without these responsible day-carers mothers were reduced to unmanageable circumstances, as the case of Ann Riley indicates. Ann was a single mother living in Bury in 1878, with a nine-month-old infant, and she was in economic difficulty. She approached her friend Mary Blackburn for help. Mary agreed to help Ann but needed the money there and then, unlike the baby-minders who could wait until the end of the week. On the second day Ann was unable to pay and was thrown out by Mary, who kept her bed and bed stock as payment for the previous night's lodging. In desperation Ann applied to the workhouse on three occasions for entry but the relieving officer rejected all of her requests – why is not known. In consequence Ann proceeded to commit infanticide.[72]

Beyond this modest though important reappraisal, it is possible to further contextualise and widen our understanding of the practice of baby-minding by closer examination of the court depositions themselves, bringing the Poor Law and baby-minders together in the fight against high infant mortality. For instance, the case of Isabella Mason contains details in her deposition statement which help us to place day-carers and baby-minders in a wider context. Although a private baby-minder, her testimony suggested she turned to the Poor Law for economic support when mothers reneged on their payments to her. When Jane Jones failed to forward payments for the care of Lewis, Mason informed her that she would in future have to send the money for his care 'to the workhouse'.[73]

The implication of her remarks is that as a baby-minder she had at least an informal understanding or arrangement with the local Poor Law Union. The non-payment of the arranged fee by Jane Jones seemingly compelled her to involve the Poor Law, which, we may surmise, would underwrite the costs incurred while she continued to care for Lewis, whom she considered to be a vulnerable infant, as an outdoor nurse.[74] Mason's action (and the actions of others like her, which will be discussed below) gives us reason to suspect that within the eyes of the Poor Law at least, baby-minders were not considered to represent a threat to infant well-being, but rather the reverse. Plainly, the idea that baby-minders were collectively viewed with suspicion during this period must be questioned.

Of course, the extent to which the Poor Law had any working relationship with baby-minders is difficult to ascertain. Alysa Levene for example argues that under the regime of the old Poor Law, 'outdoor nurses' were employed by the parish in order to address the problem posed by neglected and deserted infants; although she notes that 'the wages were often low, and it was generally practiced in restricted areas'.[75]

Although the numbers of these nurses may have been small throughout, advantages could be gained through their use to nurse infants in the home, and they were deployed by the Poor Law as 'state sponsored' baby-carers, accepting money for the care of infants and children who were not their own.[76] After the advent of the new Poor Law, inspired by Malthusian and utilitarian doctrines that argued against costly parochial responsibilities towards paupers, this nursing policy was supposedly frowned upon.[77] The new policy towards mothers needing surrogate child care was to oblige them to go into the workhouse with their children. The separation of the mother and infant would then ensue and the parish would provide care for infants through 'outdoor nurses'. Due to the high regard with which these nurses were held for their help to new mothers and vulnerable infants, as Dr Edward Smith testified, the practice continued, although on a reduced scale, well into the nineteenth century.[78] The change in policy is reflected in nineteenth-century overseer account books, which indicate that pensions – which often represented payment for nursing, either in the form of baby-minding or day-caring, undertaken on behalf of the Parish – declined markedly in areas like Bolton, Bradford, Leeds and Wakefield following the reforms of 1834.[79]

The diminished scale of outdoor nursing may be clear, but a close examination of the Poor Law records illustrates that the practice continued. The Wakefield Union minute books, for example, state that Clara Rogerson was in a working relationship with the Poor Law, receiving £23 from them whilst caring for a child which was clearly not her own.[80] Furthermore, the Wakefield Union minutes also record that 'Ann Brear, a person having the care of Sarah Ann Sampson's illegitimate child, states that on Monday next there will be an arrear of 16/- due to her from Sarah Ann Sampson in respect of the maintenance of such child.'[81] Rather than remaining aloof from 'private' maternal arrangements like these, Poor Law documentation illustrates that officials actively intervened in these cases, as the Wakefield minute books relates that 'the Clerk was to write to Ann' on this matter.[82] Dr Edward Smith comments on this child care practice in Helmsley, North Yorkshire, where infants were 'put out to nurse', although neither names nor numbers of the women who did this are noted.[83] Fanny Moses, who lived in Leeds in 1871, tells us that she was looking after Thomas Dyson, an illegitimate nursed child, but we do not know whether she was employed by the Poor Law to do so.[84]

We can be certain that the nurses in Helmsley were state-sponsored baby-minders.[85] These arrangements suggest that the Wakefield and Leeds Unions were dealing with outdoor nurses such as Clara and Ann in the same way that the Manchester Guardians appear to have dealt with Isabella Mason, who was quite clearly a baby-minder. Indeed, it is no wonder that Mason remarked on her relationship with the Poor Law for she was able to show the clear mark of respectability required by both Poor Law indoor and outdoor nurses. She was married to Henry who worked at the iron foundry and had four children herself.[86] It is likely, therefore, that Elizabeth Seddon was paid by the Poor Law when caring for Emily Jones: she enjoyed respectable married status, evidenced by having two children, being head of the household and an experienced carer of children. Elizabeth's reputation was intact after the death of Emily for, as recorded in the 1881 census, she continued to look after other children after Emily died, and was confident enough in her standing as a baby-minder to record that Mary Drury, was her 'nurse child' and lived with her.[87]

The working relationship of these nineteenth century outdoor nurses with the Poor Law appears to compare favourably with their eighteenth-century counterparts. Providing child care to mothers who needed it gave women like Ingham and Seddon a wage, although we do not know its exact level, and we see the Poor Law increasing its care of infants out of the workhouse, rather than reducing it, continuing with the age-old practice of using 'outdoor nurses' within its confines. Discussion of these quasi-professional relationships that tied these women to the Poor Law is new in the historiography of child care, and this study indicates that the women who performed child care, in all its guises, were accepted and respected within northern Unions. Given this, doubt must be cast on the attribution of the high IMR in the nineteenth-century north to these women and their child care practices. With the help of wages from the Poor Law, Mason was able to buy food, in addition to 'a hat, a frock, a petticoat, a shirt, a pair of socks and a pair of slippers' for Lewis.[88] This raises the important question as to how she was able to afford these items without alternative sources of income. It certainly seems that she and other carers were in receipt of money from the Poor Law for the services they performed, though her baby-minding occupation is merely implicit in the 1881 census. We can merely surmise as to the reason why she declined to register her job. If contractual relationships did indeed exist, then this raises the question as to what the rationale was behind this co-operation. One possibility may have been that contrary to the neglectful stereotype, these women were engaged in a form of 'policing' of maternal practices, which would imply that, as the Poor Law bankrolled them, they were considered to be part of the solution to the high IMR, rather than part of the problem. The neglect of children by some mothers in the north does not rule out this possibility. In Yorkshire for example, newspapers like *The Leeds Mercury*, *The Leeds Times* and *The Yorkshire Post,* and 1860s social commentators like Dr William Farr and John Ikin, relentlessly documented the negligent actions of mothers and posited a link between this behaviour and the IMR.[89]

Some northern mothers lacked time to pay sufficient attention to their infants, and their actions were reported on in the local press. *The Leeds Mercury*, for example, cited the case of Jane Todd, a neglectful mother who was serving a three-month prison sentence in Wakefield prison for deserting her infant. Her behaviour was far from uncommon: Rebecca Brown, Mary

Ann Murphy and Elizabeth Laycock were similarly detained in prison for desertion, whilst their infants were placed in the workhouse.[90] Indeed, the Bradford Poor Law Guardians noted that a total of 27 women had deserted their infants and children in the second half of 1857 alone.[91] The Bradford Union Administration and Discharge Book also records the names of the infants George Brown, Thomas Bradley, and Ellen Dossey, all deserted, and whose subsequent care would have been in the workhouse.[92]

Whilst not all neglected infants came under the jurisdiction of the New Poor Law, with the West Riding orphanage at Headingley Hill, Leeds, being an exception, the Poor Law remained responsible for the care of infants who were either born in the workhouse, were abandoned, or 'found'.[93] For example, when Elizabeth Laycock left her child alone in a house in Stirling Street, Bradford, Mr Wilson, the local relieving officer, stated that the infant had 'since been maintained in the workhouse at the charge of the township of Horton.'[94] As Crompton has argued, the New Poor Law was 'most assiduous in the care of these groups'.[95] Whether this was because Poor Law Unions were sensitive to the mortality rates that were published weekly in the northern press – which had the potential to reflect badly on their relief policy – is, of course, speculative. And whether this prompted northern Unions to attempt to check the IMR through the employment of baby-minders is equally speculative, but, as the case of the baby-minder Mary Hickman illustrates, this may have been a distinct possibility.[96]

Instructed by the Poor Law to oversee the delivery of the child of the unmarried Sarah Boadle, Hickman remarked that the Poor Law obliged her 'to nurse the infant of an unmarried mother' both during the confinement and afterwards.[97] These arrangements were not unusual, the Poor Law even underwriting boarding costs for outdoor nurses whilst they attended new mothers and their infants.[98] Whether the Poor Law authorities were concerned that Sarah would not care for her child, Maurice, as she had been accused of starving him, and sent Mary to care for him instead, is not known. What is known, however, is that when Mary left Sarah's house after giving Maurice, three weeks of what the court called 'due care and compassion', Sarah failed to feed Maurice, and three weeks later he was dead. Mary testified at the trial that Sarah neglected him. She said that 'Sarah would not feed the child' and that she 'did not seem to nurse him either' – and 'often found him valiantly sucking on an empty bottle' when she was *instructed* to *revisit* by the Poor Law.[99] Mary said the reason for this was that Sarah wished Maurice 'dead as he stood in the way of a marriage proposal',[100] and that her boyfriend wanted her to kill her child: 'He wants me to smother it, and then he will marry me', she said.[101]

The Poor Law's confidence in Mary Hickman and her services is evident. What is equally clear is that they deputised her to ensure the well-being of a child they had identified as being 'at risk'.[102] This suggests that the Poor Law Union considered Hickman to be a responsible and respectable carer, the court even noting her 'her high moral standing' when giving evidence against Sarah.[103] Mary Hickman was put to work to guard Sarah's infant, and her actions chime with women in London who were 'intensely hostile to those suspected of cruelty to children'. Indeed, the Poor Law were copying the model used by the NSPCC who used neighbours' testimony in prosecutions for cruelty.[104]

Due to the paucity of the archival record, it is difficult to quantify the extent of employment of baby-minders by the Poor Law in the north to negate the negligent tendencies of mothers. What is clear, however, is that the employment of third-parties like Mary Hickman and Isabella Mason to ensure the well-being of infants has a degree of historical precedent. Given the concern about infant mortality during the latter half of the nineteenth century, therefore, it is plausible that the baby-minder was a contemporary guise for a maternal strategy, entrenched for a considerable period, which sought to monitor and regulate maternal practice.[105]

It is clear that the employment of third parties to care for infants was not taken lightly by some Unions. For example, the Bradford Board of Guardians rigorously scrutinised the character of prospective infant carers, taking three weeks to decide whether George Stansfield's grandmother was respectable enough to nurse him at home.[106] Judith Wilcock's Uncle was subjected to the same vetting procedure by the Guardians before she was sent to live with him in Little Horton, Bradford.[107] These decisions appear to mirror the conclusions drawn by Steven King in respect of Bolton, where local dignitaries commented that Guardians seemed inclined to 'put out workhouse children into homes that were respectable'.[108] Hence, it was important for mothers like Isabella Mason, Elizabeth Ingham and Elizabeth Seddon to show they were married and had experience of child care, as evidenced by them having their own children. The implication behind the actions of the Poor Law Unions like Bolton is that they considered these 'surrogates' as worthy of patronage. This point may resolve in part the question posed by Steven King as to why 'Poor Law administrators might have been prone to favour a small stratum of their local poor above all the rest'.[109]

If this 'small stratum' comprised, at least in part, baby-minders, then this raises the issue of remuneration for services rendered. As we have seen, it was not unknown for Unions to provide financial assistance to these women, which in turn implies that a *value* was placed on their services. The case of Isabella Mason and others may suggest that part of this value was considered to rest in her active intervention on the maternal practices of the suspect poor, which in turn would positively feed into the IMR within the locality. Moreover, as most relief recipients were women whose opportunities to find and perform waged work were diminishing, placing infants into the hands of these trusted surrogate mothers served to deter neglect and infanticide, whilst also providing work to women who otherwise would have been idle.[110]

Clearly, the nature of these working relationships between baby-minders and the Poor Law has slipped under the radar of much existing historiography. This may be due to the complexity of developing a method of analysing these women, and also to the acceptance of the assumption held by Crompton and others that relief for infants and children was invariably provided within the workhouse. Once admitted to these institutions, children were extremely unlikely to get out.[111] This reading of Union policy is, however, overly reliant on the Admission and Discharge registers, which, as the example of Bradford clearly indicates, were neither accurate nor reliable. In particular, they distort the permeability of the workhouse. In the case of infants who lived in the workhouse, such as George Stansfield and Judith Wilcox, these registers do not record if, or when, they left the workhouse, although that there is good evidence that they did leave. This raises important questions in respect of the actual care arrangements for infants and children who were ostensibly confined within the workhouse. For if admission and discharge ledgers are no guide to residency, to what extent do they conceal the employment of surrogates within Unions?

This is a complex question that can only be addressed if Poor Law records are viewed in conjunction with other sources, such as those of the Assizes. This approach can shed important new light on the infant mortality. However, little record linkage of these sources has been undertaken. Although Pat Thane has argued that Poor Law material in particular has limited value in exploring women's issues during the nineteenth century, due to its focus on the problem of male poverty, it is clear that this opinion needs to be revised.[112] When used judiciously, and when woven with other sources such as the Assize court records, Poor Law material offers new insights and enables a more complex reading of the attitudes and actions of local relief administrations. In attempts to check the high IMR, the Poor Law was adept in exploiting the maternal alternatives offered by carers of infants and children.[113]

Conclusion

In addressing a regional dimension of the child care debate, it has been possible to argue that some of the customs and practices of northern carers reveal interesting and complex dynamics – a contrast to David Bentley and Lionel Rose's wholly critical account of the actions of women who conducted these services. Far from displaying criminal intent, they paid attention to the children placed in their care and bought them clothes. Their policing efforts indicate a professionalism in child care hitherto unnoticed by historians.

Moreover, through an innovative methodology of record linkage it is possible to place this professionalism firmly within the context of the Poor Law itself. This may well have represented a continuation of practices that were commonplace during the eighteenth century, but it is significant that provision of outdoor nurses was evident beyond the application of the New Poor Law in 1834. The sources suggest that professional carers were actively co-opted by the northern Unions named in this chapter in order to arrest excesses of maternal neglect and abandonment, and the impact of these on the IMR. Given this, it is clear that the responsible and respected carers of children noted in this chapter were not characteristic of the stereotype peddled in the contemporary media, and repeated within historical accounts. Far from being responsible for the high northern IMR, the child carers described in this chapter represented a positive and pragmatic response to the problems posed by maternal neglect. The criminal, cruel stereotype advanced by historians such as David Bentley and Lionel Rose is ill-fitted to these cases, a misleading rendition of the northern experience.

Conclusion

In the early years of the twentieth century, Margaret MacMillan expressed her concern over the high levels of infant mortality:

> It is still enormous – 120,000 die every year in this country. The great majority of these little victims, belong, of course to the poorer class. It is not hard to live, even if one is a weakly baby, when all the resources of wealth, and love, and modern science are at command. But if a weakly baby is born to a working-class mother, he cannot in many instances command even her services, and the chances of life and health are very doubtful indeed.[1]

Her call for working-class infants to access and reap the benefits from scientific medicine was misguided given the failures of this discipline during the nineteenth century to reduce death rates. The hope invested in scientific medicine and public health initiatives was not restricted to contemporary analysis, for, as we have seen, historians today reiterate the belief that science and medicine might have improved the northern IMR during the latter half of the nineteenth century were it not for the failings of northern working-class mothers.

Clearly, working-class mothers were not collectively an embodiment of the contemporary conception of the 'Angel in the House', yet this book has shown that working-class infants could 'command the services of their mothers' and the factory did not require their work, especially in Leeds, to drive a wedge between them and their mothers. These women exercised their 'right' to take their infants to work with them and carried out their maternal duty throughout industrialisation and played a significant role in ensuring that their working conditions and practices minimised the impact that waged work had on their infants. They were responsible and hardworking and did not lose sight of their maternal obligations but adopted new methods of child care to ensure their infants were not victims of their waged work, using their value as workers as leverage. Should their needs be neglected, it was well known that these valuable workers would 'go elsewhere', leaving mill owners to employ men, who worked more slowly and were less likely to undertake the domestic duties necessary to keep the factory clean. The mothers adapted the factory, turning it into a domestic environment where they could combine waged work with breast feeding and child care, thus bringing down the high northern IMR. What did lead to factory mothers' infants incurring diarrhoeal infections was the cleaning-out of the factory privy. In refusing to purchase water closets, factory owners left their female workers with no option but to undertake this insanitary task and in doing so rendering themselves and their infants susceptible to bacterial infection and disease.

Maternal elements however were but one constituent of the care provided to infants during the period. The workhouse nurse stood *in loco parentis*, and provided nursing care on a daily basis to the numerous infants both born into and brought into northern workhouses. Whilst they did on occasion act with violence and negligence, as the case of Catherine Levers at the Tadcaster workhouse illustrates, the important threats to infants were the unclean and inadequate workhouse facilities. Louisa Twining and the WVS she inspired recognised this. Despite the shortcomings of workhouse nurses their actions did little to raise the rate of infant mortality within the workhouse: their service was considered to be 'excellent' – a significant verdict given the onerous work and real time constraints they laboured under.

Equally benign was the role that the nurses played in the infants' diet in workhouses. Nutritional orthodoxy and the forced maternal separation which arose due to the prevailing philosophy of the period meant that working-class mothers' breast feeding capabilities were questioned and mothers' milk was replaced by dangerous artificially sweetened 'pap'. The rationale for this arose from the majority medical opinion that working-class mothers and their breast milk were ill equipped to feed their infants. Robert Baker was a lone voice arguing against the incorrect medical nutritional policy which supported the feeding of artificial foods, and the onward march of the high IMR was attributed to the failings of working-class women as the debilitating and deadly infantile diarrhoea and associated wasting conditions continued to take their toll.

Under instruction by doctors, workhouse nurses had no choice in administering this dangerous food, in unsterile feeding bottles which contributed to the demise of many infants, a fact easily derivable from an analysis of infant mortality in the Leeds Union workhouse. Indeed, such was the number of infants who came into the workhouse during the latter half of the nineteenth century, these feeding practices significantly increased the northern IMR.

The motive in employing day-carers in the Lancashire regions was to ensure factory mothers could earn a full-time wage. These day-carers took their roles seriously and worked *with* mothers to ensure that the infants in their care flourished. Carers were not aloof in dealings with either infant or mother, but opened their doors to ensure maternal contact with the mothers was maintained.

When day-care is placed in a broader context, as the rare sources from the Assize Court testify, important nuances appear which challenge the prevailing historical orthodoxies of child care in all its guises. The practice of day-care and baby-minding was a responsive and rational response to the needs of mothers for help in caring for their children and when dealing with the difficulties of remarriage. Indeed, the testimony from the day-carers themselves, and from doctors, reveal that these surrogates were not akin to the murderous baby-farmer stereotype propagated in the nineteenth century. Moreover, the Poor Law acknowledged the usefulness of these women's skills and developed working relationships with them, which indicates that even to contemporary eyes, the day-carer was considered to be a useful ally in providing maternal care for infants at risk or separated from their mothers. Day-carers, in the northern cases in this book at least, operated with the sanction of the Poor Law, and were a factor acting to reduce the high infant mortality rate.

In the main, working mothers in the north had their infants with them whilst at work in the fields, in the metal and salt industries, in brickyards and in the factories. They even had them sat on buffets in the corner of the room the mothers were working in if they went out washing. It is clear that surrogates were on hand to act as an effective safety net when working women had to leave their infants.

In using a wide source base, eschewing the Registrar General's material which has hitherto provided the core material base, this book challenges the deep-seated suspicions, held and expressed by nineteenth-century contemporaries and historians alike, regarding incompetent and neglectful modes of maternal and institutional care as the prime cause of the high northern IMR. It has shown that working-class mothers did care for their infants and went to extraordinary lengths to do so. This has only been made possible through the means of a thorough re-examination of the issues based on a wide evidential base which has been overlooked by many other historical accounts of IMR.

Whilst mothers cannot be entirely absolved from responsibility, it is nevertheless beyond doubt that women *collectively*, and the modes of care they employed, were not the weak link in the chain of culpability constructed by social commentators. Rather, it was a flawed medical and political class which drove up the northern IMR rates as they attempted, without success, to reduce the depressingly high levels of infant mortality experienced throughout northern industrial England during the latter half of the nineteenth century.

This book makes clear that should blame be apportioned for the high levels of infant mortality in the north during the period, then it is towards the well-meaning but misguided medical establishment and penny-pinching factory owners who refused to provide their workers with clean sanitation that we should now look. Informed by a biologically deterministic mentalité, the policies imposed by the medical men ensured that infants were separated from their mothers and condemned to be fed sweetened pap. As Edward Smith's diet sheets illustrate, this proved to be the fate of an innumerable number of infants consigned to the workhouse. In this light, it is clear that the high IMR of the nineteenth-century north was not a consequence of the uncultured maternal social world of working-class women, but was attributable to the hubris of the medical profession, whose 'wise words' and claims of paediatric knowledge were almost universally accepted.

Working class mothers were able to effectively combine waged work with child care, providing infants with breast milk by using their wit and innovation and, in doing so, hold down the northern IMR. For working mothers themselves, combining waged work with child care were two sides of the same coin. They understood the importance of the maternal bond to infant life, and they found ways to maintain the link whilst they contributed towards the family economy. The importance of infants being with their mothers was also understood by the manufacturers who accommodated them. This philosophy was also applied by surrogates, who adhered to this model in opening their doors at lunch-time to defeat the separation of mother and child, and called women from work when their infants needed breast milk. Working-class mothers, with the help of manufacturers and surrogates, lost little sight of the infants they were supposed to have neglected and harmed. Rather, they applied robust, pragmatic judgement, hence putting a brake on infant mortality.

In this respect, when working class women worked in the public sphere, took their infants with them to ensure their safety, and earned money to contribute to their family's economy then they displayed an independence and public responsibility hitherto unknown to us. Work and child care were entwined, and infant safety could be ensured. Thus, middle-class men and women were right to acknowledge the independence of working class women and wrong to malign them through their rhetoric and ill-informed evidence, wrong to enforce legislation to limit their working hours, and wrong latterly to strip mothers of the right to have their infants at work with them. This philosophy and ideology made it ever more difficult for women to work in the public sphere, hence inducing the poverty of both mother and infant. Yet, despite this hostile environment, working-class women through the latter half of the nineteenth century used their class and gender milieux to adapt their child care models to industrialised society. Their serious, responsive, effective and innovative efforts made them saviours of infant life.

Appendixes

165

Appendix 1: Female Workhouse Cohort for Years 1851, 1871 and 1891.

Female Age Cohort 15–44(%)

1851   1871   1891

Appendix 2: Length of stay, in days, for women inmates at Leeds Union Workhouse, for the half-year ended September 1875.

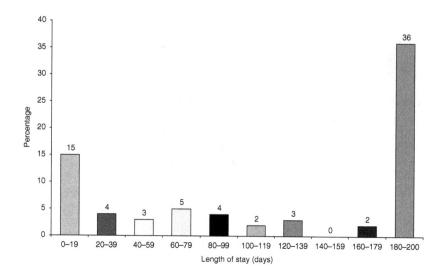

Appendix 3: Manchester Training Nurses Mid Nineteenth Century

Appendix 4: Letter to the Leeds Poor Law Board

To the overseers of the poor of the Township of Leeds, within the Leeds Union, in the County of York;-

And to all others whom it may concern.

Schedule

Whereas the Poor Law board caused an Inquiry to be made on certain days in the month of October last, by Henry Longley Esq., Poor Law Inspector, respecting the validity of the last Election of Guardians of the Poor for the West Ward of the Township of Leeds, within the Leeds union, in the County of York.

And whereas certain Witnesses, whose names are herein-after set forth, having been duly summoned, attended before the said Inspector upon such Inquiry, and did not travel more than ten miles from the said Township of Leeds, which Township, in the opinion of us, the Poor Law Board, was interested in such attendance,

Now therefore, We, the Poor Law Board, in pursuance of The powers given in and by the Statutes in that behalf made And provided, order you, the overseers of the Poor of the said Township of Leeds, to pay to the said Witnesses so attending The said Inquiry the amounts set opposites to their respective Names in the following Schedule, which We deem to be the Reasonable expenses of such Witnesses.

Example of women who attended the Board of Guardians and their expenses:

Hannah Sheard, spinster and weaver, - 2/.

Ellen Botterill, a lodging house keeper, - 3/6.

Ellen Broadley, a widow and dress maker, - 3/6

Mary Dodds, dress maker, - 3/6.

Mary Earl, widow and cloth boiler, - 2/

Sarah Glendenning, wife of Edward Glendenning, - 5/6 for both her and him

Hannah Goldthorpe, wife of James Goldthorpe, - 8/6 for both him and her.

Source: MH12/15042, p. 573/4 976 E/71.

Notes

Introduction

1. R. Woods and N. Shelton, (1997) *An Atlas* of *Victorian Mortality* (Liverpool: Liverpool University Press), pp. 47 and 51. This theory was based on the work of R.I. Woods, P.A. Watterson and J.H. Woodward, (1988) 'The Causes of Rapid Infant Mortality Decline in England and Wales, 1861–1921' Parts I and II, *Population Studies*, 42, pp. 43, 113–32 and 343–66, and N. Williams and C. Galley, (1995) 'Urban Differentials in Infant Mortality in Victorian England', *Population Studies*, 49, pp. 401–20. The recent work of Emma Griffin and Keith Morgan recognises these high rates. See E. Griffin, (2010) *A Short History of the British Industrial Revolution* (Basingstoke: Palgrave Macmillan), p. 160 and K. Morgan, (2004) *The Birth of Industrial Britain: Social Change 1750–1850* (Harlow: Pearson Longman), p. 27.
2. R. Woods and N. Shelton, (1997) *An Atlas*, pp. 49–51 and 60.
3. R. Woods and N. Shelton, (1997) *An Atlas*, p. 51.
4. J. Ikin, (1865) 'Abstract from a Paper on the Undue Mortality of Infants and Children in Connection with the Question of Early Marriages, Drugging Children, Bad Nursing, Death Clubs and Certificates of Death', *Transactions of the National Association for the Promotion of Social Science 1864* (NAPSS) (Leeds), p. 22. Ikin's research focused on anatomy and physiology. As the above quote illustrates although there are recognised differences between nineteenth-century mills and factories, the former being the forerunner of the factory which used mainly male labour and the latter which increasingly used women's, the evidence used in this work suggests that the terms were interchangeable and contemporaries used the word 'mill' to describe 'factory' during 1850–1899. This work reflects this dynamic. See also for example *The Bee Hive* 9 March 1872 which cited groups of 'mill girls' in Leeds factories and the *Leeds Evening Express* 18 March 1872 which discussed Leeds female factory workers. Cited in S.O. Rose, (1992) *Limited Livelihoods: Gender and Class in Nineteenth-Century England* (London: Routledge), p. 69 fns. 88 and 89. For an example of working environments prior to the factory in the West Riding see P. Hudson, (1983) 'From Manor to Mill: the West Riding in Transition', in M. Berg, P. Hudson and M. Sonenscher, (1983) *Manufacture in Towns and Cities Before the Factory* (Cambridge: Cambridge University Press).
5. R. Woods, (2006) 'Newman's Infant Mortality as an Agenda for Research', in E. Garrett, C. Galley, N. Shelton and R. Woods, (2006) (eds.) *Infant Mortality: A Continuing Social Problem* (Aldershot: Ashgate), pp. 18–33. See also E. Garrett, C. Galley, N. Shelton and R. Woods (2006) (eds.) in E. Garrett et al. 'Infant Mortality', pp. 4, 10, 27, 33–49, (esp. p. 38) p. 186 and 191–212 and R. Woods, et al., 'The Causes': Part II, pp. 113–32, particularly p. 115.
6. E. Griffin, (2010) *A Short History*, p. 160 and K. Morgan, (2004) *The Birth*, p. 27.
7. R. Woods and N. Shelton, *An Atlas*, pp. 51 and 47–51.
8. N. Williams and G. Mooney, (1994) 'Infant Mortality in an Age of Great Cities, London and the English Provincial Cities Compared c. 1840–1910', *Continuity*

and Change, 2, p. 191 and R. Woods and N. Shelton, *An Atlas*, pp. 48–51. See also S. Szreter and G. Mooney, (1998) 'Urbanization, Mortality and the Standard of Living Debate: New Estimates of the Expectancy of Life at Birth in Nineteenth Century British Cities', *Economic History Review*, 51, pp. 84–112.

9. R. Woods and N. Shelton, (1997) *An Atlas*, passim. Of course rural areas are important and a recent study from Pamela Birch has contributed to this under-researched area. See P. Birch, (1998) 'Factors in the Structure and Decline of Infant Mortality in the Ampthill Sub District of Bedfordshire 1873–1900'. Unpublished, B. Phil, Open University.

10. S. King and G. Timmins, (2001) *Making Sense of the Industrial Revolution; English Economy and Society 1700–1850* (Manchester: Manchester University Press), pp. 216–17.

11. P. Hudson, (1998) *Regions and Industries: a Perspective on the Industrial Revolution in Britain* (Cambridge: Cambridge University Press), p. 19; S. King and G. Timmins, (2001) *The Making*, p. 36.

12. R. Baker and W. Jevons, (1872) 'Report of the Inspector of Factories', Robert Baker's testimony, *PP* 1872 XVI, p. 89.

13. E. Griffin, (2010) *A Short History*, p. 83.

14. J. Langton and R.J. Morris, (1986) (ed.) *An Atlas of Industrializing Britain, 1780–1914* (London: Methuen), pp. 10 and 17.

15. P. Hudson, (1998) *Regions and Industries*, p. 19. For the Lancashire cotton regions see G. Timmins, (1998) *Made in Lancashire; a History of Regional Industrialisation* (Manchester: Manchester University Press) who argues that although the area experienced peaks and troughs in essence the cotton industry rose 'profoundly' from the eighteenth century onwards and that it was a key staple of the industrial revolution. For the population of towns and cities see J. Langton and R.J. Morris, *An Atlas*, p. 165.

16. See the works of Millward and Bell, and R. Woods.

17. A. Briggs, (1999) *A Social History of England* (Harmondsworth: Penguin), C. Lawrence, (1994) *Medicine in the Making of Modern Britain, 1700–1920* (London: Routledge); R. Porter, (1995) *Disease, Medicine and Society in England, 1550–1860*, (Cambridge: Cambridge University Press) and B. Harris, (2004) 'Public Health, Nutrition, and the Decline of Mortality: the McKeown Book Revisited', *Social History of Medicine*, 17, pp. 379–407.

18. E. Griffin, (2010) *A Short History*, p. 161.

19. For a general overview see H.-J. Voth, (2004) 'Living Standards and the Urban Environment', in R. Floud and P. Johnson (eds.) *Cambridge Economic History of Britain*, (Cambridge: Cambridge University Press). Among the optimists are T.S. Ashton, (1962) *The Industrial Revolution 1760–1830* (London: Oxford University Press), R.M. Hartwell, (1967) *The Causes of the Industrial Revolution in England* (London: Methuen); P. Deane and W.A. Cole, (1993) *British Economic Growth, 1688–1959: Trends and Structure* (Aldershot: Gregg Revivals); P.H. Lindert and J.G. Williamson, (1982) 'Re-visiting England's Social Tables, 1688–1812' *Explorations in Economic History*, 19, pp. 385–804. For pessimists see A. Toynbee, (1969) *The Industrial Revolution, 1852–1883* (Newton Abbott: David & Charles); S. and B. Webb, (1926) *Industrial Democracy* 2 vols. (London: Longmans Green & Co.); J.L. and B. Hammond, (1995) *The Skilled Labourer* (Abingdon: Fraser Stewart); E. Hobsbawm, (1957) 'The British Standard of Living, 1750–1850', *Economic History Review*, 10, pp. 46–48; E.P. Thompson, (1980) *The Making of the English Working Class* (Harmondsworth: Penguin); C. Feinstein (1998)

'Pessimism Perpetuated: Real Wages and the Standard of Living, During and After the Industrial Revolution', *Journal of Economic History* 58, pp. 625–658.

20. E. Griffin, (2010) *A Short History*, p. 146.

21. T. McKeown, (1976) *The Modern Rise of Population* (London: Edward Arnold), p. 52.

22. R. Millward and F. Bell, (2001) 'Infant Mortality in Victorian Britain: the Mother as Medium', *Economic History Review*, 54, p. 729 and S. Guha, (1994) 'The Importance of Social Intervention in England's Mortality Decline: the Evidence Reviewed', *Social History of Medicine*, 7, p. 113.

23. T.S. Ashton, (1969) 'Standard of Life', in P. Deane and W.A. Cole, *British Economic Growth: Trends and Structure 1688–1959* (Cambridge: Cambridge University Press), p. 27 and P.H. Lindert and J.G Williamson, (1983) 'English Workers' Living Standards During the Industrial Revolution: A New Look', *Economic History Review*, 36, pp. 1–25.

24. S. Szreter, (1988) 'The Importance of Social Intervention in Britain's Mortality Decline c.1850–1914', *Social History of Medicine*, 1, p. 31.

25. C. Feinstein, (1998) 'Pessimism Perpetuated: Real Wages and the Standard of Living, during and after the Industrial Revolution', *Journal of Economic History*, 58, pp. 625–658; S. and B. Webb, (1898) *Industrial Democracy*; E. Hobsbawm, (1957) 'The British Standard of Living 1750–1850', *Economic History Review*, 10, pp. 46–48; and E.P. Thompson, (1980) *The Making of the English Working Class* (Harmondsworth: Penguin).

26. E. Griffin, (2010) *A Short History*, p. 161 and K. Morgan, (2004) *The Birth*, pp. 33 and 111.

27. A. Wohl, (1983) *Endangered Lives*, p. 12.

28. P. Huck, (1995) 'Infant Mortality and Living Standards of English Workers during the Industrial Revolution', *Journal of Economic History*, 55, pp. 528–550.

29. T. McKeown, (1976) *The Modern Rise of Population* (London: Edward Arnold), p. 52.

30. Quoted by William Farr in A. Wohl, (1983) *Endangered Lives*, p. 18.

31. W. Farr, (1865) *Report on the Questions Submitted by Dr. Farr to the Council, Concerning the Classification of Epidemic Diseases to the Royal Society of Medicine* (London).

32. K. Morgan, (2004) *The Birth*, p. 27, F. Cartwright and M. Biddiss, (1972) *Disease and History*, (London: Hard Davis), p. 116; C. Creighton, (1965) *A History of Epidemics in Britain* (London: Cass) passim, and A. Hardy, (1993) *Epidemic Streets; Infectious Disease and the Rise of Preventative Medicine, 1856–1900* (Oxford: Oxford University Press), p. 3.

33. R. Woods and N. Shelton, (1997) *An Atlas*, p. 47.

34. R. Woods, and N. Shelton, (1997) *An Atlas*, p. 53.

35. For a detailed overview of the emergence of scientific medicine, refer to R. Porter, (1998) T*he Greatest Benefit to Mankind* (London: Fontana) chapter XI and especially p. 306.

36. R. Porter, (2001) *Bodies Politic, Disease, Death and Doctors in Britain, 1650–1900* (London: Reaktion), p. 31.

37. R. Porter, (2001) *Bodies Politic*, p. 31.

38. R. Porter, (2001) *Bodies Politic*, p. 31. My emphasis.

39. I. Loudon, (1992) 'Medical Practitioners 1750–1850 and Medical Reform in England', in A. Wear, (ed.) *Medicine in Society* (Cambridge: Cambridge University Press), p. 246. My emphasis.

40. A. Hardy, (1993) 'Lyon Playfair and the Idea of Progress', in D. Porter and R. Porter, (1993) (eds.) *Doctors, Politics and Society, Historical Essays* (Amsterdam: Rodopi), pp. 81–2.
41. See B.W. Richardson, (1876) *Hygeia, a City of Health*, in D. Porter and R. Porter, (1993) *Doctors, Politics*, p. 4.
42. D. Porter and R. Porter, (1993) *Doctors, Politics*, pp. 2–4.
43. A. Hardy, (1993) 'Lyon Playfair', p. 82.
44. A. Hardy, (1993) 'Lyon Playfair', p. 82.
45. A. Hardy, (1993) 'Lyon Playfair', p. 82.
46. I. Loudon, (1992) *Medical Practitioners*, p. 3.
47. D. Porter and R. Porter, (1993) *Doctors, Politics*, p. 6 and A. Digby, (1994) *Making a Medical Living* (Cambridge: Cambridge University Press), p. 2.
48. R. Woods and N. Shelton, (1997) *An Atlas*, p. 53; M. Hewitt, (1958) *Victorian Wives and Mothers in Victorian Industry* (London: Rockcliff), p. 146 and E. Garrett, et al., (2006) *Infant Mortality*, pp. 40 and 121.
49. A. Digby, (1994) *Making*, preface page and p. 254.
50. See Fildes' work for the vast array of eighteenth-century paediatric texts: V. Fildes, (1986) *Breasts, Bottles and Babies* (Edinburgh: Edinburgh University Press), pp. 445–49 and R. Hodgkinson, (1967) *The Origins of the National Health Service* (London: The Wellcome Historical Medical Library), p. xv.
51. S. and B. Webb, *English Poor Law History: Part II, The Last Hundred Years* (London: Cass), p. 310–311 and A. Digby, (1994) *Making*, preface page and p. 244.
52. M.W. Flinn, (1976) 'Medical Services under the New Poor Law', in D. Fraser, (ed.) *The New Poor Law in the Nineteenth Century* (London: Macmillan), p. 5.
53. R. Hodgkinson, (1967) *The Origins*, p. xvi.
54. R. Hodgkinson, (1967) *The Origins*, p. 497, and M. Rose, (1971) *The English Poor Law* (Newton Abbott: David & Charles), p. 171.
55. Dr. Eustace Smith, (1868) *The Wasting Diseases of Infants and Children* (London), p. 33.
56. W.R. Lee, (1964) 'Robert Baker': 'The First Doctor in the Factory Department Part I, 1803–1858, Part I 1803–1858 and Part II 1858 Onwards', *British Journal of Industrial Medicine*, 21, pp. 85–177. See also Herr R. Meyer, *Robert Baker, C.B., R.C.S., 1803–1880* Special Collections, f.1, in the Brotherton Library at Leeds University. This special collection was compiled by Herr. R. Meyer and was offered to the library as a gift to the Library by him. Unfortunately this publication bears no publishing date or few page numbers, however the same article has been reproduced in *British Journal of Industrial Medicine*, 1964, 21, pp. 85–93 and R. Baker, (1867) *No'butt and Never'head: A Lecture to Yorkshire Factory Girls* (Leeds).
57. R. Porter, (2001) *Bodies Politic*, p. 3; R. Porter, (1996) *Cambridge Illustrated, History of Medicine* (Cambridge: Cambridge University Press), p. 177 and R. Porter, (1987) *Disease, Medicine*, p. 63.
58. A. Hardy, (1993) *The Epidemic Streets*, pp. 3 and 21–2, F.F. Cartwright and M. Biddiss, (1972) *Disease and History*, p. 63. For the causes of death in infancy in urban and rural towns see R. Woods and N. Shelton, *An Atlas*, pp. 54 and 73. See also S. Guha, (1994) 'The Importance', p. 110 for a similar argument that diarrhoea was the biggest cause of the infant death during the latter part of the nineteenth century.
59. E. Chadwick, (1860) 'Address on Public Health', *National Association for the Promotion of Social Science*, hence forth *NAPSS*, (London), p. 580. See also K. Morgan, (2004) *The Birth*, pp. 27–9.

60. S. Halliday, (1999) *The Great Stink of London: Sir Joseph Bazalgette and the Cleansing of the Victorian Capital* (Stroud: Sutton).
61. C. Hamlin, (1998) *Public Health and Social Justice in the Age of Chadwick: Britain 1800–1854* (Cambridge: Cambridge University Press), pp. 8–9. Hamlin argues that public health measures were never meant to improve the IMR, but Chadwick clearly sees them as purpose for an amelioration of it.
62. F.F. Cartwright and M. Biddiss, (1972) *Disease and History*, p. 119.
63. A. Wohl, (1983) *Endangered Lives*, p. 81.
64. A. Wohl, (1983) *Endangered Lives*, p. 87.
65. F. Bedarida, (1970) 'Cities: Population and the Urban Explosion', in A. Briggs, *The Nineteenth Century, The Contradiction of Progress* (London: Thames and Hudson), p. 128–129; A. Briggs, (1959) *The Age of Improvement, 1783–1867* (London), p. 41 and R. Woods et al. (1989) 'The Causes', p. 113.
66. K. Morgan, (2004) *The Birth*, p. 29.
67. N. Morgan, (2002) 'Infant Mortality, Flies and Horses in Later-Nineteenth-Century Towns: a Case Study of Preston', *Continuity and Change*, 17, (2002), p. 100.
68. N. Morgan, (2002) 'Infant Mortality, Flies and Horses', pp. 97–130.
69. N. Williams, (1992) 'Death in its Season, Class, Environment and the Mortality of Infants in Nineteenth-century Sheffield', *Social History of Medicine*, 5 (1992) p. 85.
70. N. Williams, (1992) 'Death in its Season', pp. 77, 89 and 91.
71. T. McKeown, (1976) *The Modern,* passim.
72. R. Woods and N. Shelton, (1997) *An Atlas*, pp. 56 and 145.
73. S. Guha, (1994) 'The Importance', p. 109.
74. A. Hardy, (2001) *Epidemic Streets*, p. 3 and R. Woods and N. Shelton, (1997) *An Atlas*, p. 54.
75. I. Buchanan, (1995) 'Infant Feeding, Sanitation and Diarrhoea in Colliery Communities 1880–1991', in J. Oddy and D. Millar, (1995) *Diet and Health in Modern Britain* (London: Croom Helm), pp. 162 and 171.
76. A. Wohl, (1983) *Endangered Lives*, pp. 4–6 and 340–41.
77. S. King and G. Timmins, (2001) *Making Sense*, pp. 216–17.
78. R. Woods and N. Shelton, (1997) *An Atlas*, passim. Of course rural areas are important and a recent study from Pamela Birch has contributed to this under-researched area. See P. Birch, (1998) 'Factors in the Structure'.
79. A. Wohl, (1983) *Endangered Lives*, pp. 4–6 and 340.
80. R. Woods et al., (1997) *An Atlas*, pp. 33, 51 and 60.
81. R. Millward and F. Bell, (2001) 'Infant Mortality', p. 701.
82. E. Roberts, (1994) *A Woman's Place: An Oral History of Working Class Women 1890–1940* (Oxford: Basil Blackwell), p. 165.
83. P. Ford and G. Ford, (1956) *A Guide to Parliamentary Papers: What They Are: How To Find Them: How To Use Them* (Oxford: Basil Blackwell), p. 36 and P. Thompson (2000) *The Voice of the Past: Oral History*, (Oxford: Oxford University Press), p. 118.
84. G. Ford and P. Ford, *A Guide*, p. 40 and P. Thompson, (2000) *The Voice*, p. 118.
85. P. Thompson, (2000) *The Voice*, p. 118 and G. Ford, and P. Ford, *A Guide*, pp. 34–6.
86. G. Ford and P. Ford, *A Guide*, p. 35.
87. P. Thompson, (2000) *The Voice*, p. 126.
88. G. Ford and P. Ford, (1959) *A Guide*, p. 40.

89. P. Thompson, (2000) *The Voice*, pp. 126–7.
90. P. Thompson, (2000) *The Voice*, p. 126.
91. P. Thompson, (2000) *The Voice*, p. 39.
92. P. Thompson, (2000) *The Voice*, p. 127.
93. P. Thompson, (2000) *The Voice*, p. 124.
94. P. Thompson, (2000) *The Voice*, p. 123.
95. G Ford and P. Ford, (1959) *A Guide*, p. 36; P. Thompson, (2000) *The Voice*, p. 118.
96. P. Thompson, (2000) *The Voice*, p. 120.
97. E. Higgs, (1987) *History Workshop Journal*, 23, pp. 59–80 and particularly pp. 60–70 and M. Anderson, (2007) 'What Can the Mid-Victorian Censuses Tell Us About Variations in Married Women's Employment?', in N. Goose, *Women's Work in Industrial England: Regional and Local Perspectives* (Hatfield: Local Population Studies), pp. 182–208.
98. E. Roberts quoted in M. Anderson, (2007) 'What Can', p. 185.
99. Margaret Llewelyn Davies, (1915, new edition 1978) *Maternity: Letters from Working Women* (London: Virago), Letters 13, 46, 53, 83, 135 and 138.
100. Letter 26.
101. Letter 152.
102. Letter 44.
103. Letter 61.
104. http://blogs.warwick.ac.uk/angeladavis/ Here Angela Davis uses Llewelyn Davies's letters to fuel a discussion about 'pregnancy, antenatal care (or lack of it), birth and motherhood in Edwardian Britain'.
105. For an insight into the life and character of Margaret Llewelyn Davies see G. Scott, (1998) *Feminism and the Politics of Working Women* (University College London: London) and more pertinently, B. Blaszac, *The Matriarchs of England's Cooperative Movement, A Study in Gender Politics and Female Leadership, 1883–1921* (Westport: Greenwood Press), p. 126.
106. B. Blaszac, *The Matriarchs*, p. 126.
107. B. Blaszac, *The Matriarchs*, p. 116.
108. B. Blaszac, *The Matriarchs*, p. 116.
109. C. Black, (1983) (ed.) *Married Women's Work* (London: Virago), p. v, (First Published in 1915).
110. B.L. Hutchins, (1907) *Home, Work and Sweating, the Causes and the Remedies* (London: Fabian Society) and B.L. Hutchins, (1911) *The Working Life of Women* (London: Fabian Society).
111. C. Black, (1983) *Married Women's Work*, p. ii and iv.
112. C. Black, (1983) *Married Women's Work*, pp. 254–7.
113. B.L. Hutchins and E. Harrison, (1903) *A History of Factory Legislation* (Westminster: British Law: Trades and Crafts), pp. 47 and 52.
114. B.L. Hutchins, (1983) 'Yorkshire', in *Married Women's Work*, p. 146. Mother A 11.
115. L. Delap, (2007) *The Feminist Avant Garde* (Cambridge: Cambridge University Press), p. 111.
116. 1897 c8609–c.8615. To the final Reports of the Royal Commission on Vaccination in the Areas of Dewsbury, (1891–2) London (1892–3), Warrington (1892–3), Leicester (1892–3), Gloucester (1895–6), Glasgow, Liverpool, Salford, Manchester, Oldham, Chadderton, Leeds, Sheffield, Halifax and Bradford (1892–3), with c. 8615 being the final written report.
117. K.J. Carpenter, (1991) 'Edward Smith (1819–1874)', *Journal of Nutrition*, 121, pp. 1515–21.

118. K.J. Carpenter, (1991) 'Edward Smith', pp. 1515–21.
119. K.J. Carpenter, (1991) 'Edward Smith', pp. 1515–21.

1 The Scholarship on Working-class Women's Work and their Child Care Models

1. E. Higgs, (1987) 'Women, Occupations and Work in the Nineteenth-century Censuses', *History Workshop Journal*, 23, pp. 59–80, S. O. Rose, (1992) *Limited Livelihoods: Gender and Class in Nineteenth-century England* (London: Routledge), pp. 79–82; S. Horrell and J. Humphries, (1995) 'Women's Labour Force Participation Rates and the Transition to the Male Breadwinner Family, 1790–1865', *Economic History Review*, 48, pp. 89–117 and S. Horrell and J. Humphries, (1992) 'Old Questions, New Data, and Alternative Perspectives: Families' Living Standards during the Industrial Revolution', *Journal of Economic History*, 52, p. 850; M. Anderson, (2007) 'What Can the Mid-Victorian Census tell us about Variations in Married Women's Employment' in N. Goose, (ed.) *Women's Work in Industrial England: Regional and Local Perspectives* (Hatfield: Local Population Studies), pp. 182–208.
2. S. Horrell and J. Humphries, (1992) 'Old Questions', pp. 849–80.
3. S. Steinbach, (2005) *Women in England: A Social History, 1790–1914* (London: Weidenfeld and Nicolson), p. 9.
4. S. Steinbach, (2005) *Women in England*, p. 9.
5. S. O Rose, (1992) *Limited Livelihoods*, p. 76.
6. C. Malone, (2003) *Women's Bodies and Dangerous Trades in England 1880–1914* (London: Boydell Press), p. 15.
7. C. Malone, (2003) *Women's Bodies*, p. 15.
8. C. Malone, (2003) *Women's Bodies*, p. 15.
9. S. D'Cruze, (2000) 'Women and the Family', in J. Purvis, (2000) *Women's History, Britain 1850–1945: an Introduction* (London: Routledge), p. 52.
10. A. Clark, (1995) *The Struggle for the Breeches* (London: Rivers Oram Press), p. 1.
11. A. Vickery, (2009) *Behind Closed Doors: At Home in Georgian England* (London: Yale University Press), p. 291. Vickery notes 'subaltern form existed.'
12. C. Malone, (2003) *Women's Bodies*, p. 1.
13. C. Malone, (2003) *Women's Bodies*, p. 140.
14. A. Shepherd and G. Walker, (2008) 'Gender, Change and Periodization' *Gender and History*, 20, pp. 453–62.
15. P. Ayers, (1990) 'The Hidden Economy of Dockland Families: Liverpool in the 1930s', in P. Hudson and W.R. Lee, (eds.) *Women's Work in the Family Economy in Historical Perspective* (Manchester: Manchester University Press), p. 280. In J. Purvis, (2000) *Women's History*, p. 79. Pat Ayers conducted taped interviews of the wives of Liverpool Dockworkers during 1981 and 1987 to identify their spending between the wars. This quote is from a woman known as interview no. 42 who was born in 1898.
16. E. Chalus and F. Montgomery, (2005) 'Women and Politics', in H. Barker, (eds.) *Women's History Britain 1700–1850: An Introduction* (Abingdon: Routledge), p. 217.
17. G. Holloway, (2005) *Women and Work in Britain Since 1840* (London: Routledge), pp. 229–35.
18. B. Hill, (1994) *Women, Work and Sexual Politics in Eighteenth Century England* (Oxford: Basil Blackwell), p. 263.

19. H. Barker, (2005) (eds.) 'Women and Work' in H. Barker and E. Chalus, (ed.) (2005) *Women's History*, p. 142.
20. H. Barker, (2005) (eds.) 'Women and Work', p. 142. For an insight into how 'protection' has led to women being considered 'shadowy bystanders' of the economic participation of waged work see A. Shepherd, (2015) 'Crediting Women in the Early English Economy', *History Workshop Journal*, February, p. 2 viz: http://hwj.oxfordjournals.org/content/early/2015/02/18/hwj.dbv002.full.pdf
21. M. Freifeld, (1986) 'Technological Change and the Self-acting Mule: a Study of Skill and the Sexual Division of Labour', *Social History*, 11, pp. 337–9.
22. M. Reynolds, (2006) 'A Man Who Won't Back a Woman is No Man at All: the 1875 Heavy Woollen Dispute and the Narrative of Women's Trade Unionism', *Labour History Review*, 71, pp. 187–98.
23. G. Holloway, (2005) *Women and Work*, p. 109.
24. C. Malone, (2003) *Women's Bodies*, p. 21.
25. C. Malone, (2003) *Women's Bodies*, *passim*.
26. CASW, 4 April, 1891, in C. Malone, (2003) *Women's Bodies*.
27. C. Malone, (2003) *Women's Bodies*, p. 3.
28. C. Malone, (2003) *Women's Bodies*, p. 140.
29. A. Davin, (1978) 'Imperialism and Motherhood: Population and Power', *History Workshop Journal*, 5, pp. 9–65.
30. S. Steinbach, (2005) *Women In England, A Social History, 1790–1914* (London: Phoenix) pp. 12 and 23.
31. G. Holloway, (2005) *Women and Work*, p. 228.
32. E. Ewan, (1990) *Town Life in Fourteenth Century Scotland* (Edinburgh: Edinburgh University Press), J. Bennett, (1996) *Ale, Brew and Brewsters in England; Women's Changing World 1300–1600* (Oxford: Oxford University Press), p. 3; J. Burnette, (2008) *Gender Work and Wages in Industrial Revolution Britain* (Cambridge: Cambridge University Press), p. 286. For the wide ranging economic strategies of women who lived in the sixteenth Century to the twentieth see Beatrice Moring's edited version. B. M Moring, (2012) (ed.) *Female Economic Strategies in the Modern World* (London: Pickering & Chatto).
33. E. Ewan, (1990) *Town Life*; J. Bennett, (1996) *Ale, Brew and Brewsters*, p. 3. See also B. Moring, (2012) (ed.) *Female Economic Strategies*, *passim*.
34. K. E. Lacey, (2008) 'Women and Work in the Fourteenth and Fifteenth Century in London' in L. Charles and L. Duffin (eds.) *Women and Work in Pre-Industrial England*, p. 51, in J. Burnette, (2008) *Gender Work and Wages*, p. 286.
35. H. Barker, (2005) (eds.) *Women's History*, p. 135–6.
36. C. Steedman, (2009) *Lost Labours, Domestic Service and the Making of Modern England* (Cambridge: Cambridge University Press), T. Meldrum, (2000), *Domestic Service and Gender, 1660–1750, Life and Work in the London Household* (Harlow: Pearson) and L. Schwartz, (1990) 'English Servants and their Employers in the Eighteenth and Nineteenth Centuries', *Economic History Review*, 52, pp. 236–256.
37. B. Hill, (1994), *Women, Work*, p. 147.
38. C. Steedman, (2002) 'The World of Labour', in C. Jones and D. Wahrman (2002) *The Age of Cultural Revolutions in France, 1750–1820* (London: University of California Press), p. 127. L. Schwartz (1996) 'English Servants', pp. 236–56.
39. H. Barker, (2005) (eds.) *Women's History*, p. 124 and C. Steedman, 'The World of Labour', in C. Jones and D. Wahrman (2002) *The Age*, p. 127.
40. J. Burnette, (2008) *Gender, Work*, p. 57–8.

41. J. Burnette, (2008) *Gender, Work*, p. 58.
42. J. Burnette, (2008) *Gender, Work*, p. 58.
43. 'And which was originally inaugurated in 1785' C. Steedman, (2009) *Lost Labours*, pp. 37,70,115, and 130.
44. J. Bailey, (2012) *Parenting in England, 1760–1830* (Oxford: Oxford University Press), p. 22, E. Foyster, and J. Marten, (2010) *A Cultural History of Childhood and Family in the Age of Enlightenment* (Oxford: Oxford University Press) and H. Berry and E. Foyster, (2007) *The Family in Early Modern England* (Cambridge: Cambridge University Press).
45. A. Vickery, (1998) *The Gentleman's Daughter, Women's Lives in Georgian England* (New Haven, London: Yale University Press), p. 110.
46. A. Walker, (1787), *A Complete Guide for a Servant Maid, or the sure means of Gaining Love and Esteem* (London: T. Sabine), in C. Steedman, (2009) *Lost Labours*, p. 229.
47. C. Steedman, (2009) *Lost Labours*, p. 233.
48. C. Steedman, (2009) *Lost Labours*, pp. 235–6 and 238.
49. H. Barker, (2005) (eds.) *Women's History*, p. 131–2.
50. N. McKendrick, (1974) 'Home Demand and Economic Growth: a New View of the Role Women and Children in the Industrial Revolution,' in N. McKendrick (ed.), *Historical Perspectives, Studies in English Thought and Society* (London: Europa), pp. 152–210.
51. K. Gleadle, (2001) *British Women in the Nineteenth Century* (Basingstoke: Palgrave) p. 100 in S. Steinbach, (2005) *Women In England*, p. 23.
52. I. Pinchbeck, (1930) *Women Workers and the Industrial Revolution* (London: Routledge), M. Berg, (1994) *The Age of Manufactures: 1700–1820, Industry, Innovation and work in Britain* (London Routledge); M. Berg, (1993) 'What Difference did Women's Work Make in the Industrial Revolution', *History Workshop Journal*, 35, pp. 22–44 and P. Hudson, (1992) *The Industrial Revolution* (New York: Routledge), p. 162; P. Sharpe, (1998) *Women's Work*; K. Honeyman, (2000) *Women, Gender and Industrialisation in England, 1700–1870* (Basingstoke: Palgrave Macmillan) and K. Gleadle, (2001) *British Women*.
53. P. Hudson, (1992) *The Industrial Revolution* (New York: Routledge), p. 163.
54. M. Berg, (1994) *The Age*, M. Berg, (1993) 'What Difference', and P. Hudson, (1992) *The Industrial Revolution*.
55. K. Honeyman, (2000) *Women, Gender*.
56. N. Goose, (ed.) (2007) *Women's Work*.
57. T. Meldrum, (2000) *Domestic Service and Gender*, S. Todd, (2014) *The People: The Rise and Fall of the Working Class 1910 – 2010* (London: John Murray), p. 128
58. B. Hill, (1994) *Women, Work*, p. 71.
59. B. Didsbury, (1977) 'Cheshire Saltworkers', Plates 15–19 in R. Samuel (1977) (ed.) *Miners, Quarrymen and Saltworkers* (Routledge and Kegan Paul: London), and p. 155.
60. B. Didsbury, (1977) 'Cheshire Saltworkers', p. 154, *Miners, Quarrymen and Saltworkers*.
61. B. Didsbury, (1977) 'Cheshire Saltworkers', p. 154–5 *Miners, Quarrymen and Saltworkers*.
62. B. Didsbury, (1977) 'Cheshire Saltworkers', p. 154–5 *Miners, Quarrymen and Saltworkers*, p. 155.
63. B. Hill, (1994) *Women, Work*, p. 71.
64. B. Hill, (1994) *Women, Work*, p. 3, J. Stanley, and B. Griffiths (1990) *For Love and Shillings, Wandsworth Women's Working Lives* (London: History Workshop),

p. 9 and N. Verdon, (2002) *Rural Women Workers in Nineteenth Century England: Gender, Work and Wages* (Woodbridge: Boydell).

65. An advert in the *Battersea Borough News* Advertisement, 1916 in J. Stanley and B. Griffiths, (1990) *For Love and Shillings*, p. 9.
66. H. Barker (2005) (eds.) *Women's History*, p. 127.
67. A. Kussmaul quoted in B. Hill, (1994) *Women, Work*, p. 71, fn. 8. See also A. Kussmaul, *Servants in Husbandry in Early Modern England* (Cambridge: Cambridge University Press), p. 4.
68. B. Hill, (1994) *Women, Work*, pp. 73–4.
69. B. Hill, (1994) *Women, Work*, p. 71, and A. Kussmaul, (1981) 'The Ambiguous Mobility of Farm Servants', *Economic History Review*, 342, pp. 222–35.
70. D. Valenze, (1991) 'The Art of Women and the Business of Men, Women's Work and the Dairy Industry c 1740–1840', *Past and Present*, 130, p. 153.
71. A. Kussmaul, (1981) *Servants in Husbandry*. For the full gamut of female apprenticeships, and the changes and continuities in the work of husbandry, and what Snell entitled women of the 'Labouring Poor,' actually lost and gained as a consequence of enclosure, in addition to their standard of living see K. Snell, (1985) *Annals of the Labouring Poor: Social Change and Agrarian England, 1600–1900* (Cambridge: Cambridge University Press).
72. K.D.M. Snell, (1985) *Annals*, p. 279.
73. K.D.M. Snell, (1985) *Annals*, p. 279.
74. J. Humphries, (1990) 'Enclosures: Common Rights and Women: The Proletarianization of Families in the Late Eighteenth and Early Nineteenth Centuries', *The Journal of Economic History*, 50, p. 18. For the discussion of enclosure see J. D Chambers, (1953), 'Enclosure and the Labour Supply in Industrial England', *Economic History Review*, 5, pp. 319–43 and G.E. Mingay, (1968), *Enclosure and the small farmer in the Age of the Industrial Revolution* (London: Macmillan). Both old but still enormously valuable.
75. J. Humphries, (1990) 'Enclosures', pp. 23–4.
76. A. Everitt, (1999) (ed.) '"Farm Labourers"', in Thirsk, *Agrarian History*, pp. 396–465 in J. Humphries, (1990) 'Enclosures', p. 32.
77. B. Hill, (1994) *Women, Work*, p. 255.
78. J. Burnette, (2008) *Gender, Work* p. 285.
79. B. Hill, (1994) *Women, Work*, pp. 253–5.
80. T. Evans, (2005) 'Women, Marriage and Family', in H. Barker (2005) (eds.) *Women's History*, p. 66 and B. Hill, (1994) *Women, Work*, p. 241.
81. P. Laslett, (1972) 'Mean Household Size in England Since the Sixteenth Century', in P. Laslett, and R. Wall, (1972) *Household and Family in Past Time* (Cambridge: Cambridge University Press), pp. 77–8.
82. J. Burnette, (2008) *Gender, Work*, p. 77.
83. J. Humphries, (1990) 'Enclosures', p. 38. For a discussion of the straw plain industries see N. Goose, (ed.) (2007), *Women's Work in Industrial England, Regional and Local Perspectives* (Hatfield: Local Population Studies).
84. H. Barker, (2005) (eds.) *Women's History*, p. 132.
85. J. Purvis, (2000) (ed.) *Women's History*, p. 27.
86. P. Sharpe, (2000) 'Population and Society 1700–1840', in P. Clark, (2000) (eds.) *Cambridge History of Britain: II, 1540–1840* (Cambridge: Cambridge University Press), in H. Barker, (2005) (ed.) *Women's History*, p. 132
87. S. Berger, (2006) (ed.) *A Companion to Nineteenth Century Europe: 1789–1914* (Oxford: Basil Blackwell), p. xix

88. M. Anderson (2007) 'Marriage Patterns', and K.DM. Snell, (1985) *Annals.*
89. N. Goose, (2008), 'Cottage Industry, Migration, and Marriage in Nineteenth Century England' *Economic History Review*, 61, p. 799 and R. Woods, (2000) *Demography.*
90. My research into the textile areas of the West Riding shows this.
91. G. Koot, http://www1.umassd.edu/ir/resources/standardofliving/thestandardo flivingdebate.pdf and chapter 9 from E. Griffin, (2010) *A Short History of the Industrial Revolution* (Basingstoke: Palgrave, Macmillan)
92. J. Burnette, (2008) *Gender, Work*, p. 62–3.
93. J. Burnette, (2008) *Gender, Work*, pp. 229–30.
94. A. John, (1984) *By The Sweat of their Brow: Women Workers at Victorian Coal Mines* (London: Routledge & Kegan Paul), pp. 55–8.
95. J. Burnette, (2008) *Gender, Work*, pp. 229–30.
96. J. Burnette, (2008) *Gender, Work*, p. 63, A. John, *By the Sweat*, p. 40.
97. H. Barker, (2005) (eds.) *Women's History*, pp. 130–31.
98. R. Shoemaker, (1998) *Gender in English Society, 1650–1850: The Emergence of Separate Spheres?* (London: Longman), in H. Barker (2005) (eds.) *Women's History*, pp. 130–31.
99. A. John, (1984) *By the Sweat*, p. 20.
100. A. John, (1984) *By the Sweat*, p. 20.
101. A. John, (1984) *By the Sweat*, p. 230.
102. A. John, (1980) *By the Sweat*, p. 230.
103. C. Malone, (2003) *Women's Bodies.*
104. C. Malone, (2003) *Women's Bodies*, p. 34.
105. C. Malone, (2003) *Women's Bodies*, pp. 34–5.
106. C. Malone, (2003) *Women's Bodies*, p. 50.
107. C. Malone, (2003) *Women's Bodies*, p. 52.
108. C. Malone, (2003) *Women's Bodies*, p. 36. See also Richard Wall's discussion of widows in R. Wall, 'Widows, Family and Poor Relief in England from the Sixteenth to Twentieth Century' in B. Moring, (2012) (ed.) *Female Economic Strategies.*
109. S. O. Rose, (1992) *Limited Livelihoods*, p. 43
110. T. McIntosh, (2012) *A Social History of Maternity and Childbirth: Key Themes in Maternity Care* (London Routledge), L. Whaley, (2011) *Women and the Practice of Medical Care in Early Modern Europe 1400–1800* (Basingstoke: Palgrave Macmillan); L. Cody, (2005) *Birthing the Nation, Sex Science and the Conception of Eighteenth Century Britons* (Oxford: Oxford University Press); J. Grundy, (2003) *History's Midwives: Including a 17c and 18c Yorkshire Midwives Nomination Index* (Lancashire: Federation of Family History Societies); B. Ehrenreich and D. English, (2010) *Witches, Midwives and Nurses: A History of Women Healers* (New York: Feminist Press); J. Worth, (2002) *Call the Midwife* (Twickenham: Merton); D. Evenden, (2000) *The Midwives of Seventeenth Century London*, (Cambridge: Cambridge University Press); P. Allan and Moya Jolley, (ed.) (1982) *Nursing, Midwifery and Health Visiting Since 1900* (London: Faber and Faber); H. Marland, (1997) *Midwives, Society and Childbirth: Debates and Controversies in the Modern Period* (London: Routledge); H. Marland, (1993) *The Art of Midwifery: Early Modern Midwives in Europe* (London: Routledge); N. Leap and B. Hunter, (1993) *The Midwives Tale: An Oral History from Handywoman to Professional Midwife* (London: Scarlet Press); M. Chamberlain, (1981) *Old Wives' Tales: their History, Remedies and Spells* (London: Virago); O. Davies, (2003) *Cunning Folk, Popular Magic in English*

History (London: Hambledon and London); J. Hinks, (2014) 'The Representation of 'Baby Farmers' in the Scottish City, 1867–1908', *Women's History Review*, 23, pp. 560–76.

111. R. Richardson, (2013) 'The Art of Medicine: A Dismal Prospect: Workhouse Health Care', *The Lancet*, 6 July, pp. 20–21 and R. Richardson, (2001) 'From the Medical Museum', 22 December, p. 2144.

112. F. Crompton, (1997) *Workhouse Children: Infant and Child Paupers Under the Worcestershire Poor Law, 1780–1871* (Sutton: Stroud), chapters two and five and P. Allan and M. Jolley, (ed.) (1982) *Nursing, Midwifery and Health Visiting since 1900* (London: Faber and Faber).

113. E. Roberts, (1984) *A Woman's Place: An Oral History of Working Class Women, 1890–1940* (Oxford: Basil Blackwell), pp. 143–4.

114. M. Arnot, (1994) 'Infant Death Child Care and the State: the Baby Farming Scandal and the First Infant Life Legislation Act of 1872', *Continuity and Change*, 9, pp. 271–311, D. Grey, (2009) 'More Ignorant and Stupid than Wilfully Cruel: Homicide Trials and Baby Farming in England and Wales In the Wake of the 1908 Children's Act', *Crimes and Misdemeanours*, 2, pp. 60–77; L. Rose, (1986) *Massacre of the Innocents: Infanticide in Britain 1800–1939* (London: Routledge and Kegan Paul) and J. Hinks, (2014) 'The Representation'; S. Swain, (2014) 'The Baby Farmers: A Chilling Tale of Missing Babies, Shameful Secrets and Murder in 19c Australia', *Journal of Australian Studies*, 38, pp. 259–61 and S. Swain, (2012) 'Towards a Social Geography of Baby Farming', *The History of the Family*, 10, pp. 151–9.

115. S. Williams, ' "Caring for the sick poor" ": Poor Law Nurses in Bedfordshire, c. 1700–1834', in P. Lane, N. Raven, and K.D.M. Snell, (2004) (eds.) *Women, Work and Wages in England, 1600–1850* (Woodbridge: Boydell), in J. Burnette, (2008) *Gender, Work*, p. 60. For an up to date discussion about English urban midwifery in the latter half of the nineteenth century see F.J. Badger, (2014) 'Illuminating nineteenth century English Urban Midwifery: the Register of a Coventry Midwife', in *Women's History Review*, 23, pp. 683–705.

116. S. Williams, "Caring for the Sick Poor", in J. Burnette, (2008) *Gender, Work*, p. 60.

117. L. Abrams, (2012) 'The Story of the Bottle of Medicine,' *History Workshop Journal*, 73, pp. 95–117.

118. S. Steinbach, (2005) *Women In England*, p. 9

119. J. Burnette, (2008) *Gender, Work*, p. 71.

120. J. Burnette, (2008) *Gender, Work*, p. 19.

121. S.O. Rose, (1992) *Limited Livelihoods*, G. Holloway, (2005) *Women and Work*, p. 23; Patricia Hollis argues that at least 600,000 women were involved in needlework and dressmaking. S. Steinbach, (2005) *Women In England*, p. 29–34.

122. S. Steinbach, (2005) *Women in England*, pp. 32–3.

123. S. Steinbach, (2005) *Women in England*, pp. 31–4 and fn. 43 – quoted in the *Unknown Mayhew*, 149–51.

124. For works on prostitution see for example, H. Barker, (2005) (eds.) *Women's History*, p. 136; T. Henderson, (1999) *Disorderly Women in Eighteenth Century London: Prostitution and Control in the Metropolis* (London: Longman); J. R Walkowitz, (1980) *Prostitution and Victorian Society: Women, Class and the State* (Cambridge: Cambridge University Press); M. Mason, (1994) *The Making of Victorian Sexuality* (Oxford : Oxford University Press).

125. Sir John Sinclair, (1794) A Statistical Account of Scotland, Volume 13, p. 424, quoted in D. Simonton, (1998) *A History of European Women's Work* (London: Routledge), p. 126.

126. A. Sparks, (1978) *A Woman's Work* (London: Centreprise Trust Ltd.), p. 20.
127. A. Sparks, (1978) *A Woman's Work*, p. 4.
128. J. Stanley, (1990) *For Love and Shillings*, p. 11.
129. G. Halloway, (2005) *Women and Work*, p. 165.
130. G. Halloway, (2005) *Women and Work*, p. 165
131. S. Todd, (2014) *The People*, p. 127.
132. G. Halloway, (2005) *Women and Work*, p. 167.
133. G. Halloway, (2005) *Women and Work*, p. 194.
134. G. Halloway, (2005) *Women and Work*, p. 198.
135. G. Halloway, (2005) *Women and Work*, p. 203.
136. G. Joseph, (1983) *Women at Work, the British Experience* (Oxford: Phillip Allan). Quoted in J. Lewis, (1992), *Women in Britain Since 1945, Women, Family Work and the State in the Post-war Years* (Oxford: Basil Blackwell) p. 66 in G. Halloway, (2005), *Women and Work*, p. 208.
137. G. Halloway, (2005) *Women and Work*, p. 209.
138. G. Halloway, (2005) *Women and Work*, p. 210.
139. H. Barker, (2005) (eds.) *Women in Britain*, p. 125.
140. B. Hill, (1994) *Women, Work*, p. 256
141. S. O Rose, (1992) *Limited Livelihoods*, p. 76
142. T. Evans, (2005) *Unfortunate Objects, Lone Mothers in Eighteenth-Century London* (Basingstoke: Palgrave Macmillan), p. 3.
143. T. Evans, (2005), *Unfortunate*, pp. 173–202.
144. A. Levene, T. Nutt and S. Williams, (eds.), (2005) *Illegitimacy in Britain, 1700–1920* (Basingstoke: Palgrave Macmillan), p. 34 and T. Evans, (2005) *Unfortunate*, p. 98.
145. C. Steedman, (2007) *Master and Servant* (Cambridge: Cambridge University Press).
146. My emphasis.
147. C. Steedman, (2007) *Master and Servant*, p. 132. Steedman agues this is with regard to servants in husbandry only, but as we see cases of it in urban London, it is arguable that this may have been pertinent to most servants. Francis Const. (1793) 'An Act for Supplying some Defects in the Laws for the Relief of the Poor of this Kingdom'. Francis Const, *Decisions of the Court of the King's Bench, Upon the Laws Relating to the Poor, Originally Published by Edmund Bott Esq., of the Inner Temple, Barrister at Law. Revised ......by Francis Const Esq., of the Middle Temple*, 3rd edn. 2 vols. (London: Whieldon and Butterworth), vol. II pp. 516–18, in C. Steedman, (2007) *Master and Servant*, p. 133.
148. E. Griffin, (2012) 'A Conundrum Resolved? Rethinking Courtship, Marriage and Population Growth in Eighteenth Century England', *Past and Present*, 215, pp. 149–50.
149. F. Crompton, (1997) *Workhouse Children*.
150. S. Steinbach, (2005), *Women in England*, p. 11.
151. A. John, (1984) *By the Sweat of their Brow*, pp. 30 and 43
152. C. Malone, (2003) *Women's Bodies*, p. 80.
153. C. Malone, (2003) *Women's Bodies*, p. 68.
154. C. Malone, (2003) *Women's Bodies*, p. 35.
155. C. Malone, (2003) *Women's Bodies*, p. 36.
156. Quoted by C. Malone, (2003) Women's Bodies, p. 26 and cited in R. Strachey, (1978), *The Cause, A Short History of the Women's Movement in Great Britain* (London :Virago), p. 237.

157. Historians have argued that mothers either went out to work, leaving their infants with a carer, or stayed at home to care for them themselves. Jane Humphries has argued that mothers only went 'out' to work 'in crisis'. J. Humphries, (2010) *Childhood and Child Labour in the Industrial Revolution* (Cambridge: Cambridge University Press).

158. S. O. Rose, (1992) *Limited Livelihoods*, p. 93. See also M. Hewitt, (1958) *Wives and Mothers in Victorian Industry* (London: Rockliff).

159. M. Hewitt, (1958) *Wives and Mothers*, p. 130.

160. E. Roberts, (1984), *A Woman's Place, An Oral History of Working Class Women* (Oxford: Basil Blackwell) pp. 141 and 143.

161. A. Davin, (1996) *Growing Up Poor: Home, School and Street in London 1870–1914* (London: Rivers Oram Press), pp. 88–91.

162. M. Hewitt, (1958) *Wives and Mothers*, p. 129–30.

163. J. Purvis (ed.), (2000) *Women's History*, (1998), p. 59

164. M. Arnot, (1994) 'Infant Death, Child Care and the State: The Baby-farming Scandal and the First Infant Life Protection Legislation of 1872', in *Continuity and Change*, 9, pp. 271–311.

165. S. Steinbach, (2005) *Women in England*, pp. 11–12.

166. M. Hewitt, (1958) *Wives and Mothers*, p. 181 and R. Millward and F. Bell, (2001) 'Infant Mortality in Victorian Britain: the Mother as Medium', *Economic History Review*, 54, p. 702.

167. S. Steinbach, (2005) *Women in England*, p. 12.

168. C. Dyhouse, (1978) 'Working-Class Mothers and Infant Mortality in England', 1895–1914', *Journal of Social History*, 12, pp. 248–67.

169. C. Dyhouse, (1978), 'Working-Class Mothers', pp. 248–267.

170. M. Hewitt, (1958) *Wives and Mothers*, pp. 133–4.

171. R. Millward and F. Bell, (2001) 'Infant Mortality', p. 702.

172. S. O. Rose, (1992) *Limited Livelihoods*, pp. 46–7.

173. S. O. Rose, (1992) *Limited Livelihoods*, p. 76.

174. S. O. Rose, (1992) *Limited Livelihoods*, p. 76.

175. S. O Rose, (1992) *Limited Livelihoods* p. 76.

176. T. Spence (1797) 'The Rights of Infants', (London), p. 1.

177. T. Spence (1797) 'The Rights', p. 1

178. T. Spence, (1797) 'The Rights', p. 4.

179. T. Spence, (1797) 'The Rights', p. 4.

180. J. G. Williamson (1981) 'Urban Disamenities, Dark Satanic Mills and the British Standard of Living Debate', *Journal of Economic History*, 41, p. 83.

181. S.O. Rose, (1992) *Limited Livelihoods*, p. 56.

182. T. Evans, (2005) 'Women, Marriage', p. 68.

183. J. Lewis, (1986) *Labour and Love: Women's Experience of Home and Family* (Oxford: Blackwell), p. 83.

184. Quoted by Edward Bedoes, in J. Lewis, (1986) *Labour and Love*, p. 83.

185. J. M. Strange, (2002) 'She Cried a Very Little', Death, Grief and Mourning in Working-Class Culture, 1880–1914', *Social History*, 27, p. 149.

186. C. Dyhouse, (1978), 'Working-Class Mothers', pp. 248–67.

187. S. Steinbach, (2005)*Women in England*, p. 13.

188. P. Summerfield, (2005) 'Women Workers in the Second World War', in G. Holloway, *Women and Work*, p. 171.

189. G. Holloway, (2005) *Women and Work*, p. 209.

190. J. Burnette, (2008) *Gender, Work*.

191. Jo Stanley, (1990) *For Love and Shillings*, p. 9
192. G. Holloway, (2005) *Women and Work*, p. 228.
193. J. Burnette, (2008) *Gender, Work*, inside cover.
194. J. Burnette, (2008) *Gender, work*, inside cover.
195. See M. Reynolds, (2006) '"A Man Who Won't Back a Woman is No Man At All"': The 1875 Heavy Wollen Dispute and the Narrative of Women's Trade Unionism', in *Labour History Review*, 71, pp. 187–98.
196. J. Humphries, (2011) *Childhood and Child Labour*, p. 140.
197. T. Evans, (2005) 'Women, Marriage', p. 68
198. Mrs Hill, quoted in S. Steinbach, (2005) *Women in England*, p. 15, fn. 12.
199. Quoted in S. O. Rose, (1992) *Limited Livelihoods*, p. 95.
200. B. Hill, (1994) *Women, Work* p. 123. Bridget Hill tells us 'housework' is an important field of research which social historians have failed to engage with.
201. B. Hill, (1994), *Women, Work* p. 73. For Hill's discussion about female apprenticeships see pp. 85–102.
202. B. Hill, (1994) *Women, Work*, p. 253.
203. B. Hill, (1994) *Women, Work*, p. 107.
204. B. Hill, (1994) *Women, Work*, pp. 107–8.
205. B. Hill, (1994) *Women, Work*, p. 109.
206. B. Hill, (1994) *Women, Work*, p. 111.
207. B. Hill, (1994) *Women, Work*, p. 113.
208. B. Hill, (1994) *Women, Work*, p. 113.
209. J. Purvis, (2000) (ed.) *Women in Britain*, p. 66
210. S. Steinbach, (2005), *Women in England*, p. 12
211. S. Steinbach, (2005) *Women in England*, p. 12.
212. Hannah Mitchell, in J. Lewis, (1984) *Women in England, 1870–1950: Sexual Divisions and Social Change*, p. 25
213. J. Lewis, (1986) 'Reconstructing Women's Experience', in J. Lewis, (ed.) *Labour and Love, Women's Experience of Home and Family* (Oxford: Basil Blackwell), p. 7.
214. Mrs Mitchell's interview in E. Roberts, (1984) *A Woman's Place*, p. 127.
215. Mrs Mitchell's interview in E. Roberts, (1984) *A Woman's Place*, p. 127.
216. E. Roberts, (1984), *A Woman's Place*, p. 125.
217. M. Llewelyn Davies, (1978) (ed.) *Maternity: Letters from Working Women*, (Virago: London) (first published 1915), p. 6.
218. S. Steinbach, (2005) *Women in England*, p. 12.
219. A. Tomkins, (2005) 'Women and Poverty', in Hannah Barker (eds.) *Women's History*, p. 154, S. Steinbach (2005), *Women in England*, p. 13; A. Davin, (1996) *Growing up Poor*, p. 24; A. Kidd, (1999), *State, Society and the Poor in Nineteenth-Century England*, p. 146–7 and S. Horrell and J. Humphries, (1998) 'Women's Labour force participation and the transition to the male-breadwinner family, 1790–1865, in P. Sharpe, (1998) *Women's Work the English Experience, 1650–1914* (London: Arnold), pp. 172–206.
220. A. Davin, (1996) *Growing up Poor*, p. 24.
221. S. Steinbach, (2005) *Women in England*, p. 13.
222. J. Lewis, (1986) *Women in England*, p. 26.
223. J. Humphries, (2012) 'Childhood and Child Labour in the Industrial Revolution', *Economic History Review*, 66, p. 18. http://federation.ens.fr/ydepot/semin/texte11 12/JAN2012CHI.pdf
224. For a discussion about the 'family wage' see J. Humphries, (2000) 'Women and Paid Work', in J. Purvis, *Women's History*, p. 88.

225. J. Lewis, (1986) *Women in England*, p. 52, J. Purvis, (1998) *Women's History*, p. 61.
226. A. Davin, (1996) *Growing up Poor*, p. 23, A. Tomkins, (2005) 'Women in Poverty', p. 154.
227. A. Davin, (1996) *Growing up Poor*, p. 23,
228. A. Davin, (1996) *Growing Up Poor*, p. 47.
229. S. D'Cruze, (2000) 'Household Management and Family Relationships', in J. Purvis, (2000) (ed.) *Women's History*, p. 65.
230. M. Llewelyn Davies, (1978) *Maternity*, p. 159 mother 128.
231. J. Crump, *The Ups and Downs of Being Born*, (London: Vassall Neighbourhood Council) pp. 35–6.
232. A. Tomkins, (2005) 'Women and Poverty', p. 162.
233. A. Tomkins, 'Women and Poverty', p. 162.
234. J. Lewis, (1984) *Women in England*, p. 53.
235. S. D.Cruze, (2000) 'Household Management', p. 64.
236. S. D'Cruze, (2000) 'Household Management', p. 64.
237. S. Steinbach, (2005) *Women in England*, p. 15.
238. S.Steinbach, (2005) *Women in England*, p. 15.
239. A. Davin, (1978) 'Imperialism and Motherhood', p. 24.
240. A. Reid, (2006) 'Health Visitors and Enlightened Motherhood', in E. Garrett, C. Walley, N. Shelton and Robert Woods, (eds.) *Infant Mortality, A Continuing Social Problem* (Adlershot: Ashgate), p. 192
241. S. Steinbach, (2005) *Women in England*, and T. Evans, (2005) 'Women, Marriage', p. 68.
242. A. Davin, (1996) *Growing Up Poor*, p. 60.
243. J. Burnett, (1979) *Plenty and Want* (London: Scolar Press), p. 185.
244. J. Burnett, (1979) *Plenty and Want*, p. 185.
245. A. Martin, 'The Mother and Social Reform', *The Nineteenth Century and After*, May and June, 1913, p. 1069 in A. Davin, (1996) 'Loaves and Fishes: Food in Poor Households in Late-Nineteenth Century London', *History Workshop Journal*, 41, p. 188 fn. 61.
246. A. Davin, (1996) 'Loaves and Fishes', p. 188 fn. 61.
247. E. Ross, (1986) 'London's Working Class Mothers', in J. Lewis (1986) (ed.), *Labour and Love*, p. 78.
248. E. Ross, (1986) 'London's', p. 78, in Jane Lewis (ed.).
249. Evelyn Bunting et al. (1907) *A School for Mothers* (London: Marshall and Son); E. Ross, (1986) 'London's', p. 78 in Jane Lewis (ed.).
250. J. Purvis, (2000) (ed.), *Women's History*, p. 59.
251. E. Ross, (1986) 'London's Working-Class Mothers', pp. 75–7.
252. A. Davin, (1996) *Growing up Poor*, p. 89.
253. S. Alexander, (1994) *Becoming a Woman* (London: Virago), E. Griffin, (2013) *Liberty's Dawn, A People's History of the Industrial Revolution* (Hamps: Hobbs), p. 103.
254. A. Davin, (1996) *Growing up Poor*, p. 89.
255. A. Davin, (1996) *Growing up Poor*, pp. 88–91 and J. Lewis, *Labour and Love*.
256. A. Tomkins, (2005) 'Women and Poverty', p. 158.
257. J. Purvis, (2000) (ed.) *Women's History*, p. 59.
258. Jane Humphries has recently argued that the numbers of working women could be higher than we have envisaged. See J. Humphries and C. Sarasua, (2012) 'Off the Record: Reconstructing Women's Labor Force Participation in the European Past,' *Feminist Economics*, 18, pp. 39–68

259. *The Daily Chronicle*, December 1892, in C. Malone, *Women's Bodies*, p. 33.
260. *Manchester Guardian*, 22 July 1872.
261. *The Daily Chronicle*, December 1892, in C. Malone, *Women's Bodies*, p. 33.

2 Industrial Mothers

1. Quoted by Charles Dickens to Rev. J Elder Canning, (1874) 'On the Neglect of Infants in Large Towns', *National Association of the Promotion of Social Science*, *(NAPSS)* (London), p. 723. Quoted in M. Hewitt, (1958) *Wives and Mother's in Victorian Industry* (London: Rockliff), p. 99. Dickens however was not the only contemporary to think that mothers' factory work had a negative impact on infant health. See also W. Dodd, (1842, 1968) *The Factory System Illustrated; In A Series Of Letters To The Right Hon. Lord Ashley* (London: John Murray; reprint London: Cass), p. 29; W.S. Jevons, W.T. Charley, Mr. Ernest Hart, Mr. George Hastings and Mr Hereford, were also severe critics of mothers' factory work, see W.S. Jevons, (1882) 'Married Women in Factories', *Contemporary Review*, January, pp. 37–53 This argument persisted through to the Twentieth Century; see G. Newman, quoted in R. Woods, (2006) 'Newman's Infant Mortality as an Agenda for Research', in E. Garrett, C. Galley, N. Shelton and R. Woods, (2006) (eds.) *Infant Mortality: A Continuing Social Problem* (Aldershot: Ashgate), pp. 18–33. See also E. Garrett, (2006) (eds.) et al *Infant Mortality*, pp. 4, 10, 27, 33–49, (esp. p. 38) 186 and 191–212.
2. Quoted by Rev. J Elder Canning, (1874) 'On the Neglect of Infants in Large Towns', *NAPSS*, p. 723.
3. B.L. Hutchins, (1983) *Women in Modern Industry* (London: Bell and Sons), p. 71.
4. Domestic service was the principle form of employment for women during the nineteenth century. Its main employee was the single woman, but some married women were also known to perform it. See the works of Sir John Simon for the bad effects of factory work on the IMR. Sir John Simon, (1872) 'Instructions to Vaccination Officers issued by the Local Government Board, 21st December 1871', First Report of the Local Government Board *PP* 1872 XXV111, pp. 77–81; G. Newman, (1906) *Infant Mortality*, (London); J. Ikin, (1865) 'Abstract on a Paper from the Undue Mortality of Infants', (Leeds) and J. Clay (1854) 'Burial Clubs and Infanticide in England; A Letter to W.M. Brown' (Preston).
5. M. Hewitt, (1958) *Wives and Mother's*, p. 50; 'Report of Commissioners into the Employment of Children in Factories', *PP* 1833 XX; 'Reports of Special Assistant Poor Law Commissioners On the Employment of Women and Children in Agriculture *PP* 1843 XII; 'Children's Employment Commission (1862). First Report of the Commissioners. With appendix. XVIII.1; 'Report of the Commissioners into the Employment of Children, Young Persons and Women in Agriculture', *PP*, 1863 XVIII; 1867–68 XVIII and 1868–9 XVII and the 'Factory and Workshops Acts Commission' *PP's* 1872 XVI; 1873 XIX; and 1876 XXX.
6. *BMJ*, 17 November 1894, p. 1135.
7. This is despite the nineteenth century having a plethora of women waged workers who went out of the home to earn a living. Female London costermongers walked the streets earning a pittance, Bel-Maiden mineworkers toiled in the Cornish mining industry as Pit Brow Lasses worked in the West Riding and Lancashire districts. Bookbinding and printing trades, cloth workers and tailoring trades, nail makers and small metal industries, were also to coax many

women away from their homes. See. A. John, (1986) (ed.)*Unequal Opportunities: Women's Opportunities in England 1800–1918* (Oxford: Basil Blackwell)

8. N. Goose, (2007) (ed.), *Women's Work in Industrial England: Regional and Local Perspectives* (Hatfield: Local Population Studies), p. 5.
9. L. Davidoff and C. Hall, (1987) *Family Fortunes; The English Middle Class 1750–1850* (London: Hutchinson), p. 275.
10. However, one way which they could retain their femininity was to omit putting their waged work status on the census.
11. The extent to which middle class women were excluded from the public sphere has been articulated by Anne Digby, however, aiming to ensure that working-class female waged work would wither and die during the nineteenth century as to perform it was anathema to their sex and would compromise their infants, social commentators sought to limit women's work with an array of Acts. See A. Digby, (1992) 'Victorian Values and Women in Public and Private', *Proceedings of the British Academy*, 78 pp. 195–216.
12. C. Patmore, (1854) *The Angel in the House*, (London). Patmore coined this phrase and it is the title of a poem which he argued characterised his wife's personality.
13. D. Valenze, (1995) *The First Industrial Woman* (Oxford: Oxford University Press), p. 144. Valenze does not give a footnote for this quote. Mary Wollstonecraft argued during the eighteenth century that these middle-class women came to adore their gilded cage. See M. Wollstonecraft, (1792) *A Vindication of the Rights of Women* (London). Carolyn Malone argues that the short-time legislation was used to limit the working hours of the women in the workshop forges, but gives little evidence to substantiate this view as the evidence she provides is made in light of the Factory Acts only. See C. Malone, (1998) 'Gendered Discourses and the Making of Protective Labor Legislation in England 1830–1914', in *The Journal of British Studies*, 37, pp. 166–91 and p. 167 in particular.
14. E. Higgs, (1987) 'Women, Occupation and Work in the Nineteenth Century, Censuses', *History Workshop*, 23, pp. 59–80 in S. O. Rose, (1992) *Limited Livelihoods: Gender and Class in Nineteenth Century England* (London: Routledge), p. 80. The extent to which middle-class women were excluded from the public sphere has been articulated by Anne Digby. Aiming to ensure that working-class female waged work would wither and die during the nineteenth century as to perform it was anathema to their sex and compromised their infants, social commentators sought to limit women's work with an array of Acts. See A. Digby, (1992) 'Victorian Values', pp. 195–216.
15. See J. Schwarzkopf, (1998) 'Gendering Exploitation: the Use of Gender in the Campaign Against Driving in Lancashire Weaving Sheds, 1886–1903', in *Women's History Review*, 7, pp. 449–73.
16. E. Garrett, et al,(2006) '*Infant Mortality*', p. 4.
17. E. Garrett et al, (2006) '*Infant Mortality*', pp. 18–19.
18. J. Ikin, (1865) 'Abstract from a Paper'.
19. J. Ikin, (1865) 'Abstract from a Paper', passim and p. 9
20. J. Ikin,(1865) 'Abstract from a paper', passim and p. 9.
21. R. Woods, (2006) 'Newman's Infant', p. 38.
22. R. Woods, (2006) 'Newman's Infant' pp. 17–33. See also E. Garrett, et al (2006) 'Infant Mortality' pp. 4, 10, 27, 33–49, (esp. p. 38), 186 and 191–212 A. Reid, 'Health Visitors and Enlightened Motherhood', in in E. Garrett, et al (2006) *Infant Mortality*, p. 192. R.I. Woods, P.A. Watterson and J.H. Woodward, (1988) 'The Causes of Rapid Infant Mortality Decline in England and Wales, 1861–1921

Parts I and II', *Population Studies*, 42, pp. 43, 113–32 and 343–66; N. Williams and C. Galley, (1995) 'Urban Differentials in Infant Mortality in Victorian England', *Population Studies*, 49, pp. 401–20 and M. Hewitt, (1958) *Wives and Mother's*.
23. R. Millward and F. Bell, (2001) 'Infant Mortality in Victorian Britain: the Mother as Medium', *Economic History Review*, 54, p. 702.
24. R. Millward and F. Bell, (2001) 'Infant Mortality', p. 702.
25. M. Hewitt, (1958) *Wives and Mother's*, p. 181.
26. S. King and G. Timmins, (2001) *Making Sense*, chapter 7.
27. I. Pinchbeck, (1969) *Women Workers and the Industrial Revolution 1750–1850* (London: Routledge) pp. 8 and 20.
28. 'Reports of Special Assistant Poor Law Commissioners On the Employment of Women and Children in Agriculture', PP 1843 XII, Evidence of Mr. Austin, p. 4; 'Report of the Commission on the Employment of Children, Young Persons and Women in Agriculture', PP 1868–9 XIII, p. 480. Despite statistics pointing to a decline of women's work, as shown by Snell, it is clear from the Commissioners discussions that farmers depended much more on married women's work than the statistics show. See 'Reports of Special Assistant Poor Law Commissioners On the Employment of Women and Children in Agriculture', PP 1843 XII, p. 6 and of Mr Henley's evidence in the 'Report of the Commission on the Employment of Children, Young Persons, and Women in Agriculture', PP 1867–68 XVII and K.D.M. Snell, (1985) *Annals of the Labouring Poor: Social Change and Agrarian England, 1600–1900* (Cambridge: Cambridge University Press).
29. R. Jefferies, (1892 and 1981) *The Toilers of the Field 1848–1887*, p. 88 in P. Horn, (1991) *Victorian Countrywomen* (Oxford: Basil Blackwell), p. 152, fn. 74.
30. Evidence of Mr Henley Report of the Commission on the Employment of Children, Young Persons, and Women in Agriculture, PP 1867–68 XVII, p. 107 and D. Valenze, (1995) *The First Industrial Woman*, p. 45.
31. 'Report of the Commissioners on the Employment of Children, Young Persons and Women in Agriculture', PP 1867–68 XVII, p. 251. Mr. Edward Coulson, Mr. Samuel Pattison, Mr. John Johnson, Mr. Andrew Ridley, Mrs. Isabella Colbeck, and Mr. W. B. Wilson were among several others who were of the same opinion.
32. Evidence of Mr. Stanhope, 'Report of the Commission on Employment of Children, Young Persons, and Women in Agriculture', PP 1867–68 XVI, p. 273.
33. Defying their label during the age of refinement these women were identified as being as 'coarse as a muckle bondager'. See G. Anderson, (1892) *The Rural Exodus: The Problems of the Village and Town*, (London: Methuen), p. 13 and 21.
34. Evidence of Mr. Stanhope, 'Report of the Commission on Employment of Children, Young Persons, and Women in Agriculture', PP 1867–68 XVI, p. 273.
35. 'Reports of Special Assistant Poor Law Commissioners On the Employment of Women and Children in Agriculture', PP 1843 XII, pp. 4–6 and 401 and Evidence of the John Bladworth J.P. For the statistics of married women's waged work during the 1860s see the Report of Inspectors of Factories to Secretary of State for Home Dept., PP 1868–1869 XVIII, p. 480 and 481.
36. M. Hewitt, (1958) *Wives and Mother's*, p. 133.
37. 'Reports of Special Assistant Poor Law Commissioners On the Employment of Women and Children in Agriculture', PP 1843 XII, p. 27 and 66 and Evidence of Mr Phelps, 'Report of the Commission on the Employment of Children, Young Persons, and Women in Agriculture', PP 1867–68 XVII, p. 386. Evidence taken from perusing the northern areas of York, Goole, Howden, Northumberland, Richmond, Hawes, Settle, Guisborough, Wakefield,

Rotherham, Driffield, Pocklington, Malton, Thirsk, and Northallerton. This child care practice was also seen in the Southern agricultural areas.

38. 'Report of the Commission on the Employment of Children, Young Persons, and Women in Agriculture', *PP* 1867–68 XVII, p. 386 and 'Reports of Special Assistant Poor Law Commissioners on the Employment of Women and Children in Agriculture', *PP* 1843 XII.

39. Quoted in *PP* 1835 Second Report 'Poor Law Commission' XXIX, p. 221 in I Pinchbeck (1930), *Women Workers and the Industrial Revolution*, (Thetford: Lowe & Brydone), p. 85.

40. 'Reports of Special Assistant Poor Law Commissioners On the Employment of Women and Children in Agriculture', *PP* 1843 X11, p. 66. Evidence of Mrs. Britton. 'Report of the Commission on the Employment of Children, Young Persons, and Women in Agriculture', *PP* 1867–68 XVII, p. 386.

41. 'Reports of Special Assistant Poor Law Commissioners On the Employment of Women and Children in Agriculture', *PP* 1843 XII, p. 59

42. P. Horn, (1991) *Victorian Countrywomen*, p. 153.

43. D.E.C. Eversley, (1965) 'Epidemiology as Social History', introduction to C. Creighton, A *History of Epidemics in Britain*, 2nd edn., 2 vols., (London: Cass) vol. 1, p. 35.

44. See 'Reports of Special Assistant Poor Law Commissioners on the Employment of Women and Children in Agriculture', *PP* 1843 XII, p. 10.

45. Report of the Commissioners on the Employment of Children, Young Persons and Women in Agriculture, *PP* 1867–68 XVII, p. 251. Mr. Edward Coulson, Mr. Samuel Pattison, Mr. John Johnson, Mr. Andrew Ridley, Mrs. Isabella Colbeck, and Mr. W. B. Wilson were among several others who were of the same opinion.

46. Evidence of Mr. Stanhope, 'Report of the Commission on the Employment of Children, Young Persons, and Women in Agriculture', *PP* 1867–68 XVI, p. 306.

47. P. Horn, (1991) *Victorian Countrywomen*, passim. Evidence of Mr Henley, 'Report of the Commission on the Employment of Children, Young Persons, and Women in Agriculture', *PP* 1867–68 XVII, p. 107; Evidence taken from the 'Farming Townships of Richmond and Yorkshire areas, see R. Millward and F. Bell, p. 701 who argue that the IMR amongst factory workers was 32/1000. Evidence taken from the 'Farming Townships of Richmond and Yorkshire areas'.

48. I. Pinchbeck, (1930) *Women Workers*, pp. 270–78 and J. Rendall, (1990) *Women in an Industrialising Society* (Oxford: Basil Blackwell) p. 25.

49. R. H. Sherard, (1897) *The White Slaves of England* (London) p. 357 and p. 363; J. Rendall, *Women in an Industrialising Society*, p. 25 and 'Report on the Commission into the Employment of Children, Young Persons, and Women in Agriculture', *PP* 1867 XVII, p. 54.

50. 'Report of the Employment of Children, Young Persons and Women in Agriculture', *PP* 1868–9 XVIII, p. 295.

51. 'Report of the Employment of Children, Young Persons and Women in Agriculture', *PP* 1868–9 XVIII, p. 300.

52. 'Report of Inspectors of Factories to Secretary of State for Home Dept., May–October 1868', *PP* 1868–9 XVIII, p. 298.

53. 'Report of the Employment of Children, Young Persons and Women in Agriculture', *PP* 1868–9 XVIII, pp 298–301.

54. 'Report of the Employment of Children, Young Persons and Women in Agriculture', *PP* 1868–9 XVIII, p. 300.

55. R. H. Sherard, (1897) *The White Slaves*, pp. 220–27. It was also reported that women also took their children to work in their nests for safety *PP* 1843 XVI.
56. R. H. Sherard, (1897) *The White Slaves*, pp. 220–27.
57. Report of the Employment of Children, Young Persons and Women in Agriculture, *PP* 1868–9 XXXVII, p. 298 and M. Hewitt, (1958) *Wives and Mother's*, p. 133.
58. S. Lewenhak and H. Cremonesi, (1980) *Women and Work* (London: Macmillan), p. 148.
59. 'Report of the Employment of Children, Young Persons and Women in Agriculture', *PP* 1868–9 XVIII, pp. 295–6.
60. 'Report of the Employment of Children', *PP* 1868–9 XVIII, pp. 295–6. My emphasis.
61. R. Millward and F. Bell, (2001) 'Infant Mortality' p. 702.
62. Evidence of Mr Fitton, Factory and Workshops Acts Commission. 'Report of the Commissioners Appointed to Inquire into the Working of the Factory and Workshops Acts, With a View to their Consolidation and Amendment Together with the Minutes of Evidence, Appendix and Index. Vol I, Report, Appendix and Index, *PP* 1876 c.1443 XXIX-1, p. 112.
63. Evidence of Mr Fitton, Factory and Workshops Acts Commission, 'Report of the Commissioners' *PP* 1876 c.1443 XXIX-1, p. 112.
64. B. Didsbury, (1977) 'Cheshire Saltworkers', in R. Samuel, (1977) (ed.) *Miners, Quarrymen and Saltworkers* (Routledge & Kegan Paul: London), p. 155.
65. Reports of the Inspectors of Factories to Her Majesty's Principal Secretary of State for the Home Department for the half-year ending 30th April, 1873, *PP* 1873 c.849 XIX-223, p. 45 Here Robert Baker states he knows of the child care methods of working women who suckle their infants in the sheds. See also Factory and Workshop Acts Commission. 'Report of the Commissioners Appointed to Inquire into the Working of the Factory and Workshop Acts, with a View to their Consolidation and Amendment: Together with the Minutes of Evidence, Appendix and Index.' *PP* 1876 c.1443 XXIX-1, p. 112. Mr Fitton wrote to Mr Baker outlining the positive child care practices used by women who worked in the saltmines.
66. M. Llewelyn Davies, (1978) *Maternity*, mother 109, p. 142.
67. 'Factory and Workshop Acts Commission. Report of the Commissioners' Vol II. *PP* 1876 c.1443-1 XXX-1, pp. 303–4. The 'well beloved' Mr O'Conor was commonly referred to as O'Conor Don in the Reports. See 'Factory and Workshops Acts Commission. Report of the Commissioners' PP 1876 c.1443 XXIX-1, p. 3.
68. Mr O'Conor speaking to the Select Committee. 'Factory and Workshop Acts Commission. Report of the Commissioners', *PP* 1876 c.1443-1 XXX 1, pp. 303–4.
69. Mr O'Conor speaking to the Select Committee. 'Factory and Workshop Acts Commission. Report of the Commissioners' Vol II. Minutes of Evidence, *PP* 1876 c.1443-1 XXX-1, pp. 303–4.
70. Mr O'Conor speaking to the Select Committee. 'Factory and Workshop Acts Commission. Report of the Commissioners' *PP* 1876 c.1443-1 XXX-I, pp. 303–4.
71. Mr O'Conor speaking to the Select Committee. 'Factory and Workshop Acts Commission.' *PP* 1876 c.1443-1 XXX-1, pp. 303–4.
72. J. Humphries, (2010), *Childhood and Child Labour in the British Industrial Revolution* (Cambridge: Cambridge University Press), p. 110.

73. P. Hudson, (1992) *The Industrial Revolution* (London: Edward Arnold), p. 230 and back cover, P. Hudson, (1986) *The Genesis off Industrial Capital* (Cambridge: Cambridge University Press), p. 70.

74. M. Berg, (1985) *The Age of Manufacturers: 1700–1820: Industry, Innovation and Work in Britain* (London: Fontana), p. 146.

75. M. Berg, (1985) *The Age of Manufactures*, pp. 177 and 254–5. Berg has also argued that 'innovation affected the textile industries long before the eighteenth century'.

76. E. Gordon and E. Breitenbach, (1990) *The World is Ill Divided, Women's Work in Scotland in the Nineteenth and Early Twentieth Centuries*, (Edinburgh: Edinburgh University Press), p. 96

77. M. Berg, (1985) *The Age of Manufactures*, p. 234.

78. E. Gordon and E. Breitenbach, (1990) *The World is Ill Divided*, p. 98 and M. Berg, (1985) *The Age of Manufactures*, p. 259.

79. E. Gordon and E. Breitenbach, (1990) *The World is Ill Divided*, p. 98 and for an expose of the contribution that women made to the Industrial Revolution see M. Berg, (1993) 'What Difference did Women's Work Make to the Industrial Revolution?' *The History Workshop Journal*, 35, pp. 22–44.

80. It is very difficult to discern the true number of married women factory workers as census records were apt during this period to leave off the wife's occupation. However, Elizabeth Roberts has counted the numbers of married women textile workers in the areas of Yorkshire and Lancashire which were in 1871 was 460,009 and 700,000 in 1878. These married women worked on the different materials of cotton, woollens and worsteds, silk, flax and jute and hemp. See E. Roberts, (1988) *Women's Work*, who argues that 'the manufacture of woollens and worsteds continued to expand both in West Yorkshire and in the Border region of Scotland until the turn of the nineteenth century,' p. 34. See also J. Liddington and J. Norris, (1978 and 2000) *One Hand Tied Behind Us: Rise of the Women's Suffrage Movement* (London: Virago), p. 47 for an exploration of the Lancashire Cotton districts. The area of West Yorkshire was particularly synonymous for the numerous wool and worsted mills which employed married women. See M. Reynolds, (2006) '"A Man Who Won't Back a Woman is No Man at All"; The 1875 Heavy Woollen Dispute and the Narrative of Women's Trade Unionism' in *Labour History Review*, 71, pp. 187–97. The Leeds Denman's mill being one example of where many married women were employed and worked the power looms. These women were particularly concerned for the health of their children who worked at the factory with them.

81. M. Berg, (1993) 'What Difference', p. 27.

82. D.T. Jenkins and K. Ponting, (1982) *The British Wool Textile Industry 1770 – 1914* (London: Heinemann), p. 78.

83. M. Berg, (1993) 'What Difference', p. 24. Berg argues and the value of these female workers to the British industry during the nineteenth century therefore was 14.1% as opposed to the male dominated copper industry which contributed 0.7%.

84. E. Griffin, (2010) *A Short History of the British Industrial Revolution* (Basingstoke: Palgrave Macmillan), p. 83.

85. See the works of M. Anderson, and J. Humphries for this argument.

86. L. Shaw-Taylor, (2007) 'The Geography of Adult Female Employments in England', in N. Goose, *Women's Work*, p. 38, E. Higgs, (1987) 'Women

Occupation and Work in the Nineteenth Century Censuses', *History Workshop Journal*, 23, pp. 59–80.
87. E. Higgs, (1987) 'Women's Occupation and Work in the Nineteenth Century Censuses' in *History Workshop Journal*, 23, pp. 63–4, S. Horrell and J. Humphries, (1995) 'Women's Labour Force Participation and the Transition to the Male Breadwinner Family, 1790–1865' *Economic History Review*, 48, p. 95. and M. Anderson, (2007) 'What Can the Mid-Victorian Censuses tell us about Variations in Married Women's Employment, in N. Goose, (2007) (ed.) *Women's Work*, pp. 182–208; L. Shaw-Taylor, (2007) 'The Geography', p. 38
88. P. Branca, (1975) 'A New Perspective on Women's Work: A Comparative Typology', *Journal of Social History*, 9, pp. 129–53.
89. P. Laxton, (1986) 'Textiles', in J. Langton and R.J. Morris, *Atlas of Industrializing Britain* (London: Methuen), p. 106.
90. R. Hall, (2003) 'A Poor Cotton Weyver: Poverty and the Cotton Famine in Clitheroe', in *Social History*, 28, p. 227.
91. J. Hannam, (1989) *Isabella Ford* (Oxford: Basil Blackwell), p. 316 fn 45.
92. For an expose of the contribution that women made to the Industrial Revolution see M. Berg, (1993) 'What Difference', pp. 22–44.
93. M. Hewitt, (1958) *Wives and Mothers*, pp. 15–16.
94. L. Tilly and J. Scott, (1978) *Women, Work, and Family* (New York), p. 131.
95. L. Tilly and J. Scott, (1978) *Women, Work*, p. 128, fn. 79.
96. E. Griffin, (2010) *A Short History*, p. 83; E. Roberts, (1982) 'Working Wives and Their Families', in T. Barker and M. Drake (eds.) *Population and Society in Britain 1850–1980* (London: Batsford Academic and Educational), p. 143.
97. B.L. Hutchins, (1983) 'Yorkshire' in C. Black (ed.) *Married Women's Work*, (London: Virago), p. 135.
98. B.L. Hutchins, (1983) 'Yorkshire' p. 135.
99. B.L. Hutchins, (1983) 'Yorkshire' p. 135.
100. B.L. Hutchins, (1983) 'Yorkshire' p. 135. See for example evidence of a husband's insufficient income given by weavers A12,A16, A20, A25 and A26. Weaver A18 remarked on the drinking habits of her husband which compelled her to work. Weavers also spoke of the part which their husbands mental and physical disabilities which also gave rise to their need to work, such as A5 and A11. From Margaret Llewelyn Davies's survey see Mother 135 who worked as a rag sorter 'to help with the living'.
101. B.L. Hutchins, (1983) 'Yorkshire' p. 135.
102. B.L. Hutchins, (1983) 'Yorkshire' p. 144.
103. Information taken from the Leeds Brotherton Death Records. Emma and John Riley.
104. M.L. Davies (1978) *Maternity*. For example see letters 152, 153 and 154.
105. M.L. Davies, (1978), *Maternity*, p. 192.
106. Leeds Brotherton Death Records.
107. All taken from the 1871 Census records.
108. Many mothers in Llewelyn Davies work testifying to going short of food even when working. See for example mother 5 inM. Llewelyn Davies, (1978) *Maternity*, p. 23.
109. C. Dyhouse, (1978) 'Working-class Mothers and Infant Mortality in England 1895–1914', *Journal of Social History*, 12, pp. 73–98 and I. Pinchbeck, (1981) *Women Workers in the Industrial Revolution*.

192 Notes to Chapter 2

110. Royal Commission on Labour. The Employment of Women. Reports by Miss Eliza Orme, Miss Clara E. Collet, Miss May E. Abraham, and Miss Margaret H. Irwin (Lady Assistant Commissioners), on the Conditions of Work in Various Industries in England, Wales, Scotland, and Ireland. May E Abraham. Lady Assistant Commissioner visited Yorkshire mills, *PP* 1893–94 c6894 XXIII pp. 2 and 102.

111. 'Royal Commission on Labour. The Employment of women.', *PP* 1893–94 c.6894 XXIII, p. 102.

112. 'Royal Commission on Labour. The Employment of women.', *PP* 1893–94 c.6894 XXIII p. 306.

113. 'Royal Commission on Labour. The Employment of Women', *PP* 1893–94 c..6894XXIII p. 306.

114. R. Baker and W. Jevons, 'Report of the Inspector of Factories', Robert Baker's Testimony, *PP* 1872 XVI, p. 89.

115. D. Busfield, (1988) 'Job Definition and Inequality in the West Riding Textile Industry', in *Textile History*, 19, pp. 61–82.

116. A. Rawden, (1972) *The Rise and Fall of Shoddy and Mungo Manufacture at Batley 1830–1871*, pp. 31–40. Unpublished Book, presented at York University.

117. D. Busfield, (1979) 'Job Definition' p. 74, and H. Brown, *The Rise of British Trade Unionism 1825–1914* (London: Longman), p. 57 and S. Jubb, (1860) *History of the Shoddy Trade: It's Rise and Progress and Present Position*, (London: Houston and Wright), p. 69. Jubb also states that men favoured other employment opportunities, for example the railway and mining increasingly offered.

118. M.T. Wild, (1972) 'The Wool Textile Industry' in J. G Jenkins, (ed.) *The Wool Textile Industry in Great Britain*, (London: Routledge & Kegan Paul), p. 201.

119. 'Report of Inspectors of Factories' *PP* 1868–9, XVIII, p. 74. The entrepreneurial skills of Benjamin Law had led to the development of machines like 'the Devil', which ground up woollen rags in order for them to be blended with virgin wool, which 'gave rise to an important recycled wool industry'. See J.C. Malin, (1979) *The West Riding Recovered Wool Textile Industry, c.1813–1939*. Unpublished PhD Book, University of York, pp 214–18. Cited in C.D. Giles and I. Goodall, (1992) *Yorkshire Textile Mills, The Buildings of the Yorkshire Textile Industry 1770–1930* (London: HMSO), p. 116. This new industry inevitably prospered whenever virgin wool rose in price, and was aided by the exemption of Mungo and Shoddy from the export duty which made its competitors expensive in comparison. By 1851, the industry in Leeds was to make a significant contribution to the great exhibition with its woollen manufacturers winning fifteen medals. For further information see to J.A. Jowitt, (1986) (ed.) *Model Industrial Communities in Mid Nineteenth Century Yorkshire* (Bradford: The University of Bradford), p. 18. The Franco-Prussian War of 1870–71 was to prove equally profitable for Dewsbury and Batley as they were able to furnish Berlin and Russia with Shoddy in the form of coats and blankets without incurring an export duty see S. Jubb, (1860) *The History of the Shoddy Trade*, p. 25. M.T. Wild, (1972) 'The Wool Textile Industry', p. 201. The West Riding textile trade prior to industrialisation was characterised by 'a small clothier system' as distinct from the large-scale 'putting out system' employed elsewhere. As such, the capital of the local industry was 'diffused amongst a multitude of small clothiers, most of whom operated on the basis of family working units', p. 201.

120. M. Hewitt, (1958) *Wives and Mothers*, p. 60.

121. E. Roberts, (1984) *A Woman's Place*, p. 77.

122. E. Roberts, (1984) *A Woman's Place*, p. 78.
123. B. Turner, (1920) *A Short History of the General Union of Textile Workers*, (Heckmondwike: Labour Pioneer and Factory Times), pp. 2–3. The respectability of these women was evidenced by their male colleagues who voted for these women to represent them in a strike committee. See B. Turner, *A Short History*, pp. 85–95 and M. Reynolds, (2006) 'A Man Who Won't Back a Woman is No Man at All', pp. 187–97.
124. W. Hirst, (1844) *History, of the Woollen Trade for the Last Sixty Years Shewing the Advantages which the West Of England Trade had of those over Yorkshire up to 1813, How These were Gradually Overcome, Until 1818 when a challenge was Received and Accepted for the Author in London to Place His Goods in Competition with those in the West of England: Commencing with a Memoir of the Author and Tracing Connexion with the Progress of the Woollen Manufacture*, (Leeds), p. 25 and p. 29.
125. W. Hirst, (1844) *History*, p. 25.
126. B.L. Hutchins, (1983) *Women in Modern Industry*, p. 23
127. N. Goose, (2007) (ed.) *Women's Work*, p. 6.
128. W. Hirst, (1844) *History* p. 25. Hirst paid high wages to the workers in the early nineteenth century to get them to 'produce a good product'. As the demand for the innovative cloth morphed and rose in the nineteenth century, the Leeds mills in the nineteenth century were under the same pressure to pay their wages the same high rates.
129. W. Hirst, (1844) *History*, p. 26.
130. W.G Rimmer, (1963) William Hirst, 'Father of the Woollen Trade', *Leeds Journal*, 34, p. 205.
131. W. Hirst, (1844) *History*, p. 34.
132. Angus Reach's book, (2007) *Fabrics, Filth and Fairy Tents* (Hebden Bridge: Royd Press) notes some paupers in Leeds were unable, as a consequence of their age and illness to work in factories and that the West Riding was THE main provider of work for many young families in Leeds.
133. W. Hirst, (1844) *History*, p. 25. Hirst paid high wages to the workers in the early nineteenth century to get them to 'produce a good product'. As the demand for the innovative cloth morphed and rose in the nineteenth century, the Leeds mills in the nineteenth century were under the same pressure to pay their wages the same high rates.
134. J. Batty, (1877) *The History of Rothwell* (Leeds) p. 131.
135. E. Roberts, (1995) 'Working Wives and their Families', pp. 144–6. Seebohm Rowntree's research in 1901 led him to argue that 21s 8d was the poverty line for families. If men earned this, or near this, income then the family were 'in poverty' and their wives had to go out to work. See also Barbara Nelson for the number of mills in Leeds during the latter half of the nineteenth century. B. Nelson, (1980) *The Woollen Industry of Leeds* (Leeds: Thornton), p. 44.
136. W. Hirst, (1844) *History*, pp. 22 and 24.
137. W. Hirst, (1844) *History*, p. 25 and B.L. Hutchins, (1983) *Women in Modern Industry* (London: Bell and Sons), p. 40.
138. W. Hirst, (1844) *History*, p. 45.
139. Wages books of Holly Park Mill Records, John Briggs Mill Records and the 1871 Census.
140. Holly Park and John Briggs Mill's Wages Book.
141. W. Dodd, (1842, 1968) *The Factory System*, pp. 3 and 26. 'Report of the Inspector of Factories', Robert Baker's testimony, *PP* 1872 XVI, p. 89. The married women

would have worked in the Leeds factories owned by J & J Holroyd, Lister Bros., M. Oldroyd, J. Oates, Holly Park Mill Co., Wrigglesworth & Kent, and Booth Bros., among others. See P. Hudson, (1975) *The West Riding Wool Textile Industry: A Catalogue of Business Records From the Sixteenth to the Twentieth Century* (Edington: Pasold Research Fund Ltd.), pp. 71–402. For the Lancashire cotton mills see M. Hewitt, (1958) *Wives and Mother's*, p. 89.

142. J. Haslam, (1904) *The Handloom Weaver's Daughter* (London: S.C. Brown, Langham & Company Ltd), p. 69.
143. W. C. Taylor, (1873) 'Employment of Mothers in Manufactures: What Influence has the Employment of Mothers in Manufactures on Infant Mortality; and Ought Any, and What, Restrictions to be Placed on Such Employment?' *NAPPS*, p. 605.
144. W.C. Taylor, (1873) 'Employment of Mothers in Manufactures', p. 587
145. *The Spectator*, 23 March 1844, p. 267; W. Dodd, (1968) *The Factory System*, p. 16 and J. Perkins, (1993) *Victorian Women* (London: John Murray), p. 191. For the primary evidence see *Hansard*, 1844, vol. LXXIII col. 676 as quoted in M. Hewitt, (1958) *Wives and Mothers*, p. 10.
146. W. Dodd, (1968) *The Factory System*, p. 16 and J. Perkins, (1993) *Victorian Women*, p. 191. See also *Hansard*, 1844, vol. LXXIII col. 676 as quoted in M. Hewitt, (1958) *Wives and Mothers*, p. 10.
147. R. Gray, (1996) *The Factory Question and Industrial England, 1830–1860* (Cambridge: Cambridge University Press), p. 84.
148. B.L. Hutchins, (1983) *Women in Modern Industry*, p. 56.
149. 'Royal Commission on Labour. The Employment of Women.' *PP* 1893–94 C.6894 XXIII, p. 102 and p. 306.
150. 'Royal Commission on Labour. The Employment of women.' *PP* 1893–94 C.6894-XXIII, p. 102 and p. 306.
151. 'Reports of the inspectors of factories to Her Majesty's Principal Secretary of State for the Home Department for the half year ending 31st October 1866.' *PP* 1867 c.3794 XVI. See the numerous prosecutions given to mill overseers during the latter half of the nineteenth century for this practice.
152. J. Humphries, (1987) "The most free of moral objection", 'The Sexual Division of Labor and Women's Work in Nineteenth-Century England', *Journal of Economic History*, 47, p. 903. And J. Humphries, "Because they are too menny," 'Children, Mothers and Fertility Decline, The evidence from working-class autobiographies of the eighteenth and nineteenth centuries' *Oxford Economic and Social History Working Papers* Ref: 2006 – W64, p. 28.
153. See the numerous prosecutions given to mill overseers during the latter half of the nineteenth century for this practice.
154. R. Pearson, (1986) 'The Industrial Suburbs of Leeds in the Nineteenth Century: Community Consciousness Amongst the Social Classes'. Unpublished PhD Thesis (Leeds), p. 70. fn. 4 and J. Walvin, (1982)) *A Child's World: A Social History of English Childhood* (Harmondsworth: Penguin), p. 5
155. A. Reach, (2007) *Fabrics, Filth*, p. 63.
156. W. Jevons, 'Married Women in Factories', *Contemporary Review*, January 1882, pp. 37–53.
157. W. Jevons, 'Married Women in Factories', pp. 37–53. R. Baker, (1860) *On the State and Condition of the Town of Leeds in the West Riding of the County of York*, (Leeds), p. 29, W. Dodd, (1968) *The Factory System*, p. 139 and 'Reports of the Inspector of Factories', *PP* 1872 XVI, pp. 90–91.

158. 'Reports of the Inspector of Factories', *PP* 1872 XVI, pp. 90–91.
159. W. C. Taylor, (1873) 'Employment of Mothers', p. 605.
160. Evidence of R. Baker, Factory Inspector, 'Reports of the Inspectors of Factories', *PP's* 1872 XVI, p. 88 and 1876 XXX, pp. 68–9.
161. M. Hewitt, (1958) *Wives and Mother's*, p. 189.
162. S. Rowbotham, (1973) *Hidden from History* (London: Pluto), p. 57.
163. S. Steinbach, (2005) *Women in England: A Social History* (London: Phoenix), p. 13.
164. W.C. Taylor, (1873) 'Employment of Mothers', p. 572, W. Neff, (1966) *Victorian Working Women, an Historical and Literary Study of Women in British Industries and Professions 1832–1850* (London: Cass), p. 66 and M. Hewitt, (1958) *Wives and Mother's*, p. 24; S. Steinbach, (2005) *Women in England*, p. 26, J. Burnette, (2008) *Gender, Women and Wages in Industrial Britain*, (Cambridge: Cambridge University Press), p. 178 and S. O Rose, (1992) *Limited Livelihoods: Gender and Class in Nineteenth-century England* (London: Routledge) pp. 93–100.
165. D. Valenze, (1995) *The First Industrial Woman*, p. 102. One historian has argued that the Factory Acts were passed as a consequence of studies made during the period revealing that workers who worked 12 hours were not as productive as those who worked 10. As such, any hour worked over 10 produced little, and consequently manufacturers were keen to cut hours.
166. J. Humphries, (2010) *Childhood and Child Labour*, pp. 116–18
167. S. O Rose, (1992) *Limited Livelihoods*, pp. 93–100.
168. W.C. Taylor, (1873) 'Employment of Mothers', p. 575.
169. Evidence of R. Baker, Factory Inspector, 'Reports of the Inspectors of Factories', *PP's* 1872 XVI, p. 88 and 1876 XXX, pp. 68–9.
170. S. Barrett, (2003) 'Kinship, Poor Relief and the Welfare Process in Early Modern England', in S. King and A. Tomkins, *The Poor in England 1700–1850: an Economy of Makeshifts* (Manchester: Manchester University Press), pp. 199–227.
171. E. Waugh, (1867) *Home Life of the Lancashire Factory Folk During the Cotton Famine* (London) p. 102.
172. W. Dodd, (1968) *The Factory System*, p. 29.
173. R. Baker, (1860) *On the State and Condition*, p. 41.
174. A. Reach, (2007) *Fabrics, Filth*, p. 51.
175. W.S. Jevons, (1882) 'Married Women in Factories', p. 41 and 'Select Committee on Protection of Infant Life', *PP* XVI 1872 pp. 21, 45–46, 71 and 89–90. See also G. Newman quoted in R. Woods, (2006) 'Newman's Infant' pp. 40 and 215.
176. R. Woods and N. Shelton, (1997) *An Atlas*, (Liverpool: Liverpool University Press) pp. 51, 60 and 33.
177. Evidence of Dr. Greenhow, in M. Hewitt, (1958) *Wives and Mother's*, p. 147.
178. Evidence of R. Baker, 'Reports of the Commissioners', *PP* 1872 XVI, p. 126, Evidence of Rev. G. Thorpe, 'Select Committee on Protection of Infant Life', *PP* 1871 VII, pp. 45 and 671 and V. Fildes, (1986) *Breast, Bottles and Babies* (Edinburgh: Edinburgh University Press), p. 283.
179. Personal Communication with Dr. Andrew Williams, Consultant Paediatrician at Northampton General Hospital (2009).
180. G.N. Johnstone, (1976) 'The Growth of the Sugar Trade and Refining Industry', in D. J. Oddy and D. S. Millar (eds.), *The Making of the Modern British Diet* (London: Croom Helm), p. 60.
181. Of course there would be demographic variations in price, but nonetheless it could be fair to argue that a lower price would be passed on to the customer.

J. Burnett, (1985) *Plenty and Want, A Social History of Diet in England from 1815 to the Present Day* (London: Penguin), p. 142.

182. J. Blackman, (1976) 'The Corner Shop: The Development of the Grocery and General Provision Trade' in D. J. Oddy and D. S. Millar (eds), *The Making of the Modern British Diet* (London: Croom Helm), p. 148 and G.N. Johnstone, 'The Growth of the Sugar Trade', pp. 60–61.

183. E. Gaskell, (1987) *Mary Barton* (Oxford: Oxford University Press), p. 97 and G. Gissing, (1973) *The Nether World* (London: Dent), p. 75.

184. R. Baker, (1860) *It's No'butts and Niver Heed*, (Leeds), Evidence of Rev. G. Thorpe, 'Select Committee on Protection of Infant Life', PP 1871 VII, pp. 45 and 671. V. Fildes, (1986) *Breast, Bottles and Babies*, pp. 283.

185. See also Census County of York Volume, (1901) Table 35, pp. 246–7.

186. Causes of Death in England, *PP* 1867 XVI, p. 125.

187. Leeds Brotherton Library, Woodhouse Cemetery Burial Registers 1866–1874 – MS421/4i; MS421/4ii; MS421/5i. R. Woods and N. Shelton, (1997) *An Atlas*, p. 60.

188. B.L. Hutchins, (1983) 'Yorkshire', p. 137 and M. Tennant, (1908) 'Incompatibility of breast feeding and factory employment of mothers', in G. Tuckwell, *Women in Industry from Seven Points of View* (London: Duckworth), p. 117.

189. W. Dodd, (1968) *The Factory*, pp. 57 and 65.

190. J. Humphries, (2010) *Childhood and Child Labour*, p. 17.

191. B.L. Hutchins, (1983) 'Yorkshire', p. 137. For an in-depth discussion of nineteenth century female factory inspectors see B. Harrison and M. Nolan, (2004) 'Reflections in Colonial Glass? Women Factory Inspectors in Britain and New Zealand, 1893–1921', *Women's History Review*, 13, pp. 263–88.

192. J. Lown, (1990) *Women and Industrialization: Gender at Work in Nineteenth-Century England* (Cambridge: Polity), p. 146.

193. S. Pooley, (2010) 'All we parents want is that our children's health and lives should be regarded': Child Health, and Parental Concern in England c. 1860–1910', *Social History of Medicine*, 23, p. 536.

194. M. Llewelyn Davies, (1978) *Maternity*, mother 51, p. 78–9.

195. 'Public Health. Reports of the Medical Officer of the Privy Council and Local Government Board. New series, No.VI. Report to the Lords of the Council on Scientific Investigations, Made, under their Direction, in Aid of Pathology and Medicine,' *PP* 1875 c.1371 XL, p. 205.

196. F. Engels, (1969) *The Conditions of the Working Class in England: From Personal Observations and Authentic Sources* (St Albans: Granada), p. 172. Engels gives no primary source note for this comment, but I would hazard that it is from either – Factories' Inquiry Commission's Report, Power's Report on Leeds, *passim*; Tufnell Report on Manchester, p. 17 or 'Report of Factories' Inquiry Commission.' Testimony of Dr. Hawkins, p. 3.

197. 'To the final Reports of the Royal Commission on Vaccination in the areas of Dewsbury, (1891–2) London (1892–3), Warrington (1892–3), Leicester (1892–3), Gloucester (1895–6), Glasgow, Liverpool, Salford, Manchester, Oldham, Chadderton, Leeds, Sheffield, Halifax and Bradford (1892–3),' with c. 8615 being the final written report, *PP's* 1897 c.8609–c.8615

198. M. Hewitt, (1958) *Wives and Mother's* p. 164.

199. M. Hewitt, (1958) *Wives and Mother's* p. 164.

200. For details of these arrangements at Tean Hall Mill, refer to: http://www.bbc.co.uk/radio4/history/making_history/making_history_20080617.shtml. The mill specialised in the weaving of tape, had 352 looms.

201. M. Llewelyn Davies, (1978) *Maternity*, mother 105, p. 137, and mother 26 p. 54.
202. Mrs A 26 in Hutchins survey commented to Hutchins on her work in the Yorkshire weaving mills during the 1860s. She was interviewed at the age of 69 in 1909. She was married at 18. B.L. Hutchins, (1983) 'Yorkshire', pp. 149–50.
203. 'Factory and Workshops Acts Commission. Report of the Commissioners' *PP* 1876 c.14431 XXIX-1, p. 144.
204. M. Llewelyn Davies, (1978) *Maternity*, mother 53, p. 80.
205. Mother A26 in B. Hutchins, (1983) 'Yorkshire', p. 146.
206. Mother 105 in M. Llewelyn Davies, (1978) *Maternity*, p. 136.
207. 'Vaccination Commission. Appendix IX. To the Final Report of the Royal Commission on Vaccination. Papers Relating to Cases in Which Death or Non-Fatal Injury was Alleged or Suggested to Have Been Caused by, or Otherwise Connected with, Vaccination 1897 c. 8615, p. 314.
208. R. Pearson, (1986) 'The Industrial Suburbs' p. 67.
209. R. Pearson, (1986) 'The Industrial Suburbs' p. 67 and A. Reach, (2007) *Fabrics, Filth*, p. 18
210. R. Pearson, (1986) 'The Industrial Suburbs',
211. Mrs A 26. B.L. Hutching (1983) 'Yorkshire'. She stated however in 1909 that this practice was now outlawed.
212. 'Royal Commission on Labour. The Employment of women.' May E Abraham. Lady Assistant Commissioner visited Yorkshire mills. *PP* 1893–94 c.6894-XXIII, p. 102.
213. Mothers 3, 13, 17, 19, 37, 46, 53, 54, 83, 134, 135, 136, 138. M. Llewelyn Davies, *Maternity*
214. M. Llewelyn Davies, (1978) *Maternity*, mother 13, p. 35.
215. Mrs. Warren, (1865) *How I Managed my Children from Infancy to Marriage* (London), p. 17
216. William Hunter recommended weaning infants between the ages of 8 and 9 months. See V. Fildes, (1986) *Breasts, Bottles and Babies*, p. 391.
217. L. Twinning, (1859) 'Infant Feeding', (Ladies Sanitary Association: London), p. 24.
218. Mrs D8 in B. Hutchins (1983) Mrs D8 worked in the Yorkshire mills. She was aged 34 when she was interviewed about her child care practices by the Women's Industrial Council in 1909.
219. B. Hutchins (1983) 'Yorkshire', p. 135.
220. W. Elkin, (1983) 'Manchester' in C. Black (ed.), *Married Women's Work*, p. 169.
221. See the front cover illustration of Marshall's Mill.
222. Mary Cooper's testimony to Jill Liddington and Jill Norris, in J. Liddington and J. Norris, (1978 and 2000), *One Hand Tied Behind Us*, p. 58
223. J. Lewis, (1986) (ed.) *Labour and Love Women's Experience of Home and Family* (Oxford: Blackwell), p. 83.
224. B. Cotton, (1990) *The English Regional Chair* (Woodbridge: Antique Collectors Club), and B. Cotton, (2008) *Scottish Vernacular Furniture* (London: Thames & Hudson).
225. M. Llewelyn-Davies, (1978) *Maternity*, mother 105, p. 137, and mother 26, p. 54.
226. 'Reports of the inspectors of factories to Her Majesty's Principal Secretary of State for the Home Department for the half year ending 31st October 1866', 1867 c.3794, p. 25.
227. E. Crowe, (1874) 'The Dinner Hour', Mill Workers in Wigan.
228. T. Spence (1796) 'Rights of Infants', or, The Imprescriptable Right of Mothers to Such a Share of the elements as is sufficient to Enable Them to Suckle and

.....passim. For an insight into the mind of this English Radical Reformer see K. Armstrong, (2007) *The Hive of Liberty: the Life and Work of Thomas Spence 1750–1814* (Whitley Bay: Thomas Spence Trust) and A. Bonnett, (2007) 'The Other Rights of Man', the Revolutionary Plan of Thomas Spence, *History Today*, 57, pp. 42–8

229. J.G. Williamson (1995 argues that higher weekly wages were given to labours in exchange for working in the difficult conditions or urban industrial towns. See M. J Daunton, *Progress and Poverty: an Economic and Social History of Britain 1700–1850*, (Oxford: Oxford University Press), p. 440. See also J.G. Williamson (1981) 'Urban Disamenities, Dark Satanic Mills and the British Standard of Living Debate' *Journal of Economic History*, 41, pp. 75–83 and J.G. Williamson, (1990) *Coping with City Growth during the British Industrial Revolution* (Cambridge: Cambridge University Press).

230. Mr O'Conor confirmed the legal right of mothers to take infants to work in the factories and workshops during industrialisation. Factory and Workshops Acts Commission. Report of the Commissioners' Vol II Minutes of Evidence, *PP* 1876 c.1443–1 XXX-1, p. 303.

231. Mr O'Conor confirmed the legal right of mothers to take infants to work in the factories and workshops during industrialisation. 'Factory and Workshops Acts Commission'. Report of the Commissioners' Vol II *PP* 1876 c.1443-1 XXX-1, p. 303.

232. Mr O'Conor confirmed the legal right of mothers to take infants to work in the factories and workshops during industrialisation. 'Factory and Workshops Acts Commission. Report of the Commissioners' Vol II *PP* 1876 c.1443-1 XXX-1, p. 303.

233. *Huddersfield Daily Chronicle*, 25 August 1896. M. E. Shaw, 'The Childhood of the Working Classes in the Leeds area 1830–71', Unpublished PhD Thesis, (Leeds) p. 31.

234. M. E. Shaw, (1975) 'The Childhood of the Working Classes', p. 31.

235. June Hannam has noted the same domestic environment in Lancashire, as high rates of children and married women were employed in Lancashire as their wage was crucial to family economy. J. Hannam, (1989) *Isabella Ford*, p. 316 footnote 45. R. Pearson, (1986) 'The Industrial Suburbs', p. 336. M.E. Shaw, (1975) 'The Childhood' p. 169.

236. Reports of the inspectors of factories to Her Majesty's Principal Secretary of State for the Home Department, for the half year ending 31st October 1862', *PP* 1863 c.3076 XVIII, p. 123 and see R. Gray, *The Factory*, p. 106–7. 'Reports of the Inspectors of Factories to Her Majesty's Principal Secretary of State for the Home Department for the half year ending 30th April 1871', *PP* 1871 c.446 XIV, p. 13 or p. 637.

237. M.E. Shaw, 'The Childhood' (1975) 5,677 male and female children in in Leeds worked as 'slubbers', usually a male adult occupation, in flax mills getting the cloth ready for spinning, or 'heckled' in the 'heckling rooms' of Marshalls Temple Flax mills at Holbeck Leeds, in rooms which were a 'hive of industry as they hardly a moment of inactivity,' with the children 'toiling so quickly and dexterously never before remarked in the industry', or the 'piecing' 'slubbing' and 'spinning processes. R. Gray, (1996) *The Factory Question*, pp. 106–7. The wish to have their children in work was extremely strong for factory mothers consequently, less than 10 percent of children attended school. M.E. Shaw, (1975) The Childhood. See also R. Pearson, (1986) 'The Industrial Suburbs' p. 328. Leeds

Factory mothers therefore espoused a strong work rather than educational ethic to their children as mothers thought work more important than school. This was a theory which witnesses sympathised with as they reported schools 'were not always what they were made out to be' as they were unkempt, cold and damp. See 'Report of the Commissioners, Factory and Workshop Acts Commission', 1876 c.1443, p. 169 – It was not only mothers who considered children better at work than at school. Whateley-Cooke Taylor also argued the factory and its work offered more, as 'the tasks which children [were] employed for were not laborious, but monotonous', and that the 'children in the mill are better off than nine out of ten children of the same class in England. The mill is a better place than the mine, the ship, the forge and a very many private workshops', a remark which was confirmed by the working children', H. Heaton, (1965) *The Yorkshire Woollen and Worsted Industries* (Oxford: Oxford Clarendon Press), p. 239.

238. G. and J. Stubley Factory Certificates, KC 74, West Yorkshire Archive Service.
239. Using their female offspring to care for their younger siblings served two logical purposes. The first as a protection method as it reduced the risk of what Jane Humphries has termed 'importunate or undesirable liaisons', girls were at risk to from men both in and out of the factory.. J. Humphries, (1987) "....The most free from moral objection...." p. 903. The enormity of the part played by children, particularly male children in the industrial revolution is 'emphatically' made by Jane Humphries. Female children worked with their mothers in the West Riding district and which served two purposes. One was to provide their girls with a work ethic and moral sense of respectability, the characters of which would come into play when marriage loomed for in doing this the girls could show themselves to be a 'cut above' the female children of the Irish community who lived near them, whose mothers put them to work merely as hawkers selling matches in the street. Jane Humphries, (2010) *Childhood and Child Labour*, p. 8. Arguably, the mothers in the West Riding district sought to prevent their girls being seen as 'fast' or 'sexually unrespectable' when marriage prospects arose. The West Riding area therefore considered that the advantages of a scholarly education for working-class girls in the West Riding were little, and it made more sense to have them at work with them and learning a factory skill, thus equipping them with skills for marriage. J. Humphries, (1987) "The most free from moral objection", p. 947. S. Steinbach, (2005) *Women In England*, p. 13.
240. *Morning Chronicle*, Birmingham, 25 November 1850, in P.E. Razzell and R. W. Wainwright, (1973) *The Victorian Working Class, Selections from the Morning Chronicle* (London: Cass), p. 295–6. Rizzell and Wainwright provide a picture of women making buttons at a button factory, but the author of the picture omits to show evidence of infants at the factory, pp. 291–6.
241. *Morning Chronicle*, Birmingham, 25 November 1850, in P.E. Razzell and R.W. Wainwright (1973) *The Victorian Working Class*, p. 295–6. Razzell and Wainwright provide a picture of women making buttons at a button factory, but the author of the picture omits to show evidence of infants at the factory, p. 291.
242. M. Llewelyn Davies, (1978) *Maternity:* mother 105, p. 136.
243. A. Reach, (2007) *Fabrics, Filth*, p. 35.
244. A. Reach, (2007) *Fabrics, Filth*, p. 22.
245. A. Reach, (2007) *Fabrics, Filth*, p. 35.
246. A. Reach, (2007) *Fabrics, Filth*, p. 35.

247. A. Reach, (2007) *Fabrics, Filth*, p. 22.
248. 'Royal Commission on Labour. The Employment of Women.' *PP* 1893–94 c.6894 XXIII, p. 100.
249. 'Royal Commission on Labour. The Employment of Women.' *PP* 1893–94 c.6894 XXIII, p. 105.
250. 'Children's Employment Commission'. The Employment of Women' *PP*, 1864 XXII, evidence of J. Barron, p. 2. R. Pearson, 'The Industrial Suburbs' pp. 66–7.
251. 'Report from the Committee on the Bill to Regulate the Labour of Children in the Mills and Factories in the United Kingdom with the Minutes of Evidence, Appendix and Index' *PP* 1831–2 Vol, XV, p. 168–9.
252. M.E. Shaw, (1975) 'The Childhood', p. 268.
253. Marshall's Mill Records Handlist 6, Leeds University Library. Records of soap bought.
254. A. Reach, (2007) *Fabrics, Filth*, pp. 65–6 and 71 and *Leeds Intelligencer*, 11 July 1863 and *Leeds Mercury*, 7 May 1864.
255. *Leeds Mercury*, 29 February 1872 and *Leeds Mercury*, 2 March 1891.
256. M. Pember Reeves, (2008) *Round About Pound a Week*, (First published in 1913). This was the feeding pattern mothers in Lambeth described during 1909 – 1914, pp. 148, 153, 155, and 159. This feeding method was practiced for at least nine months. M. Llewelyn Davies, (1978) *Maternity*, passim.
257. B. Pourdeyhimi, K.C. Jackson and K. Hepworth, 'The Development of Weaving Using Automatic Looms', point 1.3 http://ulita.leeds.ac.uk/docs/Ars_Textrina/Volume4/9.The%20development%20of%20weaving.pdf
258. M. Tennant, (1908) 'Incompatibility', p. 117
259. See E. Griffin, (2010) *A Short History*, p. 95 for the problems beset by the early power looms.
260. L. Faucher, (1844) *Manchester in 1844, Its Present Condition*, (London).
261. E. Griffin, (2010) *A Short History*, p. 89.
262. E. Roberts, (1984) *A Woman's Place*, p. 166.
263. A.M. Huberman, (1996) *Escape from the Market: Negotiating Work in Lancashire* (Cambridge: Cambridge University Press), p. 9.
264. J. O'Neill's testimony in M. Brigg (1982) (ed.) *The Journals of a Lancashire Weaver 1856–1875* (S.I: The Record Society of Lancashire and Cheshire) pp. 57 and 170.
265. A. Anderson, (1922) *Women in the Factory, An Administrative Adventure, 1893–1921* (London: John Murray), p. 2.
266. 'Children's Employment Commission. Second Report of the Commissioners. Trades and Manufacturers' *PP's* 1843 c. 430 XIII, c.431 XIV.1 and c.432 XV.1, p. M10.
267. *The Reporter* 16 January – 15 March 1875; *The Huddersfield Chronicle*, 16 February – 19 March 1875 and *The Huddersfield Examiner* 16 February – 19 March 1875.
268. E.P. Thompson (1967) 'Time Work Discipline and Industrial Capitalism', *Past and Present*, 38, p. 60
269. For this understanding of time and its use see N. Elias, (1992) *Time: An Essay on Time*, (Oxford: Basil Blackwell), p. 122.
270. L. Davidoff and C. Hall, (1987) *Family Fortunes: Men and Women of the English Middle Class 1750–1850* (London: Hutchinson), p. 399. This mode of feeding was considered vulgar by middle class women who sought to do it in the 'seclusion' of the home wherever possible.

271. 'Factory and Workshops Acts Commission. Report of the Commissioners'. *PP* 1876 c.1443 XXIX-1, p. 212 or on net 342.

272. 'Reports of the Inspectors of Factories to Her Majesty's Principal Secretary of State for the Home Department, for the half year ending 31st October 1864', *PP* 1865 c.3473 XX, p. 107.

273. M. Hewitt, (1958) *Wives and Mother's*, p. 164.

274. Mrs. Layton, (1978) 'Life as we have known it: Memories of Seventy Years' in M. Llewelyn Davies, *Life as We Have Known It* (London: Virago) First published in 1931, p. 4.

275. 'Reports of the Inspectors of Factories to Her Majesty's Principal Secretary of State for the Home Department, for the half year ending 31st October 1864,' *PP* 1865 c.3473 XX, p. 109.

276. 'Report of the Industrial Revolution', *PP*, IUP, 1867–8, Vol. 8, pp. 137 and 212.

277. *Huddersfield Daily Chronicle*, 12 January 1857.

278. 'Factory and Workshops Acts Commission. Report of the Commissioners', *PP* 1876 c1443 XXIX, Vol I, p. 321.

279. 'Factory and Workshops Acts Commission, Report of the Commissioners' *PP* 1876 c1443 Vol I, p. 31.

280. Factory and Workshops Acts Commission. Report of the Commissioners'. *PP* 1876 c1443-I XXX-1]. Evidence of JH Marshall, 4 June 1875, p. 177.

281. 1871 census. Sarah Dawson lived at 67 Franchise Street, Leeds District 56.

282. W. Dodd, (1968) *The Factory System*, pp. 11 and 50. Evidence of Mr. Tennant, *Hansard*, 1844, LXXIII, col. 1379.

283. E. Roberts, (1984) *A Woman's Place*, p. 165.

284. R. Baker, (1868) *The Factory Acts Made Easy, or How to Work the Law Without the Risk of Penalties Embracing the Acts of 1853, 1856 and 1867*, (Leeds), p. 39. Engels has argued that the 1833 Factory Act, sought to provide child factory workers with some education. The 1834 Act 'forbade the employment of children under nine years of age (except in silk mills), limited the working hours of children between 9–13 to 48 per week, or 9 hours in and one day at the most' .... and 'compulsory school attendance of two hours daily was prescribed for all children under fourteen years' .... F. Engels, (1969) *The Condition of the Working Classes* (London: Panther), p. 200.

285. 'Reports of the Commissioners in to the Employment of Children, Young Persons and Women', *PP* 1868–9 XVIII, p. 80.

286. Testimony from the power loom weaver John O'Neill, in in M. Brigg, (1982) (ed.) *The Journals*, p. 170.

287. Testimony from John O'Neill, M. Brigg, (1982) (ed.) *The Journals*, p. 38.

288. 'Children's Employment Commission (1862). Second Report of the Commissioners,' *PP* 1864 c.3414 XXII.1, **pp**. Ix, 9 and 212.

289. M. Mostyn Bird, (1911) *Women at Work*: A *Study of the Different Ways of Earning a Living Open to Women* (London: Chapman & Hall) p. 21.

290. B.L. Hutchins, (1983) 'Yorkshire', p. 138.

291. G. Jewsbury, (1966) *Marian Withers*, 1851, in W. Neff, *Victorian Working Women*, p. 82.

292. R. Pearson, (1986) 'The Industrial Suburbs', p. 69.

293. A. Reach, (2007) *Fabrics, Filth*, p. 65

294. For the discussion of private spheres see A. Vickery, (1993) 'Golden Age to Separate Spheres; *A Review of the Categories and Chronology of English Women's History*, 36, p. 403.
295. *Leeds Intelligencer*, 11 March 1854.
296. K. Morgan, (2004) *The Birth of Industrial Britain, Economic Change 1750–1850*, (Harlow: Pearson) p. 29.
297. 'Royal Commission on Labour. The Employment of Women.' *PP* 1893–94 c.6894–XXIII, p. 101–3.
298. 'Royal Commission on Labour. The Employment of Women.' *PP* 1893–94 c.6894–XXIII p. 102.
299. 'Royal Commission on Labour. The Employment of Women.' *PP* 1893–94 c.6894–XXIII, p. 101–3.
300. Evidence of Maria Field, George Latham and R.D. Grainger Esq., in 'Children's Employment Commission, Second Report, Trades and Manufacturers'. *PP* 1843 c.430, c. 431 & c. 432, p. *f*124.
301. K. Morgan, (2004) *The Birth*, p. 28
302. Amy Riley: Leeds Woodhouse Death Registers. Leeds Brotherton Library, Woodhouse Cemetery Burial Registers 1866–1874 – MS421/4i; MS421/4ii; MS421/5i.
303. *Huddersfield Chronicle*, 12 January 1877.
304. See for example in the 1871 census Elizabeth Bradley (3 children), Martha Marshall who worked at Holly Park Mill (4 children), Sarah Busfield (2 children), Hannah Walsh (2 children), Eliza Day (8 children), Mary Battye (4 children), Elizabeth Sykes (4 children). For Holly Park Mill Wages Records 1868–1872 see Holly Park Mill Records, Handlist 138, note 15 for wages book 1868–1872 at Leeds Brotherton Library.
305. E. Griffin, (2010) *A Short History*, p. 83.
306. S.O. Rose, (1992) *Limited Livelihoods*, p. 151.

3 Workhouse Nurses

1. P. Thane (1978) 'Women and the Poor Law, in Victorian and Edwardian England, *History Workshop Journal*, 6, pp. 30–38.
2. F. Crompton, (1997) *Workhouse Children : Infant and Child Paupers Under the Worcestershire Poor Law, 1780–1871*, (Sutton: Stroud), p. 37 and P. Thane (1978) 'Women and the Poor Law' p. 54
3. F. Crompton, (1997) *Workhouse Children*, chapters three and five and p. 202; P. Thane (1978) 'Women and the Poor Law', pp. 29–51 and p. 30–38 and J. Reinarz and L. Schwartz (2013) (ed.) *Medicine and the Workhouse*, (New York: Rochester), p. 6 and especially chapter 9, A. Negrine, 'Practitioners and Paupers: Medicine at the Leicester Union Workhouse, 1867–1905', pp. 192–211.
4. Quoted in B. Abel-Smith, (1979) *A History, of the Nursing Profession* (London: Heinemann), p. 5.
5. S and B. Webb, (1963) *English Poor Law History, Part II, The Last Hundred Years*, Vol. 1, (London: Cass), p. 305 and 310–11.
6. S and B. Webb, (1963) *English Poor Law*, pp. 305 and 310–11.
7. J. Reinarz and L. Schwartz (2013) (ed.) *Medicine and the Workhouse*, p. 6 and especially chapter 9, A. Negrine, 'Practitioners and Paupers', pp. 192–211.
8. R. Richardson, (2013) 'The Art of Medicine: A Dismal Prospect, Workhouse Health Care', *The Lancet*, 6 July 2013, pp. 20–21.

9. L. Twining, (1892) 'Nursing in Workhouses: A Paper Read Before the Ladies Conference in Liverpool 1891', (Liverpool), p. 7 and Florence Nightingale to her Nurses, (1914) *A Selection from Miss Nightingale's Addresses to Probationers and Nurses of the Nightingale School at St Thomas's Hospital* (London), p. 84.

10. R. Richardson, (2013) 'The Art of Medicine', pp. 20–21, B. Abel-Smith, (1979) *A History*, chapters 1 and 3; F. Crompton (1997) *Workhouse Children:* and P. Thane (1978) 'Women and the Poor Law'.

11. R. Richardson, (2013) 'The Art of Medicine' pp. 20–21; B. Abel-Smith (1979) *A History*, chapters 1 and 3; F. Crompton (1997) *Workhouse Children*, chapters, three and five; and P. Thane (1978) 'Women and the Poor Law', passim.

12. S. and B. Webb, (1963) *English Poor Law*, pp. 310–11 and R. Richardson, (2013) 'The Art of Medicine', pp. 20–21.

13. L. Twining, (1898) *Workhouses and Pauperism, and Women's Work in the Administration of the Poor Law*, (London) p. 201 and L. Rose, (1986) *The Massacre of the Innocents, Infanticide in Britain 1800–1939*, (Routledge & Kegan Paul), p. 31.

14. B. Abel-Smith, (1979) *A History*, p. 15 and L. Twining, (1898) 'Nursing in Workhouses', p. 7. Anne Digby made this remark was made in light of the Strand Union Workhouse, London. See A. Digby, (1978) *Pauper Palaces* (London: Routledge & Kegan Paul), p. 246.

15. R. Richardson, (2013) 'The Art of Medicine', pp. 20–21.

16. 'Report on Metropolitan Workhouses', *PP*, 1866, LXI p. 530.

17. B. Abel-Smith, (1979) *A History*, p. 10.

18. F.P. Cobbe found this depiction of the pauper nurses during her visits to workhouses during 1861. Quoted in B. Abel-Smith, (1979) *A History*, p. 12.

19. Workhouse Visiting Society, (*WVS*) (1860–1865), p. 295.

20. D.M. Saunders, (1982) 'Sick Children's Nursing' in P. Allan and M. Jolley, *Nursing, Midwifery and Health Visiting Since 1900* (London: Faber & Faber), pp. 141–50.

21. *BMJ*, 23 March 1889, p. 682.

22. L. Twining, (1892) 'Nursing in Workhouses', p. 7. Nightingale summed up the nursing character as those who were 'too old, too weak, too drunken, too dirty, too stolid, or too bad to do anything else.' Quoted in B. Abel-Smith, (1979) *A History*, p. 5.

23. F.P. Cobbe found this depiction of the pauper nurses during her visits to workhouses during 1861. Quoted in B. Abel-Smith, (1979) *A History*, p. 12 and *BMJ*, 18 April 1868, p. 380.

24. *WVS*, (1860–1865) p. 296.

25. B. Abel-Smith, (1979) *A History*, p. 11 and F. Crompton, (1997) *Workhouse Children*, pp. 10 and 35. L. Rose, (1986) *The Massacre*, p. 32

26. The lack of knowledge as to the infants' welfare experience may be due to the workhouse being mainly seen as an instrument of adult welfare which put the adult employed to work and cared as best it could for the adult sick. The infant experience therefore, has been little told and remains mainly an enigma to modern historians. This has left a knowledge gap in light of infant inmates and as such Levene may have a point as when looking to the history of welfare, or its iconic building the workhouse we can see an overemphasis on the adult inmate. For the shifts in sentiment towards the poor, which gave rise to the New Poor Law in 1834 which can be characterised as a desire to punish the indigent and indolent adult unemployed male pauper, see G. Himmelfarb, (1983) *The Idea of Poverty*, (New York: Vintage). This was to be achieved by curtailing outdoor relief and the use of the workhouse, as a mechanism of welfare delivery operating

under the principal of less eligibility. For further information see S. and B Webb, (1963) *English Poor Law*; S. King, (2000) *Poverty and Welfare in England, 1700–1850, A Regional Perspective* (Manchester: Manchester University Press), and A. Brundage, (2002) *The English Poor Laws, 1700–1930* (Basingstoke: Palgrave).

27. N. Longmate, (1974) *The Workhouse* (London: Temple Smith), p. 174.

28. A. Levene, T. Nutt, and S. Williams, (2005) *Illegitimacy in Britain, 1700–1920* (Basingstoke: Palgrave), p. 36. This may be due to a lack of source material and the consequences of this have meant that documentation of any infant experience has had to be teased from adult testimony. This has left a knowledge gap in light of infant inmates and as such Levene may have a point as when looking to the history of welfare, or its iconic building the workhouse we can see an overemphasis on the adult inmate. For the shifts in sentiment towards the poor, which gave rise to the New Poor Law in 1834 which can be characterised as a desire to punish the indigent and indolent adult unemployed male pauper, see G. Himmelfarb, *The Idea of Poverty*. This was to be achieved by curtailing outdoor relief and the use of the workhouse, as a mechanism of welfare delivery operating under the principal of less eligibility. For further information see S and B Webb, (1963) *English Poor Law*; S. King, (2000) *Poverty and Welfare in England, 1700–1850*, and A. Brundage, (2002) *The English Poor Laws*.

29. K. Price, (2011) 'The Crusade Against Out-Relief', *The Lancet*, 19 March 2011, pp. 988–9 and T. Evans, (2005) *'Unfortunate Objects', Lone Mothers in the Eighteenth Century* (Basingstoke: Palgrave Macmillan), p. 208.

30. Historians such as Levene et al., Hollen-Lees, Price, Rose and McDonaugh have acknowledged that this treatment of single mothers was Malthus' favoured response to high bastardy rates. The role of the workhouse in policing bastardy is contested within the historiographical terrain and Arnot for example, has argued that bastardy in-and-of itself did not confer any degree of stigma on either mother or child, and therefore met with no specific welfare sanctions. Crompton, however, argues that the workhouse itself, in its New Poor Law guise, was formulated as a direct response to address the 'problem' of housing the progeny of unmarried mothers, and that attempts to confer the deserving status on infants did not come into effect until the 1870s. See F. Crompton, (1997) *Workhouse Children*; K. Price, (2011) 'The Crusade against Outdoor Relief', *The Lancet*, 19 March 2011, pp. 988–9; M. Arnot, (1994) 'Infant Death, Child Care and the State: The Baby-Farming Scandal and the First Infant Life Protection Legislation of 1872', in *Continuity and Change*, 9, pp. 271–311; A. Levene, et al, (2005) *Illegitimacy in Britain*; L. Rose, (1986) *The Massacre* ; J. McDonaugh, (2003) *Child Murder and British Culture, 1720–1900* (Cambridge: Cambridge University Press) and L.H. Lees, (1998) *The Solidarities of Strangers: The English Poor Laws and the People 1700–1949* (Cambridge: Cambridge University Press).

31. T. Evans, (2005) *Unfortunate'*, p. 208.

32. W. B. Ryan, (1862) *Infanticide: its Law, Prevalence, Prevention, and History* (London), p. 19 and p. 84–85.

33. W. B. Ryan, (1862) *Infanticide*, pp. 19 and 84–85.

34. T. Evans, (2005) *Unfortunate*, p. 146.

35. M.A. Crowther, (1981) *The Workhouse System 1834–1929: The History of an English Social Institution* (London: Batsford Academic & Educational), S. King, (2000) *Poverty and Welfare*, pp. 161–2.

36. L. Rose, (1986) *The Massacre*, pp. 46–7.
37. L. Rose, (1986) *The Massacre*, pp. 46–7.
38. A. Levene et al, (2005) 'Introduction', *Illegitimacy in Britain*, p. 42.
39. F. Crompton, (1997) *Workhouse Children*, passim.
40. L. Rose, (1986) *The Massacre*, p. 31.
41. F. Crompton, (1997) *Workhouse Children*, p. 35 and p. 47 and N. Longmate, *The Workhouse* (1974)
42. N. Longmate, (1974) *The Workhouse*, p. 173.
43. Dr. Edward Smith, 'Dietaries for the Inmates of Workhouses', Report to the President of the Poor Law Board of Dr. Edward Smith, F.R.S., Medical Officer of the Poor Law Board, and Poor Law Inspector. *PP* 1867–8 c.3660.
44. Catherine is usually just associated with the neglect of an aged woman in the workhouse but further research has revealed that the majority of the cruel and neglect cases were made against children and youngsters. See *Yorkshire Gazette*, 18 February 1865; 25 March 1865; 1 April, 1865; and *The Leeds Mercury*, 7 March, 1865.
45. *Yorkshire Gazette*, 18 February 1865; 25 March 1865; 1 April 1865; and *The Leeds Mercury*, 7 March 1865.
46. *Yorkshire Gazette*, 18 February 1865; 25 March 1865; 1 April 1865; and *The Leeds Mercury*, 7 March 1865.
47. *The Leeds Mercury*, 7 March 1865.
48. D. Roberts, (1984) 'How Cruel Was the Victorian Poor Law?', *Historical Journal*, 6, pp. 97–107.
49. *BMJ*, 20 July 1895, p. 151.
50. R. Hodgkinson, (1967) *The Origins of the National Health Service* (London: The Wellcome Historical Medical Library), pp. 164–5.
51. Refer to PRO MH9/10 Leeds and Liverpool, MH9/11 Manchester and MH9/18 Wakefield. See also MH9/11 Leeds, p. 184; MH12/15044 Hemsworth; MH12/15052 – 16062 Holbeck; MH 12/15224 Hunslet; MH12/15566 Wakefield; MH12 Manchester: MH12/6063, MH12/15249 13 July 1876, MH12/15042, p. 573/4 976 E/71, MH12/9534/162, MS12/9534/162 and MH12/15141; Southwell Union; MH12/9534/340 and MH12/15141; Bolton Archive, GBO/28/19 and GBO/28/30.
52. PRO MH9/11, p. 184.
53. PRO MH9/10; Leeds.
54. J. Rogers, (1889) *Reminiscences of a Workhouse Medical Officer* (London: F.T. Unwin), p. 9.
55. J. Rogers, (1889) *Reminiscences*, p. 9.
56. *The Lancet*, 15 July 1865.
57. Dr Edward. Smith 'Dietaries', *PP* 1866 c.3660, p. 19. See also M. Llewelyn Davies, (1978, first published 1915), *Maternity, Letters from Working Women* (London: Virago) mother no. one hundred and five, p. 137 and M. Llewelyn Davies, (1904) *The Women's Co-operative Guild*, (Kirby Lonsdale) viz: http://www.hull.ac.uk/arc/downloads/DCWcatalogue.pdf
58. MH12/9534/162; Southwell Union.
59. MH12/9534/340; Southwell Union.
60. *The Lancet*, 18 December 1886, p. 1186.
61. *The Lancet*, 18 December 1886, p. 1185.
62. Dr. Edward E. Smith 'Provincial Workhouses. Report of Dr. Edward Smith Medical Officer to the Poor Law Board, on the Sufficiency of the Existing

Arrangements for the Care and Treatment of the Sick Poor in Forty-Eight Provincial Workhouses in England and Wales; Together With an Appendix to such Report, Containing Dr Smith's Observations on each of the Workhouses in Question; &c, *PP* 1867–68, 4, p. 15.

63. *The Lancet*, 29 July 1865, *BMJ*, 6 October 1894, (Stockport), *BMJ*, 5 May 1894, (Manchester), *BMJ*, 24 May 1890 (Halifax), *The Lancet*, 18 December 1886 (Liverpool), *The Lancet*, 27 January 1877 (Liverpool), *BMJ*, 14 September 1895, (Bradford and Wakefield and Nottingham), *BMJ*, 15 December 1894, (Withington) and *The Lancet*, 20 February 1868 (Babies wards in workhouses).
64. *The Lancet*, 29 July 1865, p. 134
65. *The Lancet*, 29 July 1865, p. 134.
66. *The Lancet*, 29 July 1865 p. 134.
67. *The Lancet*, 29 July 1865, p. 134 and *The Lancet*, 20 February 1869, pp. 268–9.
68. *The Lancet*, 9 September 1865, p. 297 and *The Lancet*, 1 January 1865, p. 20.
69. Bolton Archive Service, GBO/28/19 and Bolton Archive, GBO/28/30.
70. See the case of Sarah Chambers, WYAS Bradford BU3/3/3.
71. B. Abel-Smith, (1979) *A History*, p. 5.
72. Dr. Edward Smith, 'Provincial Workhouses. Report of Dr. Edward Smith', *PP* 1867–68, 4, p. 12.
73. Dr. Edward Smith, 'Provincial Workhouses. Report of Dr. Edward Smith', *PP* 1867–68, 4, p. 12.
74. This remark was made in light of the Strand Union Workhouse, London. See A. Digby, (1978) *Pauper Palaces*, p. 246 and R. Richardson, (2013) 'A Dismal Prospect', pp. 20–21.
75. B. Abel-Smith, (1979) *A History*, p. 11.
76. B. Abel-Smith, (1979) *A History*, p. 11.
77. Dr. Edward Smith, 'Provincial Workhouses. Report of Dr. Edward Smith', *PP* 1867–68, 4, p. 12.
78. For the aged female cohort in the workhouse see S. Ottaway, L. Botelho and K. Kittredge, (2002) (ed.) *Power and Poverty: Old Age in the Pre-Industrial Past* (Westport: Greenwood Press), pp. xii-294.
79. WYAS Wakefield BG/1/1/1, Minute Book, Book II 1860–1865 pp. 232 and 241.
80. Fragile employment for women, and particularly wives of unemployed men led many women to resort to public relief in the shape of the workhouse.
81. Pauper Phoebe Smith for example who was admitted to Bradford workhouse with two small children was put to nurse, see W.R. Wythen Baxter, (1841) *The Book of the Bastilles: or The History of the Working of the New Poor Law* (London: J Stephens), p. 129.
82. WYAS Bradford Admission and Discharge Book, BU – 1857.
83. F. Crompton, (1997) *Workhouse Children*, pp. 110 and 148, *WVS*, (1861) XVI November, pp. 518–19. See G. Holloway for a further description of the duties of a domestic servant during this period: G. Holloway, (2005) *Women and Work in Britain Since 1840* (London: Routledge), p. 21.
84. A Plea, (1861) 'On behalf of the Workhouse Orphan' (London), pp. 12–13.
85. Levine Clark's work on Rye in Sussex suggests that the workhouse had to particularly cater to 'out of work' women. See M. Levine Clark, (2000) 'Engendering Relief: Women, Ablebodiedness, and the New Poor Law in Early Victorian England', *Journal of Women's History*, 11, p. 121. See also D. Valenze who remarks on the problems women experienced gaining full-time employment during

industrialisation: D. Valenze, (1997) *The First Industrial Woman* (Oxford: Oxford University Press).

86. L. Maynard-Salmon, (1901) *Domestic Service* (London), p. 316. My emphasis.
87. L. Maynard-Salmon, (1901) *Domestic Service* (London), p. 316. My emphasis.
88. G. Holloway, (2005) *Women and Work*, pp. 21–23; J. Purvis, (2000) *Women's History: an Introduction* (London: Routledge), pp. 66–7 and R.A. Smith, (1904) *Baby: Its Treatment and Care* (London), p. 99.
89. Mrs Warren, (1865) *How I Managed My Children from Infancy to Marriage* (London), pp. 25 and 34.
90. W. Cobbett, (1837) *Advice to Young Men* (London), p. 146, note 154.
91. W. Cobbett, (1837) *Advice*, p. 234 note 255.
92. J. Bailey, (2012) *Parenting* in England, *1760–1830: Emotion Identity and Generation* (Oxford: Oxford University Press), p. 218.
93. C. Steedman, (2009) *Labours Lost; Domestic Service and the Making of Modern England* (Cambridge: Cambridge: Cambridge University Press), pp. 228–54.
94. J. Bailey, (2012) *Parenting*, p. 28; A. Vickery, (1998) *The Gentleman's Daughter: Women's Lives in Victorian England* (London: Yale University Press) pp. 110, 113, 114 and 142; Mrs Anne Barker, (1770) *The Compleat Servant Maid*, (London), passim. C. White, (1792) *An inquiry into the nature and cause of that swelling in one or both of the lower extremities which sometimes happens to lying-in women; Together with an examination into the propensity of drawing the breasts, of those who give such, and also of those who do not give suck.* 2nd ed. (London).
95. This comment was made by the neighbours of Mr and Mrs Patrick Halpin who employed Mary as a domestic servant. *Huddersfield Daily Chronicle* April 28, 1879.
96. *Huddersfield Chronicle*, 6 September 1887.
97. G. Reynolds, (1853) *Mary Price, or the Memoirs of a Servant Maid* (London), p. 12.
98. M. A. Baines, (1859) *Domestic Servants, As They Are and As They Ought To Be, by a Practical Mistress of a Household*, (Brighton) and M. Baines, (1862) 'Excessive Infant-Mortality: How Can it be Stayed?' A Paper Contributed to the *NAPSS* (London), pp. 6–7.
99. L. Maynard-Salmon, (1901) *Domestic Service*, (London), p. 316.
100. L. Maynard-Salmon, (1901) *Domestic Service*, p. 113.
101. M. A. Baines, (1859) *Domestic Servants*, passim and M. Baines, (1862) 'Excessive Infant-Mortality'.
102. T. Bull, M.D., (1861) *Hints to Mothers for the Management of Health During the Period of Pregnancy and in the Lying-in Room* (London), M.A. Baines, (1862) 'Excessive Infant-Mortality'; L. Maynard-Salmon, (1901) *Domestic Service*, p. 253 and P. Jalland, (1986) *Women and Marriage and Politics 1860–1914* (Oxford: Oxford University Press), p. 137.
103. WVS, (1860–1865) p. 692 and A plea, (1861) 'The Workhouse Orphan'.
104. P. Crawford, (1986) 'The Suckling Child, Adult Attitudes to Child Care in the First Year of Life in Seventeenth-Century England', in *Continuity and Change*, 1, p. 38.
105. D. Dick, (1987) *Yesterday's Babies, A History of Baby Care*, front cover (London: Bodley Head), p. 61.
106. D. Dick, (1987) *Yesterday's Babies*, p. 62.
107. D. Dick, (1987) *Yesterday's Babies*, p. 62.
108. J. Walkowitz, (1980) *Prostitution and Victorian Society, Women, Class, and The State* (Cambridge: Cambridge University Press), p. 119.

208 Notes to Chapter 3

109. G. Reynolds, (1853) *Mary Price*, p. 12.
110. Mrs Anne Barker, (1770) *The Complete Servant Maid*, pp. 29–33.
111. WYAS Bradford BU6/1/1 Maria Brookes.
112. F. Crompton, (1997) *Workhouse Children*, p. xv.
113. See the Poor Law Records MH9/11B for the hundreds of Nurses whom the Manchester workhouse trained. B. Abel-Smith, (1979) *A History*, pp. 39–40 and 227. Refer to Appendix 3 for an illustration of the Manchester Poor Law Records showing the names of the nurses trained in the workhouse. MH9/11: Manchester, p. 225.
114. S. and B. Webb, (1963) *English Poor Law*, p. 304; M.A. Nutting and L.L. Dock, (2000) *A History of Nursing* (Bristol: Thoemmes Press), p. 502; J. Lane, (2001) *A Social History of Medicine, Health, Healing and Disease in England, 1750–1950* (London: Routledge), p. 127; B. Abel-Smith, (1979) *A History*, p. 4 and 11 and *The Leeds Mercury*, 24 June 1865.
115. Research for paid infant nurses was carried out through the hundreds of nurses employed by the Poor Law throughout the years 1860–1900. See the Poor Law Records of Registered Paid Staff in Workhouses, PRO MH9/3, Bradford; MH9/8 Hemsworth and Holbeck; MH9/10:Leeds and Liverpool; MH9/11 Manchester and Malton; North Riding of Yorkshire Manchester; MH9/20 and also MH9/18 Wakefield.
116. Manchester Poor Law Records, PRO MH12/6063, f48,49,and 50.
117. PRO MH9/11, Manchester, p. 200; and Manchester Poor Law Records, PRO MH12/6063, f48, 49,and 50.
118. J. Rogers, (1870) 'The Poor Law Medical Officers' Assocation; An Address...at a General Meeting ... November 29*th*', (London).
119. J. Wilson, (1890) *Nursing in Workhouses and Workhouse Infirmaries* (London), p. 21 and J. Rogers, (1889) *Reminiscences*, p. 10 and passim.
120. M.A. Nutting et al, (2000) *A History*, p. 502.
121. PRO MH12/15249 13 July 1876.
122. PRO MH9/Leeds. Annie resigned the same year, the reason being 'not stated'.
123. B. Abel-Smith, (1979) *A History*, p. 14. Abel-Smith quotes that this figure has been calculated from information given in the *Lancet Commission*, (1866), p. 24.
124. B. Abel-Smith, (1979) *A History*, pp. 5 and 11. Although both working-class and middle-class women sat on the Leeds Union election board during the 1870s, who were able to vote on the issues of infant care, the Leeds workhouse was run by pauper and not paid nurses. See Appendix 4.
125. Dr. Edward. Smith, 'Provincial Workhouses. Report of Dr. Edward Smith', *PP* 1867–68, 4, p. 12
126. Dr. Edward. Smith, 'Provincial Workhouses. Report of Dr. Edward Smith', *PP* 1867–68, 4, p. 12
127. L. Marks, (1993) 'Medical Care for Pauper Mothers and Their Infants: Poor Law Provision and Local Demand in East London, 1870–1929' *Economic History Review*, XLVI, 3 p. 527.
128. L. Marks, (1993) 'Poor Law Provision', p. 533.
129. L. Marks, (1993) 'Poor Law Provision', p. 528.
130. A. Sheen M.D., ST., M.R.C.S., Eng., D.P.H. Camb.,(1890) 'The Workhouse and its Medical Doctor', (London), p. 60.
131. *The Lancet*, 29 July 1865, p. 134.
132. The Lancet, 29 July 1865, p. 132.
133. *The Lancet*, 29 July 1865, p. 134 and *The Lancet*, 27 July 1866, p. 205.

134. Dr. Edward Smith 'Provincial Workhouses. Report of Dr. Edward Smith', *PP* 1867–68, 4, p. 13.
135. *The Lancet,* 4 November 1865, p. 514.
136. S & B. Webb, (1963) *English Poor Law History*, p. 311.
137. A.M. Dickens, (1976) 'The Workhouse' *Architectural Review*, CLX, No. 958. The reason why Guildford set aside enough space for two lying-in wards whilst other areas did not is not yet known, but this makes one wonder as to where a pregnant woman was to have her baby in other workhouses. The *BMJ* reported that in 1894 Truro still had no labour bed and Bath, in 1894 still no labour ward. See *BMJ*, 29 September 1894 p. 710 and *BMJ*, 7 July 1894, p. 27.
138. *BMJ*, 14 July 1894, p. 80.
139. Dr. Edward Smith 'Provincial Workhouses. Report of Dr Edward Smith Medical Officer', *PP* 1867–68 p. 105 and *The Lancet*, 29 July 1865, pp. 105 and 134.
140. Dr. Edward Smith, 'Provincial Workhouses. Report of Dr. Edward Smith', *PP* 1867–68 4, p. 105.
141. Dr. Edward Smith, 'Provincial Workhouses. Report of Dr. Edward Smith', *PP* 1867–68, 4, p. 105.
142. L. Twining, (1898) *Workhouses and Pauperism*, p. 201, L. Twining, (1892) 'Nursing in Workhouses', p. 7; L Marks, (1993) 'Poor Law Provision in East London 1870–1929', p. 529 and R. Hodgkinson, (1967) *The Origins*, p. 570.
143. Bolton Archive Service, GBO/28/30
144. Bolton Archive Service GBO280/19.
145. *The Lancet*, 9 September 1865, p. 297. *The Lancet*, 15 January 1870, p. 99.
146. L. Twining, (1898) *Workhouses and Pauperism*, p. 213.
147. *The Lancet*, 15 January 1870, p. 99.
148. Dr. Edward. Smith (1867–8), 'Provincial Workhouses. Report of Dr. Edward Smith' *PP* 1867–68 4, p. 105.
149. *BMJ*, 13 July 1895, p, 91.
150. *BMJ*, 13 July 1895, p, 91.
151. R. Hodgkinson, *The Origins*, pp. 566–7.
152. Dr. Edward. Smith 'Provincial Workhouses. Report of Dr. Edward Smith' *PP* 1867–68, 4, p. 21.
153. Dr. Edward Smith remarked that even 'small' workhouses could have up to 27 wards, which would pose real logistical problems for workhouse nurses. R. Hodgkinson, (1967) *The Origins*, pp. 566–7.
154. WYAS Bradford, BU3/3/3.
155. WYAS Bradford, BU3/3/3.
156. WYAS Leeds, LO4/19, p. 5; *The Lancet*, 21 September 1895, p. 742; *BMJ*, 13 October 1894, p. 809; Report of Dr. Edward Smith, 'Provincial Workhouses. Report of Dr. Edward Smith' *PP* 1867–68, 4, p. 105 and R.Hodgkinson, *The Origins*, p. 570.
157. *BMJ*, 23 March 1889, p. 652.
158. *The Lancet*, 12 August 1865, p. 185.
159. *BMJ*, 7 July 1894, p. 27.
160. L. Twining, (1898) *Workhouses and Pauperism*, p. 201, and *The Lancet*, 1 September 1866, p. 236.
161. K. Morrison, (1999) *The Workhouse: a Study of Poor-Law Buildings in England* (Swindon: English Heritage), p. 34; *BMJ*, 6 October 1894, pp. 764–5 and *BMJ*, 28 September 1895, p. 796.
162. K. Morrison, (1999) *The Workhouse* p. 34; *BMJ*, 6 October1894, pp. 764–5 and *BMJ*, 28 September 1895, p. 796.

163. S. and B. Webb, (1963) *English Poor Law History*, pp. 305–6.
164. *The Lancet*, 12 August 1865.
165. *The Lancet*, 27 January 1866, p. 105.
166. House of Lords, 'Inquiry into Workhouses' XXII, (216) p. 9.
167. *The Lancet*, 1 July, 1865, p. 20.
168. Dr. Edward. Smith, 'Provincial Workhouses. Report of Dr. Edward Smith', *PP* 1867–68, 4, p. 103.
169. Dr. Edward. Smith, 'Provincial Workhouses. Report of Dr. Edward Smith' *PP* 1867–68, 4, p. 103.
170. Dr. Edward. Smith, 'Provincial Workhouses. Report of Dr. Edward Smith', *PP* 1867–68, 4, p. 116
171. Dr. Edward. Smith, 'Provincial Workhouses. Report of Dr. Edward Smith' 1867–68, 4, p. 118.
172. *The Lancet*, 18 December 1886, p. 1185 and B. Abel-Smith, (1979) *A History*, p. 5, fn 3.
173. M. Pelling, (1995) 'The Women of the Family' Speculations Around Early Modern British Physicians', *The Society for the Social History of Medicine*, 8, p. 383.
174. S. Shaen, (1869) *Workhouse Management and Workhouse Justice* (London), pp. 6–8.
175. Bolton Archive Service, GBO/28/30.
176. T.M. Dolan, (1894) *Our State Hospitals, their Construction, Management and Organisation* (Leicester), p. 36.
177. L. Marks, (1993) 'Medical Care', p. 529, n. 58.

4   Workhouse Infant Diet

1. *BMJ*, 18 April 1868, p. 380.
2. *BMJ*, 18 April 1868, p. 380.
3. J. Reinarz and L. Schwartz (2013) (ed.) *Medicine and the Workhouse* (Rochester: New York), p. 6 and especially chapter 9, A. Negrine, 'Practitioners and Paupers: Medicine at the Leicester Union Workhouse, 1867–1905', pp. 192–211, R. Richardson, (2013) 'The Art of Medicine: A Dismal Prospect: Workhouse Health Care', *The Lancet*, 6 July 2013, pp. 20–21 and S. and B. Webb, (1963) *English Poor Law History, Part II, Volume I*, (London), pp. 310–11.
4. R. Richardson, (2013) 'The Art of Medicine' 20–21.
5. S. and B. Webb, (1963) *English Poor Law History*, p. 310.
6. V. Fildes, (1986) *Breasts, Bottles and Babies*, (Edinburgh: Edinburgh University Press), pp. 168–87 and pp. 281–8. Fildes gives a very good example of how medical men and philanthropists such as Joseph Hanway saw the negative influences which eighteenth-century wet-nursing could have on pauper infants. The consequences of this led to the wet-nurse experiencing an increasingly bad press becoming associated with ill-health and unrespectability: it was believed that infants fed by wet nurses would be contaminated by her illness and bad characteristics.
7. V. Fildes, (1986) *Breasts, Bottles*, p. 285.
8. Jonas Hanway (1767) *Letters on the Importance of the Rising Generation of the Laboring Part of Our Fellow-subjects: Being an Account of the Miserable State of the Infant Parish Poor; the Great Usefulness of the Hospital for Exposed and Deserted Young Children Properly Restricted; the Obligations of Parochial Officers; and an Historical Detail of the Whole Mortality of London and Westminster, from 1592 to this Time* (London:

A. Millar and T. Cadell); E. Caulfield, (1931) *The Infant Welfare Movement in the Eighteenth Century* (New York), p. 285.

9. V. Fildes, (1986) *Breasts, Bottles*, p. 281.
10. L. Rose, (1986) *The Massacre of the Innocents: Infanticide in Britain 1800–1939* (London: Routledge & Kegan Paul), p. 31, R. Woods and N. Shelton, (1997) *An Atlas of Victorian Mortality* (Liverpool: Liverpool University Press), p. 53 and S. and B. Webb, (1963) *English Poor Law History*, p. 305.
11. Dr. Edward Smith, 'Dietaries for the Inmates of Workhouses. Report to the President of the Poor Law Board of Dr. Edward Smith, F.R.S., Medical Officer of the Poor Law Board, and Poor Law Inspector.' *PP* 1867–68 c.3660, pp. 52 and 172–231.
12. Dr. Eustace Smith, (1868) *The Wasting Diseases of Infants and Children* (London), p. 33.
13. V. Fildes, (1986) *Breasts, Bottles*, pp. 268–70. See also, Proceedings of the Nutrition Society; 'Nutritional Problems in Infancy and Childhood', pp. 199–222. The reasons why this milk was not used for British infants are unclear.
14. V. Fildes, (1986) *Breasts, Bottles*, p. 302.
15. M.A. Baines, (1862) 'Excessive Infant-Mortality: How Can it be Stayed?' A Paper Contributed to the *NAPSS* (London), p. 19.
16. It is interesting that Eustace Smith was in contact with Jenner whilst Smith was writing his paper on infant feeding. See Eustace Smith, (1868) *The Wasting Diseases*, p. 33 and P.J. Atkins, (1992) "White Poison?' The Social Consequences of Milk Consumption, 1850–1930, *The Society for the Social History of Medicine*, 5, pp. 207–27. Although the arguments on milk still ensue, one would expect the milk in workhouses to be as pure as possible, costs allowing. See M.A. Crowther, (1981) *The Workhouse System, 1834–1929: the History of an English Social Institution* (London: Batsford Academic & Educational), p. 3; Charles Henry Routh, MD., MRCPE, (1860) *Infant Feeding and its Influences on Life: or the Causes and Prevention of Infant Mortality* (London), p. 199 and L. Weaver, (2007) 'Feeding Babies in the Battle to Control Infant Mortality: Glasgow 1900–1910' A paper given at the Mini-Symposium on The Origins of the Science and practice of Infant and Child Nutrition and Feeding 8–11 October, 2007.
17. Dr. Eustace Smith, (1868) *The Wasting Diseases*, p. 33.
18. V. Fildes, (1986) *Breasts, Bottles*, pp. 219, 349 and 418–20 for the numbers of doctors who suggested not boiling milk and L. Rose, (1986) *The Massacre*, p. 55.
19. A. Sheen, (1890) *The Workhouse and its Medical Doctor* (Bristol), p. 36.
20. Leeds Thackrah Museum, Leeds Union Workhouse Death Registers 1879–1883. This graph represents a total of 109 infant deaths aged 0–1 years of age. The total number of all deaths in the workhouse during the period 1879–1883 was 1,741. See also *PP* 1839, XVI, p. 87 and Causes of Death in England and Wales, *PP* 1867 XVI, pp. 123–5 and pp. 207–209 for Categories of Diseases.
21. S. and B. Webb, (1963) *English Poor Law*, p. 310.
22. T. Forbes, (1986) 'Deadly Parents: Child Homicide in Eighteenth- and Nineteenth-Century England' *Journal of the History of Medicine and Allied Sciences*, 41, p. 188 and S. Fowler, (2007) *The Workhouse*, (Kew: The National Archives), p. 97.
23. L. Rose, (1986) *The Massacre*, p. 32; F. Crompton, (1997) *Workhouse Children: Infant and Child Paupers Under the Worcestershire Poor Law, 1780–1871* (Stroud: Sutton), p. 69; F. Morton Eden, (1928) *The State of the Poor: a History of the*

Labouring Classes in England, with Parochial Reports (London) and A. Williams (2008) 'Please Sir, Can I Have Some More?', *BMJ*, 20 December, 2008..

24. Evidence of Dr. Robert Baker, Factory and Workshop Acts Commission, PP, 1876, XXX, p. 68. See also W.R. Lee, (1964) ' "Robert Baker" ', 'The First Doctor in the Factory Department, Part I, 1803–1858', in *British Journal of Industrial Medicine*, 21, pp. 85–93. See also Herr R. Meyer, *Robert Baker, C.B. R.C.S., Politics and Society*, p. 4.

25. D. F. Hollingsworth, (1976) 'Developments Leading to Present Day Nutritional Knowledge', in D.J. Oddy and D.S. Miller, *The Making of the British Modern Diet*, (London: Croom Helm), p. 189. Megandie's work was latterly to inform the work of the German physiologist, Liebig, who questioned the nutritional value of cow's milk. We can see an excellent review of the problems that milk caused to infants in the work of P.J. Atkins, "White Poison?"; M.A. Crowther, (1981) *The Workhouse System*, p. 3, and C. H. Routh, (1860) *Infant Feeding*, p. 199.

26. Dr Edward Smith, 'Dietaries for the Inmates of Workhouses', *PP* 1867–68 c.3660, p. 56.

27. Dr Andrew Williams Paediatrician at Northampton Hospital, Personal Communication (2009). Dr. Edward Smith, 'Dietaries for the Inmates of Workhouses', *PP* 1867–68 c.3660, pp. 172, 190, 192 and 224. In addition to the 48 northern workhouses which Smith visited he also visited the two southern workhouses of Boston and Wibsech and did not find this sweetener prescribed for infants there.

28. Dr Andrew Williams Paediatrician at Northampton Hospital, Personal Communication. (2009)

29. *BMJ*, 1886, Vol. I, p. 65, and A. Sheen, (1890) 'The Workhouse', p. 52.

30. V. Fildes, (1986) *Breasts, Bottles*, p. 216.

31. Accum on *Poisons*, (1820) *A Treatise on Adulterations of Food and Culinary Practices* (London), p. 78. M.A. Baines, (1862) 'Excessive Infant-Mortality', pp. 12 and 19.

32. *BMJ*, (1886), Vol. I, p. 652 and A. Sheen, (1890) 'The Workhouse', p. 52.

33. Dr. Edward Smith, 'Dietaries for the Inmates of Workhouses', *PP* 1867–68 c.3660, pp. 172–231. For the references to cow's milk see particularly p. 194. The areas which included it were Bingham, Nottingham; Easingwold, North Yorkshire; East Retford, Nottingham; Eccleshill, West Yorkshire; Ely, Cambridge; Helmsley, North Yorkshire; Hemsworth, West Yorkshire; Hunslet, West Yorkshire; Pocklington, East Yorkshire; Sculcoates, East Yorkshire; Selby, North Yorkshire; Carlton, Nottingham; and Great Preston, West Yorkshire.

34. T.M. Dolan, (1894) *Our State Hospitals, their Construction, Management and Organisation* (Leicester), p. 48.

35. Dr. Edward Smith 'Dietaries for the Inmates of Workhouses', *PP* 1867–68 c.3660 see Rotherham, Scarborough and Knaresborough, pp. 198 and 212; A. Sheen, (1890) 'The Workhouse' p. 62. Sugar loaf is lump sugar pounded. See Dr. Eustace Smith, (1868) *The Wasting Diseases*, p. 33 and A. Sheen, (1890) 'The Workhouse', p. 62. Breakfast for infants aged between 18 months and two years was 4oz bread, ½ pt milk. Dinner 2 days, 2oz bread, 4 ozs suet pudding, 1oz treacle; 2 days, 2oz bread, ¼ pt Broth, ¼ oz butter; 3 Days, 2oz bread, ¼ pt rice pudding, ¼ oz butter. Supper, 4ozs bread, ½ pt milk. See also *The Lancet*, 27 January 1866, p. 105 and p. 106.

36. See Dr. Eustace Smith, (1868) *The Wasting Diseases*, pp. 18–19 and p. 33 and A. Moncrieff (ed.) (1952) *A Textbook on the Nursing and Diseases of Sick Children* (London: Lewis), p. 211.

37. Dr. Eustace Smith, (1868) *The Wasting Diseases*, p. 33.
38. PRO MH9/11, p. 184.
39. *The Lancet*, 1 July 1865, p. 21; *The Lancet*, 15 July 1865, p. 75 and *BMJ*, 6 October 1894, p. 764. For an example of nineteenth century workhouse death registers see Southall Workhouse nineteenth century Birth and Death registers and also Leeds Union Infirmary Register of Deaths May 1879–1901. See Thackrah Museum Archive; Workhouse Death Registers and V. Fildes, (1986) *Breasts, Bottles*, p. 224–34.
40. See Dr. Eustace Smith, (1868) *The Wasting Diseases*.
41. *BMJ*, (1868), Vol. II, p. 593.
42. Quoted in M. Hewitt, (1958) *Wives and Mothers in Victorian Industry* (London: Rockliff), pp. 123–4.
43. J. Rogers, (1889) *Reminiscences of a Workhouse Medical Officer* (London), p. 15.
44. B. Abel-Smith, (1979) *A History, of the Nursing Profession* (London: Heinemann), p. 38, also p. 40 fn. 2 and J. Rogers, (1889) *Reminiscences*, p. 16.
45. J. Rogers, (1889) *Reminiscences*, p. 16.
46. Dr. Edward Smith, 'Dietaries for the Inmates of Workhouses', *PP* 1867–68 c.3660 pp. 192–3. This lying-in diet was similar to that of the Cardiff and Halifax Workhouses see A. Sheen, (1890) 'The Workhouse', p. 60 and T.M. Dolan, (1894) 'Our State Hospitals', p. 48.
47. Dr. Edward Smith, Dietaries for the Inmates of Workhouses', *PP* 1867–68 c.3660, pp. 192–3 and T. Orme Dudfield, (1879) 'M.D. Medical Officer to the Board of Guardians, SS Margaret and John, Westminster', (London) p. 6.
48. A. Levene, (2005) *Illegitimacy, Health and Mortality at the London Foundling Hospital, 1741–1800* (Manchester: Manchester University Press), p. 43.
49. Dr. Eustace Smith, (1868) *Wasting Diseases*, pp. 15–16.
50. Dr. Eustace Smith, (1868) *Wasting Diseases*.
51. Dr. Eustace Smith, (1868) *Wasting Diseases*, pp. 15–16.
52. Dr. Eustace Smith, (1868) *The Wasting Diseases*, pp. 15–16, 18–19, 33 and 37, A. Moncrieff (1952) (ed.)., *A Textbook*, p. 211.
53. Dr. Eustace Smith's Obituary. See *BMJ*, 21 November 1914, pp. 904–6.
54. The Unions which prescribed sugar for newly confined mothers were Bramley, Beverley (7oz), Doncaster, Driffield, Easingwold, East Retford, Eccleshill, Goole, Guisborough, Helmsley, Howden, Kirby Moorside, Malton, Newark, North Witchford, Pickering, Ripon, Scarborough, Selby, Sleaford, Spalding, Stamford, Stokesley, Thirsk, Willesey, Wisbech, and York.
55. A. Sheen, (1890) 'The Workhouse', p. 16.
56. Dr. Edward Smith, 'Dietaries for the Inmates of Workhouses', *PP* 1867–68 c.3660, pp. 192–3 and T. Orme Dudfield, (1879) 'M.D. Medical Officer to the Board of Guardians, SS Margaret and John, Westminster', (London), p. 6.
57. M. Hewitt, (1958) *Wives and Mother's*, p. 139.
58. *BMJ*, 15 December 1895, p. 1380.
59. *The Lancet*, 9 September 1865, p. 293.
60. T.M. Dolan, (1894) *Our State Hospitals*, p. 48.
61. Dr. Eustace Smith, (1868) *Wasting Diseases*, p. 15–16.
62. S and B. Webb, (1963) *English Poor Law*, p. 301.
63. S. and B. Webb, (1963) *English Poor Law*, p. 301.
64. WYAS, (1860–1865) BG1/1/1, Minute Book II.
65. WYAS, (1862) BG3/1/1/1, Minute Book, Book II, 17 September, p. 448.
66. WYAS BG3/1/1/1, (1862) Minute Book, II, 17 September.

67. WYAS, BG3/1/1/2, (1862) Minute Book, I p. 22; WYAS, Minute Book I BG31/1/2, p. 305; WYAS, Minute Book I, BG3/1/2, p. 9.
68. WYAS BG1/1/1, (1860–1865) Minute Book, Book II, pp. 232 and 241.
69. WYAS BG1/1/1, (1860–1865) Minute Book, Book II, p. 241. Jane was still in the Leeds Union in 1875 when she traversed between the Wakefield and Leeds Unions. See the WYAS PL5/16 Table concerning the 'Numbers of Paupers Resident within the Leeds Union' for the years 1870–1880.
70. P. Thane, (1978) 'Women and the Poor Law in Victorian and Edwardian England', *History Workshop Journal*, 6, p. 42 and Lionel Rose has also observed this rule in *The Massacre*.
71. V. Fildes, (1986) *Breasts, Bottles*, p. 281. The decline of wet-nursing infants during the eighteenth century Fildes has argued was because medical men thought the 'bad characteristics' of the wet-nurse were morphed on to the child she fed.
72. R. Hodgkinson, (1967) *The Origins of the National Health Service* (London: The Wellcome Historical Medical Library), p. 570.
73. S. King, (2000) *Poverty and Welfare in England, 1700–1850: A Regional Perspective* (Manchester: Manchester University Press), pp. 207–8.
74. S. King, (2000) *Poverty and Welfare*, p. 208.
75. M. Arnot, (2002) 'The Murder of Thomas Sandles: Meanings of a Mid-Nineteenth-Century Infanticide', in M. Jackson, *Infanticide Historical Perspectives on Child Murder and Concealment 1550–2000*, (Aldershot: Ashgate) p. 154. See the Assize records which contain female working-class testimony of this workhouse policy. See also ASSI 52/1 Mary Bennett and ASSI 52/2 Ellen Lanigan.
76. S. and B. Webb, (1963) *English Poor Law History*, p. 310–11.
77. A. Sheen, (1890) *The Workhouse* p. 36 and F. Crompton, (1986) *The Workhouse*, p. 38.
78. Dr. Eustace Smith, (1868) *The Wasting Diseases*, p. 15–16 and L. Rose, (1986) *The Massacre*, p. 31.
79. V. Fildes, (1986) *Breasts, Bottles*, p. 316 and L. Rose, *The Massacre*, p. 55.
80. V. Fildes, (1986) *Breasts, Bottles*, p. 346.
81. V. Fildes, (1986) *Breasts, Bottles*, p. 346.
82. V. Fildes, (1986) *Breasts, Bottles*, p. 347.
83. *BMJ*, 3 April 1886, p. 652.
84. V. Fildes, (1986) *Breasts, Bottles*, p. 316 and L. Rose, (1986) *The Massacre*, p. 55.
85. A. Sheen, (1890) 'The Workhouse' p. 62 and L. Rose, (1986) *The Massacre*, p. 55.
86. Dr. Eustace Smith, (1868) *The Wasting Diseases*, p. 34. *BMJ*, 15 December 1894, p. 1381; *BMJ*, 24 August 24, 1895, p. 496 and *BMJ*, 20 July 1895, p. 151.
87. *BMJ*, 24 August 1895, p. 496.

5   Day-care and Baby-Minding

1. Isabella Mason testimony at the Assizes at the case of Jane Jones – Northern Circuit Assize Records PRO ASSI 52/10.
2. 'Report from the Select Committee on the Protection of Infant Life together with the Proceedings of the Committee's Minutes and Evidence and Appendix', *PP* 1871–1872 c.372 VII, p. 107–9.
3. M. Arnot, (1994) 'Infant Death, Child Care and the State', The Baby-farming Scandal and the First Infant Life Protection Legislation of 1872', in *Continuity and Change*, 9, pp. 271–8 and L. Rose, (1986) *The Massacre of the Innocents* (London: Routledge & Kegan Paul), p. 97.

4. M. Hewitt, (1958) *Wives and Mothers in Victorian Industry* (London: Rockliff), p. 129.
5. 'Report from the Select Committee on the Protection of Infant Life', *PP* 1871–1872 c.372 VII, p. 107–9.
6. E. Roberts, (1984), *A Woman's Place, An Oral History of Working Class Women* (Oxford: Basil Blackwell), p. 141 and 143.
7. D. Bentley, 'She-Butchers: Baby Droppers, Baby Sweaters, and Baby-Farmers', in J. Rowbotham and K. Stevenson (2005) eds. *Criminal Conversations, Victorian Crimes, Social Panic and Moral Outrage* (Ohio) pp. 198–214.
8. E. Roberts, (1984) *A Woman's Place*, p. 1.
9. E. Roberts, (1986) 'Women's Strategies, 1890–1940', in J. Lewis, (1986) *Labour and Love, Women's Experience of Home and Family 1850–1940* (Oxford: Basil Blackwell), p. 225
10. E. Roberts (1986), 'Women's Strategies', p. 234.
11. For details of Emma Paterson see S. Alexander, (1994) *Becoming a Woman* (London: Virago), p. 57.
12. M. Hewitt, (1958) *Wives and Mothers*, p. 130–31.
13. E. Roberts, (1984) *A Woman's Place*, p. 145
14. J. Lewis, (1986) *Labour and Love*, p. 83.
15. J. Lewis, (1986) *Labour and Love*, p. 83.
16. 'Report from the Select Committee on the Protection of Infant Life', *PP* 1871–1872 c.372 VII, pp. 107 and 112.
17. Bentley does not give a precise numbers of baby-farmers, other than to state its number was very high. D. Bentley, (2005) 'She-Butchers: Baby Droppers, Baby-Sweaters, and Baby-Farmers', in J. Rowbotham and K. Stevenson (2005) (eds.) *Criminal Conversations, Victorian Crimes, Social Panic, and Moral Outrage*, (Ohio State University Press) pp. 198–214, and especially p. 201; J. Hinks, (2014) 'The Representation of Baby Farmers in the Scottish City, 1867–1901', *Women's History Review*, 2014; 4, pp. 560–70; J. Ikin, (1865) 'Abstract from a Paper on the 'Undue Mortality of Infants and Children, in Connection with the questions of Early Marriages, Drugging Children, Bad Nursing, Death Clubs and Certificates of Death', etc. Reprinted from the *"Transactions of the National Association for the Promotion of Social Sciences Congress* at Sheffield, Baines and Sons, (*NAPSS*), (Leeds). See also M. Arnot, (1994) 'Infant Death, Child Care and the State', and L. Rose, (1986) *The Massacre*, p. 97 and particularly chapter 11.
18. D. Bentley, (2005) 'She-Butchers', p. 201.
19. *BMJ*, 29 April 1893, pp. 899–900.
20. 'Report from the Select Committee on the Protection of Infant Life' *PP* 1871–1872 c.372 VII, p. 105.
21. 'Report from the Select Committee on the Protection of Infant Life', *PP* 1871–1872 c.372 VII, p. 105.
22. L. Rose, (1986) *The Massacre*, p. 17.
23. P. Thane, (1978) 'Women and the Poor Law', p. 29.
24. M. Anderson, (1971) *Family Structure in Nineteenth Century Lancashire* (Cambridge: Cambridge University Press).
25. M. Arnot, (1994) 'Infant Death', p. 271.
26. M. Arnot, (1994) 'Infant Death', p. 271, P. Thane, 'Women and the Poor Law', p. 32 and L. Rose, *The Massacre*, pp. 30–32.
27. See the Case of Maria Sleddin (1823) whose neighbours were extremely reluctant to allow her baby to stay in the house. Leeds Workhouse Board, 'Examinations taken in the case of Maria Sleddin' (Leeds).

28. P. Thane, (1978) 'Women and the Poor Law, in Edwardian England', *History Workshop Journal*, 6, (1978) pp. 29–51, and M. Arnot, (1994) 'Infant Death,' p. 271.
29. E. Roberts, (1984) *A Woman's Place*, pp. 141–4.
30. See *BMJ*, 1860–1870, especially the volumes of 1867, 1870 and 1876 and particularly 5 November 1870, p. 489.
31. H. Hendrick, (1994) *New Perspectives: Child Welfare 1872–1989* (London: Routledge), p. 46 and D. Bentley, (2005) 'She Butchers', p. 201. David Bentley argues this was not new as 'the practice of baby-farmers deliberately murdering, by starvation or worse, children entrusted to their care was, practiced as early as 1724'.
32. A. Davin (1978) 'Imperialism and Motherhood', *History Workshop Journal*, 5, pp. 9–65, passim.
33. A. Davin, (1978) 'Imperialism and Motherhood', p. 55.
34. J. Purvis, (2000) *Women's History: Britain, 1850–1945: an Introduction* (London: Routledge), p. 59.
35. E. Roberts, (1984) *A Woman's Place*, p. 144.
36. E. Roberts, (1984) *A Woman's Place*, p. 144.
37. Mrs A11, (1978) M. Llewelyn Davies, *Maternity*, p. 146.
38. M. Arnot, (1994) 'Infant Death', p. 284.
39. D. Bentley, (2005) 'She Butchers', pp. 208 and 206–14; J Knelman, (1998) *Twisting in the Wind: The Murderess and the English Press* (London: University of Toronto Press) especially, p. 208 and Chapter 6; L. Rose, (1986) *The Massacre*, Chapter 11.
40. This view was forwarded by Ernest Hertford, the Coroner at the Frances Rogers case, and is echoed by L. Rose, (1986) *The Massacre*, pp. 109–10, and 127.
41. PRO ASSI 45/72: Mary Ann Addey.
42. *Manchester Courier and Lancashire General Advertiser*, 6 January 1894.
43. 'Vaccination Commission. Appendix IX'. To the Final Report of the Royal Commission on Vaccination. Papers Relating to Cases In Which Death or Non-Fatal Injury was Alleged or Suggested to Have Been Caused by, or Otherwise Connected with, Vaccination. *PP* 1897 c.8615 XLVII.I., p. 296.
44. 'Vaccination Commission. Appendix IX', *PP* 1897 c.8615 XLVII.I. Case 133, p. 310–15.
45. 'Vaccination Commission. Appendix IX', 1897 [C.8615] XLVII.I, p. 296.
46. 'Vaccination Commission. Appendix IX', 1897 [C.8615] XLVII.I, Case 133 p. 310–15.
47. 'Vaccination Commission. Appendix IX', 1897 [C.8615] XLVII.I, p. 266–7
48. 'Vaccination Commission. Appendix IX', 1897 [C.8615] XLVII.I, p. 20.
49. *Leeds Mercury* 22 September 1860.
50. *The Leeds Mercury* 22 September 1860. Whether this was a custom well known to this area is not known, but could be suggested as the trade of selling humans was not only linked to infants. E.P. Thomson has shown that 'wife sales' could be common in Yorkshire. Wife selling was how the working-class practiced divorce. Should the man tire of his wife he could sell her at market. See E.P. Thompson, (1980) *The Making of the English Working-class* (Harmondsworth: Penguin) and E.P. Thompson, (1991) *Customs in Common* (London: Merlin Press)

51. This may be due to an incorrect research method, however, a significant number of Assize records were trawled through as were a significant amount of newspapers, such as the whole of the Northern Assize cases, and *The Leeds Mercury*, and *The Leeds Times* during the years 1860s to 1870s.
52. 20 baby-minding cases were found in the sources I looked at in the Assize records where mothers of the infants farmed out went on to kill their children themselves.
53. PRO ASSI 52/8: Rosanne Walker.
54. PRO ASSI 52/6: Elizabeth Ingham.
55. Elizabeth Ingham, 1881 Census. She lived at Old Road Side, Billington, Lancashire.
56. PRO ASSI 52/3: Isabella Mason. The autopsy reports concluded that the child prior to strangulation was 'well nourished'.
57. PRO ASSI 52/10: Isabella Mason.
58. PRO ASSI 52/10: Isabella Mason.
59. PRO ASSI 52/10: Isabella Mason.
60. L. Rose, (1986) *The Massacre*, pp. 93–107.
61. PRO ASSI 52/10: Jane Jones
62. Isabella seems to have acted no differently towards Lewis than mothers who as Jane Humphries has argued were an 'abiding presence' and who 'loomed large' as constant providers. J. Humphries, (2010) *Childhood and Child Labour in the British Industrial Revolution* (Cambridge: Cambridge University Press), p. 142.
63. M. Arnot, (1994) 'Infant Death' passim.
64. 'Report from the Select Committee on the Protection of Infant Life', *PP* 1871–1872 c.372 VII, p. 162.
65. 'Report from the Select Committee on the Protection of Infant Life', *PP* 1871–1872 c.372 VII, p. 153.
66. 'Report from the Select Committee on the Protection of Infant Life', *PP* 1871–1872 c.372 VII, p. 109 and p. 308 and p. 324.
67. 'Report from the Select Committee on the Protection of Infant Life', *PP* 1871–1872 c.372 VII, p. 179.
68. 'Report from the Select Committee on the Protection of Infant Life', *PP* 1871–1872 c.372 VII p. 156.
69. 'Report from the Select Committee on the Protection of Infant Life', *PP* 1871–1872 c.372 VII pp. 156 and 157
70. 'Report from the Select Committee on the Protection of Infant Life', *PP* 1871–1872 c.372 VII p. 158–9
71. 'Report from the Select Committee on the Protection of Infant Life', *PP* 1871–1872 c.372 VII, p. 303.
72. PRO ASSI 52/2: Ann Riley.
73. PRO ASSI 52/10: Isabella Mason.
74. PRO ASSI 52/10: Isabella Mason.
75. A. Levene, (2007) *Child care, Health and Mortality at the London Foundling Hospital, 1741–1800* (Manchester: Manchester University Press), p. 91. 'Wages' for these nursing duties were however 'often irregular, and rarely exceeded five shillings a week.' Although larger payments for nursing were not uncommon, these usually represent cumulative disbursements, and so mask the often modest individual payments which constituted the total sum. A. Levene, *Child care*, p. 91.
76. A. Levene, (2007) *Child care*, p. 91.

77. A. Levene, (2007) *Child care*, p. 91 and K. Morgan, (2011) *The Birth of Industrial Britain: Social Change 1750–1850* (Harlow)), pp. 69 and 71-6.

78. Dr. Edward Smith, 'Dietaries for the Inmates of Workhouses', Report to the President of the Poor Law Board of Dr. Edward Smith, F.R.S., Medical Officer of the Poor Law Board, and Poor Law Inspector. *PP* 1867-68, 4, p. 190.

79. For the case of Ann Riley see PRO ASSI 52/2: Ann Riley. Michael Rose and Steven King have argued that the north resisted many of the defining aspects of the New Poor Law Amendment Act. This change in 'nursing' policy appeared to reflect the philosophical underpinning of the 1834 reforms, which saw a marked shift away from the local parochial responsibility for the administration of relief towards a more centralised system overseen by government. This sea-change in welfare administration bound the fate of the poor to Malthusian and utilitarian doctrines which argued that poor relief bred poverty, particularly amongst poor women, and that the parochial administration of relief was both inefficient and corrupt. There are few specific references to pauper children being cared for by parish nurses made by guardians in the areas I have looked at. See the Poor Law Books of Wakefield, Leeds and Bradford. See also S. King, (2006) *Women, Welfare and Local Politics 1880–1920* (Brighton: Sussex Academic) chapter 2 and particularly pp. 29–30. Steven King argues that Bolton was an anomaly in its limited provision of pensions throughout the nineteenth century and S. King, (2000) *Poverty and Welfare, in England, 1700–1850: A Regional Perspective* (Manchester: Manchester University Press), p. 135.

80. WYAS, Wakefield, BG3/3/5/1, p. 184.

81. WYAS, Wakefield, BG3/1/1/1, p. 210.

82. WYAS, Wakefield, BG3/1/1/1, p. 210.

83. Dr. Edward Smith, 'Dietaries for the Inmates of Workhouses', *PP* 1867-68, 4, p. 191.

84. 1871 Census, Fanny and Robert Moses, 68 St James St, Leeds, (District West Leeds D57).

85. Dr. Edward Smith, (1867-8) 'Dietaries', p. 191.

86. 1891 Census records.

87. 1881 Census records.

88. PRO ASSI 52/10: Isabella Mason.

89. See the 1860s editions of *The Leeds Mercury*, such as 8 and 10 October 1864, and *The Leeds Times*, and *The Yorkshire Post*, in which 60 cases of maternal infant neglect and infanticide are reported during this period. See also N. Williams, (1994) 'Infant Mortality in an Age of Great Cities: London and the English Provincial Cities Compared, *c.*1840–1910', *Continuity and Change*, 9, p. 191.

90. See West Yorkshire Archive Service, henceforth WYAS Bradford, BU6/1/1 and *The Daily Post Liverpool*, 19 May 1874.

91. WYAS, Bradford Workhouse, Register of Admissions and Discharges. BU 6/1/1, (1857). Why these women deserted their infants is not stated in the records. Of course the reason is important historiographically, but it is not to be debated here.

92. WYAS, Bradford Workhouse, Register of Admissions and discharged BU 6/1/1, (1857). It is interesting to note that women also deserted their infants in the Parish of Oxford. See Minute Book for Bicester, and Abstracts of Outdoor Relief for Bicester, PLU2/RL/2A3 at the Oxfordshire Records Office.

93. 'Report of the Orphan Home, Headingley Hill', Leeds, 1867–1880 (Leeds 1880). This orphanage was an anomaly during this period in its housing of infants.

See Leeds Central Library Ref: L. Hea. 362 Book No. L D 05224500. See also F. Crompton, (1997) *Workhouse Children: Infant and Child Paupers under the Worcestershire Poor Law, 1780–1871* (Stroud: Sutton), p. xv.

94. *Bradford Observer* 25 June 1857.

95. F. Crompton, (1997) *Workhouse Children*, p. xv. Frank Crompton sees significance in the guardians' benevolence among the metropolitan districts and has persuasively argued that 'as many as 20 percent of workhouse inmates, or about 60 percent of inmate children, were in the category of being orphaned and deserted.

96. For example see the editorial editions of *The Leeds Mercury* on 28 September and 4 and 5 October 1864 and J. Braithwaite, (1865) 'An enquiry into the causes of the high infant death rate in Leeds', *The Thoresby Society*, 41, (Leeds), pp. 145–53.

97. PRO ASSI 52/10: Sarah Boadle. The medical doctor remarked at Sarah's trial that Maurice's death was due to starvation.

98. *BMJ*, 12 March 1888, p. 557.

99. PRO ASSI 52/10: Sarah Boadle.

100. PRO ASSI 52/10: Sarah Boadle.

101. PRO ASSI 52/10: Sarah Boadle.

102. *BMJ*, 22 March 1888, p. 557.

103. PRO ASSI 52/10: Sarah Boadle.

104. J. Lewis, (1986) *Labour and Love*, p. 83.

105. A. Wilson, (1985) 'Participant or Patient? Seventeenth Century Childbirth From the Mother's Point of View', in R. Porter, (ed.) *Patients and Practitioner; Lay Perceptions of Medicine in Pre-Industrial Society* (Cambridge: Cambridge University Press), pp. 129–44.

106. WYAS, Bradford Workhouse Admissions and Discharge Books (1857). George Stansfield, Bradford Workhouse – Minute Book: BU 2/2/2 1860.

107. WYAS Judith Wilcock Bradford Minute Book: BU 2/2/2 1860.

108. S. King, (2010) *Women*, pp. 45 and 54.

109. S. King, (2000) *Poverty and Welfare*, p. 214.

110. S. King, (2000)*Poverty and Welfare*, p. 211.

111. F. Crompton, (1997) *Workhouse Children*, p. xv.

112. P. Thane, (1978) 'Women and the Poor Law', p. 29.

113. WYAS, Bradford Admissions and Discharge Book BU6/1/1 (1857). This practice is also exercised by the Oxford Parish of Bicester see Oxford Records Office, PLU2/RL/2A3.

Conclusion

1. M. McMillan, (1905) *Infant Mortality* (London), p. 3.

References

Unpublished Primary Sources

John Briggs Mill Records: West Yorkshire Archive Service KC624.
Holly Park Mill Wages Records: 1868–1872 Brotherton Library Handlist 138. Ms200.
Leeds Woodhouse Death Registers: Leeds Brotherton Library, Woodhouse Cemetery Burial Registers 1866–1874; MS421/4i; MS421/4ii; MS421/5i.
Marshall's Mill Records: 'Ages of Hands Employed at Leeds' Leeds, Brotherton Library, Handlist 6, MS20.
G and J. Stubley Factory Certificates: KC 74, West Yorkshire Archive Service.
1871 Census.

Archive sources

Public Records Office, Kew, London.
Northern Assize Court Records.
ASSI 41/2 – 41/231: Crown Minute Books 1850–1890.
ASSI 45/72: Case Notes and Depositions from Northern and North Eastern Circuits 1857–1859.
ASSI: 52 – Case Notes and Depositions for the years 1859–1899.
ASSI 52/1 – 10 Case Notes and Depositions for the years 1877–1899.
HO27 – HO 184: Home Office – Criminal Registers for England and Wales 1805–1892.

Archive visits

West Yorkshire Archive Society: (WYAS) Poor Law Union Records:
Hemsworth: MH12/15044.
Holbeck: MH12/15052–16062.
Hunslet: MH 12/15224.
Leeds: MH12/15236–15247.
Wakefield: MH12/15566.

Manchester: MH12/6063–6068.
Preston: MH12/6120–6124.
Southwell: MH12/9534/162; MH12/9534/340.

Poor Law Union Records – Nursing Staff.
Bolton Archive: GBO/28/19; GBO/28/30.
Leeds: MH9/10.
Manchester: MH9/11 – Manchester.
Wakefield: MH9/18 – Wakefield.

Poor Law Admission and Discharge Books: Bradford, West Yorkshire Workhouse Register of Admissions and discharged. BU 6/1/1. 1857.
Poor Law Minute Books: West Yorkshire Archive Service: 1850–1880; Bradford: BU1/1/1; BU 2/2/2; BU1/8; BU2/1/2; BU 2/2/2; BU6/1/1; BU3/3; Leeds: LPC P68/38; LPC P68/39/1; LO HU/2; LO/AJ/1; LO/HO/1; PL1/1; LO4/19; Wakefield: BG3/4/1/1–12; BG3/1/1/1; BG3/1/1/2; BG3/4/1/3; BG3/1/1/1; BG3/3/5/1; Oxford

Parish: Minute Book for Bicester, and Abstracts of Outdoor Relief for Bicester, PLU2/RL/2A3.

Poor Law Death Registers: Southall Union – Nineteenth Century Register of Birth and Deaths at Southall Workhouse; John Devlin Archivist; Leeds Brotherton Library, Woodhouse Cemetery Burial Registers 1866–1874 – MS421/4i; MS421/4ii; MS421/5i; Leeds Thackrah Museum, Leeds Union Workhouse Death Registers 1879–1901; Bedfordshire and Luton Friendly Society Archive: P10/28/40.

UK Census Records: 1871 and 1881; Census of Great Britain, 1851. Population Tables, II, Ages, Civil Conditions, Occupations, and Birth-Place of the People: With the Numbers and Ages of the Blind, the Deaf-And-Dumb, and the Inmates of Workhouses, Prisons, Lunatic Asylums, and Hospitals. Vol. I. London.

Published Primary Sources

Medical journals

The Lancet Commission Report into Workhouse Nurses, 1860–1870 but especially: **1823**, Vol I, 1823, p. 439. **1858** Vol, I, p. 345. **1861** Vol: II, p. 256. **1865** 1 January, p. 20. 15 April, p. 410. 20 May, p. 544. 17 June p. 659 and p. 661. 1 July, p. 21. 15 July, p. 73–76. 29 July, p. 133–134. 12 August, p. 185. 26 August, p. 237. 9 Sept, p. 297. 21 October, p. 460–461 & p. 471. 4 November, p. 514. 23 December, p. 711. **1866** 27 January 1866, pp. 105–106. 1 September 1866, p. 236. **1868.** 22 February, p. 286. 25 April 1868, p. 538. 29 August 1868, p. 282 and p. 288. 28 November 1868, p. 615. 5 December 1868, p. 743. **1869** 6 February, pp. 195–218. 20 February, p. 268 & p. 269 10 April pp. 508–9. **1870** 15 January, p. 99. **1873.** 20 December, p. 886. **1876** 9 August, pp. 179–185. 23 December, p. 194. **1877** 27 January, p. 153. 31 March, p. 470. **1886** 18 December, pp. 1184–1186. **1895** 21 September 21 p. 742. The *BMJ* 1840–1880 and the *BMJ's Commission into Workhouse Inquiries 1890–1895*, but especially: **1857** 31 January, 1857, pp. 85–87. **1860s** 14 April 1868, p. 380. **1868** 9 May, p. 470. 1868, Vol II, p. 573. 25 January, p. 75. 8 February, pp. 127–128. 22February, pp. 175–176. 29 February, p. 197. 21 March, p. 276. 14 March, 1868. 28 March, pp. 301–302. 1 August, p. 121. **1869** March, p. 262. **1870** 25 June, p. 657. **1871** 21 January, pp. 55–79. 25 February, p. 212. **1884** 22 March, pp. 543–590. **1886** Vol, I, p. 652. **1888** 22 March, p. 557. 24 March, p. 655. **1889** 15 September, p. 632 and p. 682. 26 October, pp. 909–964. 1894 13 October, p. 809. 13 July, p, 91. 1889, Vol. I, p. 652. **1890** 4 January, pp. 1–60. 24 May, pp. 643–792. 6 December, pp. 1283–1340. **1894** 3 May, pp. 497–499. 7 July, pp. 26–7 and p. 56. 14 July, pp. 57–112, and 367–368. 22 September, pp. 671–672. 28 September, pp. 795–797. 29 September, pp. 711–712. 6 October, pp. 741–796. 3 November, pp. 1277–1278. 3 December, pp. 1221–1288. 8 December, pp. 1317–1319. 13 December, 1894. 15 December, 1894. **1895** 13 July, p. 91 14 July, p. 80–82. 20 July, pp. 151–152. 20 August, 1895, p. 457. 24 August, 1894, p. 496. 14 September, pp. 688–690. 21 September, pp. 740–742. 28 September, pp. 795–797. **1914** 21 November, 1914.

Curgenven, J.B. Infanticide, Baby-Farming, and the Infant Life Protection Act 1872, in *The Sanitary Record*, 15 July 1889, pp. 4–5.

Curgenven, J.B. Infanticide, Baby-Farming, and the Infant Life Protection Act 1872, in *The Sanitary Record*, 15 March 1890, pp. 415–17.

Peters, O.H. (1910) Observations On the Natural History of Epidemic Diarrhoea, *Journal of Hygiene*, X.

The Medico Gazette 24 May, 1873: T.F Hopgood on 'Marasmus'.

Newspapers

Bee Hive, 9 March 1872.
Bradford Observer, 18 June 1857; 25 June 1857.
Bradford Review, 5 June 1858; 19 June 1858; 26 June 1858.
Cotton Factory Times.
Dewsbury Reporter, 16 January–15 March 1875.
Huddersfield Chronicle, 25 May 1895.
Huddersfield Daily Chronicle, 12 January 1857; 25 August 1896.
Huddersfield Examiner, 16 February–19 March 1875.
Leeds Evening Express, 18 March 1872.
Leeds Mercury, 7 August 1860; 4 September 1860; 22 September 1860; 4 October 1860;
    6 October 1860; 8 October 1860; 19 October 1860; 21 October 1860; 27 October
    1860; 1 October 1864; 7 March 1865; 11 March 1865; 24 June 1865.
Liverpool Daily Post, 19 May 1874.
Liverpool Halfpenny Weekly, 2 November 1889; 5 November 1889; 9 November 1889.
Liverpool Weekly Post, 27 May 1882; 16 May 1885.
Manchester City News, 7 May 1881; 2 June 1881; 18 June 1881; 25 June 1881.
Manchester Courier & Lancashire General Advertiser, 6 April 1877.
Manchester Courier, 12 May 1877.
Manchester Examiner, 4 April 1877, 28 April 1877, 19 April 1877.
Manchester Guardian, 22 July 1872; 2 August 1877.
Manchester Times, 12 May 1860; 24 August 1867.
Medico Times and Gazette, 17 March 1860.
Morning Chronicle, 12 November 1849; 25 November 1850.
Northampton Mercury.
Northern Star.
Pall Mall Gazette.
Preston Guardian, 7 July 1869.
Sanitary Record, (London, 1874–1904).
Stockport Advertiser, 13 April 1877.
Yorkshire Factory Times.
Yorkshire Gazette, 18 February 1865; 25 March 1865; 1 April 1865.

Official documents and publications

Parliamentary Papers

PP Accounts & Papers, 1870 LXIII; 1878 LXXXIX; 1882 LXXXV; 1886 LXXXII;
    CVIII 1895; LXXXV 1889.

Royal Commissioners' Reports

PP 1831–2 XV Report of the Select Committee on Children's Labour.
PP 1833 XX Royal Commission on Employment of Children in Factories.
PP 1833 XXI Factory Inquiry Commission.
PP 1834 XIX–1 Factory Inquiry Commission.
PP 1839 XVI Reports of the Commissioners on Births, Deaths and Marriages.
PP 1840 (508) Bill for improving Dwellings of the working-classes, 111.657, m/f43.24.
PP XXII Inquiry into Workhouse Conditions, House of Lords.
PP 1842 XV Report of the Commissioners into Children's Employment in Mines.
PP 1843 VII Report from the Select Committee on Friendly Societies Bill.

PP 1843 XII Reports of Special Assistant Poor Law Commissioners on the Employment of Women and Children in Agriculture *PP* 1843 XII.

PP 1843 XIII, XIV.I and XV.I (c. 430, c.431 and c.432) Children's Employment Commission. Second Report of the Commissioners. Trades and Manufacturers.

PP IUP, 1847–8 and 1852, Report by Inspector of Factories made to the Government (8).

PP 1850 XXIII Reports of the Inspectors of Factories to Her Majesty's Principal Secretary of State for the Home Department XXIII.

PP 1863 [3170] Children's Employment Commission (1862). First report of the commissioners. With appendix. XVIII.1.

PP 1863 [3076] XVIII Reports of the inspectors of factories to Her Majesty's Principal Secretary of State for the Home Department, for the half year ending 31st October 1862.

PP 1864 [3414] [3414–I] XXII Children's Employment Commission.

PP 1865 [3473] XX Reports of the Inspectors of Factories to Her Majesty's Principal Secretary of State for the Home Department, for the half year ending 31st October 1864.

PP 1865 [3473] XX; Reports of the Inspectors of Factories to Her Majesty's Principal Secretary of State for the Home Department, for the half year ending 31st October 1864.

PP 1867 [3794] XVI Reports of the inspectors of factories to Her Majesty's Principal Secretary of State for the Home Department for the half year ending 31st October 1866.

PP 1867 XVI Causes of Death in England.

PP 1867–8 XVII Royal Commission on the Employment of Children, Young Persons and Women in Agriculture.

PP 1868–9 XIII Royal Commission on the Employment of Children, Young Persons and Women in Agriculture.

PP 1868–9 XVIII Reports of the Commissioners in to the Employment of Children, Young Persons and Women.

PP 1867–8 'Provincial Workhouses. 'Report of Dr. Edward Smith Medical Officer to the Poor Law Board, on the Sufficiency of the Existing Arrangements for the Care and Treatment of the Sick Poor in Forty-Eight Provincial Workhouses in England and Wales; Together With an Appendix to such Report, Containing Dr Smith's Observations on each of the Workhouses in Question; &c'.

PP 1867–8 'Dietaries for the Inmates of Workhouses: Report to the President of the Poor law Board of Dr. Edward Smith F.R.S. Medical Officer of the Poor Law Board and Poor Law Inspector.'.

PP 1868–9 XVI Reports of the Commissioners on Births, Deaths and Marriages during 1867.

PP 1871 VII Report as to the Best Means of Preventing the Destruction of the Lives of Infants Put Out to Nurse for Hire by their Parents.

PP 1871 XIV Reports of the inspectors of factories to Her Majesty's Principal Secretary of State for the Home Department for the half year ending 30th April 1871.

PP 1871–1872 Report from the Select Committee on the Protection of Infant Life together with the Proceedings of the Committee's Minutes and Evidence and Appendix.

PP 1872 XVI Report of the Inspector of Factories.

PP 1872 XXVII Sir John Simon, Instructions to Vaccination Officers issued by the Local Government Board, 21st December 1871.

PP 1873 c.849 XIX Reports of the Inspectors of Factories to Her Majesty's Principal Secretary of State for the Home Department for the half-year ending 30th April, 1873.

PP 1876 [1443–1] XXX. Factory and Workshop Acts Commission. Report of the commissioners appointed to inquire into the working of the factory and workshop acts, with a view to their consolidation and amendment: together with the minutes of evidence, appendix and index.

PP 1876 [1443] XXIX Factory and Workshops Acts Commission. Report of the commissioners appointed to inquire into the working of the factory and workshops acts, with a view to their consolidation and amendment; together with the minutes of evidence, appendix, and index. Vol. I & II.

PP 1893–94 [c.6894–XXIII] Royal Commission on Labour. The employment of women. Reports by Miss Eliza Orme, Miss Clara E. Collet, Miss May E. Abraham, and Miss Margaret H. Irwin (lady assistant commissioners), on the conditions of work in various industries in England, Wales, Scotland, and Ireland.

PP 1894 c. 7421 XXXV.9 Royal Commission on Labour, Filth and Final Report of the Royal Commission on Labour. Part I.

PP 1897 [c.8609] XLV Vaccination commission. Appendix III. To the final report of the Royal Commission on vaccination. Report to the commission of Dr. Sydney Coupland on the outbreak of small-pox in the Dewsbury Union in 1891–2..

PP 1897 (c.8610) XLV Vaccination commission. Appendix IV. To the final report of the Royal Commission on vaccination. Reports to the commission of Dr. Arthur Pearson Luff on outbreaks of small-pox in London in 1892–3.

PP 1897 [c.8611] XLV Vaccination commission. Appendix V. To the final report of the Royal Commission on Vaccination. Report to the commission of Dr. Thomas Dixon Savill on the outbreak of small-pox in the borough of Warrington in 1892–3.

PP 1897 [c.8612] XLV Vaccination commission. Appendix VI. To the final report of the Royal Commission on Vaccination. Report to the commission of Dr. Sidney Coupland on the outbreak of small-pox in the borough of Leicester in 1892–3.

PP 1897 [c.8613] XLVI.1 Vaccination commission. Appendix VII. To the final report of the Royal Commission on Vaccination. Report to the commission of Dr. Sidney Coupland, on the outbreak of small-pox in the city of Gloucester in 1895–96.

PP 1897 [c.8614] XLVI Vaccination commission. Appendix VIII. To the final report of the Royal Commission on Vaccination. Reports to the commission of Dr. Sidney Coupland on the prevalence of small-pox in Glasgow, Liverpool, Salford, Manchester, Oldham, Chadderton, Leeds, Sheffield, Halifax and Bradford in 1892–3, and the measures adopted by the local authorities.

PP 1897 [c.8615] XLVII.I Vaccination commission. Appendix IX. To the final report of the Royal Commission on Vaccination. Papers relating to cases in which death or non-fatal injury was alleged or suggested to have been caused by, or otherwise connected with, vaccination.

Correspondence and Bills

PP 1875–1882, 202 LVIII. Correspondence between Secretary of State and Commons 33 mf. 89.473.

PP Bill to Amend Acts Relating to Artizans and Labourers Dwellings and Houses of the Working-classes 1890 284 v. 271, mf 96.40, 1890 (375) v. 291 mf 96.40 40–41, (285), v.377 mf 96.41–42.

PP Bill to Explain part II of History of Working-Class Act 1890 (336) IV.585 mf 100.32. *Hansard*, 1844 LXXIII.

PP Hansard, 1844, LXXIII, col. 1379.

Death Registers

Leeds Thackrah Museum, Leeds Union Workhouse Death Registers 1879–1883.

Other works

Books, articles and pamphlets

'A plea for the helpless' (1861) *The Workhouse Orphan*, (London).

'The Burial Club', London, (1850), British Library. C.116.i.1.(170).

Accum on *Poisons*, (1820) *A Treatise on Adulterations of Food and Culinary Practices*, (London).

Anderson, A. (1922) *Women in the Factory: An Administrative Adventure 1893 to 1921* (London: John Murray).

Anderson, G. P. (1892) *The Rural Exodus: The Problems of the Village* and the Town, (London 1892).

Baines, M. A. (1859) *Domestic Servants, As They Are and As They Ought To Be, by a Practical Mistress of a Household*, (Brighton).

Baines, M. A. (1860) Excessive Infant-Mortality: How Can it be Stayed? A Paper Contributed to the *NAPSS* (London).

Baines, M.A (1860) The Practice of Hiring Wet Nurses; A Paper Contributed to the Public Health Department of the *NAPSS* (London).

Baker, R. (1867) *The Workshops' Regulation Act, 1867: Made as Easy as Possible; for the Use of Masters, Workpeople and Parents*, (London).

Baker, R. (1868) *The Factory Acts Made Easy, or How to Work the Law Without the Risk of Penalties Embracing the Acts of 1853, 1856 and 1867*, (Leeds).

Baker, R. (1868) *The Factory Acts Made Easy, or how to work the law without the risk of penalties embracing the acts of 1853, 1856 and 1867*, (Leeds).

Baker, R. (1860) *On the State and Condition, of the Town of Leeds in the West Riding of the County of York*, (Leeds).

Baker, R. (1867) *No'butt and Never'head: A Lecture to Yorkshire Factory Girls*, (Leeds).

Barker, A. (1770) *The Compleat Servant Maid*, (London).

Batty, J. (1877) *The History of Rothwell*, (Rothwell).

Bedoes, E. (1891) 'Slum-Mothers and Death-Clubs', *Journal of 'The Nineteenth Century'*, (London).

Black C. (1983) (ed.) *Married Women's Work: Being the Report of an Enquiry Undertaken by the Women's Industrial Council* (London: Virago).

Bull, T. (1861) M.D., *Hints to Mothers for the Management of Health During the Period of Pregnancy and in the Lying-in Room* (London).

Canning, Rev., Elder, J. (1874) On the Neglect of Infants in Large Towns, *NAPSS Transactions*.

Caulfield, E. (1931) *The Infant Welfare Movement in the Eighteenth Century*, (New York).

Chadwick, E. (1860) Address on public health, *National Association for the Promotion of Social Science*, hence forth *NAPSS*, (London 1860).

Clay J. (1854) Burial Clubs and Infanticide in England; A Letter to W.M. Brown (Preston).

Cobbett, W. (1912) *Rural Rides*, (London).

Curgenven, J.B. (1867) The Waste of Infant Life, Read at a Meeting of the Health Department of the *NAPSS*, (London).

Curgenven, J.B. (1869) On Baby-farming and the Registration of Nurses, Read at a Meeting of the Health Department of the *NAPSS*, (London).

Curgenven, J.B. (1871) *Infant Life Protection Society*, (London).

Curgenven, J.B. (1872) *Infanticide, Baby-Farming, and the Infant Life Protection Act*, (London).

Dolan, T.M. F.R.C.S., (1882) Infant Mortality: How does the Employment of Mothers in Mills and Manufactures influence Infant Mortality; and Ought Any, and if, so, What, Restrictions to be Placed on Such Employment?, *NAPSS* (London).

Dolan, T.M. M.D., (1894) *Our State Hospitals: their Construction, Management and Organisation*, (Leicester).

Doyle, M. (1851) *Rural Economy for Cottage Farmers*, (London).

Duglinson, R. M.D. (1855) *A Dictionary of Medical Science*, (Philadelphia).

Dunglisson, R. M.D. (1824) *Commentaries on Diseases of the Stomach and Bowels of Children*, (London).

Dyos, H.Y. and Wolff, M. (1873) *The Victorian City: Images and Reality*, Volume I & II, (London).

Eden, F.M. (1797) The *State of the Poor, or an History of the Labouring Classes in England, from the Conquest to the Present Period*, Vol. I, (London).

Farr, W. (1865) Report on the Questions Submitted by Dr. Farr to the Council, Concerning the Classification of Epidemic Diseases to the Royal Society of Medicine, (London).

Faucher, L. (1844), *Manchester in 1844, its present condition and future Prospects* (London: Simpkin Marshall & Co).

Francis, C. An Act for Supplying some Defects in the Laws for the Relief of the Poor of this Kingdom. Francis Const, Decisions of the Court of the King's Bench, Upon the Laws Relating to the Poor, Originally Published by Edmund Bott Esq., of the Inner Temple, Barrister at Law. Revised ... by Francis Const Esq., of the Middle Temple, 3rd edn. 2 vols. (London: Whieldon and Butterworth, 1793), vol. II pp 516–18.

Gaskell, E. (1987) *Mary Barton*, (Oxford: Oxford University Press) first published 1848.

Gissing, G. (1975) *The Nether World*, (London: Dent & Sons) first published 1889.

Herr Meyer, R., *Robert Baker, C.B., R.C.S., 1803–1880* Special Collections, f.1, in the Brotherton Library at Leeds University.

Hirst, W. (1844) *History of the Woollen Trade for the Last Sixty Years Shewing the Advantages which the West Of England Trade had of those over Yorkshire up to 1813, How These were Gradually Overcome, Until 1818 when a challenge was Received and Accepted for the Author in London to Place His Goods in Competition with those in the West of England: Commencing with a Memoir of the Author and Tracing Connexion with the Progress of the Woollen Manufacture*, (Leeds).

Hirst, W. (1844) *History of the Woollen Trade for the Last Sixty Years Shewing the Advantages which the West Of England Trade had of those over Yorkshire up to 1813, How These were Gradually Overcome, Until 1818 when a challenge was Received and Accepted for the Author in London to Place His Goods in Competition with those in the West of England: Commencing with a Memoir of the Author and Tracing Connexion with the Progress of the Woollen Manufacture*, (Leeds).

Hole, J. (1873) *A Chapter on Leeds*, (Leeds).

Hutchins B.L. (1983) Yorkshire, in C. Black (1983) (ed.) *Married Women's Work: Being the Report of an Enquiry Undertaken by the women's Industrial Council* (London: Virago). First published in 1915 by G. Bell & Son London.

Hutton, W. (1783) *History of Birmingham*, (Birmingham).

Ikin, J. (1865) Abstract from a Paper on the *Undue Mortality of Infants and Children, in Connection with the Questions of Early Marriages, Drugging Children, Bad Nursing, Death Clubs and Certificates of Death, etc.* Reprinted from *NAPSS* (Leeds).

Jefferies, R. (1892) *The Toilers of the Field* 1848–1887 (London).

Jevons, W. (1882) Married Women in Factories, in *Contemporary Review*, January pp. 37–53.

Jewsbury, G. (1851) *Marian Withers*, (London).

Johnson, G. (1866) *Diarrhoea and Cholera: Their Nature and Treatment*, (London).

Jubb, S. (1860) *The History of the Shoddy Trade: It's Rise and Progress and Present Position*, (Heckmondwike).

Mrs. Layton, (1977) Life as we have known it: Memories of Seventy Years, in M. Llewelyn Davies, (1977), (first published in 1931), *Life As We Have Known It*, (Virago: London).

Leeds (1880) 'Report of the Orphan Home, Headingley Hill, Leeds, 1867–1880' (Leeds).

Leeds Workhouse Committee, (1823) 'Examinations taken in the case of Maria Sleddin' (Leeds).

Liebig, J.F. (1867) *Food for Infants* (London).

Llewelyn Davies, M. (1978) Maternity: Letters from Working Women (London: Virago) First Published in 1915.

Longbottom, E. (1890) *Batley Business Records 1831–1885,* (Leeds).

Martin. A. (1913) The Mother and Social Reform, *The Nineteenth Century and After*, May and June.

Maynard-Salmon, L. (1897) *Domestic Service*, (London).

Newman, G. (1906) *Infant Mortality*, (London).

Nightingale, F. (1914) *Addresses to Probationers and Nurses of the Nightingale School at St Thomas's Hospital*, (London).

Orme Dudfield, T., M.D. (1870) Medical Officer to the Board of Guardians, SS Margaret and John, Westminster, (London).

Patmore, C. (1854) *The Angel in the House*, (London).

Patmore, C. (1854) *The Angel in the House*, (London).

Pember Reeves, M. (2008) *Round About Pound a Week*, (London: Persephone) First published in 1915 by G. Bell & Son London.

Power-Cobbe, F. (1861) *The Workhouse as an Hospital* (London).

Ranger, W. (1851) Report to the General Board of health on a Preliminary Inquiry into the Sewerage, Drainage, and Supply of Water, and the Sanitary Condition of the Inhabitants of the Township of Dewsbury, (London).

Report of the Orphan Home, Headingley Hill, (Leeds 1867–1880).

Reynolds, G. (1853) *Mary Price, Memoirs of a Servant Maid*, (London).

Rilliet and Barthez, (1853) *Maladies des Enfants*, Vol, I, p. 19, *Du Fait Chez la Femme*, 8vo, (Paris).

Rogers, J. (1870) The Poor Law Medical Officers' Assocation; An Address ... at a General Meeting ... November 29th, (London).

Rogers, J., M.D. (1889) *Reminiscences of a Workhouse Medical Officer*, (London).

Routh, C.H., M.D. (1860) *Infant Feeding and its Influences on Life: Or the Causes and Prevention of Infant Mortality*, (London).

Ryan, W.B. (1862) *Infanticide its Law, Prevalence Prevention and History*, (London).

Shean, S. (1865) *Workhouse Hospitals* (London).

Shean, S. (1869) Workhouse Management and Workhouse Justice: a Further Letter, (London).

Sheen, A. (1890) *The Workhouse and its Medical Doctor,* (Bristol).

Sherard, R.H. (1897) *The White Slaves of England,* (London: James Bowden).

Smith Edward (1867–8) *Provincial Workhouses: Report of Dr Edward Smith, Medical Officer to the Poor Law Board, on the Sufficiency of the Existing Arrangements for the Treatment of the Sick Poor in Workhouses in Forty Eight Provincial Workhouses in England and Wales: Together with an Appendix to Such Report, Containing Dr Smith's Observations On Each of the Workhouses in Question:* &c, (London).

Smith, E. (1968) *The Wasting Diseases of Infants and Children,* (London).

Spence T. (1796) *Rights of Infants,* (London: The Hive of Liberty).

Spottiswoode, C. (1891) *Urban Sanitary Authority of the Borough of Leeds, For the Year 1890,* (Leeds).

Stallard, J.H. (1864) Workhouse Management and Workhouse Justice, in W.E. Page, *Introductory Address Delivered at St Georges Hospital* (London).

Taylor, W.C. (1873) Employment of Mothers in Manufacturers', What influence has the Employment of Mothers in Manufacturers on Infant Mortality; and ought any, and what, Restrictions to be placed on such Employment, *NAPSS.*

Tennant, M. (1908) Incompatibility of breast feeding and factory employment of mothers, in G. Tuckwell, *Women in Industry from Seven Points of View,* (London: Duckworth).

Twining, L. (1858) *Workhouses and Women's Work,* (London).

Twining, L. (1861) *Workhouse Visiting Society,* 1859–1863, XVI (London).

Twining, L. (1892) Nursing in Workhouses and Workhouse Infirmaries; A paper read before the Ladies Conference in Liverpool 1891, (Liverpool).

Twining, L. (1898) *Workhouses and Pauperism, and Women's Work in the Administration of the Poor Law,* (London).

Twining, L., *Journal of the Workhouse Visiting Society* January 1859 – January 1863, *(WVS)* (London 1865).

Vernois and Becquerel, (1777) *Treatise on the Management of Pregnant and Lying-in Women,* Charles White, M.D. 8vo, 2nd ed.

Walker, A. (1787), *A Complete Guide for a Servant Maid, or the sure means of Gaining Love and Esteem,* (London: T. Sabine).

Warren, Mrs. (1865) *How I Managed My Children from Infancy to Marriage,* (London).

Waugh, E. (1867) *Home Life of the Lancashire Factory Folk During the Cotton Famine,* (London).

White, C. (1792) *An inquiry into the nature and cause of that swelling in one or both of the lower extremities which sometimes happens to lying-in women; Together with an examination into the propensity of drawing the breasts, of those who give such, and also of those who do not give suck.* 2nd ed. (London).

Wilson, J. (1890) *Nursing in Workhouses and Workhouse Infirmaries,* (London).

Wollstonecraft, M. (1985) *A Vindication of the Rights of Women,* (London, Dent). First published in 1792.

Wythen-Baxter, W.R. (1841) *The Book of the Bastilles,* or The New Poor Law, (Warwick).

Young, A. (1772) *A Six weeks Tour, Through the Southern Counties of England and Wales,* (London).

Young, A. (1804) *General View of the County of Hertfordshire* (London).

Reports

TUC Library Report, 1884.

1901 Census County of York Volume, Table 35.

Pictures
'Dinner Hour in Wigan', by Eyre Crowe, at Manchester City Art Gallery.

Secondary Sources

Books

Abel-Smith, B. (1979) *A History of the Nursing Profession* (London: Heinemann).

Abrams, L. (2002) *The Making of the Modern Woman: Europe 1789–1918* (Harlow: Longman).

Alexander, S. (1994) *Becoming A Woman* (London: Virago).

Allan P. and Jolley M. (1982) (ed.) *Nursing, Midwifery and Health Visiting Since 1900* (London: Faber and Faber).

Anderson, M. (1974) *Family Structure in Nineteenth Century Lancashire* (London: Cambridge University Press).

Aries, P. (1962) *Centuries of Childhood*, (Harmondsworth: Penguin).

Armstrong, K. (2007) *The Hive of Liberty: the Life and Work of Thomas Spence 1750–1814* (Whitley Bay: Thomas Spence Trust).

Ashton, T.S. (1962) *The Industrial Revolution 1760–1830*, (London: Oxford University Press),.

Bailey, J. (2012) *Parenting* in England, *1760–1830: Emotion Identity and Generation*, (Oxford: Oxford University Press).

Barker, H. Chalus, E. (2005) (ed.) *Women's History: Britain, 1700–1850: an Introduction* (London: Routledge).

Behlmer, G. (1992) *Child Abuse and Moral Reform in England 1870–1908* (Stanford California: Stanford University Press).

Behlmer, G. *Friends of the Family: The English Home and its Guardians*, (Stanford California: Stanford University Press).

Bennett, J. (1996) *Ale, Brew and Brewsters in England; Women's Changing World 1300–1600* (Oxford: Oxford University Press).

Berg M. (1994) *The Age of Manufactures: 1700–1820, Industry, Innovation and Work in Britain* (London: Routledge).

Berger S. (ed.) (2006) *A Companion to Nineteenth Century Europe: 1789–1914* (Blackwell: Oxford).

Berry H. and Foyster, E. (2007) *The Family in Early Modern England*, (Cambridge: Cambridge University Press).

Black, C. (1983) (ed.) *Married Women's Work*: Being the Report of an Enquiry Undertaken by the Women's Industrial Council (London, 1983) First Published in 1915 by G. Bell, London.

Blaszac, B. (2000) *The Matriarchs of England's Cooperative Movement: A Study in Gender Politics and Female Leadership, 1883–1921*, (Westport: Greenwood Press).

Boyson, R. (1970) *The Ashworth Cotton Enterprise: The Rise and Fall of a Family Firm, 1818–1880* (Oxford: Oxford Clarendon Press).

Brigg, M. (ed) (1982) *The Journals of a Lancashire Weaver 1856–1875*, (S.I: The Record Society of Lancashire and Cheshire).

Briggs, A. (1959) *The Age of Improvement, 1783–1867* (London: Longman).

Briggs, A. (1970) *The Nineteenth Century, The Contradiction of Progress*, (London: Thames and Hudson).

Brown, H. (*The Rise of British Trade Unionism 1825–1914* (London: Longman).

Brundage, A. (2002) Th*e English Poor Laws, 1700–1930* (Basingstoke: Palgrave).

Burke, P. (2004) *What is Cultural History* (Cambridge: Cambridge University Press).

Burnett, J. (1979) *Plenty and Want* (London: Scholar Press).

Burnette, J. (2008) *Gender Work and Wages in Industrial Revolution Britain* (Cambridge: Cambridge University Press).

Cartwright F.F. and Biddiss, (1972) M. *Disease and History*, (London: Hard Davis).

Caulfield, E. (1931) *The Infant Welfare Movement in the Eighteenth Century*, (New York).

Chamberlain, M. (1981) *Old Wives' Tales: their History, Remedies and Spells*, (London: Virago).

Clark, A. (1995) *The Struggle for the Breeches: Gender and the Making of the British Working Class* (London: Rivers Oram Press).

Clark. A. (1982) *Working Life of Women in the Seventeenth Century* (London: Routledge).

Cody, L. (2005) *Birthing the Nation, Sex Science and the Conception of Eighteenth Century Britons* (Oxford: Oxford University Press).

Cotton B. (2008) *Scottish Vernacular Furniture*, (London, Thames & Hudson).

Cotton, B. *The English Regional Chair*, (Woodbridge, 1990).

Creighton, C. (1965) *A History of Epidemics in Britain* 1847–1927 (London: Cass).

Crompton F. (1997) *Workhouse Children: Infant and Child Paupers Under the Worcestershire Poor Law, 1780–1871* (Stroud: Sutton).

Crowther, M.A. (1981) T*he Workhouse System 1834–1929: The History of an English Social Institution* (London: Batsford Academic and Educational).

Crump, J. (1980) *The Ups and Downs of Being Born*, (London: Vassall Neighbourhood Council).

Daunton, M.J. (1995) *Progress and Poverty: An Economic and Social History of Britain 1750–1850* (Oxford: Oxford University Press).

Davidoff L. and Hall C. (1987) *Family Fortunes: The English Middle Class 1750–1850* (London: Hutchinson).

Davies, O. (2003) *Cunning Folk, Popular Magic in English History* (London: Hambledon and London).

Davin, A. *Growing Up Poor: Home, School and Street in London 1870–1914*, (London 1996).

Deane P. and W.A. Cole, (1993) British Economic Growth, 1688–1959: Trends and Structure, (Aldershot: Greg Revivals).

Delap, L. (2007) *The Feminist Avant Garde*, (Cambridge: Cambridge University Press), p. 111.

Dick, C. (1987) *Yesterday's Babies; A History of Baby Care*, (London: Bodley Head).

Dickens, A.M. (1976) 'The Workhouse' Architectural Review, CLX, No. 958.

Digby, A. (1978) *Pauper Palaces* (London: Routledge & Kegan Paul).

Digby, A. (1994) *Making a Medical Living*, (Cambridge: 1994).

Dodd, W. (1968) The Factory System Illustrated, (London: Cass).

Dony, J.G. (1942) *A History of the Straw Hat Industry* (Luton: Gibbs, Bamforth & Co).

Drake, B. (1984) *Women in Trade Unions*, (London: Virago).

Ehrenreich B. and English, D. (2010) *Witches, Midwives and Nurses: A History of Women Healers* (New York: Feminist Press).

Elias, N. (1992) *Time: An Essay*, (Oxford: Blackwell).

Elkin, W. (1983) 'Manchester' in C. Black (ed.), (1983), Married Women's Work, (London: Bell).

Emsley, C. (1987) *Crime and Society in England 1750–1900* (London: Longman).

Engels, F. (1969) *The Condition of the Working-class in England*, (London: Panther).

Evans, T. (2005) *'Unfortunate Objects', Lone Mothers in Eighteenth Century London*, (Basingstoke: Palgrave Macmillan).

Evenden, E. (2000) *The Midwives of Seventeenth Century London* (Cambridge: Cambridge University Press).

Ewan, E. (1990) *Town Life in Fourteenth Century Scotland* (Edinburgh: Edinburgh University Press).

Fildes, V. (1986) *Breasts, Bottles and Babies, A History of Infant Feeding* (Edinburgh: Edinburgh University Press).

Floud R. Wachter K. and Gregory A., (1990) *Height, Health and History: Nutritional Status in the United Kingdom, 1750–1980*, (Cambridge: Cambridge University Press).

Ford, P. and G. Ford, (1956) *A Guide to Parliamentary Papers: What They Are: How To Find Them: How To Use Them* (Oxford: Basil Blackwell).

Fowler, S. (2007) *The Workhouse: The People, The Places, The Life Behind Doors* (Kew: National Archives).

Foyster, E. and Marten, J. (2010) *A Cultural History of Childhood and Family in the Age of Enlightenment*, (Oxford: Berg).

Fraser, D. (1980) *A History of Modern Leeds*, (Manchester: Manchester University Press).

Garrett, E. Galley, C. Shelton N. and Woods R. (2006) (eds.), *Infant Mortality, A Continuing Social Problem*, (Aldershot: Ashgate).

Garrett, E. Reid, A. Schurer, K. Szreter, S. (2001) *Changing Family Size in England and Wales, Place, Class and Demography 1891–1911* (Cambridge: Cambridge University Press).

Giles C. and Goodall, I.H. (1992) *Yorkshire Textile Mills, The Buildings of the Yorkshire Textile Industry 1770–1930*, (London: HMSO).

Gissing, G. (1973) *The Nether World*, (London: Dent).

Gleadle, K. (2001) *British Women in the Nineteenth Century* (Basingstoke: Palgrave Macmillan).

Goffman, E. (1991) *Asylums, Essays on the Social Situation of Mental Patients and Other Inmates*, (London: Penguin).

Goose, N. (2007) *Women's Work in Industrial England*: Regional and Local Perspectives (Hatfield: Local Population Studies).

Gordon E. and Breitenbach, E. (eds), (1990) *The World is Ill Divided, Women's Work in Scotland in the Nineteenth and Early Twentieth Centuries*, (Edinburgh: Edinburgh University Press).

Gray, R. (1996) *The Factory Question and Industrial England 1830–1860* (Cambridge: Cambridge University Press).

Griffin, A. (2012) *The Politics of Gender* in Victorian Britain: Masculinity, Political Culture and The Struggle for Women's Rights, (Cambridge: Cambridge University Press).

Griffin, E. (2010) *A Short History of the Industrial Revolution* (Basingstoke: Palgrave Macmillan).

Griffin, E. (2013) *Liberty's Dawn, A People's History of the Industrial Revolution*, (Hamps: Hobbs).

Grundy, J. (2003) *History's Midwives: Including a 17c and 18c Yorkshire Midwives Nomination Index*, (Lancashire: Federation of Family History Societies).

Halliday, S. (1999) *The Great Stink of London: Sir Joseph Bazalgette and the Cleansing of the Victorian Capital* (Stroud: Sutton).

Hamlin, C. (1998) *Public Health and Social Justice in the Era of Chadwick*, Britain 1800–1854 (Cambridge: Cambridge University Press).

Hammond, J.L. and B. (1995) *The Skilled Labourer* (Abingdon: Fraser Stewart).

Hannam, J. (1989) *Isabella Ford*, (Oxford: Basil Blackwell).

Hardy, A. (2001) *The Epidemic Streets: Infectious Disease and the Rise of Preventive Medicine* 1856–1900 (Oxford: Oxford University Press).

Hartwell, R.M. (1967) *The Causes of the Industrial Revolution in England*, (London: Metheun).

Haslam, J. (1904) *The Handloom Weaver's Daughter* (London: S.C. Brown, Langham & Company Ltd).

Heaton, H. (1965) *The Yorkshire Woollen and Worsted Industries*, (Oxford: Clarendon Press).

Henderson, T. (1999) *Disorderly Women in Eighteenth Century London: Prostitution and Control in the Metropolis* (London: Longman).

Hendrick, H. (1994) *Children; New Perspectives, Child Welfare in England, 1872–1969*, (London: Routledge).

Hewitt, M. (1958) *Wives and Mothers in Victorian Industry*, (London: Rockliff).

Hill, B. (1994) *Women, Work & Sexual Politics in Eighteenth-Century England*, (Canada: McGill Queen's University Press).

Hill, C. (1972) *The World Turned Upside Down*: Radical Ideas During the Industrial Revolution (London: Temple Smith).

Himmelfarb, G. (1985) *The Idea of Poverty. England in the Early Industrial Age* (New York: Vintage).

Hobsbawm, E. (1968) *Industry & Empire*: An Economic History of Britain (London: Weidenfield & Nicolson).

Hobsbawn, E. (1962) *Age of Revolution: Europe 1789–1848* (London: Weidenfield & Nicolson).

Hodgkinson, R. (1967) *The Origins of the National Health Service*, (London: Welcome History Medical Library).

Holloway, G. (2005) *Women and Work in Britain Since 1840* (London: Routledge).

Honeyman, K. (2000) *Women, Gender and Industrialisation in England, 1700–1870* (Basingstoke: Palgrave Macmillan).

Horn, P. (1991) *Victorian Country Women* (Oxford: Basil Blackwell).

Howe, G.M. (1976) *Man Environment and Disease in Britain; A Medical Geography through the Ages*, (Harmondsworth: Penguin).

Hudson, P. (1975) *The West Riding Wool Textile Industry: A Catalogue of Business Records From the Sixteenth to the Twentieth Century*, (Edington: Pasold Research Fund Ltd).

Hudson, P. (1986) *The Genesis of Industrial Capital: a Study of the West Riding Wool Textile Industry c. 1750–1850* (Cambridge: Cambridge University Press).

Hudson, P. (1989) *Regions and Industries: a Perspective on the Industrial Revolution in Britain*, (Cambridge: Cambridge University Press).

Hudson, P. (1992) *The Industrial Revolution* (London: Edward Arnold).

Humberman, A.M. (1996) *Escape from the Market: Negotiating Work in Lancashire* (Cambridge: Cambridge University Press).

Humphries, J. (2010) *Childhood and Child Labour in the Industrial Revolution* (Cambridge: Cambridge University Press).

Hutchins B.L. and Harrison, E. (1903) *A History of Factory Legislation*, (Westminster: British Law: Trades and Crafts).

Hutchins, B.L. (1911) *The Working Life of Women*, (London: Fabian Society).

Hutchins, B.L. (1907) *Home, Work and Sweating, the Causes and the Remedies*, (London: Fabian Society).

Hutchins, B.L. (1915) *Women in Modern Industry*, (London: Bell and Sons).

Jackson, M. (2002) *Infanticide, Historical Perspectives on Child Murder and Concealment 1550–2000*, (Aldershot: Ashgate).

Jalland, P. (1986) *Women and Marriage and Politics 1860–1914*, (Oxford: Clarendon Press).

Jenkins D.J. and Ponting, K.G. (1982) *The British Wool Textile Industry: 1770–1914* (London: Heinemann).

John, A. (1984) *By The Sweat of their Brow: Women Workers at Victorian Coal Mines*, (London: Routledge & Kegan Paul).

John, A. (1986) (ed.),*Unequal Opportunities; Women's Opportunities in England 1800–1918*, (Oxford: Basil Blackwell).

Joseph G. (1983) *Women at Work: the British Experience* (Oxford: Phillip Allan).

Jowitt, J.A. (ed) (1986) *Model Industrial Communities in Mid Nineteenth Century Yorkshire*, (Bradford: University of Bradford).

Kidd, A. (Macmillan Press) (1999) *State, Society and the Poor in Nineteenth-Century England*, (Basingstoke: Macmillan).

Kilday, A.-M. (2013) *A History of Infanticide in Britain; c. 1600 to the present*, (Basingstoke: Palgrave Macmillan).

Kilday, A.-M. *Women and Violent Crime in Enlightenment Scotland*, (Woodbridge: Boydell Press).

King S. and Timmins, G. (2001) *Making Sense of the Industrial Revolution*, (Manchester: Manchester University Press.

King S. and Tomkins, A. (ed.) (2003) The Poor in England: an Economy of Makeshifts, (Manchester: Manchester University Press).

King, S. (2000) *Poverty and Welfare in England, 1700–1850: A Regional Perspective*, (Manchester: Manchester University Press.

King, S. (2006) *Women, Welfare and Local Politics, 1880–1920*, "We Might be Trusted" (Brighton: Sussex Academic).

Knelman, J. (1998) *Twisting in the Wind: The Murderess and the English Press*, (London: University of Toronto Press) .

Kussmaul, A. (1981) *Servants in Husbandry in Early Modern England* (Cambridge: Cambridge University Press).

Lane, J. (2001) *A Social History of Medicine, Health, Healing and Disease in England, 1750–1950*, (London: Routledge).

Langton, J. and R.J. Morris, (1986) *Atlas of Industrialising Britain: 1780–1914* (London: Methuen).

Lawrence, C. (1994) *Medicine in the Making of Modern Britain, 1700–1920* (London: Routledge).

Leap N and Hunter, B. (1993) *The Midwives Tale: An Oral History from Handywoman to Professional Midwife* (London: Scarlet Press).

Lees, L.H. (1998) *The Solidarities of Strangers: The English Poor Laws and the People 1700–1948* (Cambridge: Cambridge University Press).

Levene, A. (2007) *Childcare, Health and Mortality at the London Foundling Hospital, 1741–1800*, (Manchester: Manchester University Press).

Levene, A. Nutt, T. and Williams, S. (eds.) (2005) *Illegitimacy in Britain, 1700–1920* (Basingstoke: Palgrave Macmillan).

Lewenhak, S. and Cremonesi H. (1980) *Women and Work*, (London: Macmillan).

Lewis, J. (1984) *Women in England, 1870–1950: Sexual Divisions and Social Change* (Brighton: Wheatsheaf).

Lewis, J. (1986) *Labour and Love: Women's Experience of Home and Family* (Oxford: Blackwell).

Lewis, J. (1992) *Women in Britain Since 1945: Women, Family Work and the State in the Post-war Years* (Oxford: Basil Blackwell).

Liddington J. and Norris J. (1978) *'One Hand Tied Behind Us': The Rise of the Women's Suffrage Movement'*, (London: Virago).

Longmate, N. (1974) *The Workhouse* (London: Temple Smith).

Lown, J. (1990) *Women and Industrialisation: Gender at Work in Nineteenth-Century England* (Cambridge: Polity).

Malcolmson, P. (1986) *English Laundresses; a Social History, 1850–1930* (Urbana: University of Illinois Press).

Malone, C. (2003) *Women's Bodies and Dangerous Trades in England 1880–1914* (Royal Historical Studies in History: Rochester NY: Boydell Press).

Marland, H. (1987) *Medicine and Society in Wakefield and Huddersfield 1780–1870* (Cambridge: Cambridge University Press).

Marland, H. (1993) *The Art of Midwifery: Early Modern Midwives in Europe* (London: Routledge).

Marland, H. (1997) *Midwives, Society and Childbirth: Debates and Controversies in the Modern Period* (London: Routledge).

Marshall, W. (2005) The Rural Economy of Gloucestershire, (Stroud: Nonsuch).

Mason, M. (1994) *The Making of Victorian Sexuality* (Oxford: Oxford University Press).

McDonough, J. (2003) *Child Murder & British Culture, 1720–1900* (Cambridge: Cambridge University Press).

McFeely, M.D. (1988) *A Lady Inspector; the Campaign for a Better Workplace, 1893–1921*, (Oxford: Basil Blackwell).

McIntosh, T. (2012) *A Social History of Maternity and Childbirth: Key Themes in Maternity Care* (London Routledge).

McKeown, T. (1976) *The Modern Rise of Population*, (London: Edward Arnold).

Meldrum, T. (2000) Domestic *Service and Gender, 1660–1750: Life and Work in the London Household* (Harlow: Pearson).

Mingay, G.E. (1968) *Enclosure and the Small Farmer in the Age of the Industrial Revolution* (London: Macmillan).

Moncrieff A. (ed). (1952) *A Textbook on the Nursing and Diseases of Sick Children*, (London: Lewis).

Morgan, C.E. (2001) *Women Workers and Gender Identities, 1835–1918: The Cotton and Metal Industries in England*, (London: Routledge).

Morgan, K. (2004) *The Birth of Industrial Britain: Economic Change 1750–1850* (Harlow: Pearson Longman).

Moring's B. (ed.) (2102) *Female Economic Strategies in the Modern World* (London: Pickering & Chatto).

Morrison, K. (1999) *The Workhouse: a Study of Poor Law Buildings in England*, (Swindon: English Heritage).

Mostyn Bird, M. (1911) *Woman at Work*: A *Study of the Different Ways of Earning a Living Open to Women*, (London: Chapman and Hall).

Neff, W. (1966) *Victorian Working Women: a Historical and Literary Study of Women in British Industries and Professions* (London: Cass).

Nelson, B. (1980) *The Woollen Industry of Leeds* (Leeds: Thornton).

Nutting M.A. and Dock L.L. (2000) *A History of Nursing* (Bristol: Thoemmes Press).

Oddy D.J. and Millar D.S. (eds.) (1976) *The Making of the Modern British Diet* (London: Croom Helm).

Pember Reeves, M. (2008) *Round About Pound a Week*, (London: Persephone) First published in 1913 by G. Bell.

Perkins, J. (1993) *Victorian Women* (London: John Murray).

Pinchbeck I. and Hewitt, M. (1969) *Children in English Society, Vol. I, From Tudor Times to the Eighteenth Century* (London: Routledge & Kegan Paul).

Pinchbeck I. (1930), *Women Workers and the Industrial Revolution*, (Thetford: Lowe & Brydone).

Pinchbeck, I. (1969) *Women Workers and the Industrial Revolution* (London: Routledge).

Pinchbeck, I. (1981) *Women Workers in the Industrial Revolution 1750–1850*, (London: Virago).

Pollock, L. (1983) *Forgotten Children: Parent–child Relations from 1500–1900* (Cambridge: Cambridge University Press).

Porter, D. and Porter R. (1993) *Doctors, Politics and Society: Historical Essays* (Amsterdam: Rodopi).

Porter, R. (1987) *Disease, Medicine and Society in England 1550–1860* (Basingstoke: Macmillan Education).

Porter, R. (1996) *Cambridge Illustrated History of Medicine*, (Cambridge: Cambridge University Press).

Porter, R. (1998) *The Greatest Benefit to Mankind: A Medical History of Humanity* (London: Fontana).

Porter, R. (2001) *Bodies Politic, Disease, Death and Doctors in Britain, 1650–1900* (London: Reaktion).

Porter, R. (ed.) (1985) *Patients and Practitioner; Lay Perceptions of Medicine in Pre-Industrial Society* (Cambridge: Cambridge University Press).

Purvis, P. (2000) (ed.) *Women's History: Britain, 1850–1945: An Introduction* (London: Routledge).

Razzell P.E. and Wainwright, R.W. (1973) *The Victorian Working Class, Selections from the Morning Chronicle*, (London: Frank Cass).

Reach, A. (1972) *Manchester and the Textile Districts in 1849*, (Rossendale: Helmshore Local History Society).

Reach, A. (2007) *Fabrics, Filth and Fairy Tents: The Yorkshire Textile Districts in 1849* (Hebden Bridge: Royd Press).

Reinarz J. and Schwartz L. (2013) (ed.) *Medicine and the Workhouse*, (New York: Rochester).

Rendall, J. (1990) *Women in an Industrializing Society: England 1750–1880* (Oxford: Blackwell).

Roberts, E. (1995) *Women and Families: An Oral History* (Oxford: Basil Blackwell).

Roberts, E. (1984) *A Woman's Place: An Oral History of Working Class Women 1890–1940* (Oxford: Basil Blackwell).

Roberts, E. (1988) *Women's Work, 1840–1940* (Basingstoke: Macmillan).

Rose, L. (1986) *Massacre of the Innocents: Infanticide in Britain 1800–1939* (London: Routledge and Kegan Paul).

Rose, M. (1971) *The English Poor Law* (Newton Abbott: Charles & David).

Rose, S.O. (1992) *Limited Livelihoods: Gender and Class in Nineteenth-century England* (London: Routledge).

Rosen, M. (1994) *Penguin Book of Childhood* (London: Viking).

Rowbotham, J. and Stevenson, K. (2005) (eds.) *Criminal Conversations, Victorian Crimes, Social Panic, and Moral Outrage* (Ohio: Ohio State University Press).

Rowbotham, R. (1977) *Hidden from History, 300 Years of Women's Oppression and the Fight Against It*, (London: Pluto Press).

Rubenstein W.D. (1994) *Capitalism and Culture & Decline in Britain* (London: Routledge).

Schwarzkopf, J. (2004) *Unpicking Gender, The Social Construction of Gender in the Lancashire Cotton Weaving Industry, 1880–1914* (Aldershot: Ashgate).

Scott G. (1998) *Feminism and the Politics of Working Women: The Women's Co-operative Guild, 1880s to the Second World War* (London: UCL Press).

Sharpe, P. (1998) *Women's Work: The English Experience* (London: Arnold).

Shoemaker, R. (1998) *Gender in English Society, 1650–1850: The Emergence of Separate Spheres?* (London: Longman).

Showalter, E. (1987) *The Female Malady: Women, Madness and English Culture, 1830–1980* (London: Virago).

Simonton, D. (1998) *A History of European Women's Work* (London: Routledge).

Smart, C. (ed.) *Regulating Womanhood, Historical Essays on Marriage, Motherhood, and Sexuality,* (London: Routledge).

Smith, R.A. (1904) *Baby: Its Treatment and Care* (London).

Snell K.D.N. (1985) *Annals of the Labouring Poor: Social Change and Agrarian England, 1600–1900* (Cambridge: Cambridge University Press).

Sparks, A. (1978) *A Woman's Work* (London: Centreprise Trust Ltd.).

Stanley, J. and Griffiths B. (1990) *For Love and Shillings: Wandsworth Women's Working Lives* (London: History Workshop).

Steedman, C. (2007) *Master and Servant: Love and Labour in the English Industrial Age* (Cambridge: Cambridge University Press).

Steedman, C. (2009) *Labours Lost; Domestic Service and the Making of Modern England,* (Cambridge: Cambridge University Press).

Steinbach, S. (2005) *Women in England: A Social History, 1790–1914* (London: Phoenix).

Stone, L. (1979) (Ab. version) *The Family, Sex and Marriage in England 1500–1800* (Harmondsworth: Penguin).

Strachey, R. (1978) *The Cause: A Short History of the Women's Movement in Great Britain* (London: Virago).

Summerfield, P. (2012) *Women's Workers in the Second World War* (London: Routledge).

Szreter, S. (1986) *The Importance of Social Intervention in Britain's Mortality Decline C.1850–1914: a Re-interpretation of the Role of Public Health,* (London: Centre for Economic Policy Research).

Szreter, S. *Fertility,* (1996) *Class and Gender* in Britain 1860–1940 (Cambridge: Cambridge University Press).

Thompson, E.P. (1980) *The Making of the English Working-class,* (Harmondsworth: Penguin).

Thompson, E.P. (1991) *Customs in Common* (London: Merlin Press).

Thomson, P. (2000) *The Voice of the Past; Oral History* (Oxford: Oxford University Press).

Tilly L. and Scott, J. (1978) *Women, Work & Family,* (New York: Holt, Rinehart & Winston).

Timmins, G. (1998) *Made in Lancashire; a History of Regional Industrialisation* (Manchester: Manchester University Press).

Todd, S. (2014) *The People: The Rise and Fall of the Working Class 1910 – 2010* (London: John Murray).

Toynbee, A. (1969) *The Industrial Revolution, 1852–1883,* (Newton Abbott: David & Charles).

Tuckwell, G., Smith, C. MacArthur, M. Tennant, M. Adler, N. Anderson, A. Black, C. (1908) *Women in Industry from Seven Points of View,* (London: Duckworth).

Turner, B. (1920) *A Short History of the General Union of Textile Workers,* (Heckmondwike: Labour Pioneer & Factory Times).

Valenze, D. (1995) *The First Industrial Woman* (Oxford: Oxford University Press).

Verdon, N. (2002) *Rural Women Workers in Nineteenth Century England: Gender, Work and Wages* (Woodbridge: Boydell).

Vicinus M. (ed.) (1972) *Suffer and Be Still, Women in the Victorian Age*, (London: Methuen).

Vickery, A. (1998) *The Gentleman's Daughter: Women's Lives in Victorian England*, (London: Yale University Press).

Vickery, A. (2009) *Behind Closed Doors: At Home in Georgian England* (London: Yale University Press).

Walkowitz, J.R. (1980) *Prostitution and Victorian Society: Women, Class and the State*, (Cambridge: Cambridge University Press).

Walvin, J. (1982) *A Child's World: A Social History of English Childhood* (Harmondsworth: Penguin).

Watson, K. (2004) *Poisoned Lives, English Poisoners and their Victims*, (London: Hambledon and London).

Wear A. (ed.), (1992) *Medicine in Society* (Cambridge: Cambridge University Press).

Webb, S. & B. (1963) *English Poor Law History, Part II: The Last Hundred Years*, (London: Cass).

Webb, S. & B. (1926) *Industrial Democracy: 1859–1947* (London: Longmans Green & Co.).

Weeks, J. (1981) *Sex, Politics and Society: The Regulation of Sexuality Since 1800* (London: Longman).

Whaley L. (2011) *Women and the Practice of Medical Care in Early Modern Europe 1400–1800* (Basingstoke: Palgrave Macmillan).

Whittington-Egan, M. (2001) *The Stockbridge Baby-Farmer*, (Glasgow: N Wilson).

Williamson, J.G. (1990) *Coping with City Growth during the British Industrial Revolution* (Cambridge: Cambridge University Press).

Wohl, A. (1983) *Endangered Lives: Public Health in Victorian Britain* (London: Dent).

Woods R. and Shelton, N. (1997) *An Atlas of Victorian Mortality* (Liverpool: Liverpool University Press).

Woods, R. (2000) *The Demography of Victorian England and Wales* (Cambridge: Cambridge University Press).

Woods, R. (2000) *The Demography of Victorian England and Wales* (Cambridge: Cambridge University Press).

Woods, R. (2006) *Children Remembered: Responses to Untimely Death in the Past* (Liverpool: Liverpool University Press).

Worth, J. (2002) *Call the Midwife* (Twickenham: Merton).

Yeandle, S. and S. Pantry (1993) *Women of Courage, 100 Years of Factory Inspectors*, (London: HMSO).

Chapters in books

Anderson, M. (2007) 'What Can the Mid-Victorian Census tell us about variations in married women's employment?' in N. Goose (ed.) *Women's Work in Industrial England; Regional and Local Perspectives* (Hatfield: Local Population Studies) pp. 165–182.

Andrews, J. (2002) The Boundaries of Her Majesty's Pleasure: Discharging Child-Murderers from Broadmoor and Perth Criminal Lunatic Department, C. 1860–1920, in M. Jackson, *Infanticide: Historical Perspectives on Child Murder and Concealment 1550–2000*, (Aldershot: Ashgate) pp. 216–248.

Arnot, M.L. (2000) Understanding Women Committing Newborn Child Murder in Victorian England, in S. D'Cruze (ed.) *Everyday Violence in Britain, 1850–1950: Gender and Class,* (Harlow: Pearson) pp. 55–69.

Arnot, M.L. (2002) The Murder of Thomas Sandles: Meanings of a Mid-Nineteenth-Century Infanticide, in M. Jackson, (ed) *Infanticide, Historical Perspectives on Child Murder and Concealment, 1550–2000,* (Aldershot: Ashgate) pp. 149–167.

Ashton, T.S. (1969) Standard of Life, in Phyllis Deane and W.A. Cole, *British Economic Growth: Trends and Structure 1688–1959,* (London: Cambridge University Press).

Ayers, P. (1990) The Hidden Economy of Dockland Families: Liverpool in the 1930s, in P. Hudson P. and W.R. Lee (eds.) *Women's Work in the Family Economy in Historical Perspective,* (Manchester: Manchester University Press) pp. 271–290.

Barker, H. (2005) Women and Work in H. Barker and E. Chalus (eds) (2005) *Women's History Britain 1700–1850* (London: Routledge), pp. 125–151.

Barrett, S. (2003) Kinship, Poor Relief and the Welfare Process in Early Modern England, in S. King and A. Tomkins, *The Poor in England 1700–1850: an Economy of Makeshifts,* (Manchester: Manchester University Press) pp. 199–227.

Bedarida, F. (1970) Cities: Population and the Urban Explosion, in A. Briggs, *The Nineteenth Century, The Contradiction of Progress,* (London: Thames and Hudson) p. 128–129.

Bentley, D. (2005) She-Butchers: Baby Droppers, Baby-Sweaters, and Baby-Farmer, in J. Rowbotham and K. Stevenson (eds.) *Criminal Conversations, Victorian Crimes, Social Panic, and Moral Outrage,* (Ohio: Ohio University Press) pp. 198–214.

Blackman, J. (1976) The Corner Shop: The Development of the Grocery and General Provision Trade, in D. J. Oddy and D. S. Millar (eds), *The Making of the Modern British Diet,* (London: Croom Helm).

Blythell, D. (1993) Women in the Workforce, in P. O'Brien and R. Quinault (ed.) (1993) *The Industrial Revolution and British Society,* (Cambridge: Cambridge University Press) pp. 31–53.

Buchanan, I. (1995) Infant Feeding, Sanitation and Diarrhoea in Colliery Communities 1880–1991, in D. J. Oddy and D.S. Millar, *Diet and Health in Modern Britain,* (London: Croom Helm) pp. 148–177.

Burn, W.L. (1987) The Age of Equipoise; A Study of the Mid-Victorian Generation, in S. Kent, *Sex and Suffrage in Britain 1860–1914,* (London: Routledge).

Chalus E. and Montgomery, F. Women and Politics, in H. Barker (eds.) *Women's History, Britain, 1700–1850: an Introduction* (London: Routledge) pp. 195–216.

D'Cruze, S. (2000) Women and the Family, in J. Purvis, (2000) *Women's History, Britain 1850–1945: an Introduction* (London: Routledge), pp. 51–84.

Dickinson, J. and Sharpe, J.A. (2002) Infanticide in Early Modern England: the Court of Great Sessions at Chester, 1650–1800; in M. Jackson, *Infanticide, Historical Perspectives on child Murder and Concealment, 1550–2000* (Aldershot: Ashgate).

Dupree, M. (2007) Women Workers in the 19th Century Pottery, in N. Goose, (ed) *Women's Work in Industrial England: Regional and Local Perspectives,* (Hatfield: Local Population Studies).

Evans, T. (2005) Women, Marriage and Family, in H. Barker (eds.) (2005) *Women's History, Britain, 1700–1850: an Introduction* (London: Routledge) pp. 57–77.

Flinn, M. (1976) Medical Services Under the New Poor Law, in D. Fraser, (ed.), *The New Poor Law in the Nineteenth Century,* (London: Macmillan) pp. 45–66.

Goose N. (2008), Cottage Industry, Migration, and Marriage in Nineteenth Century England *Economic History Review,* 61, pp. 798–819.

Hall E. and Drake, M. (2006) Diarrhoea: The Central Issue?, in Garrett, E., Galley, C., Shelton N., Woods R (ed.), *Infant Mortality : A Continuing Social Problem*, (Aldershot: Ashgate) pp. 149–168.

Hardy, A. (1993) Lyon Playfair and the Idea of Progress, in D. Porter and R. Porter, (eds.) *Doctors, Politics and Society, Historical Essays*, (Amsterdam: Rodopi).

Higginbotham, A. (1992) Sin of the Age: Infanticide and Illegitimacy in Victorian London, in K.O. Garrigan (ed.) *Victorian Scandals: Representations of Gender and Class* (Ohio: Ohio University Press) pp. 257–288.

Hollingsworth, D.F. (1976) Developments Leading to Present Day Nutritional Knowledge, in D. J. Oddy & D. S. Millar (eds), *The Making of the Modern British Diet*, (London: Croom Helm) pp. 189–195.

Horrell S. and Humphries J. (1998) Women's Labour Force Participation and the Transition to the Male-breadwinner Family, 1790–1865, in P. Sharpe, (1998), *Women's Work the English Experience, 1650–1914* (London: Bloomsbury Academic) pp. 172–206.

Humphries, J. (2000) Women and Paid Work, in J. Purvis, (2000) (ed.) *Women's History Britain: 1850–1945: An Introduction* (London: Routledge), pp. 85–106.

Jefferies, R. (1892 and 1981) *The Toilers of the Field* 1848–1887 in P. Horn, (1991) *Victorian Countrywomen*, (Oxford: Basil Blackwell).

Johnstone, G.N. (1976) The Growth of the Sugar Trade and Refining Industry, in D. J. Oddy and D. S. Millar (eds.), *The Making of the Modern British Diet*, (London: Croom Helm).

Kilday, A.-M. (2002) Maternal Monsters: Murdering Mothers in South-West Scotland, in Y.G. Brown, R. Ferguson, Rona (ed.), *Twisted Sisters: Women, Crime and Deviance in Scotland Since 1400* (East Linton: Tuckwell Press) pp. 156–189.

Kilday, A.-M. (2005) Women and Crime, in H. Barker, E. Chalus, (ed.), *Women's History: Britain, 1700–1850: an Introduction* (London: Routledge) pp. 174–193.

Kilday, A.-M. (2007) 'The Lady-Killers': Homicidal Women in Early Modern Britain, in K.D. Watson, (ed.), *Assaulting the Past: Violence and Civilization in Historical Context* (Newcastle: Cambridge Scholar Publication) pp. 203–221.

Lacey, K.E. (2008) Women and Work in the Fourteenth and Fifteenth Century in London, in Charles L. and Duffin L. (eds.) (2008) *Women and Work in Pre-Industrial England*, (London: Croom Helm) pp. 1–23.

Laslett, P. (1972) Mean Household Size in England Since the Sixteenth Century, in P. Laslett, and R. Wall, (1972) *Household and Family in Past Times* (Cambridge: Cambridge University Press), pp. 125–157.

Laxton P. (1986) Textiles, in J. Langton and R.J. Morris, *Atlas of Industrializing Britain*, (London: Methuen).

Lewis, J. (1986) Reconstructing Women's Experience, in J. Lewis, (ed.) *Labour and Love, Women's Experience of Home and Family* (Oxford: Basil Blackwell), pp.

Loudon, I. (1992) Medical Practitioners 1750–1850 and Medical Reform in England, in A. Wear (ed.), *Medicine in Society*, (Cambridge: Cambridge University Press) pp. 219–247.

Marland, H. (2002) 'Getting Away with Murder', Puerperal Insanity, Infanticide and the Defence Plea; in M. Jackson, (ed.), *Infanticide: Historical Perspectives on Child Murder and Concealment 1550–2000*, (Aldershot: Ashgate) pp. 168–92.

Masciola, A.L. (2002) 'The Unfortunate Maid Exemplified': Elizabeth Canning and Representations of Infanticide in Eighteenth-Century England, in M. Jackson, *Infanticide: Historical Perspectives on Child Murder and Concealment 1550–2000*, (Aldershot: Ashgate) pp. 52–72.

McKendrick, N. (1974) Home Demand and Economic Growth: a New View of the Role Women and Children in the Industrial Revolution, in N. McKendrick (ed.), *Historical Perspectives, Studies in English Thought and Society*, (London: Europa), pp. 152–210.

Negrine, A. (2013) Practitioners and Paupers: Medicine at the Leicester Union Workhouse, 1867–1905, pp. 192–211., in J. Reinarz and L. Schwartz (ed.) *Medicine and the Workhouse*, (New York: Rochester).

Pooley, S. (2009) Child Care and Neglect in the Late Nineteenth Century, in L. Delap B. Griffin and A. Wills, (eds.) *The Politics of Domestic Authority in Britain since 1800*, (Basingstoke: Palgrave Macmillan).

Quinn, C. (2002) Images and Impulses: Representations of Puerperal Insanity and Infanticide in Late Victorian England, in M. Jackson, *Infanticide: Historical Perspectives on Child Murder and Concealment, 1550–2000*, (Aldershot: Ashgate) pp. 193–255.

Reid, A. (2005) The Influences of Health and Infant Mortality of Illegitimate Children in Derbyshire 1917–1922, in A. Levene, S. Williams, T. Nutt (ed.), *Illegitimacy in Britain, 1700–1920*, (Basingstoke: Palgrave Macmillan), pp. 168–89.

Reid, A. (2006) Health Visitors and Enlightened Motherhood, in E. Garrett, C. Galley, N. Shelton and R. Woods (eds.), *Infant Mortality, A Continuing Social Problem*, (Aldershot: Ashgate), pp. 191–212.

Richardson, B.W. (1993) *Hygeia, a City of Health*, (London, 1876) in D. Porter and R. Porter, *Doctors, Politics, and Society: Historical Essays*, (Amsterman: Rodopi).

Roberts, E. (1982) Working Wives and Their Families, p. 143, in T. Barker and M. Drake (ed) *Population and Society in Britain 1850–1980*, (London: Batsford Academic and Educational).

Ross, E. (1986), London's Working Class Mothers, in J. Lewis (1986) (ed.) *Labour and Love, Women's Experience of Home and Family* (Oxford: Basil Blackwell), pp. 73–98.

Saunders, D.M. (1982) Sick Children's Nursing in P. Allan and M. Jolley, in *Nursing, Midwifery and Health Visiting Since 1900*, (London: Faber & Faber) pp. 141–50.

Scharlieb, M. (1987) What it Means to Marry in S. Kent, *Sex and Suffrage in Britain 1860–1914*, (London: Routledge).

Sharpe, P. (2000) Population and Society 1700–1840, in P. Clark (ed.), *Cambridge History of Britain: II, 1540–1840* (Cambridge: Cambridge University Press) pp. 491–528.

Shaw-Taylor, L. (2007) Diverse Experiences: The Geography of Adult Female Employment in England and the 1851 Census, in N. Goose, (ed.), *Women's Work in Industrial England: Regional and Local Perspectives*, (Hatfield: Local Population Studies) pp. 29–50.

Smart, C. (1992) Disruptive Bodies and Unruly Sex: the Regulation of Reproduction and Sexuality in the Nineteenth Century, in C. Smart, (ed.) *Regulating Womanhood: Historical Essays on Marriage, Motherhood and Sexuality*, (London: Routledge) pp. 7–32.

Stearns, P.N. (1972) Working-Class Women in Britain, 1890–1914, in M. Vicinus (ed.), *Suffer and be Still: Women in the Victorian Age*, (London: Methuen) pp. 100–120.

Steedman, C. (2002) Service and Servitude in the World of Labour: Servants in England, 1750–1820, in C. Jones and D. Wahrman, (ed.), *The Age of Cultural Revolutions: Britain and France, 1750–1820* (Berkeley: London: University of California Press), pp. 124–36.

Steedman, S. (2002) Servants and Servitude in the World of Labour: Servants in England 1750–1820, in C. Jones and D. Wahrman (2002) *The Age of Cultural Revolutions: Britain and France, 1750–1820* (London: University of California Press) pp. 124–136.

Tennant, M. (1908) Incompatibility of breast feeding and factory employment of mothers, in G. Tuckwell, G., *Women in Industry from Seven Points of View*, (London: Duckwell) p. 117.

Tomkins, A. (2005) Women and Poverty, in Hannah Barker (eds.) *Women's History, Britain 1700–1850: an Introduction* (London: Routledge) pp. 152–73.

Voth, H.-J. (2004) Living Standards and the Urban Environment, in Floud and Johnson (eds.) *Cambridge Economic History of Britain*, (Cambridge: Cambridge University Press).

Wall, R. (2012) Widows, Family and Poor Relief in England from the Sixteenth to Twentieth Century, in B. Moring, (ed.) *Female Economic Strategies in the Modern World*, (London: Chatto) pp. 11–32.

Wild, M.T. (1972) The Wool Textile Industry, in J. G. Jenkins, (ed.), *The Wool Textile Industry in Great Britain*, (London: Routledge & Kegan Paul) pp. 185–234.

Williams, S. (2004) 'Caring for the sick poor': Poor Law Nurses in Bedfordshire, c. 1700–1834, in P. Lane, N. Raven, and K.D.M. Snell, (eds.) *Women, Work and Wages in England, 1600–1850*, (Woodbridge: Boydell) pp. 141–169.

Wilson, A. (1985) Participant or Patient? Seventeenth Century Childbirth From the Mother's Point of View, in R. Porter, (ed.) *Patients and Practitioner; Lay Perceptions of Medicine in Pre-Industrial Society* (Cambridge:Cambridge University Press) pp. 129–144.

Woods, R. (2006) Newman's Infant Mortality as an Agenda for Research, in E. Garrett, C. Galley, N. Shelton, R. Woods, (2006) *Infant Mortality: A Continuing Social Problem*, (Aldershot: Ashgate) pp. 18–33.

Wrigley, E.A. (2004) The occupational structure of England in the mid-nineteenth century, in E. A. Wrigley, *Poverty, Progress and Population* (Cambridge: Cambridge University Press) pp. 129–203.

Articles

Anderson, M., (1976) Marriage Patterns in Victorian Britain: An Analysis Based on Registration District Data for England and Wales 1861, *Journal of Family History*, 1, pp. 55–78.

Arnot, M.L., (1994) Infant Death, Child Care and the State: The Baby-farming Scandal and the First Infant Life Protection Legislation of 1872, *Continuity and Change*, 9, pp. 271–311.

Atkins, P.J., (1992) 'White Poison?' The Social Consequences of Milk Consumption, 1850–1930, *Society for the Social History of Medicine*, 5, pp. 207–227.

Badger, F.J., (2014) Illuminating nineteenth century English Urban Midwifery: the Register of a Coventry Midwife, *Women's History Review*, 23, pp. 683–705.

Behlmer, G., (1979) Deadly Motherhood: Infanticide and Medical Opinion in Mid-Victorian England, *Journal of Medical History*, 34, pp. 403–427.

Beresford, M., (1988) East End, West End: The Face of Leeds During Urbanisation 1684–1842, *The Thoresby Society*, LX and LXI, pp. 60–61.

Berg, M. (1993) What Difference Did Women's Work Make to the Industrial Revolution? *History Workshop Journal*, 35, pp. 21–44.

Bonnett, A., (2007) 'The Other Rights of Man', the Revolutionary Plan of Thomas Spence, *History Today*, 57, pp. 42–8.

Bornat J. and Diamond, H., (2007) Women's History and Oral History, Developments and Debates, *Women's History Review*, 16, pp. 19–39.

Braithwaite, J., (1865) An enquiry into the causes of the high infant death rate in Leeds, *The Thoresby Society*, Vol. 41, (Leeds).

Branca, P., (1975) A New Perspective on Women's Work: A Comparative Typology, *Journal of Social History*, 9, pp. 129–53.

Busfield, D., (1988) Job Definition and Inequality in the West Riding Textile Industry, *Textile History*, 19, pp. 61–82.

Carpenter, K.J., (1991) Edward Smith (1819–1874), *Journal of Nutrition*, 121, pp. 1515–1521.

Chambers, J.D., (1953), Enclosure and the Labour Supply in Industrial England, *Economic History Review*, 5, pp. 319–343.

Crawford, P., (1986) The Suckling Child, Adult Attitudes to Child Care in the First Year of Life in Seventeenth-Century England, in *Continuity and Change*, 1, pp. 23–52.

Cuthbertson, D.P., C.B.E., D.SC., M.D., (1963) Nutritional Problems in Infancy and Childhood, *Proceedings of the Nutrition Society One Hundred and Fifty-Sixth Scientific Meeting, Great Ormond Street, London*, 22, (London) pp. 119–121.

D'Cruze, S., (2000) (ed.) Everyday Violence in Britain, 1850–1950: *Gender & Class*, (Harlow: Longman) pp. xii – 233.

Davin, A., (1978) Imperialism and Motherhood, *History Workshop Journal*, 5, pp. 9–65.

Dickens, A.M., (1976) The Workhouse, *Architectural Review*, CLX, No. 958 pp. 345–52.

Didsbury, B., (1977) Cheshire Salt Workers, in R. Samuel (eds.) Miners, Quarrymen and Saltworkers, (London: Routledge & Kegan Paul), pp. 136–204.

Digby, A., (1992) Victorian Values and Women in Public and Private, *Proceedings of the British Academy*, 78, pp. 95–216.

Dyhouse, C., (1978) Working-class Mothers and Infant Mortality in England 1895–1914, *Journal of Social History*, 12, pp. 248–267.

Endfield, G.H., and Nash, D., (2005) 'Happy is the Bride the Rain Falls on': Climate, Health and 'the Woman Question' in Nineteenth-Century Missionary Documentation. *Transactions of the Institute of British Geographers*, 30, pp. 368–386.

Feinstein C., (1998) Pessimism Perpetuated: Real Wages and the Standard of Living, during and after the Industrial Revolution, *Journal of Economic History* 58, pp. 625–658.

Forbes, T., (1986) Deadly Parents: Child Homicide in Eighteenth and Nineteenth Century England, *Journal of the History of Medicine*, 41, pp. 175–199.

Freifeld, M., (1986) "Technological Change and the Self-acting Mule: a Study of Skill and the Sexual Division of Labour, *Social History*, 11, pp. 337–9.

Glennie, P., (1990) Distinguishing Men's Trades: Occupational Sources and Debate for Pre-census England, *Historical Geography Research Series*, 25, *Institute of British Geographers*, pp. vi –141.

Goose, N., (2006) How Saucy did it Make the Poor? The Straw Plait and Hat Trades, Illegitimate Fertility and the Family in Nineteenth-Century Hertfordshire, *History*, 91, pp. 530–556.

Griffin, E., (2012) A Conundrum Resolved? Rethinking Courtship, Marriage and Population Growth in Eighteenth Century England, *Past and Present*, 215 pp. 149–150.

Guha, S., (1994) The Importance of Social Intervention in England's Mortality Decline, *Social History of Medicine*, 7, pp. 89–113.

Hall, R., (2003) A Poor Cotton Weyver: Poverty and the Cotton Famine in Clitheroe, *Social History*, 28, pp. 226–250.

Harris, B., (2004) Public Health, Nutrition, and the Decline of Mortality: the McKeown Book Revisited, *Social History of Medicine*, 17, pp. 379–407.

Harrison B. and Nolan M., (2004) Reflections in Colonial Glass? Women Factory Inspectors in Britain and New Zealand, 1893–1921, *Women's History Review*, 13, pp. 263–88.

Henriques U., (1968) How Cruel Was the Victorian Poor Law? *Historical Journal*, 11, pp. 365–716.

Higgs, E., (1987) Women, Occupation and Work in the Nineteenth Century, Censuses, *History Workshop* 23, pp. 59–80.

Hill, B., (1993) Women's History: A Study in Change, Continuity or Standing Still? *Women's History Review*, 1, pp. 5–22.

Hinks, J., (2014) The Representation of 'Baby Farmers' in the Scottish City, 1867–1908, *Women's History Review*, 23, pp. 560–576.

Hobsbawm, E., (1957) The British Standard of Living, 1750–1850, *Economic History Review*, 10, pp. 46–48.

Homrighaus, R.E., (2001) Wolves in Women's Clothing: Baby Farming and the British Medical Journal 1860–1872 *Journal of Family History*, 26 pp. 350–372.

Hornell, M., and Oxley R. (2009) Measuring Misery, *Explorations in Economic History*, 46, pp. 93–119.

Horrell S. and Humphries, J., (1992) Old Questions, New Data, and Alternative Perspectives: Families' Living Standards during the Industrial Revolution, *Journal of Economic History*, 52, pp. 849–80.

Horrell S. and Humphries, J., (1995) Women's Labour Force Participation and the transition to the male breadwinner family, 1790–1865, *Economic History Review*, 48, pp. 89–117.

Huck, P., (1995) Infant Mortality and Living Standards of English Workers During the Industrial Revolution, *Journal of Economic History*, 55, pp. 528–550.

Humphries, J., (1987) '...The most free from moral objection...' The Sexual Division of Labor and Women's Work in Nineteenth-Century England, *Journal of Economic History* (1987), pp. 929–949.

Humphries, J., (1990) Enclosures: Common Rights and Women: The Proletarianization of Families in the Late Eighteenth and Early Nineteenth Centuries, *The Journal of Economic History*, 50, p. 18.

Humphries, J., (1991) 'Bread and a penny worth of treacle': Excess Female Mortality in England in the 1840s, *Cambridge Journal of Economics*, 15, p. 464.

Humphries, J., (1991), Lurking in the Wings...: Women in the Historiography of the Industrial Revolution, *Business and Economic History*, 20, pp. 32–44.

Hunt, A., (2006) Calculations and Concealments: Infanticide in Mid-Nineteenth Century Britain, *Victorian Literature and Culture*, 34, pp. 71–94.

Hurren, E.T., (2004) 'A Pauper Dead-House': The Expansion of the Cambridge Anatomical Teaching School under the late-Victorian Poor Law, 1870–1914, *Medical History*, 48, pp. 69–94.

Kilday, A.-M. and Watson, K.D., (2008) Infanticide, Religion and Community in the British Isles, 1720–1920: Introduction, *Family & Community History*, 11 pp. 84–99.

Kilday, A.-M., (2008) 'Monsters of the Vilest Kind': Infanticidal Women and Attitudes to their Criminality in Eighteenth-Century Scotland, *Family & Community History*, 11/12, pp. 100–115.

Kilday, A.-M. and Watson, K.D., (2005) Child Murder in Georgian England, *History Today*, 55, pp. 40–46.

King, S., (2011) Welfare Regimes and Welfare Regions in Britain and Europe c1750–1860s, *Journal of Modern European History*, 9, pp. 44–67.

Lee, W.R., (1964) Robert Baker, The First Doctor in the Factory Department, Parts I and II, 1803–1858, *British Journal of Industrial Medicine*, 21, pp. 85–177.

Levene, A., (2008) *Medical History*, 52, pp. 545–547.

Levine Clark, M., (2000) Engendering Relief: Women, Ablebodiedness, and the New Poor Law in Early Victorian England, *Journal of Women's History*, 11, pp. 107–30.

Levine-Clark, M., (2000) Engendering Relief: Women, Ablebodiedness, and the New Poor Law in Early Victorian England, *Journal of Women's History*, 11, pp. 107–130.

Lindert P.H., and Williamson, J.G. (1982) Re-visiting England's Social Tables, 1688–1812, *Explorations in Economic History*, 19, pp. 385–804.

Lindert P.H., and Williamson, J.G. (1983) English Workers' Living Standards During the Industrial Revolution: A New Look, *Economic History Review*, 36, pp. 1–25.

Lomax, E., (1973) The Uses and Abuses of Opiates in Nineteenth Century England, *Bulletin of the History of Medicine*, 47, pp. 167–176.

Malcolmson, P.E., (1981) Laundresses and the Laundry Trade in Victorian England, in *Victorian Studies*, 24, pp. 439–462.

Malone, C., (1998) Gendered Discourses and the Making of Protective Labor Legislation in England, 1830–1914, *Journal of British Studies*, 37, pp. 166–191.

Marks, L., (1993) Medical Care for Pauper Mothers and their Infants: Poor Law Provision and Local Demand in East London, 1870–1929, *Economic History Review: New Series*, XLVI, 3, pp. 518–542.

Millward R., and Bell, F. (2001) Infant Mortality in Victorian Britain: The Mother as Medium, *Economic History Review*, LIV, 4, pp. 699–733.

Mood, J., (2009) 'If We're Petticoat Clothed, We're Major Minded', working-class women and the meat boycott of 1872, *Women's History Review*, 18:3, 409–426.

Morgan, N., (2002) Infant Mortality, Flies and Horses in Later-Nineteenth-Century Towns: a Case Study of Preston, *Continuity and Change*, 17, pp. 97–130.

Pelling, M., (1995) The Women of the Family? Speculations around Early Modern British Physicians, *Society for the Social History of Medicine*, 8, pp. 383–401.

Pooley S., (2010) 'All we Parents Want is That Our Children's Health and Lives Should Be Regarded': Child Health, and Parental Concern in England c. 1860–1910, *Social History of Medicine*, 23, pp. 528–48.

Reynolds M., (2006) 'A Man Who Won't Back a Woman is No Man at All': The 1875 Heavy Woollen Dispute and the Narrative of Women's Trade Unionism' *Labour History Review*, 71 pp. 187–198.

Richardson, R., (2001) From the Medical Museum, *The Lancet*, 357, p. 2144.

Richardson, R., (2013) The Art of Medicine: A Dismal Prospect: Workhouse Health Care, *The Lancet*, 382, pp. 20–1.

Rimmer, W.G., (1963) William Hirst, 'Father of the Woollen Trade', *Leeds Journal*, Vol. 34, pp. 205–208.

Roberts, D., How Cruel Was the Victorian Poor Law? *Historical Journal*, 6, (1984).

Saito, O., Who Worked When: Life-time Profiles of Labour Force Participation in Cardington and Corfe Castle in the Late Eighteenth and Mid Nineteenth Centuries, *Local Population Studies*, (1979) pp. 209–207.

Sauer, R., Infanticide and Abortion in Nineteenth-Century Britain, *Population Studies*, Volume 32, (1978) pp. 81–94.

Schwartz, L., (1990) English Servants and their Employers in the Eighteenth and Nineteenth Centuries, *Economic History Review*, 52, pp. 236–256.

Schwarzkopf J., Gendering Exploitation: The Use of Gender in the Campaign Against Driving in Lancashire Weaving Sheds, 1886–1903, *Women's History Review*, 7, (1998) pp. 449–473.

Steedman, C., A Boiling Copper and Some Arsenic: Servants, Childcare, and Class Consciousness in Late Eighteenth-Century England *Critical Inquiry*, 34, (2007).

Strange, J.-M., (2002), 'She Cried a Very Little', Death, Grief and Mourning in Working-Class Culture, 1880–1914, *Social History*, 27, p. 149.

Strange, J.-M., 'Only a Pauper Whom Nobody Owns': Reassessing the pauper grave c. 1880–1914, *Past & Present*, 178, (2003) pp. 148–175.

Strange, J.-M., 'Tho' Lost to Sight, to Memory Dear': Pragmatism, Sentimentality and Working-Class Attitudes Towards the Grave, c.1875–1914, p. 145, *Portality*, 8, (2003) pp. 144–159.

Styles, J., Spinners and the Law: Regulating Yarn Standards in the English Worsted Industries 1550–1800, *Textile History*, 2013, 44, pp. 145–170.

Swain, S., (2012) Towards a Social Geography of Baby Farming, *History of the Family*, 10, p. 151–59.

Swain, S., (2014) The Baby Farmers: A Chilling Tale of Missing Babies, Shameful Secrets and Murder in 19c Australia, *Journal of Australian Studies*, pp. 259–261.

Szreter S. and Mooney G., (1998) Urbanization, mortality and the standard of living debate: new estimates of the expectancy of life at birth in Nineteenth Century British Cities, *Economic History Review*, 51, pp. 84–112.

Szreter, S., (1988) The Importance of Social Intervention in Britain's Mortality Decline C.1850–1914: a Re-interpretation of the Role of Public Health, *Social History of Medicine*, 1, pp. 1–37.

Szreter, S., (1994) Mortality in England in the Eighteenth and the Nineteenth Centuries: a Reply to Sumit Guha, *Social History of Medicine*, 7, pp. 269–282.

Thane, P., (1978) Women and the Poor Law in Edwardian England, *History Workshop Journal*, 6, pp. 29–51.

Thompson, E.P., (1967) Time, Work Discipline and Industrial Capitalism, *Past and Present*, 38, pp. 56–97.

Vickery, A., (1993) and (2007) Golden Age to Separate Spheres; A Review of the Categories and Chronology of English Women's History, *Historical Journal*, 36, pp. 383–414.

Ward, T., (1999) The Sad Subject of Infanticide: Law, Medicine, and Child Murder, Social and Legal Studies, VIII, pp. 369–86.

Williams A., (2008) Please sir can I have some more? *BMJ*, 337, a2722.

Williams N., and Galley, C., (1995) Urban Differentials in Infant Mortality in Victorian England, *Population Studies*, 49, pp. 401–20.

Williams, N., (1992) Death in its Season: Class, Environment and the Mortality of Infants in Nineteenth-century Sheffield, cited in *Social History of Medicine*, 5, pp. 71–94.

Williams, N., and Mooney, G., (1994) Infant Mortality in an Age of Great Cities: London and the English Provincial Cities Compared, c. 1840–1910, *Continuity and Change*, 9, pp. 185–212.

Williamson J.G., (1981) Urban Disamenities, Dark Satanic Mills and the British Standard of Living Debate, *Journal of Economic History*, 41, pp. 75–83.

Woods, R.I., Watterson P.A. and Woodward, J.H., (1988) The causes of rapid infant mortality decline in England and Wales, 1861–1921, Parts I and II, *Population Studies,* 42 pp. 343–66 and 43, pp. 113–32.

On-line sources

For Margaret Llewelyn Davies Co-Operative Guild information see:.
http://www.hull.ac.uk/arc/downloads/DCWcatalogue.pdf.
Pourdeyhimi, B., Jackson K.C. and Hepworth, K., The Development of Weaving Using Automatic Looms, point 1.3. http://ulita.leeds.ac.uk/docs/Ars_Textrina/Volume4/9. The%20development%20of%20weaving.pdf.
TUC Library Records 1880–1884. Ann Ellis http://www.tuc.org.uk/about-tuc/union-history/tuc-archive-collection-modern-records-centre.
http://blogs.warwick.ac.uk/angeladavis/.
http://ulita.leeds.ac.uk/docs/Ars_Textrina/Volume4/9.The%20development%20of %20weaving.pdf.
http://www.bbc.co.uk/radio4/history/making_history/making_history_20080617. shtml –.
http://www.teanhallmills.co.uk/history.html.
http://www1.umassd.edu/ir/resources/standardofliving/thestandardoflivingdebate. pdf.

Unpublished works

Birch, P. (1998) Factors in the structure and decline of infant mortality in the Apthill sub district of Bedfordshire 1873–1900. Unpublished, B. Phil, Open University.
Brennan K.M., Infanticide Past and Present: Law, History and Culture, Unpublished PhD. book, University College Dublin, (2006).
Collier, F. (Author) R.S. Fitton, (ed.) (1964) The Family Economy of the Working-class in the Cotton Industry, 1783–1833, (Collier's MA Thesis, Manchester).
Grey, D. (2008) Representations of Infanticide, Ph.D Book, Roehampton University.
Humphries, J., 'Because they are too menny.' Children, mothers and fertility decline. The evidence from working-class autobiographies of the eighteenth and nineteenth centuries. University of Oxford Discussion Papers in Economic and Social History. Number 64, September, 2006.
Malin, J.C., The West Riding Recovered Wool Textile Industry, *c.*1813–1939 Unpublished PhD Book, (University of York, 1979).
Minoletti, P. (2011) The Importance of Gender Ideology and Identity: The Shift from Factory Production and its Effect on Work and Wages in the English Textile Industries, 1760–1850 Unpublished D.Phil (Oxford).
Pearson, R. (1986) The Industrial Suburbs of Leeds in the Nineteenth Century: Community Consciousness Amongst the Social Classes (PhD Thesis, Leeds).
Rawden, A., The Rise and Fall of Shoddy and Mungo Manufacture at Batley 1830–1871, 1972, pp 31–40. Unpublished Book, (University of York 1972).
Rose, M., The Administration of the Poor Law in the West Riding, 1820–1855, Unpublished Ph.D. Book (Oxford 1965).
Shaw, M.E. (1975) The Childhood of the Working Classes in the Leeds area 1830–1871, (PhD Thesis, Leeds).

Index

Printed in the USA
CPSIA information can be obtained
at www.ICGtesting.com
LVHW060856160823
755086LV00028B/529